Kindly mention THE ANNALS *when writing to advertisers*

Term Life Insurance – supplementary protection at attractive rates

One of the benefits of your AAPSS membership is the availability of a Term Life Insurance Plan initiated as a new service to individual members of the Academy.

Eligible members may request Term Life Insurance for themselves ranging from $10,000 to $50,000 (in units of $10,000) with lesser amounts for spouse and dependent children. All requests for coverage are subject to evidence of insurability requirements.

This Plan is offered at attractive rates and when dividends are earned, the cost can be even lower. However, future dividends and credits cannot be promised or guaranteed.

The information is yours without obligation. Simply return the coupon. Now may be the best time to re-evaluate your present life insurance coverage.

THE SEVENTY-NINTH ANNUAL MEETING OF THE AMERICAN ACADEMY OF POLITICAL AND SOCIAL SCIENCE

APRIL 11 AND 12, 1975
THE BENJAMIN FRANKLIN HOTEL
PHILADELPHIA, PENNSYLVANIA

The Annual Meeting will be addressed at each session by prominent scholars and officials and will be devoted to

Adjusting to Scarcity

Approximately 1,000 persons will be in attendance sometime during the two days of sessions, representing a wide variety of cultural, civic and scientific organizations.

Members are cordially invited to attend and will automatically receive full information.

- Proceedings of this 79th Annual Meeting will be published as the July issue of THE ANNALS

- FOR DETAILS WRITE TO: THE AMERICAN ACADEMY OF POLITICAL AND SOCIAL SCIENCE • BUSINESS OFFICE • 3937 CHESTNUT STREET, PHILADELPHIA, PENNSYLVANIA 19104

VOLUME 417   JANUARY 1975

THE ANNALS

of The American Academy *of* Political
and Social Science

RICHARD D. LAMBERT, *Editor*

ALAN W. HESTON, *Assistant Editor*

DRUGS AND SOCIAL POLICY

Special Editors of This Volume

RALPH M. SUSMAN
Former Associate Director
National Commission on Marihuana and
Drug Abuse

LENORE R. KUPPERSTEIN
Former Assistant Director
National Commission on Marihuana and
Drug Abuse

PHILADELPHIA

PATRICIA J. ENNIS, *Copy Editor*

JOANNE S. SMITH, *Book Review Copy Editor*

International Standard Book Numbers (ISBN)

ISBN 0-87761-185-8, vol. 417, 1974; paper—$4.00

ISBN 0-87761-184-X, vol. 417, 1974; cloth—$5.00

Issued bimonthly by The American Academy of Political and Social Science at Prince and Lemon Sts., Lancaster, Pennsylvania 17604. Cost per year: $15.00 paperbound; $20.00 clothbound. Add $1.00 to above rates for membership outside U.S.A. Second-class postage paid at Lancaster and at additional mailing offices.

Editorial and Business Offices, 3937 Chestnut Street, Philadelphia, Pennsylvania 19104.

CONTENTS

BOOK DEPARTMENT

CONTENTS

PAGE

GOVERNMENT AND POLITICS

SOCIOLOGY

ECONOMICS

PREFACE

Since the second half of the nineteenth century when opium use was first recognized in the United States as a social evil to be eliminated, policy makers and program administrators have persistently battled with the now institutionalized though still elusive social problem of "drug abuse." Over the years, as the meanings of the term itself, and therefore the definitions of the drug problem, have changed and the degree of public concern and symbolic importance attached to the problem have heightened, those charged with the formation and development of drug policy have created, in the words of the National Commission on Marihuana and Drug Abuse, a "drug abuse industrial complex" to deal with it.

The crisis intervention method characteristic of drug policy development in the United States, however, has never allowed for full comprehension, or even recognition, of the complexity and inherent dynamics of "the drug problem." As such, the formulation of drug policy at the federal, state and local levels has proceeded, for the most part, on the basis of outmoded definitions, untested and often unwarranted assumptions and inappropriate perspectives, generally without the benefit of proper planning or reliable and valid data.

The purpose of this volume is to highlight some of the major political, legislative, economic and social concerns which underlie drug policy in the United States; to examine the policy development process; and to cast some direct light on the capabilities and limitations of various institutional resources and responses in their pursuit of solutions to the drug problem as they perceive it. The first section is devoted to the policy development process.

Joseph R. Gusfield opens the discussion with an analysis of the relationship between knowledge and public policy. He suggests that the visibility of policy statements, the meanings and symbolic importance attached to drugs and drug use, and the context within which the drug problem is defined explain the limitations on the use and usefulness of knowledge and social science research in the formation of public policy regarding drug use and abuse.

Ralph M. Susman turns his attention to Congress and examines its fact-finding process and legislative efforts designed to deal with drug abuse. He discusses in some detail the perspective from which Congress has operated in this endeavor, traces the role of the law enforcement and criminal justice bureaucracy in the formulation and development of drug policy, and calls into question the degree of public accountability and the standard of performance maintained by Congress over the years in its response to the problem of drug use and abuse.

Selma Mushkin discusses the political and economic issues which have influenced and shaped the government's response to heroin and other drug use. These issues include the change in public opinion; the geographic spread of the problem; the changing character of the drug using population; the increasing number of, and social costs attendant to, drug-related crime; the significant increase in resources allocated for drug abuse programs;

the cost-effectiveness of drug abuse prevention and control; the impact of drug treatment programs; and the prognosis for the future.

In the last paper in this section, Stuart M. Matlins examines the interaction between the planning process and the utilization of resultant data. He finds that planning activity is often isolated from the total management system within which it takes place and which it is intended to serve, thus rendering largely useless the products of the planning process. With respect to drug abuse, he suggests that our drug policy has faltered significantly precisely because of the insufficient attention given to the management of activities and the failure of planning and planning process research activity to have a significant impact on decision making.

The second section of this volume is concerned with some fundamental drug policy issues and selected institutional responses to drug abuse. More specifically, Frederic Suffet and Richard Brotman discuss the concept of prevention and analyze the limitations of the four major preventive strategies—coercion, persuasion, correction and substitution—designed to reduce the demand for drugs.

Drug-related crime generally captures the headlines in political and social commentary on drug abuse even though the relationship is complex, difficult to measure and often misunderstood. Jared R. Tinklenberg addresses some of the difficulties in assessing the effects of drug use on antisocial behavior.

The belief that the immoderate, nonmedical use of mood-altering drugs is widespread and increasing underlies much of the current public apprehension and demand for legal or medical intervention. Yet, we still have no adequate data base and no reliable and valid means of estimating the number of drug, especially opiate, users in the United States. Lenore R. Kupperstein discusses some of the problems in assessing the nature and dimensions of the drug problem and reports on the efforts made by the National Commission on Marihuana and Drug Abuse to provide some guidance and direction in this area.

Whenever new developments threaten established values, society looks for a convenient villain or scapegoat. In the case of psychoactive drug use, the villain has been the mass media. F. Earle Barcus and Susan M. Jankowski present a detailed examination of the various charges leveled against the mass media and an analysis of issues and evidence in the current controversy over the purported role of the mass media in the recent escalation of drug use and abuse.

Colleges and universities form yet another set of social institutions which have come under increasing attack for their apparent failure to deal adequately with drug abuse in their midst. Although formerly entrusted with the power to act in loco parentis, recent challenges to the concept and the practice have led many colleges and universities to reduce, if not to abandon, control over nonacademic aspects of student life, including the use of psychoactive drugs. Nonetheless, increasing drug use on campus and mounting concern voiced by parents and educators have required that these institutions develop and implement drug policies. Gerald L. Robinson and Stephen T. Miller examine these administrative responses, explore the policy development process, and reflect on the impact and effectiveness of the drug policies currently in force throughout our nation's institutions of higher learning.

Lastly, we turn to the response of the federal government, particularly the National Institute of Mental Health (NIMH). Since shortly after the turn of the century, drug abuse has been defined and treated, at least in part, as a public health issue. In his paper entitled "Drugs and Public Health: Issues and Answers," Dr. Bertram S. Brown, Director of NIMH, highlights some of the activities and accomplishments of his agency relative to drug abuse and discusses some significant issues, demands, weaknesses and directions of the national drug program in its pursuit of solutions to public health problems related to the use and abuse of psychoactive drugs.

RALPH M. SUSMAN
LENORE R. KUPPERSTEIN

ANNALS, AAPSS, **417**, Jan. 1975

The (F)Utility of Knowledge?: The Relation of Social Science to Public Policy toward Drugs

By JOSEPH R. GUSFIELD

ABSTRACT: This paper discusses the ambiguities and levels of public policy, with emphasis on the consequences of the visibility of policy statements. The symbolic aspects of public policy are analyzed, and the character of meanings other than those attributed by scientific experts is discussed. Implications of "drugs" as related to youth and cultural change help to explain limitations on the use of knowledge in public policy. A distinction is drawn between visible policy and the policy of day-to-day action. Several ways in which knowledge does contribute to policy are then specified.

Joseph R. Gusfield is a Professor of Sociology at the University of California, San Diego. He holds a Ph.D. from the University of Chicago (1954) and has taught at the University of Chicago, Hobart and William Smith Colleges and the University of Illinois, Urbana. He has written and conducted research in a variety of fields, including social movements, sociology of education and comparative political sociology. In the field of drug and alcohol policy he has published a number of papers and Symbolic Crusade: Status Politics and the American Temperance Movement. *Currently he is completing a book on the relation of knowledge to public policy toward drinking, driving and auto accidents.*

This paper was prepared during the period (1973–74) when the author was a recipient of a Fellowship from the John Simon Guggenheim Foundation. I am grateful to the Foundation for its support.

TESTIFYING in 1968 before the President's Commission on Racial Disorders, Kenneth Clark looked back over 40 years of such commissions and doubted their efficacy. He pointed to the similarity of their findings to those of many past commissions and studies. Despite the accumulation of much knowledge, very little active change had occurred:

I read that report . . . of the 1919 riot in Chicago, and it is as if I were reading the report of the investigating committee on the Harlem Riot of '35, the report of the investigating committee on the Harlem Riot of '43, the report of the McCone Commission on the Watts Riot.

I must again in candor say to you members of this Commission—it is a kind of Alice in Wonderland—with the same moving picture reshown over and over again, the same analysis, the same recommendations, and the same inaction.[1]

This skeptical assessment of the importance of knowledge in the formation of public policy can be contrasted with a more optimistic view, perhaps the conventional perspective of the social scientist in support of the public efficacy of social science research. It too is drawn from a presidential commission:

We were appointed not to fan public anxiety, but to convert it into meaningful constructive proposals. This can be done only by refusing to accept at face value many of the common assumptions about drugs and the drug problem. . . . Confident social action comes from the understanding of the problem and from an impartial assessment of the impact of alternative strategies. . . .

We are convinced that public policy, as presently designed, is premised on

incorrect assumptions, is aimed at the wrong targets, and is too often unresponsive to human needs and aspirations.[2]

The second viewpoint by no means finds knowledge as futile a lever for new and improved social policy as does the first. There is a decided ring of confidence in its contrast between ignorance, partiality and mistaken relationships and the fruits of study found in correct knowledge, impartiality and the correct assessment of relations between action and outcome.

The aim of this paper is not the support or condemnation of either of these two perspectives. It serves to analyze some of the ways in which knowledge has, and has not, played a part in public policy toward drug use and abuse in recent years in the United States. Of necessity, some things of a general nature are said about knowledge and policy as well as about the specific area of drugs. As might be expected from any scholarly paper, the conclusions are critical of both perspectives for being too simplistic. For tactical purposes, however, criticism of the second perspective will be highlighted. Whether the relationship of knowledge to policy appears futile depends upon the expectations and criteria by which the reader judges it.

AMBIGUITIES OF PUBLIC POLICY

Clarification of a problem often usefully begins by examining the words which characterize a topic. In this case the words reveal an ambiguity which provides a framework for analysis.

1. Report of the National Advisory Commission on Civil Disorder (New York: New York Times Co., 1968), p. 483.

2. National Commission on Marihuana and Drug Abuse, Drug Use in America: Problem in Perspective (Washington, D.C.: Government Printing Office, March, 1973).

The word *public* is frequently used in at least two different senses. One is akin to the meaning of public interest. The word here refers to a collective attribute, that is, a goal or objective and accompanying action which is justified by reference to the interests of the total group. It is distinguished from private interest, meaning the objective of special, exclusive groups. In this sense, public policy is usually enunciated by public officials, agency members, judges, police and elected representatives.

In a second meaning, the opposite of *public* is *private*, as in acts conducted in a public arena versus those conducted behind the scenes. Public acts are conducted where many people can observe them; private acts are not. In Kenneth Burke's useful paradigm, the emphasis of the first meaning of *public* is on the *agent*; the emphasis of the second is on the *scene*.[3]

Again, using Burke's terms, *policy* has two meanings, one of *act* and one of *agency*. As agency, policy is a statement of general and deliberate direction which purports to inform and determine individual and specific acts. Thus: "The policy of Her Majesty's government enunciated in the Prime Minister's recent address on the import price of Bermuda onions." Here the policy is a document, statement or specific justification for a series of individual, situated actions. It places responsibility, or justification, for the action onto a higher agency; it provides direction for the individual actor. "Sorry sir, it's the policy."

As act, policy has meaning which reverses the hierarchy of policy as

agency. Here it is used to refer to the outcomes of a multiplicity of acts viewed as if they were designed; the policy is found in the direction or pattern which is followed by those carrying it out. It refers to the general pattern created by individual acts without reference to any directive statement. Thus we refer to court policy or police policy by imputing a direction to them, a deduction to the instant case from a hypothetical general principle.

REFERENTS OF PUBLIC POLICY

This linguistic and literary analysis leads to several useful insights. It provides a means by which to analyze drug use *policies* in a more realistic and complex manner. Possible conflicts and inconsistencies which are sustainable within one so-called public policy are as follows:

1. The idea of policy as deliberately stated directive implies its existence as visible. It is addressed to an audience, whether it be an organization or a nation. It is communicated and attributed to someone and some office. Of course, that visibility is a matter of degree. The statements of the president have wider news coverage and visibility to a national audience than do the policy statements of a county sheriff to his deputies.

2. The more diverse the audience of the policy statement, the more it is cast in terms of public interest. The ambit of presidential policy is wider than that of the county sheriff and less likely to refer only to internal needs of the organization. Yet both, coming from public officials, will find their

3. This paradigm can be found in the opening chapters of Kenneth Burke, *A Grammar of Motives* (New York: Prentice-Hall, 1945).

justifications in public statements of the collective interest. It must be emphasized that I am not referring here to personal or party or other private motives, but only to the form in which public statements are made.

3. Public policy, in the sense of visible and general statements of direction, states the publicly acceptable definition of public interest or morality. I am not saying that it is a response to a definitive and proven public to which it responds. Instead, I am asserting that such statements provide the visible evidence of what is public interest. Governments, in their action as public and visible officials, make conscious the attribution of collective values. The censoring agency, in defining a policy of X-rated movies, displays to the watchers the public moral criteria.[4]

4. Simply because policy exists, or has meanings, on the levels of agency and of act, there is no necessary connection between public and visible policies and those carried out in day-to-day actions. The latter are less visible and the imputations of policy depend on complex monitoring and communication to wider audiences. In the analysis of governmental actions, what is said at the highest levels of authority is frequently contravened at the level of the immediate, the local and the situational. One example will illustrate. Although legislative policy in almost all states directs that persons convicted of driving while intoxicated be subjected to a temporary suspension of driving licenses, suspension rarely occurs following a first offense.[5]

In order for situated, day-to-day actions to be visible, a complex system of monitoring and a corps of monitors must observe, analyze and transmit observations. Journalists, social scientists and the media of communications may perform this function.

QUESTIONS FOR ANALYSIS

The framework of the above discussion raises two questions relating to issues of drug use. In answering them, I hope to clarify relationships between knowledge and policy in the field of drugs.

1. How does knowledge affect drug policy as public and visible statements defining and asserting collective interests, values and moralities? In this question, drug policy is viewed as being policy directed toward the public arena, conducted in full view of interested laymen and imbued with a complex of divergent meanings and conflicts.

2. How does knowledge affect drug policy in the sense of actions carried out by public officials and agents in day-to-day routines? In this question, policy has a different quality and meaning, attracts different kinds of interests and serves

4. For an excellent analysis of governmental actions from this perspective, see, Murray Edelman, Politics as Symbolic Action (Chicago: Markham Press, 1973).

5. Richard Zylman, "Are Drinking-Driving Laws Enforced?" Police Chief 37 (September, 1970), pp. 48–52; Joseph Gusfield, "A Study of Drinking Driving in San Diego County," mimeographed (San Diego City: Urban Observatory, 1972).

different functions than those implied in the first question. Indeed, even the object of policy—drugs and drug users —may be considerably different in the two levels of policy.

CONFERRAL OF PUBLIC SIGNIFICANCE

There is a long history to the use of various mood-altering substances. Alcohol, marihuana, opium, heroin and other substances which induce alterations of the mind have appeared in many cultures throughout recorded history. Although alcohol is probably the oldest, most widespread and most frequently used substance, others are by no means recent in their use.[6] Except for alcohol, however, the control and possible extension of drug use has not been a major public issue until recently.[7]

For much of the nineteenth and early twentieth centuries, the issues of alcohol control and prohibition were high on the agenda of American political life. While other substances were in use, their consumption was not noticed as a widespread phenomenon, nor did they achieve the status of a public problem. During the early part of the twentieth century, however, both marihuana and opium began to occupy legislative attention and to come under legal limitations of use and sale. During the 1930s there was a greater interest in marihuana control. While alcohol control had receded as a major public issue by the mid-1930s, interest in other substances had increased in legislative concern. Not until the 1960s, however, did nonalcoholic drugs of various kinds become the significant issue that has spawned news coverage, dramatic productions, academic research, and governmental and legal activity. Zinberg and Robertson report that on a day chosen at random (August 14, 1970) when there was no major news item concerning drugs, stories about drugs nevertheless occupied 11 columns in the *Boston Globe*, 16 in the *Washington Post* and 19 in the *New York Times*.[8]

It is vital to distinguish between an existent situation—drug usage— and public awareness or perception of usage. The attention of public media to a problem gives it status as an issue. The attention of government and other public agents to a problem accentuates, in turn, its position on the public agenda. "Society" is not an object that is revealed by its own light. It is too wide in scope to be seen with the naked eye. It gains its shape from the reflected light of public exposure. There is, then, a crucial interaction between that which interests the public and that which is available to their interest.

In this sense, even the effort to obtain knowledge or to develop programs provides a way in which the situation is given importance. The existence of new agencies, mechanisms and literature pro-

6. Richard H. Blum and Associates, *Society and Drugs* (San Francisco: Jossey-Bass, 1969), ch. 1–5.

7. The following are useful analyses of legislative attempts to control use of mood-altering substances: Blum et al., *Society and Drugs*; Howard S. Becker, *Outsiders* (Glencoe: The Free Press, 1963); Joseph Gusfield, "Prohibition: Experiment in Political Utopianism," in John Braeman, Robert Bremner, and David Brody, *Change and Continuity in Twentieth-Century America: 1920s* (Columbus: Ohio State University Press, 1968).

8. Norman Zinberg and John Robertson, *Drugs and the Public* (New York: Simon and Schuster, 1972), p. 30.

nounces the significance of the issue. So-called experts maintain that the detrimental effects of alcohol are both greater and far more common in the United States than are those of addictive drugs such as heroin, opium, cocaine and morphine. A glance at current newspapers or bookshelves will not show this to be a common belief.

Public policy statements and public, governmental actions have effects which stem from their rhetorical and communicative aspects; they are not only means to an end. When governing officials commission a report on drugs, or when a law is debated, the issue is public. The signal has been made that the public interest is being defined, and action, or inaction, must result. The issue has been placed in the political realm, and it requires a governmental response.

MEANINGS OF DRUGS AND DRUG USE

In the study of human behavior, people are often viewed as responding to stimuli. It is important to recognize, however, that human beings also help to construct or create their own stimuli. They select, interpret and place connotations on objects and events; they give meanings to often amorphous experience. What appears to the observer as the character of stimuli may not be at all consistent with the character attributed to that stimuli by its receivers. This is certainly the case in public orientations to drugs.

Let us begin with the object itself —the drug. What has attracted attention, provided news, and been the basis of television drama has not been the substance of drugs as the medical or pharmacological pro-fession would define it. The public definition of drugs refers less to the treatment of illness than to the socially disturbing elements which prompt attention to these substances. *Drugs* and *drug abuse* are linked together in the public mind. There is a tendency to use the term *drugs* without differentiation. Persons are reported in the news to be arrested for drug use with no distinction being made between marihuana and what so-called experts consider to be addictive substances.[9] Public discussion of the drug problem has excluded many substances which pharmacologists, physiologists and physicians might well include.[10] Prescription drugs, such as tranquilizers and barbiturates, are often excluded. Alcohol commands little attention as a drug and has not been included as part of the drug problem by the Department of Health, Education and Welfare.

Drugs are viewed as being problematic and disturbing within a particular historical context. Alcohol abuse and the effects of prescribed drugs lack the news value which television writers and news reporters seek. While alcohol has not disappeared as a public problem, it is an old issue, the outlines of which are generally known. Public policy has been formed and has ceased to be either interesting or puzzling. The detrimental consequences of prescription drugs have not yet achieved widespread recognition. It is those substances which are defined as illegal and which have increased in use in recent years that stir interest and policy debate.

At the outset, then, the object under discussion and scrutiny is by

9. Ibid., pp. 37–42.
10. National Commission on Marihuana and Drug Abuse, *Drug Use in America*, pp. 9–14.

no means the same for everyone. The word *drugs* has different meanings for the public than for the professionals who maintain and generate the corpus of knowledge on the subject.

SYMBOLIC MEANINGS OF DRUGS

This section focuses on the public aspect of policy as visible and signifying—as activity which must be distinguished from its direct and instrumental impact on drug use. The rules of public action and their importance are under scrutiny. "The public level of existence becomes increasingly important in itself . . . actions come to have a publicity effect largely independent of their private effects."[11]

This mode of analysis differs from those which stress the mood-altering consequences of drugs or the detrimental aspects of addiction. America has long been able to accept mood-alteration in the form of alcohol. The punitive drug legislation of the 1960s cannot be understood as a response of a pragmatic and work-oriented society to the passivity and abstention which drug use entails nor as concern for the mental health of addicts. The addictive use of heroin and cocaine has been a source of concern for more than half a century. The penalties for alcohol use, even during Prohibition, applied only to its manufacture for sale or the sale itself. Possession alone was not illegal, as it has been for marihuana, heroin, opium and other "hard" drugs.

Inherent in the public debate over drugs and drug use are symbolic meanings and connotations which tap emotive elements and which

are more metaphorical than matter-of-fact. They cannot be proven true or false since they constitute the way in which the events or objects have been given dramatic value.[12] For much of the history of public controls over alcohol, marihuana and narcotics, the character of the users has been crucial to understanding public conflict and the depth of emotional commitment.

American concern with narcotics is more than a medical or legal problem—it is in the fullest sense a political problem. The energy that has given impetus to drug control and prohibition came from profound tensions among socioeconomic groups, ethnic minorities and generations—as well as the psychological attraction of certain drugs.[13]

The conflicts over alcohol control and prohibition in the nineteenth and the early twentieth centuries illustrate the symbolic meaning of a substance in public conflict. The social and cultural differences between users and nonusers were clues to the emotive character of the political struggles.[14] As long as ethnic, occupational and religious groups were opposed to each other on alcohol questions, the political controversies were also indicia of the status, prestige and moral standing of the users and nonusers.

11. Jack D. Douglas, *American Social Order* (New York: The Free Press, 1971), p. 238.

12. The analysis of metaphor has occupied much attention from philosophers and literary critics. *See*, especially, Kenneth Burke, *The Philosophy of Literary Forms* (New York: Vintage Books, 1957), pp. 121–144; Philip Wheelwright, *Metaphor and Reality* (Bloomington: Indiana University Press, 1964); Max Black, *Models and Metaphors* (Ithaca: Cornell University Press, 1962), ch. 1–3, 13.

13. David F. Musto, *The American Disease: Origins of Narcotic Control* (New Haven: Yale University Press, 1973), p. 244.

14. Joseph Gusfield, *Symbolic Crusade: Status Politics and the American Temperance Movement* (Urbana: University of Illinois Press, 1963).

While the instrumental consequences, measured in amount and
kind of drinking, were part of the
issue, they were by no means all
of it. Passage of legislation, statements of public figures and decisions of appellate courts are all
ways in which a public morality
is stated and defined. What was at
stake was the answer to the question: Whose morality will prevail?

After the Civil War and following
intensive immigration from Europe,
ambivalence about the use of alcohol
was overlaid with conflict between
rural Protestants and urban Roman
Catholics. The conflict also concerned cultural dominance of the
former group over the latter. The
opposing cultures were couched in
terms of public legitimacy toward
differing concepts of leisure, internal discipline and standards of
moral character. The repeal of Prohibition was a phase in the weak-
ened dominance of the older American culture. Alcoholic drinking was
and is a metaphor for cultural opposition and conflict.

DRUG USERS AND CULTURAL
CHANGE

Until recently, public awareness
of the use of marihuana and addictive drugs had been associated
mainly with social and/or cultural
minorities or marginal communities.
The world of the jazz musician,
the criminal underworld, the black,
brown and yellow worlds of Negro,
Mexican and Oriental life, the
Bohemian and offbeat elements of
society—these had been the depicted locales of the drug user.
Usage may have been wider than
such imagery implied. The use of
addictive drugs by members of the
medical profession and the presence
of opiates in patent medicines sug-

gest this. However, in the public
debate over drug use, it is the less
conventional and/or less powerful
segments of the society that are
singled out. Thus, in the passage
of marihuana control legislation
during the 1920s, the Mexican-
American was seen as the recipient
of the action:

Whether motivated by outright ethnic
prejudice or by simple discriminatory
disinterest, the proceedings before state
legislatures resembled those in Texas
in 1923. There was little, if any, public
attention and no debate. Pointed references were made to the drug's Mexican origins and sometimes to the criminal conduct which invariably followed
when Mexicans ingested the killer
weed.[15]

As long as drug use was clearly
seen as being confined to marginal
and minority social groups, it was
possible to confine it to a limited
place on the agenda of public actions. Both law and practice upheld
the dominance of conventional and
powerful social groups by upholding
the dominance of norms controlling
mood-altering commodities. Drug
use provided no threat to the culture or the social position of those
for whom the public norms were
enunciated. The moral order was upheld by legislative passage and court
actions.

The emergence of marihuana use
and public awareness of addictive
and hallucinatory experiences with
drugs among middle class youth
have created a crisis of another kind.
Not only is drug usage new among
culturally dominant groups, but it is
also part of general cultural changes

15. National Commission on Marihuana
and Drug Abuse, *Marihuana: A Signal of
Misunderstanding*, Appendix, vol. 1 (Washington, D.C.: Government Printing Office,
1972), pp. 482–485.

in which young people are at the center. An important part of the political disturbances of the 1960s involved young people who represent in the public image marihuana users and experimenters with drugs like LSD and amphetamines. Much of what has come to be seen as the moral and sexual revolution of the 1960s is centered among the same youth. The connections between drug use and cultural change are readily symbolized.

Two aspects of the recent public awareness of drug use differentiate it from earlier periods: (1) the new group perceived as users—middle class youth—can not be clearly construed as a social or cultural minority, and (2) the use of drugs, especially marihuana, is linked to issues of cultural change, both through the users and through its relation to new and deeply contested life styles. Public policy must be seen in light of these meanings. Public affirmations and negations take place in the context of these broader issues and possess meanings unrelated to those of experts in scientific knowledge about drugs.

DRUGS AND YOUTH CULTURE

The first of the two aspects of the symbolic meaning of drug use is its status as an activity of youth, including visible and significant proportions of middle class and upper middle class youth, both male and female. The current drug "scare" developed in the context of a "youth problem" in the United States. To analyze the causes of that problem is beyond the scope of this paper. It is sufficient to recognize that

16. For introduction to the literature on youth and for analysis of "youth culture," see, Bennett Berger, *Looking for America* (Englewood Cliffs, N.J.: Prentice-Hall, 1971).

youth, in the United States as well as in many other countries, has increasingly become a separate and separable age group. The cultural activities and standards of that group have given it distinctiveness. Its institutions and communications have provided an internal structure. The music of youth, the journals of youth, youth hostels—all of these are visible manifestations of a profound trend that has culminated in the now popularly accepted term "youth culture."[16]

The use of marihuana and some of the hallucinogens among university students has been very important in fixing public attention on middle class youth as drug users. The importance of middle class and university student usage lies not only in its relation to youth culture, but also in its newsworthy character. It is puzzling, anxiety-provoking and therefore of intrinsic interest. The fact that drug use is illicit enhances its newsworthiness.

Two facets of the relation between drug use and youth are significant. First, the idea of drugs has been closely related to youth culture in public discussion. What is meant is not the concept of drugs as defined by experts but the concept of drugs and drug users connected with the youth culture. Second, drugs within this meaning connote a style and usage which distinguishes youth from adulthood. Alcohol, for example, has long been seen as something with which young people experiment. Such experimentation, however, has also been interpreted as part of growing up, as an act of socialization. Drug use, however, is not readily seen as part of socialization. It is viewed as "growing away" rather than growing up.

This relationship between drugs and youth accentuates and deepens the attention and anxiety about youth and the rise of the youth culture among consumers of public news and entertainment. It solidifies and strengthens parental fears and guilt. Television drama and movies have given prominence to the myth of the guilty parents—parents whose busied concern for financial and social success has kept them from active control and guidance of their children. Drugs and drug use are seen to be caused by parental neglect. Discussion of drugs often provokes anxious questioning, soul-searching and intense emotional responses among adults.

Public attention to drugs as an object and as a problem is not, however, a simple case of American Puritan concern about mood-alteration per se. Rather, it is concern about the form and character of mood-alteration which occurs outside the scope and control of adult agencies and models.

DRUGS AND THE 1960s REVOLUTIONS

The second major aspect of the symbolic importance of drug use lies in its relationship to major cultural issues of the 1960s. I refer especially to what has been labeled "the moral revolution," that is, the issues surrounding questions of sexual conduct, abortion, pornography, personal privacy and life styles. I refer secondarily to the issues connected with changing social structure, especially racial, sexual and age group equality.

As stated above, attitude toward mood-alteration is not the dominating source of anxiety over drug use in the United States. However, the issues of moral change that have developed in recent years have

touched off new debates about hedonism, sexuality, individual and public responsibilities and personal ambition. This re-emergence of life style as a central problem is epitomized in the attention and controversy surrounding the "hippie" movement and communes. The drugs in question are those associated with the heightening of experience, ecstatic and extraordinary sensations, and the retreat from active and aggressive behavior. The idea of the validity of an "alternative consciousness," though voiced only by a few intellectualized advocates of marihuana and hallucinogens, is nevertheless inherent in the way in which the drug controversy has been posed as an attack on conventional social life.[17]

The equalitarian revolution has brought marginal and subterranean activity into the mainstream of attention. In the past, lack of involvement of public agencies and mass media with the lives of minorities may have diverted public concern from issues of drugs involving minorities. In the changed atmosphere of equalitarian movements, the opposite is true. Whether actuated by minority interests, fear of crime, or the newsworthy character of minority happenings, drug use among less advantaged social groups has merged with other forces making drug use a matter of public interest and attention.

SYMBOLIC IMPORT OF DRUG POLICY

Statements of policy made in the open arena of public forums become statements about the speaker and his or her stance toward cultural changes of the time. They are

17. Zinberg and Robertson, *Drugs and the Public*, pp. 30–32.

endorsements or condemnations of changes taking place among young people today. Made by public officials, they assure or create anxieties in listeners. Public policies, as deliberate and visible directives, have a strong ritualistic component. Whatever their effects on drug users, they persuade listeners that public interest and its agencies grant legitimacy to one side and withhold it from another.

Within the context of the symbolism of drugs I discern two major strategems. One is legal; it has consisted of officially labeling drugs as illicit items. Coupled with this has been a punitive pattern of mandatory sentences. Both the illicitness and the punitive patterns maintain public condemnation of drug users and the consequent reinforcement of the legitimacy of those values threatened by cultural change.

The other strategy is therapeutic. It consists of defining the user as pathological. The solution lies not in punishment but in treatment. As a strategy it softens the condemnation of the user. He or she is not quite as morally condemned since the behavior is a form of illness and the user is absolved of full responsibility. Hence the symbolic significance is less reinforcing to the legitimacy of past values.

It is noteworthy that these strategies involve different groups and occupations responsible for gathering information, apprehending users and preventing the occurrence and recurrence of drug use. The legal approach fixes attention on legislators, police, judges and lawyers. The therapeutic approach places responsibility on physicians, pharmacologists, psychologists, sociologists and educators.

KNOWLEDGE AND SYMBOLIC POLICY

Knowledge consists of statements about a world of reality in which means are used to achieve ends. It provides instruments to achieve agreed-upon goals. Do we want to improve the balance of payments deficits? Economics will tell us what to do. Do we want a better way to treat slipped discs? Medical science will discover it. Do we want to decrease the use of drugs? Sociology will tell us how. However, the above discussion of ritual and symbolism in public policy suggests that such knowledge may not be completely relevant to the broader issues addressed in drug policy.

Insofar as gatherers of knowledge about drug use operate at the "how to" level, their findings support or diminish policy measures which align them with one or another perspective regarding questions of youth culture and moral change. The knowledge with which specialists work is specifically about the causes, uses and abuses of drugs, and strategies of drug continuance or discontinuance. For the lay public there are other issues which are not addressed by the experts. Even to choose between the legal and the therapeutic strategies is to engage in the conflict of tough versus tender attitudes toward drug users. The relation between knowledge experts and the public is not a direct relation between professional servants and clients, since the findings of science may be irrelevant to the latent meanings and values of the clientele.

Fearfulness toward experts in matters of public policy and drug issues arises in the strategies of both law and therapy, though more so in the former than in the latter. Both strategies operate within what Jack

Douglas calls the "myth of absolutist morality."[18] The legal rule presumes a homogeneity of moral values within the society so that the legislators and judges speak for "the public interest." Therapy operates with concepts of illness and health.[19] The drug user commits a legal offense and thus acts in opposition to public welfare. The drug user, by his act of use, shows that he is sick and needs to be cured. Both strategies uphold an official, public view of morality.

Especially in the field of drugs, knowledge has played a deeply subversive role. The consensus of findings about drug use, well illustrated in the report of the President's Commission, adds up to loud raspberries directed at the official public and accepted versions of the drug problem.

In much recent discussion of drug problems, professional experts have cast considerable doubt on the character of the drug problem as depicted in the public arena. Knowledgeable persons have criticized the prevailing concept that drugs are necessarily harmful or more harmful than prescription medicines or alcohol. They have revised the idea of the drug user as a deviant, antisocial or disturbed person. They have begun to suggest that many of the problems connected with drug use, such as crime, are functions of the social control responses to drug use rather than consequences of the primary behavior.

Experts have told the public and the practitioners that they have been misled; the problem is not a large one, the addictive consequences are

18. Douglas, *American Social Order*, ch. 7.
19. For the analysis of sickness as one form of deviance, *see*, Eliot Freidson, *Profession of Medicine* (New York: Dodd, Mead and Co., 1972).

not highly detrimental, even to health; marihuana and the hallucinogens are by no means as destructive of physical or social behavior as is alcohol. Further, many of the problems connected with drug use, such as criminal behavior, are consequences of efforts to solve the problem.

How does such knowledge affect policy? If public programs establish and sustain an official public morality, is science relevant? If public policies maintain a needed illusion of a common, stable culture, can expertise have any impact?

KNOWLEDGE AND SOCIAL CONFLICT

A major message of the body of scientific work on drugs, delivered by physiologists, pharmacologists, sociologists and psychologists, has functioned to break down the public appearance of a united and consensual society on the question of drug use. As indicated above, removal of the pathological character of the drug user destroys both the view of the drug user as being in need of therapy and the belief in a social consensus. The drug user, like the alcohol user, becomes someone who follows a different, yet morally acceptable, life style. The drug abuser, like the chronic alcoholic, may be seen as a social problem, but that is not to say he is a social deviant. Rather, it is an admission of the plural character of the society and a legitimation of behavior which is morally reprehensible and anxiety-provoking for many people. The experts have legitimized the youth culture and the moral revolution of the 1960s. They have not done so in a logical and explicit fashion but in a symbolic sense, because the issue had taken on a meaning within that context. Furthermore, in underlining the character of cultural conflict implicit in drug use, they have made law and therapy appear as matters of cultural domination rather than agencies of societal consensus.

A distinction should be drawn at this point between scientific and political knowledge. Scientific knowledge in the field of drug use is the body of facts and theories related to the uses of drugs. Political knowledge concerns public attitudes and organization toward drug use, including scientific knowledge. This paper deals with political rather than scientific knowledge and may be construed as one source of advice for political officials engaged in the management of change and conflict through public acts. Scientific knowledge can be only one of a number of factors which bear upon the symbolic and instrumental character of official public action. The politician, in Robert Bales' frequently used nomenclature, is both task leader and social-emotional leader.[20] He is often aware that his statements and actions serve to monitor for his audience the direction of social events. He has an ability to influence the polarization or unity of the political process.

KNOWLEDGE AND PUBLIC DISCUSSION

Much doubt has been cast herein on the utility of knowledge for social and cultural change relating to drug use. In much of the above, the perspective of Kenneth Clark, which began this paper, is reiterated. However, while knowledge makes less difference than conventional theory will admit, it nevertheless plays

20. Robert Bales, *Interaction Process Analysis* (Cambridge, Mass.: Addison-Wesley, 1950).

significant roles under particular conditions and in particular ways in relation to public policy, both in its highly visible form and in its localistic, day-to-day form.

The place accorded knowledge and expertise in the idiom of public discourse constitutes one such role. Discussion in the public arena often seems to be one chorus after another of chaotic, fighting voices. Yet there are rules to the game which demand that ideas be set forth in the language and tactics of rational debate and analysis in terms of public rather than private interest. The participants must appear to be rational and informed persons, and they must persuade rather than influence the listeners. It is a game of persuasion. The expert assumes importance in this game because he or she assumes an informed and impartial position. As knowledge is disseminated, it sets limits to the public acceptability of all ideas.

In his classic study of the Negro in America in the early 1940s, Gunnar Myrdal attributed changes in white attitudes largely to the decline of scientific support for the theory of racial inferiority. Not only was this theory no longer credible, but also a white person could not maintain it and still perceive himself to be a rational, informed and understanding person. He had to face the conflicts in himself and the society. Science, through its pronouncements, made it difficult for many people to rationalize prejudice.

This process is noticeable in public discussion of drugs. The belief in the addictive character of marihuana or in its great physiological harm has ceased to be conventional wisdom. In the late 1960s, those who attacked the view that marihuana is addictive and harmful did so from the posture of a minority view. Today the situation is reversed. The context has been changed and the supporter of punitive marihuana legislation must attack a new conventional wisdom.

THE EVERYDAY LEVEL OF PUBLIC POLICY

Much of the above discussion concerns highly visible public policy. Here the debate and the statement of policy have an abstract quality about them. The typologies presented are fixed and definitive. In the world of daily existence there is much more ambivalence, ambiguity and contradiction than the generalized rules and formulations of public policy can admit. In the immediacy and flux of specific actions, the application of rules involves what H. L. A. Hart calls their "open texture."[21] Rules are formulated in general terms, but they are applied in specific situations. There is no exact method for determining when an instant case is subsumed under a general category. In the process of policy enforcement, the general is given a meaning, often changing the direction and thrust of policy.

It is not the open quality of language alone that provides opportunities for variance between highly visible statement of public officials and day-to-day formulations of individual acts. The fervor and emotion inherent in the symbolic nature of public events is less apparent in the reality of coping with defendents, parents, attorneys, hospital organizations and the multiple elements in daily existence. A parent has one attitude toward public

policy, and the courts grapple with the organizational difficulties in prosecuting and enforcing laws. The less than punitive enforcement of severe laws against marihuana possession illustrate the process by which policy, trapped at one level by its symbolic import, is changed at another by the situational exigencies of organizational life.[22]

In 1951 Robin Williams coined the phrase "patterned evasion of norms" to describe the regularized process by which illegal, deviant or illicit activities continue in a regularized and predictable fashion with relatively few official sanctions. Such activities as gambling, prostitution and abortion persist in a quasi-permitted manner. This discrepancy between the ritual world of public statements and the real world of situated activities has constituted a significant part of the drug scene in the United States. Rejection of the conventional view of drug usage, even though the generalized version of policy remains unaffected, enables the daily and local level of policy to change more easily.

KNOWLEDGE AND PUBLIC ISSUES

The discrepancy between policy at different levels of application and visibility suggests one way in which social policies undergo revision: not by the definitive and deliberate embrace of one doctrine or theory, but by the slow accretion of individual acts. The difficulties en-

21. H. L. A. Hart, *The Concept of Law* (Oxford: Clarendon Press, 1961), pp. 120–132.

22. Studies of state enforcement of marihuana laws find that "the trend is undoubtedly to invoke the marihuana possession laws only when the behavior (possession) comes out in the open." Only one-third of the arrests sampled led to a sentence and only six percent were sent to jail. *Marihuana, A Signal of Misunderstanding* (Washington, D.C.: Government Printing Office, 1972).

tailed ultimately become more than the organizational commitments can sustain. The "game is not worth the candle" and even the experts agree.

Stated another way, publics become tired of issues even though it is difficult to ignore the symbolic moral issues created by public pronouncements. There is a sense today that the drug problem has passed the apex of public attention and concern. The broader issues that gave it a deeper meaning either have abated or have been accepted, or at least many people have learned to live with them. The limitations to legislative solutions have become apparent. Marihuana use has neither abated nor decreased. Drug addiction has become a recognized problem for which organized solutions have supposedly been created, and in that sense it is under control. Adults have learned from youth culture, and many who were in youth cultures are now themselves beyond thirty.

The accumulation of knowledge receives a better hearing in this atmosphere. In fact, by turning to expertise, the polarized groups can find a way to diminish the ardor of the issue without having to admit a costly defeat. The high-level, often moralistic and conventional public utterances that pass for much policy permit the officials, experts and practitioners to carry out their often quite different orientations. The politician is thus a useful insulator between publics and between levels of policy. He engages in what Kenneth Burke called "secular prayer." By invoking morals and values which are being dishonored and circumscribed in behavior, he prevents an open conflict between disputants. The losers are satisfied by the appearance of their culture at the level of public interest, while the winners are satisfied because their behavior is permitted *de facto*.

The United States is no longer a society in which any one social group or culture has such clear-cut hegemony that it can hold forth its moral standard, its style of life, as the example for the rest to follow. We have neither a hierarchy of authoritative nobility nor a disciplined revolutionary society. In place of such order, we follow a complicated pattern of ignorance, knowledge and change which goes on at different levels and in different directions. In this pattern, the experts are neither social engineers nor unemployed workers.

Drug Abuse, Congress and the Fact-Finding Process

By RALPH M. SUSMAN

ABSTRACT: This article concerns Congress, its fact-finding process and its legislative efforts designed to deal with problems related to narcotic and drug abuse. In essence, it examines the perspective within which Congress has defined and has attempted to solve the "drug problem" and traces the manner in which the law enforcement and criminal justice bureaucracy gradually came to be the principal architects and purveyors of drug control legislation. It also addresses the matter of public accountability and bureaucratic and congressional performance relative to fact-finding and the policy formulation process. Lastly, it provides an assessment of what is required of Congress if it is to undertake more rational and responsible action in reference to the problems of drug use and abuse.

Ralph M. Susman received his Ph.D. from New York University. He has held various administrative and research posts in the criminal justice area and was formerly Director of the Office of Juvenile Delinquency and Youth Development, Department of Health, Education and Welfare, and Acting Director of the 1970 White House Conference on Children and Youth. He recently served as Associate Director, National Commission on Marihuana and Drug Abuse.

16

THIS article concerns Congress, its fact-finding process and its legislative efforts designed to deal with problems related to narcotic and drug abuse.

Although history records the use of mood-altering drugs, especially opium, for more than two thousand years, concern about opium *usage* did not develop in the United States until the second half of the nineteenth century. At that time, it was brought to public attention within the context of social reform activities, particularly the temperance-prohibitionist movement.

It should be noted, however, that some early efforts were made by the United States to discourage American nationals or United States registry ships from participating in the lucrative international opium *trade*. These early measures included the Treaty of Amity and Commerce of 1833 between the United States and Siam; the Treaty of Wang Hea of 1844 with China; a subsequent treaty with China in 1880; and a treaty with Korea in 1882. None of these measures, however, was particularly effective, owing in part to lack of enforcement machinery, official indifference and the substantial profits being realized by prominent ship owning and trading companies.[1]

It was within the context of social reform, however, that Congress first defined the "drug problem" and attempted to construct its solutions. In essence, the underlying philosophy of early drug control legislation was that opiate addiction was a nasty and immoral vice

and that continued use of drugs was a willful act. As such, in all instances, early legislative efforts were directed toward the prohibition of *all* narcotic drugs for *all* persons except those suffering from terminal diseases or those who, because of age and infirmity, would likely die without the continued administration of narcotic drugs.[2]

Between 1870 and 1915, national concern over the problem of drug abuse centered on two classes of users and two substances. First was the highly visible social outcast typified by poor Chinese laborers who were brought to the United States, who settled in sizable communities in San Francisco, Seattle, New York and other major port cities, and who were exploited as a source of cheap labor, particularly by the railroads. Many of these Chinese laborers were opium smokers and a small number were opium eaters. The second major group of users, far less visible, included professionals, businessmen and others normally thought to constitute the dominant force of the community. Women—housewives and mothers—comprised a sizable proportion of this group and outnumbered men by three to two. Opium consumption among this group of users generally involved, for the most part, various over-the-counter remedies or morphine in pill form or by injection. Although a small number of marginal individuals—derelicts, criminals, prostitutes, seamen and others— were known to engage in drug use, their numbers were insignificant in the total national picture of this period.

1. *Treaty of Amity and Commerce*, 20 March 1833, 8 Stat. 454, T.S. No. 321. *See also*, N. Ansley, "International Efforts to Control Narcotics," *Journal of Criminal Law, Criminology and Police Science* L (July-August, 1959), pp. 105–113.

2. J. A. Clausen, "Social and Psychological Factors in Narcotics Addiction," *Law and Contemporary Problems* 22 (Winter, 1957), pp. 34–51.

The early moralistic, social reform outlook has continued to pervade the judgments of those who have shaped legislation directed toward the control of both narcotic and non-narcotic mood-altering substances. But today the moral reformers of old have been replaced by self-appointed moral entrepreneurs who now combine the talents and prejudice of the three traditional major interest groups: criminal justice officials, police and medical personnel, particularly psychiatrists. With respect to drug abuse, they carry on the late nineteenth and early twentieth century crusade against what they perceive as behavior antithetical to the work ethic and its requirements for moral responsibility and striving for success.

An official publication of the United States Government Printing Office lists 54 different public laws (federal) which relate to drug abuse and which were enacted between February, 1909 and October, 1968.[3] Since that time, federal legislation in this area has continued to proliferate at a great rate. The rapid amendment, replacement and succession of legislative provisions provides substantial evidence of the lack of fundamental understanding of the problem to which all of this legislation has been addressed.

CONGRESS, ITS CLIENTS AND DRUG POLICY FORMULATION

The formulation of public policy by Congress is virtually always a shared responsibility between the legislative branch and the bureau-

cracy. In part, this has evolved as a consequence of the growth of "big government," increasingly complex technological developments, and the tendency for bureaucratic organizations to expand and develop broad constituencies.[4]

In the matter of drug legislation and policy formulation, the primary client group or constituency upon which Congress has relied over the years has been the criminal justice system. As is the case with other special interest groups, however, Congress has received from the criminal justice bureaucracy highly selected information consonant with its goals. As such, the development and administration of federal drug legislation enacted since the Harrison Licensing Act of 1914 bears the unmistakable marks of its principal purveyors.

For many years, the most preeminent personality representing the criminal justice approach to drug control was Harry J. Anslinger. Mr. Anslinger, an executive in the old prohibition enforcement program, became Commissioner of the Federal Bureau of Narcotics at that agency's creation in 1930 and remained in the post until his retirement in 1962. His bureaucratic achievements and his capacity to influence and lead docile and uninformed congressional committees for the many years of his tenure is probably unmatched in the history of the nation. During his reign, the enforcement bureaucracy expanded considerably, many new laws were enacted and budgetary outlays increased very significantly.

Thus, over time, the criminal justice/law enforcement bureaucracy —beginning with the old Bureau of

3. G. C. Udell, ed., *Opium and Narcotics Laws* (Washington, D.C.: Government Printing Office, 1968).

4. J. M. Pfiffner and R. K. Presthus, *Public Administration*, 5th ed. (New York: Ronald Press, 1967), p. 54.

Prohibition in the Treasury Department and continuing through the Federal Bureau of Narcotics, the Bureau of Narcotics and Dangerous Drugs and the current Drug Enforcement Administration—has continually expanded its scope of influence and operation. Until very recently, it provided the major impetus for all drug control legislation and has assumed principal responsibility for defining the drug problem, categorizing the offenses, labeling the violators, enforcing the laws, discouraging new approaches to the problem, and periodically returning to Congress to press for new legislation and increased funding levels.

Although in recent years the enforcement bureaucracy has made room for the treatment and research interests represented principally by the medical and psychiatric community, this sharing of the fiscal pie is more a matter of strategy than a belief in the mutually beneficial results of such a cooperative effort. In plain terms, the promises made to Congress over the years by the enforcement bureaucracy have not been fulfilled and, in hindsight, they never could have been. Only as a result of considerable pressure from state and local political figures, the news media and local law enforcement officials, did Congress and its federal drug bureaucracy reluctantly expand the field and include the treatment and research community. It is useful to point out that even such a recent measure as methadone maintenance, originally acclaimed as a treatment modality, was ultimately sold to the public as a crime prevention and control (law enforcement) mechanism. Thus, treatment continues to be subordinated to what remains essentially a criminal

law approach to the problems of narcotic addiction and drug abuse.

Particularly noteworthy in the history of federal drug policy development is the increasingly greater share of the policy formulation process which the bureaucracy has pared away from Congress and the executive branch of the government.[5] As the executive tries to grapple with policy making in the few critical or high priority areas which continually unfold, and as the legislature becomes increasingly dependent upon the bureaucracy for its policy inputs, the bureaucracy has expanded its authority significantly without any increase in its accountability. In this way, the democratic values of American society, which are purportedly guarded by Congress, administered by the executive and judged by the judiciary, have become blurred and somewhat diminished by the bureaucratic agencies in the name of administrative efficiency.[6]

DRUG ABUSE, FACT-FINDING AND CONGRESSIONAL PERFORMANCE

Stephen K. Bailey has enumerated three general propositions relative to the achievement of a desirable standard of performance by Congress. They are: (1) that Congress should act responsibly, that is, it should act in such a way that the voting public may be able to hold individual members and the separate parties reasonably accountable for their actions; (2) that Congress should act democratically, that is, it should formulate policy through a process of majority

5. Ibid., p. 60.

6. M. E. Dimock, G. O. Dimock, and L. W. Koenig, *Public Administration*, rev. ed. (New York: Holt, Rinehart & Winston, 1961), p. 348.

rule while allowing for the free expression of minority opinions rather than vice versa; and (3) that it should act in the public interest rather than in the sole interest of local or narrowly vested group pressures.[7]

In the matter of narcotics and other dangerous drug control legislation, Congress has failed to achieve a satisfactory mark when its performance is measured against the three propositions stated above. Little if any real evidence exists to show that the more than 50 significant legislative actions passed by Congress in this century in any way reflect a genuine consensus or call for action on the part of congressional constituents. It can easily be observed, however, that in nearly all cases the impetus for legislation arose from within the federal bureaucracy. Especially problematic is the fact that the resulting legislation does not in any manner reflect a public consensus or broad professional discussion.

A careful review of the testimony pursuant to the passage of major drug control legislation reveals the following: nowhere was a significant case made for the fact that the public was demanding some action, nor was any attention given to public sentiment or judgment concerning the various solutions which were proposed by the legislative architects. In fact, solutions such as mandatory minimum sentences, denial of parole, no-knock entry and death sentences, which were recommended and later enacted into law, have been shown in many instances to be contrary to broad public sentiment. The same can certainly be said for more recent schemes such as methadone maintenance. Lastly, the testimony also reveals little concern about, or interest in, minority or dissenting opinion.

It might be noted here that the level of uninformed, misguided or otherwise prejudiced judgment relative to the development of drug control legislation seems to have been distributed equally over both major political parties in the Senate as well as in the House of Representatives.[8]

In all, the many hearings pursuant to enactment of the federal drug laws can best be characterized as a charade deemed necessary to satisfy some formal requirement, but with the outcome well established in advance.[9] Witnesses were carefully selected by the bureaucrats in an effort to minimize the input of opposition opinions.[10] In

7. S. K. Bailey, *Congress Makes a Law* (New York: Columbia University Press, 1950), p. ix.

8. J. P. Heinz, R. W. Gettleman, and M. A. Seeskin, "Legislative Politics and the Criminal Law," *Northwestern University Law Review* 64 (July–August 1969), p. 280.

9. U.S., House of Representatives, Committee on Ways and Means, *Taxation of Marihuana* (hearings on H.R. 6385, 75th Cong., 1st sess., 1937, pp. 5–17, hereinafter cited as *House Marihuana Hearings*); U.S., Senate, Committee on the Judiciary, *Illicit Narcotics Traffic* (hearings before the Subcommittee on Improvements in the Federal Criminal Code on S. 3760, 84th Cong., 1st sess., 1956, pt. 1, pp. 17–18, 30, 33–34, 44–45, hereinafter cited as the *Daniel Subcommittee Hearings*).

10. U.S., Senate, Committee on Finance, *Taxation of Marihuana* (hearings on H.R. 6906, 75th Cong., 1st sess., 1937); U.S., House of Representatives, Committee on Ways and Means, *Control of Narcotics, Marihuana and Barbiturates* (hearings on H.R. 3490, 82d Cong., 1st sess., 1951, pp. 1–238, hereinafter cited as *Boggs Subcommittee Hearings*, 1951). *See also*, U.S., Senate, Committee on Finance, Report No. 1051, 82d Cong., 1st sess., 19 October 1951. In this instance, the Senate did not even bother to schedule hearings on a most significant piece of criminal legislation which, in the course of House testimony,

the rare instances in which "opposition" witnesses were permitted to testify, indifference to their viewpoints by committee members was clearly evidenced by the fact that they posed few or irrelevant questions to such witnesses following their presentations.[11] In fact, committee members frequently demonstrated impatience bordering on antisocial behavior toward those persons whose testimony was contrary to specific bureaucratic interests and practices.[12]

Finally, these hearings clearly demonstrate a very low level of preparation and understanding by committee members. As indicated earlier, committee members have traditionally received and relied almost exclusively upon data provided by bureaucratic executives. Despite the fact that these data have generally come to serve as the basis for congressional judgment and action, rarely have the underlying assumptions, the methods of

data collection, or the interpretation of the results been subject to any meaningful or informed questioning or challenge.[13]

Rather, committee members have generally appeared to be satisfied with statistical reports of progress and program success supplied by agency executives who routinely appear before them in well orchestrated and sometimes theatrical imitations of the fact-finding process. No substantial evidence exists to indicate that the hard or "gut" questions are ever posed to law enforcement, treatment or research bureaucrats by Congress.

One must conclude, therefore, either that Congress does not know what to ask or that there are areas of activity about which Congress would prefer to remain in splendid ignorance. Understanding of certain practices, or knowledge about what is really happening in the community regarding drug abuse, would place Congress in the position of having to report to the public the true situation and what it intends to do about it.

All of this raises once again the subject of accountability. It is clear from the above that one of the outstanding characteristics of resultant drug control legislation and the process through which it develops is the lack of any real accountability by the bureaucratic agencies of the executive branch to Congress, and by Congress, in turn, to the public.

---

slandered and viciously castigated the federal judiciary while moving toward a restriction of judicial discretion by imposing mandatory minimum penalties. The committee report was four and one-half pages long, noted favorable reports on H.R. 3490, and recommended passage without amendment. See also, U.S., Senate, Committee on Foreign Relations, Convention on Narcotic Drugs (Executive Report No. 11, 90th Cong., 1st sess., 3 May 1967). In this connection, see also, New Republic (8 July 1967), p. 7.

11. See, Boggs Subcommittee Hearings, 1951, pp. 1–238; U.S., House of Representatives, Committee on Ways and Means, Traffic in and Control of Narcotics, Barbiturates and Amphetamines, 84th Cong., 2d sess., 1956, pp. 510–529, 638–641, 1147–1148, 1219–1228; Daniel Subcommittee Hearings, 1956, pt. 2, pp. 338–350; pt. 6, p. 2149 (hereinafter cited as Boggs Subcommittee Hearings, 1956).

12. House Marihuana Hearings, 1937, pp. 87–121; Boggs Subcommittee Hearings, 1956, pp. 528–529. See also, Daniel Subcommittee Hearings, 1956, pt. 2, pp. 338–350.

13. Boggs Subcommittee Hearings, 1951, p. 111. See also, H. W. Mattick, "The Epidemiology of Drug Addiction and Reflections on the Problem and Policy in the U.S.," Illinois Medical Journal 130 (October, 1966), p. 444; and R. H. Blum and M. L. Funkhouser, "Legislators on Social Scientists and a Social Issue: A Report and Commentary on Some Discussions with Lawmakers about Drug Abuse," Journal of Applied Behavioral Science 1 (March, 1965), pp. 84–112.

That Congress has been a willing, albeit largely uninformed, partner in all of this for more than 60 years is totally inexcusable and demonstrates a serious weakness in the legislative process. Furthermore, it raises some very fundamental questions about the role of the bureaucracy in a free and democratic society, expecially in those cases where the principal agencies involved have police or regulatory powers.[14]

THE BASIS OF DRUG CONTROL LEGISLATION

Over the years, the enactment of each new piece of drug legislation has been justified on the grounds that the drug problem, however defined, was worsening and that harsher and more punitive measures, some of doubtful constitutionality,[15] were needed to deal with it. In hindsight, however, it is clear that the increasingly harsher provisions of the drug control laws constructed by the bureaucracy and guild interests and adopted in great profusion by Congress could never accomplish what they were supposedly formulated to achieve. The reason is that in all cases these punitive laws have been formulated on the basis of false or erroneous premises concerning the nature of opiate addiction and drug abuse and the roles of the participants. In the case of heroin addicts, both the law and enforcement practices reveal the absence of basic understanding of the role, status and interaction

14. S. K. Bailey, *Congress Makes a Law*, pp. 53, 539–554.

15. *See, Agnello* v. *U.S.*, 269 U.S. 20 (1925); *Johnson* v. *U.S.*, 333 U.S. 10 (1948); *Rochin* v. *California*, 342 U.S. 165 (1952); *Jones* v. *U.S.*, 362 U.S. 267 (1960); *Wong Sun* v. *U.S.*, 371 U.S. 471 (1963); *Ker* v. *California*, 374 U.S. 23 (1963).

which takes place among the smugglers, the peddlers or middlemen, and the addicts themselves.

In essence, Congress has consistently failed to take cognizance of the fact that heroin trafficking is a highly organized, relatively low risk, lucrative commercial venture. As with other organized criminal activities, it simply could not continue to exist on any significant scale without the complicity and cooperation of law enforcement authorities and criminal justice personnel at all levels of government, not only in foreign countries but in the United States as well. Yet, Congress consistently ignores this fact and continues to act in response to the bureaucratically convenient view which centers around pursuit and prosecution of the addict.

From the standpoint of the law enforcement bureaucracy, however, this congressional stance is useful in that the addict, who is visible, vulnerable and in constant supply, can continue to provide the data for positive "box scores" needed by federal and local law enforcement officials and politicians. Obviously, it is much more difficult and politically sensitive to root out those well protected and largely invisible figures who profit handsomely from the human misery of heroin addiction. Over the years, the arrest and conviction of large numbers of heroin addicts, along with young middle class poly–drug users and marihuana smokers, has provided law enforcement agencies and prosecutors with a very substantial basis (which they believe and need) for telling the public how much progress is being made in eliminating the drug problem and how much safer our communities are becoming, now that these societal menaces are being "dealt with" properly.

It should be noted, however, that at no time since the very beginning of federal or state drug control efforts has there ever been an objective, reliable and valid estimate of the nature, magnitude and dimensions of the drug problem. In fact, we still do not have an adequate measure of the incidence, prevalence or patterns of heroin use, marihuana use, or use of any of the controlled substances.[16] Rather, in many instances nothing exists but guesstimates published by various bureaucratic officials in order to justify their budgetary requests and the political requirements of their superiors.

VICTIMS OF DRUG CONTROL LEGISLATION

It is almost inconceivable, and certainly inexcusable, that Congress has been satisfied to remain so uninformed about the problems and characteristics of persons who are the objects of their legislative handiwork. At the time of the Harrison Act, the principal victims were Chinese and other "outsiders" who were looked upon as morally weak or unworthy. The Marihuana Tax Act of 1937 incorporated the myth of the dope fiend and was directed at Mexican Americans, musicians, avant-garde artisans, and others who were characterized as, and stigmatized for, being outside of conventional social morality and at odds with the dominant value system of the society.[17] Heroin use in the big city slums became widespread following World War II, and Congress enacted very punitive laws during the 1950s to deal with this new population of "social inferiors." The heroin users of the 1950s, however, were principally the poor slum-dwelling blacks, Puerto Ricans and Mexican Americans whose misery was increased as a consequence of efforts to fill federal and state institutions with them[18] and blithe acceptance of the word and attitudes of law enforcement officials as the definitive judgment.

In retrospect, it is difficult to understand why Congress never asked itself some obvious questions about the results of its legislative judgments. The problems as defined by law continued to focus on slum-dwelling minorities who were outsiders in every sense of the term: outside the economic, social and normative mainstream of America. Still, Congress failed to understand the implications of its actions. Not until the late 1960s, when the impact of the law began to be felt by white, middle class young people in communities and on college campuses, did a counter pressure begin to develop. For the

16. A. Blumstein, P. C. Sagi, and M. E. Wolfgang, "Problems of Estimating the Number of Heroin Addicts," in National Commission on Marihuana and Drug Abuse, *Drug Use in America: Problem in Perspective*, Appendix, vol. 2 (Washington, D.C.: Government Printing Office, 1973), pp. 201–211. See also, National Commission on Marihuana and Drug Abuse, *Drug Use in America: Problem in Perspective* (Washington, D.C.: Government Printing Office, 1973), pp. 41–97.

17. H. S. Becker, *Outsiders: Studies in the Sociology of Deviance* (New York: The Free Press, 1963).

18. U.S., Department of Justice, Bureau of Prisons, *Report on the Work of the Federal Bureau of Prisons* (Washington, D.C.: Government Printing Office, 1957). See also, *Proceedings of the White House Conference on Narcotic and Drug Abuse* (Washington, D.C.: Government Printing Office, 1963). p. 230.

first time in the twentieth century, the objects of the drug control laws were persons from the dominant middle class whose value system served as the basis for the development and enforcement of the criminal code.

As more and more white, middle class young people experimented with marihuana and ethical psychotropic drugs, public concern heightened. Initially, community concern centered on the fact that tens of thousands of young people were being arrested and prosecuted, and many were being sent to jail or prison under the rather strict and punitive provisions of federal and state laws. Not until a number of youthful drug experimenters went on to try other, more dangerous drugs such as heroin and cocaine, and not until public reaction mounted due to some well-publicized drug-related deaths, medical and psychiatric problems, and the branding of many young people as criminals, did Congress, along with state legislative bodies, begin a hasty re-examination and reassessment of existing laws, practices and programs.

This reassessment has resulted in the development of new laws and practices designed to provide a maximum of flexibility in the handling of drug users by "encouraging" them to seek treatment. At the same time, the new laws have expressed increasing determination to stop the importation of illicit drugs—marihuana, heroin and cocaine—and to eliminate diversion into the illicit market of ethical psychotropic drugs. No hard and independent evidence exists, however, to indicate that the determination of Congress has been matched in any way by the performance of enforcement agencies. In recent years, however, we have witnessed an explosion of heroin treatment programs, many of which are based upon methadone maintenance. In addition, a host of other treatment approaches have developed, including so-called drug-free programs, intensive psychotherapeutic, institution-based programs, and numerous other variations ranging from very conventional to esoteric religious-philosophical cultist programs.

Despite many claims of success, especially by large government-supported programs and others resulting from political commitments, no hard, independently developed data exist to show that these programs, with their considerable expenditure of public funds, have had any significant impact either on heroin dependence or on poly-drug use. Rather, findings to date point to the fact that a significant number of these large and costly programs have been grossly mismanaged, their funds squandered and their results nil.[19] The situation is rendered all the more appalling by the manner in which bureaucratic officials, politicans and project officials have conspired to provide "facts" showing results that in reality have never been achieved. The White House Special Action Office for Drug Abuse Prevention (SAODAP), the Justice Department and the National Institute of Mental Health (NIMH) have been the principal purveyors of funds and statistical fairy tales designed to assure the public of their investment's worth and to assure politi-

19. Research Concepts Incorporated, "An Evaluation of the Management of U.S. Methadone Treatment Centers," in National Commission on Marihuana and Drug Abuse, *Drug Use in America: Problem in Perspective*, Appendix, vol. 2 (Washington, D.C.: Government Printing Office, 1973), pp. 334–359.

cians and tax payers alike that matters are indeed getting better.

In reality, federal agencies have been passing out tens of millions of dollars in research and action grants and in contracts to a fairly well developed network of clients, particularly those with powerful political connections, friends and acquaintances in the academic research mills, or colleagues in various other organizations and agencies who have developed the proper lines to funding sources. All the while, Congress continues to appropriate funds and to ask only those questions which are prepared in advance by the bureaucrats. The frequently outrageous political decisions made by SAODAP or the endless string of NIMH research grants, which are made in the "old boy" manner and are frequently duplicative or ill-conceived, are virtually never questioned by Congress.[20]

These issues, along with the uncoordinated proliferation of drug-related programs throughout the federal government, have seriously and rightly undermined public confidence in those who insist that many improvements have been made due to their respective efforts.

RESPONSIBLE CONGRESSIONAL ACTION

A curious situation now exists in which the law enforcement bureaucracy, which previously dominated the drug scene, has a

most willing ally in the treatment-research community. The two are seemingly no longer in competition for funds on Capitol Hill since Congress has seen fit to fund both areas very substantially and to ask few questions. Congress apparently remains satisfied that, because it has funded all possibilities, the desired results will flow naturally.

Now more than ever before, however, a demonstration of responsible congressional action is required. Congress should make an independent assessment of the total federal drug bureaucracy which it has created, with a view to reducing it and making its various components more effective and responsive. It should also undertake an independent assessment of the nature, scope, incidence and prevalence of the drug problem for which it legislates funds. Next, the relevant committees of Congress should enlist and maintain staff and consultant advisors who are free of the bureaucracy and who can advise the members of Congress on the real issues and the results being obtained.

Perhaps the most significant step would be for Congress to set performance standards for the agencies receiving the taxpayers' money. Promises cloaked in questionable data and research jargon should not be accepted by Congress as the standards against which program results will be measured. Rather, Congress itself should set standards of performance for all agencies involved in the drug area, and it should make these agencies responsible and accountable for performing as directed or for providing sufficient and appropriate justification for failure to achieve established goals.

Only when Congress shows and maintains such initiative will the

20. S. J. Mushkin et al., "Federal Funding and Intergovernmental Coordination for Drug Addiction Programs," in National Commission on Marihuana and Drug Abuse, *Drug Use in America: Problem in Perspective*, Appendix, vol. 2 (Washington, D.C.: Government Printing Office, 1973), pp. 5–125.

investment of public confidence and money be justified, and only under such conditions will we begin to understand in a rational manner what the problems really are, what our limitations of action are, what results can be reasonably expected and with what consequences. A continuation of what we have had for more than 60 years simply will not do. In the matter of drug use and abuse, Congress must take the initiative to become informed and to determine what is best for the nation. Congress can no longer rely exclusively on the bureaucrats and special interests to tell its members what in the end is best . . . for themselves.

ANNALS, AAPSS, **417,** Jan. 1975

Politics and Economics of Government Response to Drug Abuse

By SELMA MUSHKIN

ABSTRACT: Relative numbers and relative costs define the type and size of political response to drug abuse in the United States. Those who are damaged by the crime originating in drug abuse outnumber the abusers. While the total cost of crime attributed to drug abuse is high and exceeds efforts of control, intractability of the problem stands in the way of effective action. This paper presents an alternative to the "get-tough" policies represented by action recently taken in New York and the priorities of the federal 1975 budget. It is a second chance of self-help in a new life. Analysis of this proposal is a next step. Its potential adoption, given the relative numbers, is not favorable, and the preferred approach is likely to be incremental. But there is reason to expect that incremental solutions are not sufficient.

Selma Mushkin is a Professor of Economics and Director of the Public Services Laboratory of Georgetown University. She received her Ph.D. from the Graduate Faculty of the New School for Social Research in 1956. Prior to 1964 she was in government service, mostly in the Department of Health, Education, and Welfare. Since then, she has taught at George Washington University, Urban Institute and Georgetown. She has been a consultant to numerous international, federal, and state and local organizations, including PAHO, Unesco, IIEP and OECD, and has written extensively about public services and their financing.

GOVERNMENT response to drug abuse appears to be continually shifting direction. The shifts have their origins in changes in public opinion, in the geographic spread of the problem, and in an expanding knowledge about the nature of drug abuse. Viewed for a long time as an individual problem, mostly of "undesirables," the heroin problem with which this paper is concerned came to be defined as a problem of crime, and later still as one of social disorganization and economic dependency. It was not until 1972, with the enactment of the Drug Abuse Treatment Act, that primary emphasis was given to drug abuse as a health problem.

Historically, heroin abuse was concentrated in New York City. It was a disease of the big city, of the "black belts." Only gradually, as reports of addictions came in from most major cities and even from suburban areas, did the nation comprehend the extent of drug abuse.[1]

Fiscal resources for drug abuse prevention and control have increased. Federal expenditures for all abuse activities that are specific to drugs are expected to rise to $754 million in 1975;[2] expenditures over the nation as a whole are not documented, but perhaps they will be no more than double that sum.

The rise in outlays has been dramatic—some tenfold for the federal government in a decade. But the amounts for federal, state and local governments are still small per drug abuser—perhaps $1,000 to $2,500—and represent only a fraction of the gains that could be made if the disease and the crime associated with it could be brought under control.

At best, even today there is only a reaching out for an answer as to how to prevent drug addiction and reduce its impact. Perhaps due to the complexity of the "system" in which drug abuse issues are presented for public action, much emphasis has been placed on current program evaluation and research. Yet the data on which policy judgments can be made remain meager, and barriers to understanding originate in the entrenched attitudes of those involved in existing drug abuse programs.

SOME POLITICAL ASPECTS

The politics of drug abuse has posed sharply the issue of control. Crime in this day ranks high among the nation's problems, and crime and narcotics are interlocked. In January 1973, Governor Nelson Rockefeller, proposing new legislation for New York State, said, "We must have the understanding and courage to take the stern measures that can protect our people— measures tough enough to deter hard drug pushers, measures tough enough to deal with addicts who commit violent crimes."[3] Existing laws were deemed ineffective and the court processes lax; of 20,762

---

1. Richard Brotman et al., "Suburban Towns Respond to Drugs: A Study of Decision-Making in Contiguous Communities," in the Technical Papers of the Second Report of the National Commission on Marihuana and Drug Abuse, *Drug Use in America: Problems in Perspective*, Appendix, vol. 2, Social Responses to Drug Use (Washington, D.C.: Government Printing Office, 1973), pp. 288–333.

2. *Special Analyses: Budget of the United States Government*, Fiscal Year 1975 (Washington, D.C.: Government Printing Office, 1974), p. 153.

3. Nelson A. Rockefeller, *Testimony at Joint Hearing before Senate and Assembly Codes Committee* (press release), (Albany, New York, 30 January 1973), p. 1.

narcotics arrests in New York City, only 418—just two percent—resulted in prison sentences.

The public agenda includes protection for the thousands victimized by the drug-related crime of drug abusers. While efforts have been made to quantify the extent of crime originating in heroin addiction, the larger pressures for political action originate in the climate that the crime breeds. "Are we," Governor Rockefeller said, "going to accept the degradation, the deaths, the violence, the terror, the immense social and financial pillage that the pushing of drugs is inflicting on our society? . . . The people want this nightmare ended. The preservation of our society and individual security demand it."

The climate is one of fear for person and property, aggravated in some families by anxiety about the spread of heroin use in the schools and the threat that such spread may victimize their children. Those who live in fear of crime can lose the strength of belief and reason from which political democracy draws its vigor. Damage is enlarged by corruption—a corruption that comes from the inability to control narcotics production, to stop drug importation, and to deter illicit trading. Profits high enough to warrent great risk continue to encourage import and trading despite tightened laws. Corruption involving some public officials and law enforcement agents in the crimes further drains strength from the body politic.

The politics of the arithmetic of drug abuse is apparent in the treatment accorded it in former President Nixon's 1974 State of the Union message. Under the caption "Ending Drug Abuse," the progress made and new legislation required were presented in a space equal to or greater than that given culture and communication, rural development, and help for disaster victims, and almost equal to that given the nation's economic security.[4]

Estimates of the costs of crime associated with heroin use are supported by data extracted from analytical studies. The size of the problem has been quantified in terms of: (1) the quantity of heroin demanded; (2) the price of heroin; (3) the nature of the source of funds supporting that demand; and (4) the amount in property thefts that produce those funds. Quantification of those costs requires, in addition to a fairly accurate count of the number of drug abusers, data that range from prices of heroin to "fence" fees or discounts on stolen goods.

Data on numbers are at best partial. Estimates range from about 100,000 to more than 10 times that figure.[5] According to a nationwide survey made for the Commission on Marihuana and Drug Abuse, about 1.5 million Americans between the ages of 12 and 18 have used heroin at least once.[6]

4. Richard M. Nixon, *State of the Union Message* (Washington, D.C.: Government Printing Office, 1974), pp. 34–35.

5. Alfred Blumstein, Philip C. Sagi, and Marvin E. Wolfgang, "Problem of Estimating the Number of Heroin Addicts," in the Technical Papers of the Second Report of the National Commission on Marihuana and Drug Abuse, *Drug Use in America: Problems in Perspective*, Appendix, vol. 2, Social Responses to Drug Use (Washington, D.C.: Government Printing Office, 1973), p. 205.

6. Selma J. Mushkin et al., "Federal Funding and Intergovernmental Coordination for Drug Addiction Programs," in the Technical Papers of the Second Report of the National Commission on Marihuana and Drug Abuse, *Drug Use in America: Problems in Perspective*, Appendix, vol. 2, Social Responses to Drug Use (Washington, D.C.: Government Printing Office, 1973), p. 6.

Price data are needed on heroin per bag, yet price data are not easy to come by in an illicit market. However, data have been quoted on prices, by city, in several studies.[7]

The number of bags of heroin used per day by the addict, another frequently quoted estimate used in arriving at daily costs of supporting addiction, appears to those who have studied the question to be exaggerated. John Holahan, in attempting to measure the market for heroin, notes that the increasing difficulty of obtaining the necessary funds to pay for increasing heroin dosages imposes an upper limit on most habits.

The Hudson Institute has estimated daily consumption to average 55 milligrams, but with a wide distribution among users. The method developed by Mark Moore involved classifying addicts into seven categories ranging from "joy poppers," at four bags per day, to large habit dealers using 18 bags per day.[8]

Cost of acquiring the heroin varies by the size of the market, but certainly in some cities it takes time and involves risk to find the market. The size of the heroin market, determined as a product of number of users, patterns of use, size of dosage per day and price, helps to define the supply—the amount of illicit trade and the amount of profits and size of import.

To convert estimates of data on purchases of heroin into the "crime generated" by maintaining the heroin habit requires knowledge on sources of funds used. Sources of funds for heroin have been estimated by Moore as follows:

Shoplifting	22.5%
Burglary	19.0
Pickpocketing	5.4
Larceny	7.4
Robbery	3.4
Confidence games	4.7
Prostitution	30.7
Welfare	3.0
Other, legal sources	3.9
	100.0%

Information on sources of funds is not sufficient; information is also required on percent in cash and percent in property. Cash can be used directly, but property must be sold to raise the cash; thus a further assumption is needed with respect to the fence or market return on stolen property.[9] The costs to the victims in property loss exceed the amounts received by the addict as a consequence of marketing costs of stolen goods.

The literature on costs of drug-related crime has grown. President Nixon, in his remarks to Congress when he established the Special Action Office for Drug Abuse Prevention (SAODAP), estimated these costs at $2 billion.[10] The Drug Abuse Council arrived at an estimate of $1.7 billion, assuming 250,000 drug addicts, and $2.4 billion,

7. John F. Holahan, "The Economics of Heroin," in *Dealing with Drug Abuse: A Report to the Ford Foundation* (New York: Praeger Publishers, 1972), p. 291.

8. Max Singer and Jane Newitt, *Policy Concerning Drug Abuse in New York State*, Final Report, vol. 1, The Basic Study (Croton-on-Hudson: Hudson Institute, 1970), pp. 54–59, and Mark Moore, vol. 2, Economics of Heroin Distribution (Croton-on-Hudson: Hudson Institute, 1970), p. 64.

9. President's Commission on Law Enforcement and Administration of Justice, *Task Force Report: Narcotics and Drug Abuse* (Washington, D.C.: Government Printing Office, 1967), p. 10.

10. Richard M. Nixon, *Statement to Congress establishing the Special Action Office for Drug Abuse Prevention* (17 June 1971).

assuming 350,000.[11] In New York City alone, crime-related heroin abuse has been estimated to range from $250 million to more than $2 billion per year.[12]

In addition to the personal losses attributable to heroin-related thefts, there are the "public direct costs," represented by costs to taxpayers for public safety and correctional institutions, and social costs of loss in production, both during the time drug abusers are confined and afterwards, for those with criminal records. Those public and social costs are determined by, and are a determining factor in, the risk of arrest per crime committed, the risk of conviction per arrest, and the risk of imprisonment following conviction.[13]

The costs of crime to support drug habits have counterpart costs in the attempts through public safety agencies and the correctional system to apprehend criminals, punish crimes, and rehabilitate offenders. The costs are both direct and indirect. Among the direct costs are those parts of the following which are attributable to law enforcement: police surveillance, police apprehension, intelligence and customs control, court operations (including legal defense, bonding, etc.), correctional institu-

tions and halfway houses (maintenance and capital outlays), added surveillance and arrest costs attributable to complicity.

Indirect costs are composed of: loss in man-years of work in the economy while persons are in correctional or other institutions; earnings attributable to those losses in man-years of work; and loss in earnings due to unemployment of persons with criminal records. (Other costs in human product that may be attributed to drug abuse are not necessarily attributable to crime, and are enumerated in a later section.)

Another type of political process is at issue, however, in the decisions to finance drug programs rather than others, to favor deterrents rather than treatment. The number of drug abusers, though too large in terms of the realities of hard drugs, is small as a group pressuring for public action on drug abuse prevention and commitment of financial resources. Many more persons are victims of addicts than are drug abusers, and, as indicated earlier, the value of property loss is greater for the victims than is the gain for the addicts. In the numbers lies the crux of the problem of preference for control. To quote Governor Rockefeller, "the people want this nightmare ended." The spending priorities are for drug control and crime prevention. The 1975 national budget calls for less of a rise in expenditures for drug abuse prevention than in expenditures for manpower and other resources for control. The increase in preventive expenditures proposed is less than the amount required to maintain present programs, given the price increases expected. Treatment, information, and education programs do not receive as yet the same priority as drug control that

11. Holahan, "Economics of Heroin," p. 293.

12. Mushkin, "Federal Funding," p. 15.

13. David Lawrence Sjoquist, "Property Crime and Economic Behavior: Some Empirical Results," *American Economic Review* 63, no. 8 (June 1973), pp. 439–446; Simon Rottenberg, "The Clandestine Distribution of Heroin, Its Discovery and Suppression," *Journal of Political Economy* 76, no. 1 (January/February 1958), pp. 78–90; William M. Laudes, "An Economic Analysis of the Courts," *Journal of Law and Economics* 14, no. 1 (April 1971), pp. 61–107; T. S. Schelling, "Economics and Criminal Enterprise," *Public Interest* 7 (Spring 1967), pp. 61–78.

could reduce the inflow of drugs and sales. This is so despite the fact that the analytical work that has been done raises the question: Is the restrictive policy making the price too high to society?

There is a balance of forces, moreover, that results in less spending for drug programs of all kinds than the costs—personal, direct and social—would support. This situation is not unusual. In many programs, when the number of beneficiaries is small and not representative of majority concerns, the priorities are not favorable for use of scarce resources. In the present circumstances of the national budget formulation, expansion of resources for full-scale attack on the illness of drug abuse is unlikely.

As long as the taxpaying public is asked to pool collective resources to finance an attempt to reduce or eliminate the drug abuse problem, the distribution of public funds must be paralleled by a continuing and publicly available estimate of just what effect those resources are having in achieving the purposes sought. There is little doubt that at some level of commitment the taxpayers will feel that other public programs will take precedence over additional allocations to drug abuse abatement.

Focusing the politics on the facts is difficult because of the problem's many components. While the punishment approach to dealing with drug abuse appears to be the favored solution, we do not have the data required to confront action and public discussion with fact. For example, we do not know how many users of mind-altering drugs there are in the United States, nor how many ex-users. The complexities have been characterized graphically: "In some ways the drug problem is like a balloon—squeezed in one place it tends to expand in another."[14]

ECONOMIC ASPECTS

Economic analysis of drug abuse starts with a concept of program purposes and asks how those purposes are to be met in a cost-effective way. The basic economic concept is that of optimum use of scarce resources. When resources are applied to drug abuse prevention, they involve the cost of the resources, a cost evident in the opportunities foregone for alternative programs and activities. A decision to provide methadone or other treatment for every addict who seeks it means that less is available for food, housing, or other public and private uses. A decision in favor of stiffer criminal sanctions and imprisonment means that fewer resources are available for preventive activities in drug abuse or for other health or education measures. The opportunity costs of one or another program policy depend upon our value judgments about the purposes of society and the quality of personal development and environment. The costs of a policy pursued are costs in other societal purposes foregone, in other programs that offer promise of enhancing the lives of people.

Why drug abuse control? What payoff is expected? The starting point necessarily is a formulation of objectives as backdrop against which to assess the costs and gains. The specific objectives have been enumerated as follows:

14. Thomas E. Bryant et al., *A Perspective on "Get Tough" Drug Laws* (Washington, D.C.: Drug Abuse Council, 1973), p. 5.

—to decrease the amount of drug addiction-related crime;

—to lower the number of drug addiction-related deaths;

—to rehabilitate the drug addict as a "useful" citizen within the community (employability);

—to decrease the number of new drug addicts;

—to enforce the laws pertaining to the flow of hard drugs and reduce the number of drug addicts;

—to reduce the number of drug addiction-related illnesses;

—to minimize the transfer of antisocial attitudes to other areas (crime, alcohol, other drugs).[15]

The economics of heroin-related crime is viewed in the literature from the perspective of Gary Becker's and George Stigler's work on crime and law enforcement.[16] To Becker, criminal activity generally is a subset of activities that cause diseconomies. Persons become criminals and affect the utility of others, not because of motives that differ from others, but because their benefits and costs differ. This approach implies that there is a function relating the number of offenses by a person to the probability of his conviction, probability of punishment if convicted, income available from legal and other illegal activities, the frequency of nuisance arrests, and the willingness to commit an illegal act. Willingness in part is related to risk preference. Whether crime pays depends upon the attitude of offenders to risk, with the risk itself determined by public policy.

By raising the probability of conviction so that it approaches one, offenses could be deterred. The appropriate public policy is dependent, then, upon the cost of raising the probability of conviction. Or, in Jeremy Bentham's words, "the evil of the punishment must be made to exceed the advantage of the offense."[17]

Optimal policy decisions are decisions that minimize the social loss in income from offenses, losses that are the sum of damages, costs of apprehension and conviction, and costs of punishment. Income from the offense of heroin sales is dependent upon market conditions. The factors determining price define damages and establish the supply response in the light of the costs of apprehension and conviction. Higher price increases the costs of euphoria, the amount of theft required, and the incentives to undermining enforcement activities.[18]

Heroin demand is usually viewed as price inelastic within a margin, but, clearly, alternatives such as methadone increase the elasticity. Demand for heroin tends to drop when prices rise and substitution of product occurs. Substitution effects are part of the "balloon" characteristics of drug abuse that make so difficult and uncertain the effect and policy prescription.

Higher heroin prices encourage more clandestine activity. The analytical framework of criminal behavior is extended by viewing

15. Mushkin, "Federal Funding," p. 21

16. Gary S. Becker, "Crime and Punishment: An Economic Approach," *Journal of Political Economy* 76, no. 2 (March/April 1968), pp. 169–217; George J. Stigler, "The Optimum Enforcement of Laws," *Journal of Political Economy* 78, no. 3 (May/June 1970), pp. 526–536.

17. As quoted in Becker, "Crime and Punishment," p. 191.

18. Edward Erickson, "The Social Costs of the Discovery and Suppression of the Clandestine Distribution of Heroin," *Journal of Political Economy* 77, no. 4, pt. 1 (July/August, 1969), pp. 484–488.

the enterprise of heroin supply in two parts. Simon Rottenberg divides the supply firm operation into an enterprise supplying a service or good and an additional enterprise concealing the activities of that heroin supply, including bribes of law enforcement officials.[19] The decisions on heroin supply require choices between the costs of security and the degree of concealment. While increase in the probability of interception has the effect of reducing supply and raising prices, increases in costs of security operations tend also to raise prices.

Characteristics of the distribution line in heroin make the probability of concealment lowest at the retail sales end of the trade where the accessibility to the addict determines the market. Possibly because a unit of concealment is more costly at that end of the trade, price of heroin at retail is reported to be eight times that at wholesale, and about 150 times that at point of importation.

Because the political emphasis is on tightening the laws, the assessment must determine the possible "payoff" in reduced crime for the action taken. A payoff is uncertain, however, for a number of reasons, including: the shift to other drugs; the high cost of institutional isolation; the contamination of those in prison who were not drug abusers when entering the institution; and the large incentives to organized crime to maintain its product and its market.

Much less analysis has been done on treatment modalities than on the criminal aspects of heroin. Those analyses that have been done are partial at best.

19. Rottenberg, "Clandestine Distribution."

Treatment necessarily starts from an understanding of the nature of the disease. Some persons have argued that the model of a medical problem fits the current drug addiction problem. Drug addiction has characteristics of a communicable disease. While the cause of addiction is not known, it appears to be transmitted by social interaction; it is passed among closely associated individuals having some common social affinity, such as the same job, school, gang or friends. One estimate is that one addict is likely to infect 20 others. Further fact gathering suggests that heroin users are infectious for only a relatively short period. About 80 percent of reported users had infected their successors within a year.

Uncertainty surrounds treatment modalities. Knowledge is limited on what causes the drug problem, how it can be prevented, and how to cure it. In terms of sureness of return, the policy directions are far from clear. The capacity is not at hand to yield information that could permit governments to respond with certainty.

The New York State Addiction Control Commission identified seven different treatment modalities: psychiatric, correctional, interdisciplinary, ex-addict therapeutic, maintenance, drug antagonist and ambulatory care. Each approach has given evidence of providing rehabilitation opportunities for segments of the drug-dependent population.

One major task in determining the payoff is to determine through evaluation which programs are effective with what particular types of addicts. A successful treatment modality for some drug addicts does not mean that it would be useful for all. Data for program assessment are lacking—important data on the number of addicts who are rehabilitated and who remain free of drug use for a given period of time, as well as on those at the other end of the spectrum who do not seek rehabilitative help.

In perhaps no other public service area has as much evaluation been encouraged.[20] Use of the various treatment modalities to derive some findings on potential program payoffs is beginning to yield results.

Costs of the various treatment options are being evaluated, including direct costs, both capital and operation, and staffing patterns. Among the operating cost components are: wages and salaries of personnel, including administrative staff; fringe benefits of staff; equipment; professional fees of consultants; supplies; and transportation services. For comparability among modalities, food, clothing, and residential costs of therapeutic communities ought to be pruned down to the "extra" costs attributable to the treatment, excluding the costs that would be involved in substitute living arrangements. The value of patient services provided would have to be counted as part of direct costs, as would the value of other services and goods contributed without charge.

Indirect costs include, as stated earlier: the cost in manpower lost as a consequence of drug abuse (or the number of days of work lost); the cost in earnings lost for the days not at work; and costs due to un-employment of convicted persons. In the analysis of indirect costs, account must also be taken of:

—the deterioration of skill level and lower earnings potential;
—the production losses attributable to inability to concentrate, apathy, and lessened physical activity;
—the added costs of production attributable to wastes of material and industrial accidents; and
—the costs of continuing unemployment for those with criminal records.

There are still other costs to be reflected—costs that bear on inter-generational impacts of heroin use and addiction.

TYPES OF TREATMENT

One study of 37 federally funded drug treatment programs operating at 80 sites throughout the country analyzed three treatment modalities —methadone, residential therapeutic community program, and outpatient abstinence programs—to determine costs, client utilization of services, and staff productivity. The measures used in assessing each modality are those listed above, and are applied sequentially in examining four best programs of each modality type. Such a study marks a step toward understanding cost of differing modalities.[21]

In assessing gains, it is important to ask what would have been the employment and productivity ex-

20. Special Action Office for Drug Abuse Prevention, *First Annual Report* (1973); National Commission on Marihuana and Drug Abuse, *Drug Use in America: Problems in Perspective*, Second Report of the National Commission on Marihuana and Drug Abuse (Washington, D.C.: Government Printing Office, 1973).

21. Marvin R. Burt et al., *Staffing and Efficiency of Drug Treatment Programs*, vol. 5 of *An Analysis of the Staffing Patterns for Comprehensive Health Centers, Family Planning Projects and Drug Treatment Programs* (Bethesda, Maryland: Burt Associates, 1973).

perience without the drug prevention program. Or, if persons under treatment are employed, is the employment a consequence of the treatment, or is it attributable to other factors? In brief, are the earnings gained added earnings?

The New York Temporary Commission to Evaluate Drug Laws reports that addicts in treatment are becoming able to function and are available for training and jobs. Jobs have been found to be an important component of rehabilitation, and one of the best predictors of successful treatment is prior employment. Yet only a beginning has been made to remove barriers to the employment of those who are addicts. This is the general handicap for men and women with criminal records.

One of the reasons for reliance on follow-up and evaluation is to determine what approach works and for how long. The commitment, however, of those directing a project to the chosen design and operation often stands in the way of hard evaluation. Correction for this bias is not simple, for it is a commitment to work and cure that is a vital input to the treatment modality itself. Another difficulty in fact gathering and evaluation lies in the known characteristics of drug abusers, which indicate a deterioration of person that underlies behavior, encourages cheating and lying, and makes fact gathering difficult.

Methadone

As a modality, methadone has perhaps received more publicity than other treatment methods. Objectives of methadone programs have been diverse, but perhaps most weight has been given to reducing crime and assimilating heroin ad-

dicts into society.[22] The Johns Hopkins evaluation study of modalities measures outcome in terms of: (1) continued heroin use; (2) criminality; (3) economic productivity; (4) social coping; and (5) health and psychological adjustment. Some studies point to effectiveness of such programs in terms of the added earnings of the addicts served.[23] Lesser criteria of success are often used, including annual cost per patient and percent completions of course of treatment. One study of 40 programs selected as targets for interview sought to assess these programs with the findings, questioning the feasibility of assessment when programs differ and have varied purposes and management procedures. "The loose central management controls in individual methadone projects and apparent over funding raise some serious questions as to the integrity of some program managers."[24]

Methadone use that reduces crime and opens paths to employment of the drug abuser can have large payoffs. In making the demand for heroin less price inelastic, the availability of methadone reduces prices for the heroin addicts.

22. Wallace Mandell et al., *An Evaluation of Treatment Programs for Drug Abusers*, vol. 2, Summary (Baltimore: Johns Hopkins University, School of Hygiene and Public Health, 1973).

23. William H. McGlothlin et al., *Alternative Approaches to Opiate Addiction Control: Costs, Benefits and Potential* (Washington, D.C.: Department of Justice, Bureau of Narcotics and Dangerous Drugs, 1972).

24. Research Concepts, Inc. "An Evaluation of the Management of U.S. Methadone Treatment Centers," in the Technical Papers of the Second Report of the National Commission on Marihuana and Drug Abuse, *Drug Use in America: Problems in Perspective*, Appendix, vol. 2, Social Responses to Drug Use (Washington, D.C.: Government Printing Office, 1973), p. 345.

Some qualifications about methadone projects are:

—increased use of supplementing drugs (number of users);
—spread of addiction to methadone of those who have not used heroin (number of users and wastes in treatment costs);
—uncertainties about methadone's physical effects over a long period of use (may cause added future costs); and
—on-again-off-again use of heroin that is encouraged by ready access to methadone centers (number of users).

A COMPARISON OF APPROACHES

Stiffening the law

The component costs of crime were discussed earlier. New York State in 1973 officially moved away from five years of experimentation with programs that treated drug offenders medically to imposition of life sentences for the sale of hard drugs. For sales of a pound or more of heroin, cocaine, morphine or opium, a minimum sentence of 15 to 25 years is decreed, with a maximum of life without possibility of parole. Strong penalties for smaller amounts of a wider range of drugs are also specified. For possession of one-eighth to one ounce of major narcotics, the law calls for sentences of 1 to 15 years for first offenders and 4½ to 25 years for second offenders.

Evaluation of New York State's move calls for determination of costs and effectiveness in the quarantine of the user in the jails and prisons of the nation. Among the costs, if the method results in higher rates of imprisonment, are the cost of maintaining prisoners in jails—perhaps $5,000 to $6,000 per prisoner per year—and the costs of overcrowding of jails in further crime, loss of life, and spread of addiction. Does the threat of imprisonment serve as a real deterrent? Little evidence exists to suggest the deterrent effects of tight laws.

Much is unknown about the number and characteristics of addicts already in penal institutions and of those directed by the courts to rehabilitation and treatment. The cause-and-effect relationship of heroin and other drug abuse and criminal behavior is still unknown. Some persons using heroin would engage in criminal behavior even if they were not addicts. Data are not available on the number of persons who commit crimes simply to purchase heroin, as underscored by Jared Tinklenberg in his study of drugs and crime.[25] What would be the costs of attempting to use undercover methods to determine drug sales? Will the new law be effective? Will it increase consumption? Will it cause a shift in product of the crime market? A study by the Drug Abuse Council details the historical experience with similar penalties over the years, noting that by the early 1960s many groups, including the Federal Bureau of Prisons, criticized mandatory minimums as being cumbersome and ineffective in controlling drug abuse. Furthermore, the same report notes other changes that could come about, including:

—a rise in alcoholism;
—an immediate and large rise in use of barbiturates; and

25. Jared Tinklenberg and R. C. Stillman, "Drug Use and Violence," in Daniels et al., eds., *Violence and the Struggle for Existence* (Boston: Little, Brown & Co., 1970).

—the use of new and more potent psychoactive drugs with unknown side effects.

In his study, John Holahan concludes: "It is ironic that our national policy, by resorting almost exclusively to criminal sanctions to eliminate addiction, has bred a thriving illegal market that can be sustained only by criminal activity."[26] The two factors identified as basic incentives are the small amount of opium needed to supply the heroin demand (since only a small output is needed at point of origin, control is impossible) and the large profits which make it unlikely that the risk will be high enough to force dealers out of business.

The second chance community

If assumptions are made about the isolation of the addict who spreads the disease and about the role of employment and personal dignity in a "cure," an alternative to the "get-tough" laws offers itself. The get-tough laws are an attempt to deal with the drug problem from three perspectives: (1) as punishment for users or dealers; (2) as deterrent to potential users or dealers; and (3) as rehabilitation and cure primarily for users. The weakness of punishment as an effective deterrent has been discussed. Now we turn to isolation and self-help as potential cure.

Inherent in the notion of incarceration is the idea that addicts must be isolated from the population at large. Isolation may in fact be applicable for certain types of drug-dependent persons—those likely to addict others, those with high rates

26. Holahan, "Economics of Heroin," p. 293.

of recidivism after other forms of treatment, and those who come from a social milieu conducive to drug use. But are there not better, more productive isolation methods than long term imprisonment? It is assumed here that isolation can be achieved earlier and better by developmental self-help communities that offer a second chance. Assumption of responsibility by the national government for treatment and rehabilitation of drug abusers opens the way to the design of such public sponsored mutual-help communities.

Historic precedent exists for second chance communities. The records of history point to the colonization of New Zealand, Australia and the United States by those whose crimes led to imprisonment in the home country, but who were permitted migration and resettlement in a second chance new home.

Addicts who enroll voluntarily, or those coming through the criminal system, could be given the opportunity to build a new community and, by inference, a new life in an isolated setting. The government's role would be one of sponsorship and catalyst. Isolated communities could be defined in a geographic sense as being far removed from population concentrations, or in a social sense as having no easy interaction with the city or community at large. Addicts would participate in site selection and in the actual building and design of the communities. They would be given the opportunity to maintain their family units and to participate in community government. Maximum use—with governmental technical assistance—would be made of income maintenance payments, medicaid, housing allowances, public service employment, and the like by residents of the second chance community. An integral part of the community would be specific forms of drug treatment for the drug abuser's withdrawal: methadone maintenance, encounter groups and/or therapy groups.

No complete or detailed formulation is attempted here, but in any proposal of this kind some important questions must be considered. A decision would have to be made about the level of funding in terms of the type of subsidies, the manner in which subsidies are extended, the savings in existing public programs, and the savings in social costs. Several classes of subsidies should be considered: (1) subsidized public services—health care, education and food stamps, for example—equivalent to those available to all communities; (2) subsidies for economic enterprise; and (3) subsidies for housing and community facilities.

Presumably a special office would have to be established to administer the second chance community. Its functions would include: (1) responding to addicts seeking to establish or join second chance communities; (2) providing assistance with site selection; (3) aiding in subsidizing land, equipment, and building acquisitions on behalf of the community; (4) facilitating access to the Small Business Administration, Veterans Administration, Economic Development Administration, and other agencies which provide loans to economic enterprises; (5) assisting in obtaining access to and securing other public services such as vocational training and technical assistance; (6) monitoring participation in the communities; and (7) performing other functions of management and administration as required.

The approach of isolation without prison combines public supervision of drug abusers with a strong emphasis on a new life and the support of the community in meeting stressful situations. The nation would assume little authority over various aspects of living by participants. The intention is to foster economically viable communities in which the participants undertake to eliminate their drug dependency, build a history of job training and employment experience, and make, with their families if they so elect, a new life.

Initial eligibility for participation in the program may be defined in several ways. It could be opened to all comers. It could be made an option to imprisonment, a later stage precondition for parole, or an alternative to halfway community houses for those on parole. Once initial eligibility were established by the administering authority, community members would be encouraged to establish rules and procedures for those desiring entry and participation.

Communities could differ on their entry rules. One might require evidence of a specific drug-free period as a precondition. Others might have as part of their program a specific method of drug treatment, and require a demonstrated interest in that mode of therapy.

Provisions for exit from the program would have to be clearly defined. Exit would have to be safeguarded both for volunteer entrants as well as those coming through the penal system. Evidence of non–drug use for a substantial period of time would be the main condition. The most difficult exit requirement question would apply to the volunteer. Could he leave voluntarily? Or, having made the election, would he also be required to be free of drug use for a substantial period? If the second chance communities are an option to prison, individuals would have the option of returning to prison. Failure to comply with community rules may require imprisonment as a sanction as well. Again, maximum flexibility might be incorporated into the approach, at least at the beginning when experimental possibilities are being tested.

Perhaps among the major blocks to the second chance community is acceptance by neighboring communities. There is a long and well documented history of neighborhood fear of, and resistance to, the nearby location of treatment centers for drug abusers, mental patients, parolees or run-aways. Self-built, self-run programs by drug abusers coming from another locale are likely to encounter strong local objections.

The problem may be compounded, but just as possibly ameliorated, by the fact that the program is not conceived as a temporary home for a large stream of addict-inmates. One of its inherent features is the potential that program participants will become drug-free—the primary definition of cure and provision for exit—and will choose to stay in the community, committing themselves to the new life they have built. Thus, area residents may feel greater reluctance to allow not just a treatment center, but the establishment of a "new town in town," or a new neighborhood.

In summary, experience with the existing modalities, when they are drawn together and analyzed, moves toward meeting the problems of a response from government. The past experience, evaluated in depth, provides a way to help ensure the generating of new ideas that will cope better with critical drug abuse. But the experience that will be drawn from these evaluations is likely to be interpreted as calling for incremental change that will meet the public desires for action as evidenced in public opinion polls. A less incremental approach is suggested here, and the option of second chance communities is outlined. The proposal requires in-depth evaluation. It could provide, however, a foundation for a long term attack based on reasoned action. Too tough, too soon is not the answer.

Planning: A Personal View and Some Practical Considerations

By STUART M. MATLINS

ASTRACT: Because planning is often viewed as being external to the total management process, planning activities are often isolated from the management system within which they take place and which they are intended to serve. As a result, the use and utility of the planning product as a tool for management decision making and a more rational approach to the allocation of society's resources are significantly diminished. To a large extent, the "drug crisis" and society's response to it has suffered from this isolation of planning activity from the management process. This article addresses the practical side of the process as it actually takes place and concentrates on the major factors that affect the ultimate use, or nonuse, of the product. More specifically, it describes the various purposes for research data in the area of drugs and social policy; defines and describes the different types of planning activities that may be used to obtain the data needed; describes the major approaches to planning as currently utilized; highlights some of the problems in current planning activities; and recommends some improvements that can be made in the planning process and in the use of its products.

Stuart M. Matlins, Vice President of Booz, Allen & Hamilton, Inc., Management Consultants, is Managing Officer of the firm's Institutional and Public Management Division. His practice covers the functions of planning, organization and evaluation for governmental, institutional and commercial clients that have included the National Commission on Marihuana and Drug Abuse, International Council on Alcohol and Addictions, National Council on Alcoholism, National Institute on Alcohol Abuse and Alcoholism, and other federal, state and local government organizations and privately operated programs. He holds a B.S. from the University of Wisconsin and an A.M. from Princeton University.

THE PLANNING process and the utilization of data resulting from it have been the subject of much consideration and discussion as society becomes increasingly aware of the interaction in the real world of seemingly unrelated actions. Much of the discussion has focused on the need for planning and the techniques of doing it. This article addresses the practical side of the process as it actually takes place and concentrates on the major factors that affect the ultimate use—or nonuse—of the product. It argues particularly that planning too often has been viewed as being outside of the total management process and that this tendency to isolate planning activity from the management system must be overcome if the product is to be useful. Otherwise, planning will become an increasingly esoteric activity of declining interest to all but the planners themselves. Instead of being a tool for optimizing more rationally the allocation of society's resources, it will become another drain on them. At that point, the current disuse of many of the products of planning will be followed by disuse of the planners themselves.

The following material concentrates on planning in general but gives specific attention to its application in the area of drugs and social policy. Its aim is to:

—describe the different purposes for research data in the area of drugs and social policy;
—define and describe the different types of planning activities that may be used to obtain the data needed;
—describe major approaches to planning as currently done;
—highlight some of the problems in current planning activities; and
—recommend some improvements that can be made in the process of planning and in the use of its products.

THE PROBLEM OF PURPOSE

All data may be interesting, but not all of it is equally interesting or equally useful. In order for the planning process—data collection, analysis and the development of recommendations—to be useful, a careful preselection process is essential. The purpose for which data will be used must be clearly understood by participants in the effort and clearly articulated by them to ensure that a common understanding exists between them and the ultimate consumer of their product. This purposeful approach to planning must then take place within the context of the total management process. The attack on the abuse of drugs and other substances and the social policy developed to carry out the attack have faltered significantly as a result of problems in the management of the effort. While preoccupied with doing something to meet "the crisis," we have given insufficient attention to the management of our activities. This performance in the drug crisis is not an isolated one. It is typical of approaches to many other social problems, from the war on poverty to the crisis in our cities.

Planning: servant of the management process

There are several elements in the successful management of any endeavor. Planning is but one of them and should be seen as the servant of them all. These elements are:

—understanding the need to undertake the endeavor;

—defining goals and objectives;

—making specific plans to achieve those defined objectives;

—mustering the necessary resources to carry out the plan;

—structuring the resources within an organization that equalizes responsibility with authority at all levels;

—creating incentives to enhance the goal-orientation of the people in the system;

—scheduling and execution of monitoring activities, a follow-up to test whether the planned operations continue to be implemented as planned; and

—scheduling and execution of evaluation activities, an examination to determine if implementation of the plan is producing the desired result. Evaluation must feed back into the entire process of goal definition, planning and action.

Data collection: defining the purpose

The data to be collected and the research effort to be carried out must begin by defining clearly the purposes to be served. These purposes might include:

—guilding the specific development of the endeavor's activities and the services or products it is to produce;

—organizing and staffing to provide the resources for carrying out the activities and the framework within which they will be managed;

—controlling the endeavor's activities once they are underway to ensure that they remain targeted on the end to be reached;

—coordinating activities within the one organization involved in the endeavor or among different organizations, each of which may have a role to play in reaching the agreed-upon goal; and

—evaluating the results of the activities actually carried out to determine whether they are the ones most appropriate to achieving the agreed-upon goal and to guide future activities.

Purpose of politicking

In addition to these fairly traditional purposes of data use, one other must be given its proper place: the purpose of politicking, that is, drawing attention to the existence of the problem and the need to do something about it, and motivating the decision makers to allocate resources to attacking the problem. In the early 1960s, when Great Britain's recurring balance of payments problem became a subject of almost constant attention in our daily newspapers, the prime minister was asked at a press conference why his country had not experienced similar problems during the nineteenth century. His answer was that many factors were different at the earlier time, the most important of them being "no statisticians." The appearance of a problem worth addressing by the society may not be its existence, but our ability to recognize it. It may be a problem in our perception rather than in its existence. The collection of data may serve importantly the objective of pointing out a problem's existence. This, too, is a worthwhile purpose.

The purpose of politicking was highly visible in the early stages of this society's attempt to address the drug use and abuse problem. The problem was frequently defined as those in control of the governmental machinery wanted to see it. Data, incomplete at best, were arrayed to focus the country's attention as desired rather than to present a balanced view of the problem as it really existed. As a result, much of the resources expended in the initial attack were spent on solving the wrong problems or perhaps even problems that did not exist.

As in all of the instances cited above, planning must be viewed in the context of the purpose to be served. The sponsors of the effort must know what they want and what they need. This is not to suggest that data collection should be skewed to give us the answers we want; rather, it should be tailored to a specified purpose so that it is relevant as well as objective. And, despite much evidence to the contrary, planning is not an end in itself.

THE HIERARCHY OF TIME AND ORGANIZATION

Once the purpose for the planning activity is defined, its focus must be sharpened by recognizing that movement toward a goal takes place over time and at different levels in an organization. Different types of planning take us out over different parts of the time continuum leading to ultimate achievement of a goal. A cartoon that appeared recently in the *New Yorker* illustrates the point. It shows two pilgrims in seventeenth century dress standing and chatting together on the deck of a Mayflower-like sailing ship. They are talking about the reasons for their journey to the New World, and one explains to the other: "Religious freedom is my immediate goal, but my long-range plan is to go into real estate."

The basic function of the planning process is to assist in the allocation of scarce resources among less scarce alternative uses for those resources. This is much like the definition of economics as provided by the English economist Lord Robbins in the 1930s when he called economics "the science which studies human behavior as a relationship between ends and scarce means which have alternative uses." Successful planning is, then, a way of thinking about the world as it is and as we would like it to be and the development of a guide to get us from one point to the other. This movement takes place over time and is recognized by two different types of planning: strategic and operational.

Strategic planning

The strategic planning process identifies major long term problems and proposes broad strategies for dealing with them. It looks to the future, perhaps 5 to 10 years. It is comprehensive in scope and looks at all the factors operating in the environment without the constraint of whether the unit for which the plan is being made has any control over those factors. The strategic planning process is long range and is used to identify strategies which should:

—be reflected in the operational programs of sub-units;
—require changes that can be made within the authority of the units; and
—require action by third parties.

In terms of those matters under the unit's direct control, the strategic planning process provides the framework for the annual operating plans of each constituent sub-unit. In a highly formal system, a strategic planning process provides quantified output targets; the sub-unit operating plans develop the detailed resource requirements for reaching those targets. Less formal systems look to the strategic planning process for qualitative rather than quantitative guidance for operational planning.

The strategic plan can be captured in a single document at periodic intervals, or it can exist as a continuous stream of analyses, recommendations and strategic decisions on salient issues. The format is less important than the capability to identify and address strategic issues.

In the federal government's approach to the drug problem, the need for a strategic plan was recognized and the development of a strategic plan for drug abuse traffic and prevention was mandated by the Drug Abuse Office and Treatment Act of 1972. Responsibility for the development of the plan was given to a Strategy Council comprised of secretaries of state, treasury, defense, and health, education and welfare, the attorney general, the administrator of the Veteran's Administration, the director of the Special Action Office for Drug Abuse Prevention, and the director of the Office for Drug Abuse Law Enforcement. The product of the Strategy Council's effort appeared in March, 1973, several months after the deadline specified in the act.

Operational planning

Operational plans translate targets developed in the strategic plan into operational terms. The operational plan is built around each sub-unit's particular area of responsibility. The planning process involves the identification and analysis of the alternative means that the sub-unit might use to reach specified performance targets. The operating plan is generated annually and issued as a basis for controlling and evaluating performance during the operating year.

Unlike strategic plans, operating plans are always formal documents produced at regular annual intervals within a framework of detailed procedures. Because analyses conducted as part of an operating plan cycle compare alternative means for meeting the same specified ends, the analytical sophistication of operating plan analyses can be quite high.

At each level of the planning process—strategic and operational —and within each, the need for data and the uses of that data must be articulated clearly. There must be a plan within the plan.

Function of Planning

The basic function of planning and the research activities that take place as part of the planning process is to improve the quality of decisions made over time. The most striking characteristic of many planning systems is their failure to impact on the decision making process. While planning in a vacuum often produces documents that are impressive from the point of view of technical craftsmanship, such planning rarely impacts on decisions. Planning's reason for existence is to improve the quality of decisions. An effective system features products which can be understood and used by decision makers, not planners. This means that the planning process must be designed to involve decision makers at key points. It also means that the methodologies involved in planning must be credible to decision makers. These requirements most often are met by systems which are simple and systematic rather than highly sophisticated.

In turn, the data collection systems that will provide the raw inputs for the planning process must be simple and systematic. They must be designed for easy use by the people who will actually collect the raw data. In the drug field, the basic data collection systems designed at the federal level and mandated on other levels of government and individual programs failed, in my experience, to recognize this important issue. They tended to be highly sophisticated and comprehensive and were far beyond the technical capacities of the people in the field. As a result, system implementation was and is an unending problem.

Getting decision makers to understand and use planning system products is usually the most serious constraint in planning system implementation. Getting planners to tie the products of their activities into the decision makers' management process is often the most serious constraint in the use of planning products.

At all times, whether short or long range in scope, plans must have the following characteristics in common:

— identification of need;
— stated objectives; and
— definition of success.

The development of data, whether on a continuous reporting basis or through special studies that focus on particular issues, must relate to meeting a purpose that ties into one or more of these plan characteristics and into the process of managing to meet objectives.

PROBLEMS IN THE CURRENT PROCESS

Planning may be carried out through a variety of organizational means. If the organization to be served is large enough, it may have its own separate planning unit. If it is not large enough to sustain planning as a separate activity, or if it does not have the right mix of talents available internally, it may obtain planning assistance for the whole plan or specific parts, such as special studies, by using outside resources. These outside resources usually fall into one of four categories, particularly in the substance abuse planning field: (1) academic institutions; (2) individual "experts;" (3) private contract research firms; or (4) private management consulting firms.

Importance of involvement

The designation of the most appropriate source of outside assistance is as varied as are the individuals involved in making the selection. The most important distinction to be made is between those internal, as well as external, planning and research resources that set themselves, or allow themselves to be set, apart from the decision makers and managers the planning activity is intended to serve. As stated previously, planning exists to assist in the decision making process. The conduct of the planning activity, therefore, must involve the decision makers at all stages. Whether performed by an internal planning unit or an external contract research firm, the planning activity must function in a counseling mode, forming a team of planners, managers and decision makers. Within the organizational hierarchy, the process must be both "top down" and "bottom up" so that people at all levels participate in determining the paths they must follow and in designating the measures by which their performance will be judged.

Domination of form over substance

All too often, the planning activities that have taken place to help allocate resources in the drug field have been characterized by their separation from the reality of the world, as well as the reality of the organization intended to carry out the plan. Federally mandated requirements to plan are laudable in intent and frequently laughable in result. The planning activity is often seen as an onerous chore that must be carried out in order to receive federal funds. So-called experts are brought in to piece together a set of words that meet the federal guidelines. The plan is approved and put on a shelf to gather dust until next year's cycle begins.

In such a system, the planning process has been used primarily to produce the "paper plans" needed to satisfy federal requirements and get the funds distributed within the state, rather than to identify need, establish priorities among competing objectives, and allocate resources systematically. Monitoring of activity against plans of this kind simply becomes a self-fulfilling prophesy. Evaluation cannot be conducted in any meaningful way because clearly articulated goals and objectives were not set for individual unit performance at the start. Though obvious, it seems little recognized that if you have not determined what you want to get, you cannot tell when you have it—or do not have it. At the other extreme, simplistic and inappropriate statements of goals can be useful to the recipient of federal funds if the statement is accepted. I have always envied the managers of a drug program whose federally funded grant application I reviewed two years ago. Their objective for the full year was clearly articulated: establish a drug program at 201 Second Street. Success was theirs immediately.

The efforts of federal officials in the drug establishment to require adherence to planning guidelines have been good on the whole. They have backed up the requirements they have mandated by withholding funds until an adequate plan is developed, even in the face of significant political pressure. Their failure has taken place, however, after the paper product exists. The commitment or the resources, or both, have not been present to ensure that the plan, once completed, becomes a working tool rather than an artifact.

Proposal season

At the federal level, research that is potentially of significant assistance to the more rational allocation of resources is carried out too often under less than optimally rational conditions. Too often research follows the boom-bust cycle of "proposal season," the commitment of funds for research each spring so that they do not have to be returned to the Treasury Department on July 1. This type of research activity is often ill-conceived, and its products little used. In the rush to spend, there is little time for the coordination of inter- and even intra-agency activities. The selection of researcher, contractor or consultant may become a highly political process. The amount committed to the effort becomes a function of what is left in the budget rather than what is needed in fact. Guidelines for future decision making, themselves planned and developed in a less than rational process, are poor tools for use in building the future—and the cycle continues.

A vision of the future

The development of clearly defined goals and objectives within a hierarchy of priorities is essential to the efficient and effective allocation of limited resources to help us accomplish our goals. In practice, this can be an extremely threatening process. Perhaps the threat comes from the possibility that our potential failure will be obvious if we commit ourselves to a precise goal; perhaps it comes from the obviousness of the need and our reluctance to do the obvious. For whatever reason, a threat exists. I have participated in planning workshops in which professionally responsible adults have been so threatened by the task at hand that they have resorted to the refuge of nonparticipation through a variety of means. For example, one otherwise sober individual used the opportunity of the dinner break to anaesthetize himself against the pain with alcohol and spent the evening work session insisting that the primary objective of his unit was to provide a happy work environment for his people. Another professional with a position of pub-

lic responsibility spent a day and a half reading the same issue of the *Wall Street Journal*, an arduous task at best, intermittently arguing that there was so much to do that there was no time for the planning workshop. These people, and others whose behavior was less dramatic, highlight the reluctance to take the first steps toward more rational decision making. Those initial steps, the setting of clearly articulated goals and objectives, involve the making of clear choices among competing goals and objectives, among alternative uses of resources. It is a competition. There are winners and there are losers. The individual who can use the system will gain power over the use of his own resources and the potential for getting more resources from others who can not or will not commit themselves clearly to providing a social return for society's investment.

Management of the effort

The "we don't have time for this" argument carries through frequently to the execution of the plan itself. Sometimes it is correct; the plan may be so voluminous or sophisticated as to be unusable in a day-to-day world of operating pressures. It must be recognized, however, that preparation of the plan is only the beginning of the process. The plan document, the research product, is only a way of stabilizing thought at a point in time. The planning process must be run as part of the management process so that it becomes a way of thinking about what is done on a day-to-day basis. This means that managers must take the time to produce a plan that is useful to them for managing and then use it. This approach must be communicated downward by example from each management level in an organization. It requires that managers have the courage to make clear decisions that resolve the conflicts between organizations whose goals and objectives compete and conflict in their operational activities. This can be seen, for example, in the competition between law enforcement agencies that seek arrests to demonstrate their success and treatment programs that seek to avoid the arrest of clients who may have lapses while showing progress toward rehabilitation.

Identification of need

The massive federal effort to combat drug abuse began and continued for much of its history without identifying effectively the nature and extent of the problem or the need for different types of drug abuse prevention activities. This applies to programs and activities of preventive education and law enforcement as well as of treatment and rehabilitation. Most federal agencies relied on applicants and state agencies to identify and assess need in a given area. The state agencies primarily responsible for identifying program requirements did not have the resources or the sophistication required to assess need on an objectively measured basis. They frequently passed the responsibility down to grant applicants and local government bodies. As a result, existing and potential service providers relied on subjective evaluations to identify need. These evaluations often coincided with self-interest. Objective assessment of need on a con-

tinuing basis is a task essential to the rational allocation of resources.

Closing the loop

Planning is a continuous process. A planning system of ongoing data collection and special studies produces products in the form of analyses, recommendations and decisions, but it never produces "the plan." The system must provide for routine reassessment of basic objectives and a continuing evaluation of the adequacy of earlier decisions. It must be used by managers on a routine basis as they make the decisions that take them from where they are to where they want to be.

USE: THE MEASURE OF SUCCESS

The best measure of the success of a planning effort is whether it is used. This does not mean that the paper product must be followed as an unalterable road map to some destination. Rather, it means that the process of plotting the course to a desired future has allowed the decision makers to make initial choices among alternative uses of resources and to discern when it is necessary or desirable to remake them.

Priorities of decision makers

For planning to influence decision making effectively, planners must be aware of the priorities of the decision makers. Good information and analysis or a good system does not increase rational decision making unless it focuses on the needs of those people who can make important resource allocation decisions.

Information and analysis

Once planners are aware of the top priorities of the decision makers, they must be able to produce the information and analysis that is required to improve the quality of decision making. Planning that is action-oriented must be able to recommend actions that attack the major problem areas of an issue, not just the problem areas that appear to be important on the surface.

To promote implementation, planning must be part of a system that disseminates information and analysis to groups outside the planner's own unit in such a way that future planning and implementation activities are coordinated better and are more comprehensive. Such a system requires an information flow that translates planning information and analysis into program budgeting decisions and finally into evaluation feedback.

Operational usefulness

The operational usefulness of planning or research activity must be kept in mind from the beginning if implementation is to be achieved. This is particularly important when goals and objectives are developed initially. It is difficult to plan when objectives are vague. Plans are rarely any better than the objectives they address. Any planning system depends on the clearest feasible articulation of the objectives of the organization's key decision makers. This is an extremely difficult task. Many of the legitimiate differences between decision makers are in fact differences in view about objectives to be pursued by public programs. While the job of defining objectives is always difficult, the ideal toward which planners should lead decision makers is the "operationally useful objective." The operationally useful objective meets the following criteria:

— it focuses on the output or end product or service provided by the organization, not on the means for providing that service;
— it can be translated into quantifiable measures of output or benefits;
— it is defined with sufficient precision to permit the identification of competing or inconsistent objectives.

Role of the consumer

Sometimes, no matter what those involved in the planning or research process do, the products are little used, used improperly, or disused entirely. This reflects on the role of the ultimate consumer of the planning effort, the manager or decision maker, or on how that role is played. In a theatrical production, the successful performance of each of the actors is dependent not only on their individual efforts, but also on the dramatic tension that is created by their interaction. The actors play "against" each other in a wholly constructive sense. So too in other endeavors, each of the players must act out his role fully, or the tension that holds the endeavor together and allows it to use its energies to move forward will be absent. Energy will be used to move in place. The appearance of activity may be impressive, but results will only be an apparition.

Decision makers and managers must understand their roles and play them fully. Frequently, full-time managers of social and other programs do not perceive their functions correctly. They do not plan and manage their own activities, let alone those of their subordinates. Distracted by activity, they forget about purpose. They flatter themselves by thinking that in the drama of their lives they move from crisis to crisis. In fact, like a 1940s "Our Gal Sunday," they move from episode to episode, each day's trauma having within it the seeds of the next day's distraction. Managing by episode, they do not reserve a part of their time to carry out their unique function—looking to the future and setting the course for reaching it.

When decision making or the setting of direction through the making of policy is reserved to a board of directors or other multiheaded governing body, the problem of getting use out of the planning process and its products is frequently compounded. While the involvement of many heads in directing an endeavor may be better than one head and may serve desirable social purposes such as community involvement, a governing body is not better simply because of its existence. It must work to be better. Board members, typically part-time people who have been selected for membership because of the position they already have in the community, frequently are overcommitted. They carry out their board role in the time left over from other occupations. Since decision makers are often underskilled, overworked and poorly prepared, decisions are made in an atmosphere where interpersonal and political considerations dominate. Until the board members concentrate on meeting their obligations as part of a deliberative body, the functioning of the organization must of necessity be impaired.

For the effective efforts of planners and researchers to optimize the rational use of resources, the decision makers, managers and governing body must accept and meet the unique responsibilities of their own roles. The planner or researcher need not be passive in this area. His obligation is not met by the delivery of the paper product. He must actively reach out to the decision makers to involve them in the process and explain the use of the product.

The end must be considered from the beginning

The planning process should begin with the end. The planner should ask himself:

—What am I going to do with all this stuff once I've got it?
—How much of the organization's resources will be used to get it?
—Is the benefit worth the cost?

The means do not justify the ends. The results of the process must be the justification for its taking place. The desired result at all times is improving the quality of decision making. In the area of drugs and other issues of social policy, the decision making often may be dominated by political considerations. In a study of how resources are allocated to drug-related functions, conducted for the National Commission on Marihuana and Drug Abuse by Booz, Allen & Hamilton, we concluded that "resources usually are allocated on the basis of political need as perceived by politicians." While it would be naive to expect the resource allocation system to be apolitical, it is equally naive to assume that the current system must be accepted in resignation.

A practical planning process managed by realistic professionals can be used to provide decision makers with the information they need to make better decisions. The perception of need can be sharpened and focused. The management of activities can be made goal-oriented. The results of those activities can be evaluated in terms of their efficient and effective movement toward the goal, and they can feed back into guiding what we will do to take us from where we are to where we want to be. An active, result-oriented planning activity that concentrates on and involves itself with these management issues can improve the rationality of resource allocation and produce more benefit for the society.

ANNALS, AAPSS, **417**, Jan. 1975

The Concept of Prevention and Its Limitations

By RICHARD BROTMAN AND FREDERIC SUFFET

ABSTRACT: The concept of prevention was first developed in the field of public health and epidemiology. Since the 1960s, it has been applied increasingly to illicit drug use, thus standing alongside law and treatment as a major form of social control over drugs. While a strict epidemiologic, or "contagion," model of drug use is held by some, we find this model to be of limited utility for discussing the broad range of efforts commonly defined in the field as preventive. An economic, or supply-demand, model is proposed instead. Under this model, prevention is defined as the attempt to reduce the demand for drugs. Four strategies for reducing demand are discussed: (1) coercion, or the threat of formal punitive sanctions; (2) persuasion, or education in the harmful consequences of drug use; (3) correction, or the eradication of the presumed causes of drug use; and (4) substitution, or the provision of alternatives to drug use. The limitations of each strategy are discussed, and because of the prevalence of recreational patterns of moderate drug use, it is concluded that the prevention of all illicit drug use is not an achievable goal.

Dr. Richard Brotman is a Professor in the Department of Psychiatry, New York Medical College, and Director of the college's Division of Community Mental Health. He has published widely on drug use and alcoholism and has conducted research for the National Commission on Marihuana and Drug Abuse. He has also designed drug education programs for inner-city and suburban schools, and has taught at the City College of New York and Barnard College.

Frederic Suffet is an Instructor in the Department of Psychiatry, New York Medical College, and Research Associate in the college's Division of Community Mental Health. He has been involved in a number of drug education programs and, with Dr. Brotman, has published articles on various aspects of drug use. He collaborated on research conducted for the National Commission on Marihuana and Drug Abuse. Mr. Suffet has taught at Finch College and New York University.

ALTHOUGH the United States has frequently been characterized as a drug-oriented society, the use of certain drugs for purposes of pleasure or stress relief has, historically, been socially and legally proscribed. Drugs subject to proscription have included heroin and other opiates, cannabis preparations such as marihuana and hashish, LSD and other psychedelics, cocaine, and amphetamines and barbiturates when not used under medical supervision.

Broadly speaking, the proscription has two main sources. First, the use of such drugs is seen as potentially injurious to the physical and mental health of the user, particularly when use is immoderate. Second, their use, especially for reasons of pleasure, has been widely regarded as antithetical to the complex of moral values, including industriousness and maintaining control of ones rational faculties, often designated by the terms "work ethic" or "Protestant ethic." The former assertion hardly requires elaboration. Evidence for the latter may be found in many places, most recently in a survey of a national sample of adults sponsored by the National Commission on Marihuana and Drug Abuse. The survey revealed, for example, that 59 percent of the respondents thought marihuana use makes people lose their desire to work, and 64 percent said using marihuana is morally offensive.[1]

Historically, the loci of responsibility for enforcing the proscription, that is, for the control of illicit drug use, developed initially in two main institutional realms—law and medicine. Stated briefly, the intended function of legal control has been to deter the use and distribution of banned drugs by threat of punitive sanctions. The intended function of medical control, as expressed through various approaches to treating drug users—chemotherapy and therapeutic communities, for example—has been to terminate individual drug use careers. However, as the so-called drug explosion of the 1960s showed, both forms of control largely failed. The law apparently did not deter many persons from becoming involved in illegal drug activities, probably because the risk of arrest was demonstrably low. Few drug users came into contact with drug treatment programs, and of those who did relatively few stopped using drugs permanently.

Consequently, there was, starting in the mid-1960s, a rising demand for another form of control which would complement law and medicine. This was a demand for prevention, for programs which would somehow keep people from entering into the world of illicit drug use. And, since in the 1960s drug use was seen mainly as a problem of the young, the demand focused primarily on the need to create or update school-based programs.

The upward curve of this demand, and the remarkable speed with which it became the basis of a significant aspect of national drug control policy, may be charted by federal appropriations over the past five years for drug education and information programs. In fiscal year 1969, $2.7 million was appropriated, followed by $10.3 million in 1970, $24.1 million in 1971, $43.7 mil-

1. Herbert Abelson, Rueben Cohen, and Diane Schrayer, "Public Attitudes Toward Marihuana," in National Commission on Marihuana and Drug Abuse, *Marihuana: A Signal of Misunderstanding*, Appendix, vol.

lion in 1972, and $40.5 million in 1973.[2] These funds, disbursed through various federal agencies to establish programs at national, state and local levels, scarcely reflect the magnitude of the burgeoning drug prevention "industry," for an incalculable amount of money and effort for preventive programs has been generated by businesses, foundations, voluntary organizations, and other groups in the private sector. While it is probably true that most programs are based in the schools (a National Commission on Marihuana and Drug Abuse survey showed that, as of 1971, twenty-four states required drug education at secondary school level, and in the other states many, if not most, local school districts had developed programs on their own initiative[3]), it should be pointed out that many programs operate outside the schools in forums as diverse as the national television networks, local churches and civic groups, and so on.

It is clear, then, that the prevention of illicit drug use has become a major area of planned social action. It is also quite clear, as critics have begun to point out, that programs in this area, with few exceptions, have not been evaluated.[4] As a result,

there are few empirical clues as to what drug prevention actually accomplishes; no one really knows whether preventive programs, by and large, achieve their goals. Moreover, the assumption that the concept of prevention is applicable to illicit drug use has largely gone unquestioned. So strong has this assumption been, constituting as it does the fundamental premise of the entire preventive enterprise, that only within the past year or two has it been asked: Is the prevention of illicit drug use a realistic, achievable goal? Or is it just wishful thinking?

The purpose of this paper is to examine the concept of prevention as it relates to the use of illegal drugs and to make explicit some of its limitations. In doing this we outline a model, or classificatory scheme, in which we can locate the various approaches to prevention.

THE CONCEPT OF PREVENTION

The concept of prevention was first developed in the field of public health and epidemiology. In the classic epidemiologic formulation, the spread of contagious disease among people depends on the interaction of an agent (the disease germ) with a host (the human organism) as mediated through a particular environment (physical and social). Given this formulation, which is greatly oversimplified here, prevention may, according to standard public health categories, occur at three levels. *Primary* pre-

2 (Washington, D.C.: Government Printing Office, 1972), p. 893. For a classic analysis of the values which drug use is said to violate, see, Howard S. Becker, *Outsiders: Studies in the Sociology of Deviance* (New York: Free Press, 1963), ch. 7.

2. Reported in National Commission on Marihuana and Drug Abuse, *Drug Use in America: Problem in Perspective* (Washington, D.C.: Government Printing Office, 1973), p. 348.

3. "Marihuana and Education," in *Marihuana: A Signal of Misunderstanding,* Appendix, vol. 2, p. 1204.

4. For example, see, Patricia M. Wald and Annette Abrams, "Drug Education," in Drug

Abuse Survey Project, *Dealing with Drug Abuse: A Report to the Ford Foundation* (New York: Praeger Publishers, 1972), pp. 123–172.

vention is aimed at keeping the agent from infecting potential hosts by, for example, immunizing the uninfected parts of the population or quarantining those already infected. *Secondary* prevention, through early case finding and diagnosis, seeks to limit the disease process among infected individuals in whom the process is not far advanced. *Tertiary* prevention aims at limiting disabilities among, and if possible rehabilitating, persons in whom the disease process has reached an advanced stage.[5]

As employed in the field of drugs, the concept of prevention has usually meant primary prevention and, to some extent, secondary prevention. In other words, the aim of preventive efforts has been to keep nonusers from becoming illicit drug users, and to help experimental or occasional users revert to nonuse, or at least to keep them from progressing to patterns of heavy use. Those who have reached the point of heavy involvement with drugs are typically seen as candidates for treatment; they are beyond the reach of preventive efforts. In this paper we shall adhere to the meaning of prevention commonly understood in the drug field; programs of treatment and rehabilitation for those already seriously involved with drugs will be considered herein to fall outside the area of prevention.

Since it is by now indisputably clear that most people are introduced to illicit drugs by intimate associates—usually friends, sometimes relatives—and not by the

mythical pusher who loiters near schools, some persons in the field uphold a "contagion" or epidemiological model of drug use which views use as spread by direct contact. Under the auspices of this model, they propose classic public health measures, such as quarantining known users, or chemically immunizing nonusers.[6] It should be noted that these measures are usually recommended with respect to heroin addiction.

In our view, however, the contagion model has a significant shortcoming. Namely, unlike the case of an infectious disease, people contract the disease of drug use willingly; they *choose* to use drugs. There is, in short, an element of volition in drug use which the epidemiological model fails to encompass adequately. Given this shortcoming, the model is of limited utility for discussing the wide range of efforts coming under the rubric of prevention. We therefore employ a different model, one which better fits the empirical facts. This is an economic model, first developed for somewhat different purposes by James V. Koch and Stanley E. Grupp, which treats factors of supply and demand as the organizing principles of analysis.[7]

5. For a full discussion of the epidemiologic approach to prevention, *see*, Hugh Rodman Leavell and E. Gurney Clark, *Preventive Medicine for the Doctor in His Community: an Epidemiologic Approach* (New York: McGraw-Hill, 1958), esp. pt. 1.

6. For a statement recommending that drug addicts be quarantined, *see*, James L. Markham, "Quarantining of Drug Addicts Urged to Halt Epidemic," *New York Times*, 8 May 1972. In regard to immunization, the suggestion has been made that it may be possible to do this by implanting biodegradable silastic vehicles containing a narcotic antagonist in "at risk" individuals. *See*, for example, Max Fink, "Narcotic Antagonists in Opiate Dependence," *Science* 169 (4 September 1970), pp. 1005–1006.

7. James V. Koch and Stanley E. Grupp, "The Economics of Drug Control Policies," *International Journal of the Addictions* 6, no. 4 (December 1971), pp. 571–584.

Under the terms of this model, prevention in its broadest sense may be said to include, first, all efforts aimed at reducing the supply of drugs, and second, all efforts aimed at reducing the demand for drugs. Attempts to reduce the supply of drugs, especially through monitoring and interdicting the illegal drug traffic, fall, generally speaking, into the domain of law enforcement. Such activity may validly be called preventive to the degree that it curtails the drug supply and, in turn, restricts opportunities for drug use. However, since in the drug field the term *prevention*, as commonly used, does not cover this kind of law enforcement activity, we shall eschew further consideration of the supply side of the equation and focus instead on the demand side, where virtually all preventive efforts, in the usual meaning of the term, may be located analytically.

In what follows we review the main approaches to prevention—that is, the strategies for reducing demand—and point out what appear to be the limitations of the various approaches. These are discussed under four headings: (1) coercion, or the threat of formal punitive sanctions; (2) persuasion, or education in the harmful consequences of drug use; (3) correction, or the eradication of the presumed causes of drug use; and (4) substitution, or the provision of alternatives to drug use.

Coercion

Throughout most of the twentieth century, the basic means American society has employed to reduce the demand for illicit drugs is the threat of punitive sanctions, as expressed through formal penalties codified in the law. This has been true at least since the passage of the Harrison Act in 1914, and the general trend, in response to the stubborn persistence of illegal drug use, has been to increase the severity of the penalties.[8] The major exception to this trend has been the reduction, over the past few years, of penalties for marihuana possession.[9]

The theory behind the drug laws is that the threat of punishment will act as a deterrent, that through the instrument of the law people can be coerced into acting in their own best interests. But despite its preventive intent, the law, viewed as a strategy to reduce the demand for drugs, has clearly not proved effective. One could discourse at length on why this is so; but since the detection and arrest of drug possessors, like the case of drug traffickers, is typically considered a law enforcement matter and not a form of prevention, let us consider another kind of coercion, one which is often closely linked to programs generally recognized as preventive in nature. This is the application of extra-legal administrative sanctions by certain organizations, schools in particular, to individuals discovered to be in possession of illegal drugs.

Schools, from elementary to college level, have become the key site for preventive programs, and

8. For comprehensive historical treatments of the United States drug laws, *see,* Alfred R. Lindesmith, *The Addict and the Law* (Bloomington: Indiana University Press, 1965); Rufus King, *The Drug Hang-Up: America's Fifty-Year Folly* (New York: W. W. Norton, 1972); and David Musto, *The American Disease: Origins of Narcotic Control* (New Haven: Yale University Press, 1973).

9. For a recent survey of changes in the marihuana laws, *see, Shafer Commission News,* 31 October 1972.

for two reasons. First, young people are seen as the primary "population at risk" in regard to drug use; and second, school settings permit an in-depth presentation and discussion of drug information. The substantive aspects of such programs are treated below. Here we note that school-based programs, especially at secondary and college levels, often include, in addition to the strictly educational aspects of the program, a warning to students that administrative sanctions may be applied to any of them discovered to be drug users. Typically, these sanctions involve the possibility of suspension or expulsion from school, although in some cases school policy may include notifying the police.[10] Whatever the arguments pro and con concerning the use of these sanctions, it is clear that such warnings are not always a hollow threat. In two noteworthy instances, midshipmen at the United States Naval Academy have been expelled for marihuana use.[11] A national survey of schools conducted for the National Commission on Marihuana and Drug Abuse showed that 50 per cent of the 363 secondary schools sampled had suspended at least one student for involvement in a drug-related incident, and 21 percent had expelled at least one.[12]

Despite these facts, the use of administrative sanctions, considered purely as a means to reduce drug demand, has an important limitation. Most students, knowing school policy regarding illicit drugs, are not likely to use drugs in situations where there is a risk of detection by the school authorities. Given the high rate of campus drug use, it may be inferred that most drug-using students do not view detection as a significant possibility. It may also be, for obvious reasons, that many school administrators do not seriously attempt to identify drug users among their student populations. Thus it would seem that the most important function of the enactment of policies which include administrative sanctions is not to reduce the demand for drugs, but rather to placate parents, legal authorities and other interested parties outside the school, assuring them that the school administration is "doing something" about drugs.

No one, of course, pretends that administrative sanctions form the core of any prevention program; rather, they are ancillary to the main effort, which is to prevent drug use through nonpunitive means. From all indications, the most prevalent approach along these lines is education, or the attempt to persuade people by dint of information to abstain from drugs.

10. For a review of elementary and secondary school policies and college and university policies, *see,* respectively, Robert F. Boldt, Richard R. Reilly, and Paul W. Haberman, "A Survey and Assessment of the Current Status of Drug-Related Instructional Programs in Secondary and Elementary Educational Institutions," and Gerald L. Robinson, Leon R. Young, and Martin E. Duffy, "Review of College and University Policies Concerning Illegal and Unprescribed Drugs and Narcotics," in National Commission on Marihuana and Drug Abuse, *Drug Use in America: Problem in Perspective,* Appendix, vol. 2 (Washington, D.C.: Government Printing Office, 1973), pp. 455–546, and pp. 548–570.

11. "Thirteen Midshipmen Face Dismissal in Marihuana Case at Annapolis," *New York Times,* 22 February 1968; and "Seven Middies Expelled in Cloud of Pot," *New York Post,* 6 March 1972.

12. Boldt, Reilly, and Haberman, "A Survey," p. 492, table 27.

Persuasion

The effort to reduce drug demand through persuasion rests on a key rationalist assumption ". . . that given valid information about the consequences of alternative courses of action, most people will not elect the course most likely to result in self-harm."[13] In a similar vein, Donald A. McCune, in his report on drug education to the National Commission on Marihuana and Drug Abuse, said:

The general consensus among the public at large as well as many in the drug bureaucracy has been that primary prevention can best be achieved through effective education. The traditional rationale has been very simplistic: if an individual knows about the drugs and their harmful effects and if he understands fully the variety of social controls and punishments associated with the use of drugs, he will abstain from using such substances in order to avoid the consequences.[14]

In their review of school drug education curricula, Robert Boldt, Richard Reilly and Paul Haberman found that, "This concept, expressed in different ways, is the pervasive theme of all the drug curricula reviewed."[15] Indeed, in their national survey of drug education practices of 342 elementary and 363 secondary schools, they discovered that, in the academic year 1972–73, the physical and psychological effects of drugs on the user was the single most emphasized topic in educational programs, with an identical proportion—85 percent—of the schools at both levels reporting this emphasis.[16] They found, furthermore, that the most frequently utilized educational technique, presumably used to convey this information, was audiovisual presentation (reported by 67 percent of the elementary schools and 70 per cent of the secondary schools).[17]

The schools, of course, are only the most conspicuous example of this form of prevention. Persuasion has also been attempted at the national level through brief television messages, some developed with the support of the National Institute of Mental Health, which describe the dangers of various kinds of drug use.[18]

The sheer proliferation of drug education programs of one kind or another suggests that the rationalist assumption which underlies them —that is, that knowledge of the possible consequences of drug use will promote nonuse—has in effect become an article of faith, one which until recently has gone unquestioned.[19] It is becoming clear, however, that this approach to prevention has certain limitations.

First of all, attempts to persuade people not to use drugs, by force of information, fly in the face of a commonplace observation: even

16. Ibid., pp. 498–499, tables 37 and 38.
17. Ibid., pp. 504–505, tables 44 and 45.
18. For a review of drug education programs conducted through the national media, see, Wald and Abrams, "Drug Education," pp. 150–155.
19. For a critique of this assumption as it applies generally to health behavior, see, Jon Colby Swanson, "Second Thoughts on Knowledge and Attitude Effects upon Behavior," Journal of School Health 42, no. 6 (June 1972), pp. 363–365.

13. Richard Brotman and Frederic Suffet, "Marihuana Use and Social Control," Annals of the New York Academy of Sciences 191 (31 December 1971), p. 242.
14. Donald A. McCune, "An Analysis of the Role of the State in Drug Education," in Drug Use in America: Problem in Perspective, Appendix, vol. 2, p. 394.
15. Boldt, Reilly, and Haberman, "A Survey," p. 461.

when they accept the information as valid, people often discount the risks and act against their own best interests. The use of cigarettes in this country is a classic case in point. This behavior might be termed the "not me" syndrome, which expresses the individual's belief that harm will not befall him, only someone else. For example, a study of 155 narcotics addicts undergoing treatment in the California Rehabilitation Center showed that 81 percent of them claimed that when they first began to use narcotics they did not believe they would become addicted.[20]

Second, information may not be believed by its intended audience because its source is not seen as being credible. Several studies of students have indicated, for instance, that they often discredit drug information offered by law enforcement officers, clergymen, and school guidance counselors on the grounds that such persons are trying to promote "official" moral values.[21]

Third, drug information offered by an education program may not be in accordance with information individuals obtain from friends or from firsthand observations of drug use. In the event of such discordance, the discrepancy may be resolved by crediting only the latter kinds of information, since these generally indicate to the individual that the risks attached to drug use are not nearly so high as official sources would have him believe.[22] Howard S. Becker has pointed out that the drug subculture has its own informal ways of doing "research" on drug effects, and that the body of knowledge which results and is disseminated among users may be quite different from the information disseminated by official sources.[23] In fact, officially produced information often may be faulty. For example, the National Coordinating Council on Drug Education recently evaluated 220 films on drug use and rated 84 percent of them unacceptable. Council president Robert M. Earle said that, "The majority of these films are inaccurate, unscientific and psychologically unsound."[24]

The use of inaccurate information, especially that which exaggerates the dangers of drugs like marihuana, may produce, as a number of researchers have observed, an unfortunate "boomerang" effect. That is, if a program's audience disbelieves information on drugs which in their experience are not terribly dangerous, they may also discredit information on drugs whose dangers are more certain, and thus be induced to try them.[25]

20. Troy Duster, The Legislation of Morality: Laws, Drugs, and Moral Judgment (New York: Free Press, 1970), p. 180.

21. See, for instance, Richard A. Bogg, Roy G. Smith, and Susan D. Russell, Drugs and Michigan High School Students (Michigan Department of Public Health, 1968), pp. 33–34; and Richard H. Blum and Associates, Students and Drugs (San Francisco: Jossey-Bass, 1969), pp. 346–347.

22. Peter T. Adler and Lynn Lotecka, "Drug Use among High School Students: Patterns and Correlates," International Journal of the Addictions 8, no. 3 (1973), pp. 537–548. Although the authors do not touch on the point concerning discrepancy, their data show that among personal sources of drug information (that is, excluding the mass media), students view friends as the most trusted source.

23. Howard S. Becker, "Consciousness, Power and Drug Effects," Society 10, no. 4 (May/June 1973), pp. 26–31.

24. "Drug Abuse Films Termed Harmful," New York Times, 13 December 1972.

25. Herbert Blumer and his associates were among the first to make this observa-

One might assume that the latter problem can be solved by having programs issue only accurate information. However, as the National Commission on Marihuana and Drug Abuse has noted, drug education programs face a special dilemma:

Prevention programs may proclaim goals which stress the prevention of high-risk drug use, or of drug dependence, or use of particular drugs, but in practice they must try to curtail *all* illicit drug use. Programs which expressly emphasize the harm of certain use patterns imply that other patterns are relatively harmless and thus tacitly condone them. Since this is unacceptable, education-information programs usually take the opposite tack; they suggest that all use patterns are equally harmful, because all are likely to evolve into undesirable behavior.[26]

The fourth limitation to the persuasion approach is that educational programs, even when they take care to deliver accurate information, may actually stimulate drug use rather than deter it. This possibility is suggested by the research of Richard B. Stuart, to our knowledge the only research designed to assess the effects of a drug education program on the drug use behavior of its audience.[27] Space limitations prohibit details, but the research was done in experimental form, with 935 students in two suburban junior high schools being randomly assigned to experimental drug education or to control groups. The experimental group was given a ten-session fact-oriented drug curriculum, taught over a ten-week period. Pre- and post-measures were made of the use and sale of various drugs, as well as of drug-related knowledge and attitudes. For some students, follow-up data were obtained four months after the program (all data were collected in the 1971-72 academic year). The key findings, for this discussion, were that the experimental group, compared with the controls, showed a sizable increase in the use of alcohol, marihuana and LSD, and also became more involved in the selling of the latter two drugs.

Given these findings, a difficult problem arises: If programs which present distorted information induce a certain amount of illicit drug use through a "boomerang" effect, and if programs which strive for honesty also induce a certain amount of use (perhaps by a combination of increasing knowledge and reducing worry about possible harm, as Dr. Stuart's research suggests), is there a viable role for drug education programs? Are efforts based on persuasion a tenable means of reducing the demand for illicit drugs? The definitive answers to these questions are not known, but at the moment the evidence is not promising. It is not surprising, then, that in early 1973 both the National Commission on Marihuana and Drug Abuse and the federal Special Action Office for Drug Abuse Prevention called for a moratorium on production and dissemination of new drug education materials.[28] It should be noted that

tion. *See, The World of Youthful Drug Use* (Berkeley: School of Criminology, University of California, 1967), p. 55.

26. *Drug Use in America: Problem in Perspective*, p. 351.

27. Richard B. Stuart, "Teaching Facts about Drugs: Pushing or Preventing?," *Journal of Educational Psychology* 66, no. 2 (Washington, D.C.: American Psychological Association, April 1974), pp. 189–201.

28. *Drug Use in America: Problem in Perspective*, p. 355.

neither agency recommended a complete halt to drug education efforts, but a moratorium would allow time for evaluation and critical appraisal of the goals, methods and results of programs currently in operation.

Correction

An approach to prevention which has recently gained currency is correction, or the attempt to reduce drug demand indirectly by dealing with the presumed causes of illicit drug use. A vast body of research on the etiological factors involved in drug taking indicates that the causes are multiplex, ranging from the individual level (personality attributes), to the interactional level (differential access to and involvement in drug-using groups), to the macrosocial level (for example, the evolutionary trend in our society toward acceptance of mildly hedonistic forms of recreation).

Obviously, some causal factors are beyond the reach of preventive efforts. For instance, a number of recent studies show that youthful drug users come disproportionately from families in which the parents use alcohol, tobacco, and prescription drugs.[29] These youngsters, in effect, socially inherit a predisposing orientation to substance use which facilitates their decision to try illegal drugs when introduced to them by peers. The problem, of course, is that by the time a youngster is exposed to a prevention program, the substance use patterns of his or her parents have probably had their effect; there is no way to

go back in time and try to change these patterns.

Because of such difficulties, preventive efforts which address causal factors tend to focus on the attributes of the individual, in particular his or her value system. The key approach along these lines, as practiced in many school-based programs, is what has been variously called "affective education," "humanistic education," or "value clarification." The thrust of this approach is to help youngsters, through a number of techniques such as role playing, to form their values consciously, so that in time they will become autonomous individuals, capable of making rational decisions based on those values. A typical statement of this approach is one made by Henry A. Kane and Doris Pearsall:

Students should be helped to develop a sense of inherent self-worth and uniqueness which will lead to the choice of positive and viable alternatives in life rather than self-destructive ones. . . . Assistance for each student in the clarification of individual values and value systems for himself and in relation to his individual choice of life style should pervade all areas of discussion. Students should be helped to develop a mutuality of respect for others who hold different values from their own, while at the same time developing a confidence and trust in ones own values and a willingness to live ones life in accordance therewith.[30]

The assumption apparently underlying this approach is that once an individual's values are "clarified," he or she will refrain from drug

29. These studies are cited and their implications discussed by Erich Goode, in *The Drug Phenomenon: Social Aspects of Drug Taking* (Indianapolis: Bobbs-Merrill, 1973), pp. 23–24.

30. Henry A. Kane and Doris Pearsall, "Youthful Drug Abuse . . . The Schools of the City of Boston . . . and the Challenge of Preventive Education," in *Drug Use in America: Problem in Perspective*, Appendix, vol. 2, p. 449.

use. But given the current absence of evaluation data, that remains, empirically, an open question.

Theoretically, the approach has an important limitation; that is, the overriding values it recommends—as distinct from whatever specific values students may form —may foster rather than inhibit drug use. The above quotation, taken on face value, advocates self-construction of individual values rather than unquestioning acceptance of received values; individual choice of life style rather than unthinking conformity to dominant life styles; and tolerance of differences of others. These are precisely the kinds of values which many studies have found illicit drug users to hold, and which distinguish them from nonusers to a large degree.[31] These studies have shown that drug users, as compared with nonusers, tend to be more self-exploratory, more open to experimentation with different life styles, and more tolerant of unconventional behavior. If the affective education or value clarification approach truly promotes these values, then in the long run, whatever its other potential merits, this approach may do little to reduce the demand for drugs.

Substitution

A final approach to reducing drug demand is substitution, or the pro-

vision of alternatives to drug use, especially natural or nondrug "turn-ons." This approach is often recommended in prevention literature, but it is undoubtedly less widely practiced than are the approaches discussed above, at least in the sense of its forming the basis of actual programs.

The approach rests on the premise that there is something in the drug experience which users seek, and that this can be gained through nondrug means. For example, the National Commission on Marihuana and Drug Abuse has recommended that ". . . drug use prevention strategy, rather than concentrating resources and efforts in persuading or 'educating' people not to use drugs, emphasize alternative means of obtaining what users seek from drugs: means that are better for the user and better for society."[32]

The question, of course, is: What do users seek through drugs? Some theorists see drug use as resulting from a lack of meaningful experiences, or a lack of relevant "connectedness" to others, a kind of socio-psychological isolation, as it were. They recommend that opportunities be made available for people to become involved in pursuits—community work, the arts, craft skills, and new recreational programs—which will provide personal fulfillment and a sense of meaningful involvement with others.[33]

Others believe that drug users basically seek altered states of con-

31. *See,* for example, Bogg, Smith, and Russell, *High School Students;* Blum and Associates, *Students and Drugs;* Edward A. Suchman, "The 'Hang-Loose' Ethic and the Spirit of Drug Use," *Journal of Health and Social Behavior* 9, no. 2 (June 1968), pp. 146–155; Erich Goode, *The Marihuana Smokers* (New York: Basic Books, 1970), ch. 2; and Richard Brotman and Frederic Suffet, "Some Social Correlates of Student Drug Use," *Crime and Delinquency* 16, no. 1 (January 1970), pp. 67–74.

32. *Drug Use in America: Problem in Perspective,* pp. 353–354.

33. An example of this point of view is provided by Stanley F. Yolles, "Managing the Mood Changers," *New York University Education Quarterly* 2, no. 3 (Spring 1971), pp. 2–8.

sciousness. Drug authority Andrew Weil holds that the desire occasionally to experience such states is an innate drive.[34] Accordingly, somewhat more esoteric alternatives are recommended which will induce altered states of consciousness, including yoga and meditation.[35]

The limitation to this approach is that, in principle, none of these alternatives is necessarily mutually exclusive with drug use. It may be perfectly possible to become intensely involved in community work, or in the arts, or to practice yoga—and still use drugs. Indeed, several studies of student drug users have shown that, compared with nonusers, they are more involved in political activities and in artistic pursuits.[36]

More important, perhaps, is the real possibility that none of the alternatives provides what users seek from drugs. Marihuana users, for example, typically report that the drug is a sensory intensifier, that it greatly increases their enjoyment of music, food and sex.[37] If this is one of the significant reinforcing aspects of the marihuana experience, it is difficult to see what can substitute for it.

34. Andrew Weil, *The Natural Mind* (Boston: Houghton Mifflin, 1972), pp. 19–20.
35. *See,* for instance, Allan A. Cohen, "Psychedelic Drugs and the Student: Educational Strategies," in Richard E. Horman and Allan M. Fox, eds., *Drug Awareness* (New York: Avon Books, 1970).
36. Suchman, "The 'Hang-Loose' Ethic;" Brotman and Suffet, "Some Social Correlates;" and James L. Carey, *The College Drug Scene* (Englewood Cliffs, N.J.: Prentice-Hall, 1968), esp. pp. 122–144.
37. Probably the most detailed study of marihuana's effects, as reported by users, is Charles T. Tart, *On Being Stoned: A Psychological Study of Marihuana Intoxication* (Palo Alto, Cal.: Science and Behavior Books, 1971). *See also,* Goode, *The Marihuana Smokers,* ch. 7.

CONCLUSION

Using a simple supply-demand model, we have asserted that most efforts at prevention, as the term is ordinarily understood, are strategies intended to reduce the demand for drugs. We have reviewed four major strategies or approaches: coercion, persuasion, correction, and substitution. And we have pointed out what appear to be the limitations of each.

The picture, frankly, is not hopeful. If the goal of prevention is to curtail *all* illicit drug use, then it is fair to say that, on the basis of currently available evidence, none of the approaches has proved effective.

Perhaps the time has come, as several observers have suggested, to admit that the prevention of all illegal drug use is not an achievable goal.[38] Perhaps the time has come to adjust our goals and focus our preventive efforts primarily on high-risk patterns of use—on those patterns, that is, where drug involvement demonstrably and significantly increases the chances of self-harm. (This is not to suggest, incidentally, that prevention programs should not continue to reinforce those who have already decided to abstain from drugs. This is an important group, one which should not be neglected, and their decision should be given sustained support.)

Whether any of us likes it or not, reality intrudes. The reality is that some forms of drug use, particularly patterns of moderate recreational use, are firmly institutionalized in

38. For statements to this effect, *see,* Boldt, Reilly, and Haberman, "A Survey," p. 462; and Richard H. DeLone, "The Ups and Downs of Drug-Abuse Education," *Saturday Review of Education* (11 November 1972), pp. 27–32.

certain sectors of society. While the most troubling aspect of the drug problem—the high-risk patterns of use—becomes ever more visible and unquestionably warrants our deepest concern, we should not overlook the fact that there is an underlayer of episodic, moderate or low-risk drug use which is resistant to change. To try, then, to prevent all illicit drug use merely diffuses our energies, with the probable result that we will accomplish less than we otherwise could.

Assessing the Effects of Drug Use
on Antisocial Behavior

By JARED R. TINKLENBERG

ABSTRACT: Nonmedical drug taking and antisocial behavior are both complex, dynamic processes; consequently,
the impact of these behaviors on each other is difficult to
assess. Among the multiple factors to be considered are the
pharmacological properties of the drug, the psychological
characteristics of the individual, the social environment, and
the various categories of antisocial behavior. Many
methodological problems are inherent in research that
attempts to define relationships between illicit drug use and
antisocial behavior. Sampling problems are common since
deviant individuals are generally not used in controlled
laboratory studies, whereas field studies often are confined
to inherently deviant populations such as prison inmates.
Field studies are limited by lack of information about
pharmacological variables as well as the difficulty in obtaining adequate control groups. The extreme forms of antisocial
behavior are not amenable to laboratory study. Thus,
research on illicit drug use and assaultive or sexual crimes is
usually restricted to retrospective field studies which often
indicate both forms of deviance present in the same
individual. A cause and effect relationship cannot be
inferred from retrospective studies; both behaviors often
appear to be covariants of the same developmental process.

---

*Jared R. Tinklenberg is an assistant Professor of Psychiatry at Stanford
University. He is also an Associate Director of the Stanford University
Laboratory of Clinical Psychopharmacology and Psychophysiology and a Research Associate at the Palo Alto Veterans' Administration Hospital. He received
his M.D. from University of Iowa in 1965. Dr. Tinklenberg serves as consultant on
drug abuse to numerous public and private agencies. His research interests lie in
the field of clinical psychopharmacology and the effects of drugs on deviant
behavior.*

ASSESSING the relationship between drug use and antisocial behavior involves a number of complex questions. How do the pharmacological effects of each specific drug influence aggression or other forms of deviant behavior? What dose levels of the drug were involved, what were the previous patterns of drug use? What were the personality predispositions of the user, especially the previous tendencies toward psychopathology or antisocial activity? In what psychological and social setting did the drug use take place? Since both drug use and antisocial behavior are dynamic processes which involve changing variables, an alteration in either of them may influence the interaction between the two and, consequently, the behavioral outcome. Unfortunately, most research in this area has necessarily been restricted to specific populations, such as prison inmates, who frequently use a variety of drugs in different circumstances and who also engage in various forms of antisocial behavior, again in varying conditions. The dynamic character of these two processes is a central problem in assessment; generally static points along the process continuum are observed rather than longitudinal interactions of these two behaviors.

The following outlines some of the major variables that must be considered in assessing the interactions of drug use and antisocial behavior. The antisocial behaviors discussed are those activities that seriously violate the legal norms of the community, with particular emphasis on the enhancement of assaultive and sexual offenses. The form of drug use discussed in this paper is non–medically supervised self-administration, often termed illicit drug use. Illicit drug use may in some instances be a form of self-medication—an attempt to deal with chronic anxiety or depression, for example. Nevertheless, it may be assumed that repetitive, non–medically supervised self-administration of drugs involves a deliberate attempt to alter one's usual consciousness.

People may use drugs in non-medical settings to achieve or maintain a state of homeostasis and to avoid or alleviate unpleasant emotional states. Central nervous system depressing drugs such as barbiturates are sometimes used in social settings to control anxiety; central nervous system stimulants such as amphetamines are used, sometimes unknowingly, to ameliorate chronic depression.

The self-medication factor in illicit drug use raises the important question: Do the drug effects sought in self-medication with illicit drugs have an impact on the reduction of antisocial behavior, as suggested by some observers?[1] This aspect of the impact of drug use on antisocial behavior is difficult to assess but must not be omitted from an objective evaluation of the relationship between drug use and behavior.

A primary consideration in assessing drug effects in humans is the large element of unpredictability, for it is difficult to predict with certainty how an individual is going to react to a given drug under different circumstances. During controlled laboratory conditions,

1. Herbert Blumer et al., *ADD Center Project Final Report: The World of Youthful Drug Use* (Berkeley: University of California Press, 1967); J. R. Allen and L. J. West, "Flight From Violence, Hippies and the Green Rebellion," *American Journal of Psychiatry* 125 (1968), pp. 364–370.

most people demonstrate singular reactions to a given dosage of a specific drug; however, when drugs are taken in social settings, the unpredictability of reaction increases.

It is important to remember, however, that drugs can only modify processes and capabilities already present in the individual. Thus, although they may contribute, sometimes significantly, to specific behaviors, they do not compel the individual to any particular type of action.

PHARMACOLOGICAL FACTORS

While the basic pharmacological properties of most commonly used illicit drugs are fairly well understood, the specific physiological mechanisms by which they influence human behavior are less well known. For example, laboratory and clinical studies may determine that a specific drug induces analgesia and sedation; however, the specific brain mechanisms whereby these effects are exerted have not yet been completely elucidated. In addition, there is considerable variability in psychoactive drug influences on basic brain mechanisms among different individuals.

Assessing the behavioral effects of drugs is further compounded by the propensity of many drug users toward multi-drug use. The ingestion of more than one drug at the same time or sequentially poses the possibility of a drug-drug interaction that may induce effects different from the effects of each drug taken alone. For example, in social settings wine and marihuana are often taken together. Subsequent behavioral changes may be erroneously attributed to one of the drugs, but may actually derive from the

other or from a synergistic effect. Also, uncontrolled studies of nonmedical drug use necessarily rely on self-reporting which always contains an element of risk that the user did not receive the putative drug or dose.

Dose-related response is another pharmacological variable in drug effects which influences assessment. Dose-related response patterns are not necessarily linear— that is, an increase in dosage may not simply induce an increase in the same effects. Instead, complex, sometimes curvilinear behavioral responses may occur: the same behavioral effects increase up to a point and then other effects appear. Several commonly used drugs provide salient examples of the dose-response variable. Low doses of alcohol, for instance, are commonly associated with a reduction in tension and increased conviviality, but at higher doses, hostility and aggressiveness may increase. Finally, at very high doses, all assertive behavior is usually reduced as the individual becomes stuporous. Cannabis also induces different effects as dosage is increased. Low doses of cannabis generally induce a mild euphoria and a pleasant relaxation. But high doses of cannabis are associated in some individuals with a panic reaction and marked perceptual distortions. Indeed, with very high doses most psychoactive drugs will induce a toxic psychosis which can include aberrant, antisocial behavior.

Drug influences on behavior also change as tissue levels of drug concentration increase and decrease. This phenomenon, known as the time-action course of a drug, is sometimes relevant to antisocial episodes. Acute intoxication may have one effect on behavior while declining drug levels may have quite a different effect, especially if the drug has been used repetitively. For example, the initial effects of alcohol are often associated with the general feeling of relaxation and conviviality; however, in some individuals decreasing concentrations of alcohol are associated with irritability and hostility. An assessment of the time-action factor depends upon specific knowledge of the particular drug as well as drug-taking patterns and possible cumulative effects.

Cumulative effects of drug use have been shown to be of special importance with a number of psychoactive substances since behavior associated with chronic drug use may be markedly different from that observed in acute, transient intoxication. Researchers have observed that some alcoholics respond to alcohol ingestion with increased anxiety and hostility rather than with mild euphoria generally experienced by less frequent users.[2] Perhaps the most dramatic example of the effects of cumulative drug use on antisocial behavior is that observed among high-dose intravenous amphetamine users. Extremely violent and aberrant behavior has been described in connection with a marked change in the patterns of repetitive amphetamine use, such as a sudden increase in dosage or abrupt cessation of drug intake.[3] Transient paranoid reactions have been experimentally induced in normal subjects by the repeated administration of large doses of amphetamines.[4] These findings suggest that pharmacological factors per se can exert a primary effect on antisocial behavior and that other factors, such as predisposing personality characteristics and the social setting, can in some instances be less salient.

PSYCHOLOGICAL AND ENVIRONMENTAL FACTORS

Controlled studies have shown that psychological and environmental factors can exert important influences on behavioral responses to drug effects.[5] Subjective reports from users of various drugs, especially marihuana and the psychedelics, often stress the importance of these factors on the kind of drug experience they have. Especially at lower doses, the expectation of the user and the environment in which he takes the drug seem to cue responses that tend to meet these expectations. At high doses, however, the pharmacological properties of the drug tend to override psychological factors.

When set and setting factors have been systematically controlled with marihuana intoxication, experienced users have reported subjective marihuana drug effects after having smoked a placebo cigarette.[6] This placebo effect has been attributed to the users' expectations of getting "high" which are maintained by the various cues involved in the drug-taking procedure. It

2. N. K. Mello (personal communication, March 1971).
3. E. H. Ellinwood, "Assault and Homicide Associated with Amphetamine Abuse," *American Journal of Psychiatry* 127 (1971), pp. 1170–1175.

4. J. D. Griffith et al., "Dextroamphetamine: Evaluation of Psychomimetic Properties in Man," *Archives of General Psychiatry* 26 (1972), pp. 97–100.
5. R. T. Jones, "Tetrahydrocannabinol and the Marihuana Induced Social 'High' or the Effects on the Mind of Marihuana," *Annals of the New York Academy of Sciences* 191 (1971), pp. 155–165.
6. Ibid.

appears that if the drug-taking setting is one in which personal and group expectations are of relaxed social interactions, it is likely that the drug experience will follow the expected pattern. Another example of the importance of set and setting is provided by secobarbital, which is commonly taken under medical supervision at bedtime in quiet surroundings to induce sleep. However, the same drug, which is termed "rowdy reds" in some nonmedical settings, is used to foster assertive, aggressive interaction which sometimes leads to violent crime.[7]

Individual psychological predispositions as well as poorly understood biological factors contribute to individual variations so that, even within the same setting at the same dose levels, individuals may differ in drug responses. The factor of individual variation limits generalizations about the impact of drug use on antisocial behavior, particularly from studies using hospital or prison populations. Any associations found between drug use and antisocial behavior in such deviant populations must be interpreted with caution. Many apprehended offenders demonstrate varying degrees of sociopathy, a complex condition often characterized by unusual drug reactions. Sociopaths, those individuals who account for a considerable portion of the statistical correlation between drugs and antisocial behavior, are discussed at greater length below.

SUBJECTIVE DRUG EFFECTS

Virtually all commonly used chemical substances exert effects on subjective states and moods. In general terms, central nervous system depressants tend to reduce anxiety and disinhibit certain parts of the personality normally held in check by internalized social controls. Central nervous system stimulants increase the sense of well-being, relieve depression, and raise the general level of arousal and activity. Psychedelics alter perception and enhance sensory experiences, while the opiates relieve pain and satiate primary drives such as hunger. Repeated drug use is an indication that the particular alteration is perceived by the drug user as pleasant or valuable. It is important to have a defined picture of the subjective effects experienced by the user in order to ascertain whether these have an impact on the user's antisocial behavior. Unfortunately, since subjective effects by definition do not represent the data researchers often collect, with few exceptions, little is known about the role and function various drugs have in the subjective experiences of users.

In a recent California study, users were asked how various drugs affected them, which drug they preferred and why, and which drugs made them more inclined to be assaultive.[8] An analysis of drug-related current convictions for these subjects showed that they had accurately evaluated drug effects on their assaultive behavior. Those convicted of assaultive crimes and those convicted of nonassaultive crimes both tended to describe secobarbital as the drug most likely to enhance their violent behavior. Alcohol was their second choice. These were the two drugs most often implicated in drug-

7. J. R. Tinklenberg et al., "Drug Involvement in Criminal Assaults by Adolescents," *Archives of General Psychiatry* 30 (1974), pp. 685–689.

8. Ibid.

involved assaults. Conversely, both groups tended to identify marihuana as the drug most likely to decrease assaultive tendencies. Of interest is that the nonassaultive group showed a definite preference for marihuana.

Similarly, other researchers have observed a connection between psychedelics and a "flight from aggression."[9] The possibility that illicit drugs are being used by certain individuals as a form of self-medication or in an effort to enhance certain behaviors or control others is worthy of serious research and is in fact a logical necessity in the development of a clear understanding of the impact of drug use on behavior, especially antisocial behavior.

The question follows: If certain sub-groups of the criminal population are using drugs for specific subjective effects, how much of their behavior is a result of pharmacological properties of the drugs and how much is a result of peer norms and expectations of the drugs, that is, psychological and environmental factors? It should be noted that a smaller sub-group in the Tinklenberg study insisted that drugs had no effect on their behavior, and they also tended to describe no pronounced subjective drug effects. Thus, the subjective effects of drugs appear to be an important factor in drug-related behavior, even though individual variation in subjective effects necessarily limits generalizations.

TYPES OF ANTISOCIAL BEHAVIOR

The antisocial behavior examined in this article has been simply defined as those behaviors that seriously violate the legal norms of the community. Illicit drug use itself is considered antisocial, so the assessment to be made is the effect of one form of legally defined antisocial behavior upon another form—criminality. As was discussed earlier, when considering the problem of measuring the impact of drug use on antisocial behavior, it is important to view both behaviors as dynamic coexistents.

The term *antisocial* also requires further specification, because at least two sub-groups can be delineated. First, a large portion of the overall group called antisocial could better be described as dyssocial, a term which connotes that they subscribe to the norms of their particular sub-group but violate the norms of the dominant society.[10] Dyssocial individuals are often encountered among ethnic and socio-economic minorities. Certain behaviors, such as the use of physical violence to right wrongs or to maintain one's group status, appear to be socially acceptable within certain subcultures despite their illegal status within the dominant legal system.

A second sub-group that requires special definition is the group usually called sociopathic. Sociopathic individuals exhibit behaviors contrary to community as well as general legal norms in many areas of their lives; indeed, their behavior is characterized by a consistent inability to form an allegiance with any group or code, a lack of any meaningful sustained personal relationships, and a failure to learn

9. J. R. Allen and L. J. West, "Flight From Violence."

10. American Psychiatric Association, *DSM-11 Diagnostic and Statistical Manual of Mental Disorders* (Washington, D.C.: American Psychiatric Association, 1968).

from experience.[11] They are often the hard core repeaters in the criminal justice system and are notoriously resistant to legal intervention and rehabilitation. Assessing the impact of drug use on the antisocial behavior of sociopaths is extremely difficult since they often exhibit unusual reactions to drugs but also tend to exhibit consistent antisocial behavior from an early age, regardless of their patterns of drug consumption.

Problems in Methodology

In the previous section, a number of influential factors were enumerated about which the investigator must have fairly specific data in order to assess relationships between drug use and antisocial behavior. Unfortunately, each of the two general sources of information —controlled laboratory or clinical studies and uncontrolled field or naturalistic studies—provides only partial information regarding the two processes involved. Controlled laboratory studies can provide dose and time action information as well as drug-drug interaction data; however, certain powerful psychological and environmental variables that also influence behavior are absent. In addition, controlled laboratory or clinical studies of drug effects on human behavior often contain a sampling bias since such studies usually omit deviant, disturbed, or otherwise abnormal individuals who may be especially susceptible to idiosyncratic drug reactions. More importantly, it is difficult to extrapolate from laboratory-based behavior to the complex, multi-dimensional situations of real life. The full aggression process cannot be studied in the laboratory because the total complex series of events of human aggressive attacks cannot be practically or ethically replicated. Some measurement of change in mood, attitude and perception can be made, but important psychological and environmental variables are necessarily absent. Consequently, the responses of individuals in controlled studies cannot be fully generalized to other situations. In contrast, field studies can provide information about social and environmental variables, but they lack controls for personality predisposition, drug dosage, time-action and possible drug-drug interaction. Field studies may also contain a population bias since most studies are conducted among accessible but deviant populations such as patients or prisoners.

In assessing interactions between drug use and antisocial behavior, there is also the methodological problem of generalizing across different age levels. It is quite possible that the relative influence of drug effects on behavior changes with the level of maturation of the individual. Young people who are in the process of developing and incorporating behavioral responses to the demands of life situations may respond differently to specific drugs than do mature adults. Therefore, generalizing to adolescents from studies of adults must be done with caution.

A further complication in investigating drug-antisocial interactions stems from the observation that some sociopathic individuals experience a spontaneous decrease in tendencies toward both antisocial behavior and illicit drug use. This

11. R. D. Hare, *Psychopathy: Theory and Research* (New York: John Wiley and Sons, 1970).

spontaneous amelioration of deviant tendencies most commonly occurs when the individual is in his thirties or early forties.[12] These changes in behavior over time illustrate the dynamic character of these processes and that the maturational process may be an important factor at several different age levels.

Another question faced in considering methodology is: Are drug influences for individuals who have incorporated antisocial behaviors into their repertoire of responses the same as they are for others with less established antisocial patterns? The study of adolescent offenders in California discovered a small group of individuals who were physically violent in a wide range of provocative situations.[13] They insisted that if the situation were one in which they would customarily respond with violence, they would do so regardless of their drug consumption. In contrast, many other adolescent offenders claimed that they ordinarily did not respond to provocation with violence, but when under the influence of certain drugs (in this study it was usually alcohol, secobarbital or both), they would become aggressive. These differences in reported drug-related behavioral patterns illustrates the important variable of baseline, nondrug antisocial tendencies which are derived from personality characteristics, subcultural group norms, and other factors.

Establishing baseline pre-drug behavioral patterns is a methodological problem. Retrospective self-reporting is always subject to distortion, particularly if the individual is required to describe events in the distant past or episodes which are embarrassing. Nevertheless, differences in basic pre-drug response pattern must obviously be taken into consideration when assessing the possible influence of drug use on antisocial activities. In order to establish the potency of the drug variable, it is necessary to determine the probability of aggressive responses without the drug factor.

All of the several methods of research that have been applied to the investigation of drug use and antisocial behavior have certain methodological limitations. One method of study is the retrospective case analysis which lists crimes committed by drug users or enumerates the number of drug users among criminal populations. While these retrospective case studies provide useful descriptive data and show that many apprehended antisocial individuals are also drug users, without control groups for other important ethnic, psychological and social factors, retrospective case studies are severely limited. A superficial review of events after the fact can usually give the impression that events have a cause and effect relationship even though a multitude of unknown developmental forces have intervened which are not accessible to measurement. Studies which have attempted to determine primacy of antisocial behavior or drug use have provided mixed findings. Since in some instances drug use has preceded the criminal behavior and in others the opposite has been found, arguments about progression from one form of deviant behavior to another cannot be resolved.

12. Charles Winick, "Maturing Out of Narcotic Addiction," *Bulletin on Narcotics* 14 (1962), pp. 1–7; L. N. Robins, *Deviant Children Grown Up* (Baltimore: Williams and Wilkins Co., 1966).

13. J. R. Tinklenberg et al., "Drug Involvement."

Some studies are limited because not all drugs are investigated. For example, failure to include alcohol in investigations of antisocial behavior and drugs is an especially glaring omission, since in both adults and adolescents alcohol is generally the drug most often linked with serious crime.[14] The omission of alcohol precludes comparisons across studies and populations and, more importantly, excludes from investigation the single drug which is most frequently implicated in antisocial behavior.

Ethnic variables, which necessarily include different subcultural mores and values, are another major consideration in analyzing the effects of drugs on antisocial behavior. For example, on the basis of small samples, the California adolescent study previously cited suggests that, in general, white subjects use drugs more frequently and especially reported heavier use of the psychedelics. Both white and Chicano youths tended to commit crimes more frequently during drug intoxication, while blacks committed more offenses in a nondrug state. Ethnic differences, however, did not differentiate among drugs involved in violent crimes; alcohol and secobarbital were most common for all groups. More research is required regarding the significance of ethnic differences and drug-related antisocial behavior.

The importance of sociological variables is also demonstrated by Erich Goode in a retrospective study of 559 young, male marihuana users and nonusers designed to determine significant differences in criminal behavior attributable to marihuana use per se.[15] He found that when several sociological variables were applied simultaneously—race, education, age, the use of other drugs, and having drug-using friends—less than one percent of the variance in committing offenses could be attributed to the use of marihuana per se. Again, as with other field studies, certain methodological limitations pertain: the study is dependent upon self-reports of criminal behavior; drug dosage was unknown; and the data did not necessarily reflect behavior during drug intoxication, since drug use during the preceding 24 hours was the criterion for drug involvement in the offense. Nevertheless, the important point is, as Goode indicated, that the application of sociological variables cannot obviate an important pharmacological variable. In other words, if the antisocial behavior had resulted directly from marihuana use per se, other factors would be less significant.

Finally, one of the more perplexing difficulties in assessing the impact of drug use on antisocial behavior is that to a considerable degree both behaviors appear to stem from a common matrix. In other words, the same forces which generate antisocial behavior also seem to contribute to excessive nonmedical drug use. Individuals who demonstrate one or both forms of these behavioral problems are often described as deviant from early childhood, having had dif-

14. J. R. Tinklenberg, "Alcohol and Violence," in *Alcoholism: Progress in Research and Treatment*, ed. P. G. Bourne and R. Fox (New York: Academic Press, 1973), pp. 195–210.

15. Erich Goode, "Marihuana Use and Crime," in *Marihuana: A Signal of Misunderstanding*, First Report of the National Commission on Marihuana and Drug Abuse (Washington, D.C.: Government Printing Office, 1972), pp. 446–459.

ficulties in school, truancy and discipline problems, and other indications of psychological disturbance. The possibility that certain individuals are, from an early age, predisposed toward both drug abuse and antisocial behavior does not mean that the use of drugs has no effect on their antisocial tendencies. As suggested above, the use of certain drugs in some settings may discernably increase propensities toward assaultiveness; it is also possible that the use of other drugs may decrease antisocial inclinations.

Assessing the Nature and Dimensions of the Drug Problem

By LENORE R. KUPPERSTEIN

ABSTRACT: Over the years, various attempts have been made to define, describe and measure the nature and dimensions of psychoactive drug use in the United States. The purpose of this article is to address the problems of definition associated with the traditional concept of "drug abuse"; to examine the various formulations of "the drug problem"; to assess the efficacy of the survey method and other research techniques currently utilized to estimate the nature and extent of drug use; and to report on some of the efforts made by the National Commission on Marihuana and Drug Abuse to provide guidance and direction in this area to researchers and policy makers alike.

Lenore R. Kupperstein holds an A.M. in Criminology from the University of Pennsylvania and is presently a Ph.D. candidate in Sociology at the same institution. She was formerly on the research staff of the Commission on Obscenity and Pornography and recently served as Assistant Director of the National Commission on Marihuana and Drug Abuse. She is currently the Evaluation and Program Development Officer at international headquarters of the International Planned Parenthood Federation in London, England.

ATTEMPTS to define, describe, investigate and measure "the drug problem" or "drug abuse" may generally be divided into two major types: those which focus on particular classes of drugs and their dysfunctional effects upon the users, and those which concentrate on drug users and focus upon their drug using behavior and social and psychological characteristics. Those of the first type may be further divided into one which narrows its focus to a few illegal and socially disapproved psychoactive substances used mainly by the young, and another which includes in its purview the broad spectrum of drugs and substances used by various segments of the population for mood alteration. Obviously, estimates of the nature and dimensions of the drug problem and their implications for public policy vary in accordance with the formulation of the problem and the perspective of the researcher.

The intent of this article is to examine the concept of "drug abuse," to review the various formulations of "the drug problem," and to assess the efficacy of several research methods currently utilized for estimating the nature and extent of psychoactive drug use.

DRUG AS IN DRUG ABUSE

Although psychoactive drug use is commonplace in American society and the word *drug* is used daily in common parlance, this word, when attached to another—*problem* or *abuse*—instantly changes meaning. It is almost unconsciously transformed from the scientific shorthand for a "substance other than food which by its chemical nature affects the structure or function of the living organism,"[1] to an emotional and value-laden referent to particular classes of drugs, the nonmedical or unauthorized use of which is socially disapproved. As the National Commission on Marihuana and Drug Abuse has noted:

The imprecision of the term "drug" has had serious social consequences . . . because the referents of the word "drug" differ so widely in the therapeutic and social context, the public is conditioned to believe that "street" drugs act according to entirely different principles than "medical" drugs. The result is that the risks of the former are exaggerated and the risks of the latter are overlooked.[2]

The concept of drug abuse is particularly notable for its imprecision, its eclecticism, its polarity, and the degree of emotional arousal it engenders. Although the term is often employed interchangeably with drug use or the drug problem, it always connotes social disapproval and refers to a social problem of some magnitude deriving from the use of *some* drugs, under *some* circumstances, for *some* purposes and with *some* consequences. The general absence of public consensus relative to the precise meaning of the term and the multifaceted nature of the concept are clearly evident in the findings of the commission's national survey presented in tables 1 and 2.[3]

1. National Commission on Marihuana and Drug Abuse, *Drug Use in America: Problem in Perspective* (Washington, D.C.: Government Printing Office, 1973, hereinafter cited as *Drug Commission Report,* 1973), p. 9.

2. Ibid., p. 11.

3. Herbert Abelson et al. "Drug Experience, Attitudes, and Related Behavior Among Adolescents and Adults," in National Commission on Marihuana and Drug Abuse, *Drug Abuse in America: Problem in*

TABLE 1

BELIEFS ABOUT THE MEANING OF DRUG ABUSE

	ADULTS (N = 2411) (Percent)	YOUTH (N = 880) (Percent)
Any nonmedical purpose, or purpose not intended for the drug; purpose not prescribed; if prescription was not for you	30	27
Use for pleasure; to feel good; to get high; for kicks; for fun; take a trip	10	13
Taking or using marihuana, heroin, dope, acid, LSD, mescaline (or other drugs which are illegal to possess)	4	4
Taking an overdose; overdoing; taking to excess; taking too much	27	16
Anything that is addictive; habit forming; where you become dependent on it	17	15
Any use that damages health, is bad for you, does damage to the person	11	10
If it is a distortion of reality; makes you unable to cope with everyday living, work, other people	7	4
Don't know what drug abuse is; no answer	13	20

SOURCE: *Drug Commission Report*, p. 12. (See footnote 1.)
NOTE: Multiple responses; main mentions included here.

TABLE 2

WHETHER EACH OF TEN SITUATIONS IS DRUG ABUSE

	YES, DRUG ABUSE	
	ADULTS (N = 2411) (Percent)	YOUTH (N = 880) (Percent)
Context: Pills—What if someone		
took these pills just to enjoy the feeling they give	89	88
took these pills everyday . . . had to have them . . . to help cope with day	84	82
had pills prescribed by doctor, but took more than he directed	83	77
bought nonprescription pills, took more than label directed	82	76
took pills that were prescribed for someone else	73	72
took any of these pills once or twice to see effect	46	50
Context: Alcohol—What if someone had		
cocktails or highballs with lunch or dinner and in the evening	36	37
Marihuana, Heroin—What if		
someone used heroin once in a while	82	80
someone smoked marihuana once to twice a week	54	63
marihuana were made legal and someone used under these conditions	56	44

SOURCE: *Drug Commission Report*, p. 13. (See footnote 1.)

Perspective, Appendix (hereinafter cited as *Appendix to Drug Commission Report*, 1973), vol. 1 (Washington, D.C.: Government Printing Office, 1973), pp. 488–871.

Despite its multifaceted nature, however, drug use is often perceived as a unitary phenomenon; thus the precedence of concern over quantity rather than the quality of drug use. On the other hand, much of the descriptive terminology associated with drug abuse refers more directly to perceived attributes and characteristics of the individual drug user than it does to his drug-using behavior.

In view of the definitional confusion created by the term *drug abuse* and the functional disutility of its use as a referent, the commission proposed that it be deleted from the vocabulary of policy makers and recommended that the focus of policy be shifted to the "relative risks and social consequences of various patterns of drug-taking behavior."[4]

DRUGS AS REFERENTS

As noted earlier, many researchers define the drug problem in terms of drugs per se and traditionally focus on such illicit psychoactive substances as marihuana, hashish, LSD, heroin and cocaine, and the nonmedical use of controlled substances (amphetamines, tranquilizers and barbiturates), particularly by the young. With the trend toward poly–drug use by a broader spectrum of the population, however, researchers have recently broadened their perspective and expanded their list of drugs to include the gamut of tobacco, alcohol, prescription-only controlled substances and over-the-counter nonprescription drugs, as well as illicit substances.

Distinctions among the drugs forming the list can be made on the basis of: (1) their pharmacological properties; (2) their effects on the physical well-being and social functioning of the individual user;

(3) their consequences for public health, safety and welfare; and (4) the legality or degree of societal disapproval attendant to their availability, possession and use.

Possession and use of some drugs such as marihuana, hashish, LSD, heroin and cocaine, for example, are clearly illegal. Most drugs, however, fall into the licit category. Some, such as amphetamines, tranquilizers and barbiturates, are controlled substances requiring medical prescriptions for possession and use; others, such as over-the-counter drugs (OTCs) designed to suppress appetite, relax, induce sleep or keep awake, may be obtained legally without prescription.

With respect to illicit drugs, the so-called drug problem is generally couched within the framework of the youth culture and the law, and particular attention is given to the potential of illicit drug use for social harm. Drug-related crime, public health problems, social dysfunction, and the economic drain on society by heroin addicts are issues frequently raised. This perspective, however, may omit reference to the most common types of drug use in the United States and to the great majority of drug takers.

When licit drugs are included in the formulation, consideration is ordinarily given to the pharmacological properties of specific classes of drugs, their effects on the user, their availability and the degree of social acceptability accorded to their use. Thus, drugs may be hallucinogens, stimulants, tranquilizers or depressants; at the same time they are either illegal, controlled, or generally available. At one extreme, for example, is coffee—a widely used, generally available, socially acceptable mild stimulant. In between are: alcohol

4. *Drug Commission Report*, 1973, p. 14.

—a socially acceptable, widely used depressant whose availability is generally regulated by law; marihuana —a rather widely used (especially among the young), increasingly socially acceptable, illegal hallucinogen; and amphetamines and barbiturates—stimulants and depressants now believed to be widely used and available by prescription, whose use is socially acceptable only if medically motivated. At the other extreme is heroin—a powerful depressant, rarely used, illegal and socially unacceptable.

It is not unusual, in this broader, more contemporary formulation of the drug problem, to find references to the role of the mass media in the escalation of drug use; to those elements of society generally believed to be responsible for so-called drug abuse by young people, successful businessmen, physicians and middle class housewives alike; and to aroused public concern for the physical, moral and social well-being of drug takers drawn from the dominant sector of the community.

Regardless of which formulation is used, reports and commentaries focusing on drugs rather than people frequently contain a nose-count of users. These incidence and prevalence statistics often find their way, without appropriate explanation of their inherent limitations, into the releases of politicians and bureaucrats, where they are used to arouse public concern over what appears to be scientific evidence of the growth or extent of the drug problem. It should be noted, however, that these data fail to address such crucial policy questions as the meaning of drug use, the nature and dimensions of such use, and the social problems posed by it.

DRUG-USING BEHAVIOR

Of greater import for the development of public policy is the behavior of drug users. Who are the users? What kinds of drugs do they use? How did they become drug users? How do they obtain drugs? How long do they continue to use them? Under what conditions and circumstances are drugs used? How frequently and intensively are specific drugs used? How much of a specific drug (dose) is used in a given situation? What are the motivations for use? What physical and social problems do users encounter? To what extent do they become physically or psychologically dependent upon given classes of drugs? In the answers to these and other similar questions lies the meaning of drug-using behavior. As the National Commission on Marihuana and Drug Abuse has stated:

To better understand current self-defined drug use and to determine the scope of social concern, one must go beyond the cataloguing of substances (pharmacologically defined where possible), the listing of effects, and the counting of users and non-users of drugs. The inquiry must shift from drugs to people, from pharmacological effects to the meaning and function of drug use. . . . The initial step in understanding the meaning of drug use and its impact on the social order is to regard the phenomenon as we would any other human behavior . . . [to place] incidence figures in perspective, elaborating on the patterns of drug-using behavior and the individual and social factors which seem to influence individual decisions to initiate, continue or terminate the use of drugs.[5]

Until recently, data collection efforts with respect to psychoactive drug use tended to concentrate on

5. Ibid., pp. 28, 30.

questions of incidence (ever used) and prevalence (current use). Increasingly, though to a far lesser extent, attempts have been made to gather data relative to the patterns of use: frequency, intensity and duration. More detailed information on some of the questions raised above, however, remain generally absent or so fraught with definitional and methodological problems as to render them of questionable utility for policy considerations.

In an effort to provide some direction for researchers and policy makers, the commission classified drug-using behavior into five discernible types: experimental, recreational, circumstantial, intensified and compulsive drug use.[6] Assessment of the extent to which this new approach yields more fruitful results must await its application to data collection and planning efforts.

Having briefly reviewed the definitional and operational problems attendant to assessing the nature and dimensions of drug use, let us turn our attention to data collection methods and estimating techniques used in this connection.

THE SURVEY METHOD

Several methods for estimating the extent of drug use in the population are currently available. By far the most commonly employed, particularly in large scale efforts to measure the broad range of non-medical drug use, is the survey technique. During this author's tenure with the National Commission on Marihuana and Drug Abuse,

several hundred surveys were collected and reviewed. The following general conclusions can be drawn about the data they contain: although large and often irreconcilable differences exist in the populations under study, in the research and sampling methods utilized and in the terminology and operational definitions employed (thus precluding precise comparison of point estimates), the drug surveys in the aggregate provide valuable descriptive data and may be viewed as indications—not absolutes—of the use and users of psychoactive drugs in American society. As the commission has cautioned, however:

One of the unintended and unfortunate consequences of [advances in the measurement of social data, including drug use] has been the tendency of policy makers to appropriate these statistics, often taking them out of context, and to convert them directly into public policy decisions. Little or no attention is given to the assumptions and hypotheses suggested by the findings or to the limitations, reliability and validity of the data.[7]

As noted above, most drug surveys rely heavily on incidence data, as these are the easiest to gather, the most readily available and the least threatening to the respondent. They have the further advantage of inter-survey comparability, assuming, of course, that incidence (ever used) always refers to having tried a given drug at least once during one's lifetime up to the time of the survey.

Prevalence (current use) data appear in drug surveys with almost equal frequency, but these may be somewhat less reliable than incidence figures because they require that respondents admit to the com-

6. The characteristics of each of the five types of drug-using behavior may be found in *Drug Commission Report*, 1973, pp. 30–31, 93–98.

7. *Drug Commission Report*, 1973, p. 42.

mission of one or more illegal acts. They have the further disadvantage of greater variability in meaning. In the surveys reviewed, for example, current use does not always mean present use. It can refer to use within the 12 months preceding the survey;[8] it can include everything from yesterday to more than one year ago;[9] it can mean use within the past 30 days;[10] or it can define current use as less than two months preceding the survey.[11] In the commission's national survey, current use meant those "presently using."[12]

Regardless of the definition of prevalence, it is clear from the survey findings that only a fraction of those who have tried certain types of drugs—marihuana, LSD and heroin, for example—continue to use them. The crucial questions are: What proportion of the experimental users discontinue use, and how do they differ in important characteristics from more enduring users? Although several surveys address the issue of attrition, variations in terminology and inability to verify self-reports of termination

preclude any exact measures. In some instances, for example, estimates of attrition are derived from specific inquiries as to whether respondents no longer use the drug in question. In other cases, the question is not posed directly; rather, the results are inferred from other data on drug experimenters, defined in such a way as to imply discontinuation of use after one or more trials.

Obviously, data about past and present drug use provide some indication of what might be expected in the future. At least tentative answers to some of the following questions may be extrapolated from available survey data: Is society likely to witness further increases in drug use? If so, what types of use and among what classes of users? Are some types of drug use likely to pass out of fashion? Are those who have never experimented with psychoactive drugs likely to do so in the future? Can we expect young people to escalate from soft to hard drug use?

Similarly, some few indicators are available from survey findings relative to why people initiate, continue or terminate drug use; how they were first introduced to certain classes of drugs or patterns of use; what were the circumstances of their first and ensuing drug trials; and how drugs are normally obtained. All of these data, however, suffer from variability in definition and inattention to questions of reliability and validity. The same may be said for much of the now abundant survey data on the social and demographic characteristics of self-reported users.

Aside from definitional issues, probably the most important drawbacks to the use of survey data derive from sampling problems. As noted in the commission's report:

8. W. S. Ferguson and W. L. Howard, *Marihuana and Drug Use and Highway Safety: A Survey of High School Students in Virginia* (Virginia Highway Research Council, July 1971).

9. Governor's Citizen Advisory Committee on Drugs, "Drug Use Among High School Students in the State of Utah," in *Advisory Committee Report on Drug Abuse: Summary and Recommendations* (Salt Lake City, Utah: September 1969), pp. 54–112.

10. American Institute of Public Opinion, *Gallup Opinion Index: Results of 1971 Survey of College Students* (Princeton, N.J.: February 1972).

11. H. J. Parry, I. H. Cisin, and M. B. Balter, *Concomitants of Marihuana Use among Americans Aged 18–29* (Washington, D.C.: Social Research Group, George Washington University, 1972).

12. Herbert Abelson et al., "Drug Experience."

. . . the basic question is the extent to which statistics drawn from any subsegment of a population are generalizable to and representative of the total population under study. By definition, a sample represents only a small part of a larger aggregate or universe . . . about which information is sought, and the data collected in surveys of selected samples are subject to bias and variation; consequently the estimates are imprecise in absolute terms and may vary in reliability and validity, both of which are statistically measurable and dependent upon proper sampling techniques.[13]

Lastly, the survey method generally fails to address the recent trend toward multi-drug use. In the past, researchers have simply provided tabulations on the percentage of users of each of several listed drugs; they have not, however, adequately addressed the issues of simultaneous or sequential use of psychoactive substances. As of this writing, no reliable or valid method exists for estimating the nature and dimensions of multi-drug use, nor do we have much useful information on the subject.

Despite these and other comparative and analytical problems—including bias, error and expense —drug survey data, when used with care and caution, can provide meaningful guidance and direction for policy makers and program administrators. Their results, however, should not be accepted as being synonomous with precise measurements of the nature and dimensions of drug use in American society.

INCIDENCE AND PREVALENCE OF OPIATE USE

The usefulness of the survey method for estimating the incidence and prevalence of opiate

(mostly heroin) use and dependence is severely limited. Populations generally accessible to household or other types of surveys— permanent residents, school populations and military personnel, for example—simply differ in important ways from most opiate users, particularly those dependent upon heroin and living the life of the "street addict."

Several new estimating techniques were recently developed, at least in part, to overcome the difficulties presented by the survey method. They are themselves fraught with methodological problems, however, in that they depend entirely on lists or registers of known heroin users. In essence, they are as weak or as inaccurate as the lists upon which they rely.

At the request of the National Commission on Marihuana and Drug Abuse, Alfred Blumstein, Philip Sagi and Marvin Wolfgang analyzed the problems associated with reportability and registers generally, with defining addicts, and with the uses of several existing estimates of the prevalence of narcotic use and addiction.[14] What follows is a brief summary of their findings.

With respect to lists or registers, it is generally agreed that they are incomplete in coverage and unpurged of the dead, the rehabilitated and the emigrant. They are at the same time inflated by the listing of individuals whose opiate use or dependence has not been adequately verified. As such, these faulty data, when converted into estimates of opiate use, are rendered even more problematic.

13. *Drug Commission Report*, 1973, p. 71.

14. *See*, Alfred Blumstein, Philip C. Sagi, and Marvin E. Wolfgang, "Problems of Estimating the Number of Heroin Addicts," in *Appendix to Drug Commission Report*, 1973, vol. 2, pp. 201–211.

One model, for example, swells the registry of known heroin users by the proportion of unlisted (unknown) users among individuals whose deaths have been attributed to opiate use or overdose. The unwarranted, or at least untested, assumption is that death rates among the known and the unknown (listed and unlisted) are equal. If, however, it were shown that the death rate among novice heroin users still unlikely to be listed is inordinately high, the above-mentioned technique would exaggerate the magnitude of heroin use. Another untested assumption upon which this model is based is that the registry includes only currently active heroin users. This, too, is of questionable veracity.

Yet another estimating model exploits the listing of persons over successive periods of time. The basic assumption is that the probability of being identified and reported twice in two successive time intervals is a function of chance alone, and not the function of particular vulnerability to identification. The error in estimates of the total number of users calculated in this way is therefore dependent upon the extent to which special vulnerability to identification actually operates.

One further model also inflates the size of the register, this time by obtaining, from other local lists or sources of authority, estimates of underreporting. Two assumptions, equally questionable, are evident: (1) that the estimates of other local lists or contributors are more complete or accurate than the one which serves as the base, and (2) that the estimates of underreporting do not vary from area to area.

With respect to the concept of addiction, the problem of definition arises again. The narrow view of addiction incorporates and is limited to physiological dependence and the onset of withdrawal symptoms in the absence of the needed narcotic. This definition is generally more restrictive than that used by the registers. A broader view of addiction embraces an unknown number of opiate-dependent individuals who remain invisible to authorities by virtue of their social and economic position and their ability to operate within the bounds of conventional society.

Clearly, this second group differs from the stereotypical characterization of the "street addict" who is socially and economically dysfunctional and whose behavior generally involves participation in criminal or other antisocial activities. Undoubtedly, questions of treatment, rehabilitation and policy reflect and are influenced by the characteristics of the opiate users and the nature, extent and visibility of their opiate use. Blumstein, Sagi and Wolfgang conclude that:

Trend analysis is needed in order to determine whether there is stability, a decrease, or an increase in heroin addiction. Probably the most useful form of trend analysis is through birth cohorts . . . [which] would aid in our estimation of the number of heroin addicts and would further aid in determining social policies of prevention and treatment.[15]

IMPLICATIONS FOR POLICY

Undoubtedly, the preference for one problem definition, set of parameters or estimating technique over another will depend upon the inherent limitations of the method, the degree of precision required, the fiscal resources needed and

15. Ibid., pp. 209–210.

available, the time involved, the cost-effectiveness of the approach and, perhaps most importantly, the purposes for which the data are being collected and the uses to which they will be put. To the extent that these factors are likely to be overlooked in any effort to assess the nature and dimensions of drug-using behavior, the probability increases that the end result will be of limited utility for policy purposes and that the concluding recommendation will be a plea for further research and additional data.

In some instances, of course, such a recommendation is legitimate; in others it may be viewed as an ill-disguised excuse or cover for previously inadequate or improper research, indecisiveness with respect to policy, political conflict or even incompetence.

If data on the nature and dimensions of drug-using behavior are to be used effectively for policy development, policy guidelines must be adopted well before the data are collected, analyzed and interpreted. It is fruitless to base a policy decision on these kinds of data if the parameters are largely unknown, if they continue to be of questionable reliability and validity, and if the resultant policy decision bears little relation to the results of the research activity presumably carried out as part of the planning process.

ANNALS, AAPSS, **417,** Jan. 1975

Drugs and the Mass Media

By F. EARLE BARCUS AND SUSAN M. JANKOWSKI

ABSTRACT: Mass media have been described as all-pervasive cultural institutions which both reflect and project society's values. They are shown to have played a role throughout history, whenever new developments have threatened established values, and often are singled out as important facilitators and accelerators of social change. As such, it is not surprising that various charges have been leveled against the mass media for their purported role in the recent and significant escalation of psychoactive drug use and abuse. Some critics have attempted to relate the *act* of viewing or experiencing the mass media to problems of drug use; others have focused their charges on, and label as villains, the *contents* of the media, as in advertising, television entertainment and popular song lyrics. The intent of this paper is to examine some of these accusations and to explore the issues and the evidence in the current controversy over the role of mass media in the use and abuse of psychoactive drugs.

F. Earle Barcus is Professor of Communication Research at the Communication Research Center, School of Public Communication, Boston University. He was the principal investigator in a study of drug advertising on television conducted for the National Commission on Marihuana and Drug Abuse.

Susan Jankowski is a senior graduate associate at the Communication Research Center, School of Public Communication, Boston University.

MASS media have been described as all-pervasive cultural institutions which both reflect and project the values of society. As cultural arms of industrial enterprise, the media reach millions of people who invest great quantities of their money and time seeking information, entertainment and advice from them. Advertisers know they are effective in creating images and channeling attitudes, and communication researchers know that people learn from them.

The media accelerate social change. Cultures have gone through more and more rapid social changes with the successive introduction of printing of books, magazines and newspapers; the mechanical-visual technology of motion pictures; and the electronic media of radio and television.

In the history of society, whenever new developments have threatened established values, the mass media have played a role. A new political movement challenging the established order (as in the French and American revolutions) brings with it punishment to those political writings which support the movement. Any threat to current moral standards, whether it be in the popular novels of Defoe and Richardson in eighteenth century England or the X-rated films and sexually frank magazines of today, leads to acts of censorship against the publishers to protect the public morals. Other changes in life style which are perceived as too rapid to be controlled or understood bring similar responses; for example, the problems associated with the increasing use of alcohol directed attention to the content of motion picture portrayals of its use in the 1930s.

The use of chemical substances by a wider range of the public than before represents part of the process of rapid social change in life styles today. The mass media serve to carry the messages of society in their news, information and entertainment functions. Like the ancient emperors who killed the messengers conveying bad tidings, we tend to vent our own anger, borne of anxiety over change, on the modern messengers of society—the mass media. They become obvious targets when one is looking for villains who cause social problems. But in the midst of our problems, we must question whether we are looking for villains and finding only scapegoats—or whether we should be concerned with either.

POPULAR CULTURE AND THE DRUG CULTURE

Many experts in popular culture have talked about the relationship of electronic media to a life style consonant with drug use. The argument, basically, is that the very existence of the new media—rather than their content—changes our perspectives on living. Since its inception, television has been considered a "passive" medium, that is, leading to passivity in the population. There were early jokes about "TV addiction," and later, in the words of the drug culture, of "turning on" or "tuning in." Marshall McLuhan's well-known phrase, "the medium is the message" (later changed to "the medium is the massage"), indicates a similar view. More than 20 years ago, Lazarsfeld and Merton spoke of a "narcotizing dysfunction" of mass media.[1] Ac-

1. P. F. Lazarsfeld and R. K. Merton, "Mass Communication, Popular Taste and

cording to the authors, the flood of information from the media serves to narcotize rather than energize the average reader or listener. This may lead to apathy or alienation from the issues of the day.

More recently, Asa Berger suggested that the drug culture is simply one aspect of consumer culture, a culture which has trained us from childhood that the solutions to problems may be obtained through the purchase of manufactured products sold through the mass media. As Berger says, "America is a drug culture in general although most people do not recognize it as such, or themselves as 'addicts' or drug abusers."[2] From this, it is not too difficult a jump from the use of legal to illegal drugs. Larger problems require stronger remedies: ". . . it's just a matter of degree, in essence."[3] The connection with television is also made: "The kinship of the LSD and other drug experiences with television is glaringly obvious. Both depend on 'turning on' and passively waiting for something beautiful to happen."[4]

A test of this relationship was seriously attempted by Jerome Brodlie, who conducted a small experiment on "Drug Abuse and Television Viewing Patterns."[5] Noting the clinical patterns of ado-

lescent drug users whose life styles showed little involvement in school, clubs, hobbies and sports, and the boredom resulting therefrom, Brodlie hypothesized that drug taking is analogous to TV viewing, both of which provide stimulation and passivity simultaneously.

Brodlie studied 50 adolescent drug users being dealt with at the clinic, a control group of 50 adolescent nonusers, and another control group of 27 adolescents with behavioral pathologies not associated with drug use. Although he did not claim any cause and effect relationship, he did find interesting differences in TV viewing behavior among the groups. The users reported 3.8 hours per day of TV viewing (compared with 2.0 for nonusers), more Saturday and Sunday viewing, and fewer parental restrictions on TV viewing than nonusers. Seeing both drugs and TV as anxiety defenses (against boredom), Brodlie concluded that "perhaps excessive television viewing plays some role in the development of a life-style which seeks pleasure and passivity simultaneously."[6]

Although the above data attempt to relate the *act* of viewing and experiencing mass media with patterns of drug use, most charges focus on certain *contents* of mass media. Advertising, TV entertainment, newspaper coverage, and popular song lyrics are often seen as villains creating a tendency toward greater drug use in society.

This article attempts to examine some of these charges, the issues and the evidence in the current controversy over the role of mass media in the use of psychoactive drugs.

Organized Social Action," in *The Communication of Ideas*, ed. L. Bryson (New York: Harper, 1948), pp. 95–118.

2. Cited in E. H. Kramer, "A Review of Literature Relating to the Impact of the Broadcast Media on Drug Use and Abuse," in National Commission on Marihuana and Drug Abuse, *Drug Use in America*, Appendix, vol. 2 (Washington D.C.: Government Printing Office, 1973), pp. 586–611.

3. Ibid.

4. Ibid.

5. J. F. Brodlie, "Drug Abuse and Television Viewing Patterns," *Psychology* 9, no. 2 (May 1972).

6. Ibid.

DRUG ADVERTISING

The first so-called villain to be formally identified was the advertising of over-the-counter drugs on television. Senator Frank Moss—Democrat, Utah—who led the fight to remove cigarette advertising from television, was one of the first to speak out on the problem:

The drug culture finds its fullest flowering in the portrait of American society which can be pieced together out of the hundreds of thousands of advertisements and commercials. It is advertising which mounts the message that pills turn rain to sunshine, gloom to joy, depression to euphoria, solve problems, and dispel doubt. Not just pills: cigarette and cigar ads; soft drinks, coffee, tea and beer ads—all portray the key to happiness as things to swallow, inhale, chew, drink and eat.[7]

Nicholas Johnson, former commissioner of the Federal Communications Commission, holds an even stronger position, labeling TV as the prime pusher of drugs in our society:

Every indicator of drug use from cigarette sales to aspirin sales; from the use of alcohol to the use of vitamins; from sleeping pills to stay-awake pills—is increasing annually. And television is intimately involved in selling these drugs. Television is the pusher.[8]

Richard Penna, speaking for the American Pharmaceutical Association, also spoke out on the relationship between drug use and advertising:

We feel that over-the-counter drug advertising is out of control, and has become a major health problem. It is often erroneous. It exaggerates claims.

And it even attempts to convince people they have non-existent diseases.

Most critically, we feel that over-the-counter drug advertising substantially contributes to the drug orientation of our culture, and we feel that something ought to be done about it.[9]

Just what are the messages in the media which bring about such strong attacks? Two studies which investigated the specific content of drug advertising on television were submitted to the National Commission on Marihuana and Drug Abuse.[10] Both reached similar conclusions although they studied different samples of television programming.

In a 126-hour sample of commercial television in Boston, Massachusetts, 132 over-the-counter drug commercials were recorded. These represented about five-and-one-half percent of all commercial announcements, or about one per hour. Heffner Associates studied a composite week of network television representing 250 hours of program time, locating 465 drug commercials, or 13.4 percent of all network TV ads.

By product category, internal analgesics such as aspirin were the most prominent, comprising almost one-fourth of all drug ads, followed in frequency by antihistamine preparations, antacids, laxatives, vitamin and mineral preparations, sleeping aids and a host of other remedies.

7. "Another Hill Assault on Ads?" *Broadcasting Magazine* 78 (18 May 1970), p. 30.
8. Cited in Kramer, "A Review," p. 590.
9. Ibid.
10. F. E. Barcus et al., "Drug Advertising on Television," in National Commission on Marihuana and Drug Abuse, *Drug Use,* pp. 623–668; Richard Heffner Associates, Inc., "Over the Counter Drug Commercials: Network Television, Spring, 1971," in National Commission on Marihuana and Drug Abuse, *Drug Use,* pp. 669–697.

The product claims and promises of relief in these ads are perhaps the most relevant direct messages for their audiences. Both studies showed that in 80 to 90 percent of the ads, references were made to very specific ailments, conditions, or symptoms for which the drug was intended. However, the TV ads offered not only specific relief, but also frequently promised general relief from pain or discomfort. They promised relaxation, general well-being ("look better" and "feel younger"), or the maintenance of one's overall health. Psychological well-being and changes in mood were indicated as well.

Although often not stated verbally in the commercials, mood changes were frequently depicted in "before-after" scenes in which initially frowning, unhappy, and hurting faces became smiling, relaxed and happy.

Other attractions associated with drug products were suggested by the Heffner Associates study. These included solving general personality problems or improving family, job, marital or romantic and sexual relationships.

There is ample *a priori* evidence from these studies that advertising messages encourage one to swallow, chew, or otherwise ingest substances not only for medical symptoms, but also for psychological well-being. There is, of course, the question of whether these remedies are effective medically, let alone whether they improve one's psychological and social relationships. There may be either misrepresentation or overstatement of claims in the commercials.

A more important question, however, is whether these messages become translated into action or behavior. At one level the answer

to the question is rather simple: yes. It does not take a great deal of documentation or scientific evidence to demonstrate that TV advertising is effective in increasing the sale of specific products, whether they be automobiles, soaps or drugs.

On a second level, the question is more difficult to answer. The issue is not "Do people buy and consume advertised products?" but rather, "Does such advertising create a general tendency to use drugs or lead to an acceptance of drug taking as a life style?"

The charges leveled against such advertising as being the "cause" of the problem are at best an oversimplification. In a panel sponsored by the National Council of Churches of Christ, Gerhard J. Hanneman discussed drug advertising and abuse:

In relationship to the influence of drug advertising on drug abuse I should point out that there is also no evidence pointing to a cause-and-effect connection between exposure to such ads and consequent drug use.

Calling for a ban proscribing drug advertising seems premature, näive and a somewhat hysterical reaction to a society's inability to contain drug abuse. It seems to me that drug advertising has been appointed the scapegoat. That is, the media because they are so pervasive are immediately considered guilty of cause.

Yet what is probably necessary is an examination of how media wide norms, both in content and all advertising, reinforce escapism and immediate gratification. I have seen beer commercials urging the viewer to live life with gusto and be daring presented back-to-back with drug abuse ads urging caution. The two messages are strictly contradictory.

Finally, of course, all media content suggesting similar norms needs to be examined. What is needed is evidence to either support or refute the assumption that individuals make mental connections between one message and subsequent, and perhaps entirely different behavior.[11]

Donald Kanter, who also testified before the panel, has said:

To assume that advertising is the only or strongest determinant of drug abuse is, to many, unfounded. Other factors in the social as well as total media environment play an important part in the drug using culture.[12]

What comprises this "total media environment?" Other forms of media messages besides commercial advertising should be examined. These include antidrug messages, television entertainment and informational programs, newspaper and magazine coverage, motion picture content, popular song lyrics and pharmaceutical advertising to physicians.

ANTIDRUG MESSAGES

Another form of media drug message is the antidrug television message. A content analysis of antidrug communications shown in the Hartford, Connecticut area found that, similar to other public service announcements, antidrug commercials tend to be broadcast in low and inappropriate audience time periods.[13] This practice immediately raises suspicion as to their efficiency.

Not only does the content of drug abuse appear to reflect a "dump truck" approach for dissemination but the seemingly inappropriate dissemination by

broadcasters during class C and D times (lowest audience attendance) may leave them relatively ineffectual.

Such a *de facto* shotgun approach assumes that mere exposure—at any time, by any audience—results in message effect. Such assumptions ignore audience needs and attendance (e.g., do teenage drug abusers attend to television at 9), as well as the suitability of content (are drug abuse appeals about heroin use appropriately broadcast during children's cartoon shows?).[14]

Hanneman's research also suggests the need to assess the most credible medium and form of communication for reaching drug users —which appears to differ from that for nonusers.

A Canadian study by Dianne Fejer *et al.* indicates that while non–drug users rely upon the news media for their principal information on drugs, drug users will usually turn to friends and personal experiences.[15] Another study confirmed this, highlighting the need for a delineation of target audience in any attempt to transmit information on drug abuse.[16]

Whatever the role of advertising and program content in promoting the use of drugs or in creating a drug-oriented culture, studies by several researchers have found the effect of the antidrug message to be even more uncertain.

Kanter, in an analysis of antidrug commercials, suggests that the general ineffectuality of antidrug messages may be attributed to the per-

11. Cited in Kramer, "A Review," p. 592.
12. Ibid., p. 594.
13. G. J. Hanneman, "Sources of Drug Abuse Information on the College Campus" (DAIR Report no. 10, Storrs, Conn.: University of Connecticut, October 1972).

14. Cited in Kramer, "A Review," p. 599.
15. Dianne Fejer et al., "Sources of Information About Drugs Among High School Students," *Public Opinion Quarterly* 35, no. 2 (Summer 1971), pp. 235–241.
16. K. G. Smart and Dianne Fejer, "Credibility of Sources of Drug Information for High School Students," *Journal of Drug Issues* (Spring 1972), pp. 8–18.

ception by adolescents that ads are "preaching from the 'Establishment.'"[17] Elsewhere it has been suggested that antidrug commercials, instead of presenting a persuasive case against the use of drugs, may serve as a source of information which may be perceived as subtle support for their use.[18]

The anticigarette campaign provides an interesting parallel to drug researchers concerned with mass media as a vehicle for public health and safety education. Evidence collected thus far indicates the limited effects of media in changing smoking behavior.

An evaluation of the effectiveness of antismoking commercials led Timothy O'Keefe to construct five hypotheses on the potential behavior modification of such commercials. It is probable that these considerations apply to antidrug commercials as well:

Campaigns, or information, designed to influence the behavior of individuals will tend to be perceived as more successful by those persons outside the primary target audience.

One of the groups most affected by campaigns or information, designed to alter the behavior of individuals, will be composed of persons already predisposed toward the behavior advocated.

One of the groups most affected by campaigns or information, designed to alter the behavior of individuals, will be composed of persons for whom the behavior under attack is not of great importance.

Even during (or after) extensive information campaigns, many persons formerly acting contrary to the newly proposed behavior will adopt the attitude advocated and still not alter their previous behavior.

When behavior and attitude are in conflict, people will tend to maximize the perceived benefits derived from the discrepant behavior to justify their actions.[19]

Thus, while it is indicated that antidrug or antismoking commercials have limited potential for effecting change, some sort of evaluatory research is needed to determine long range implications and other possible means of using the media for positive public action.

ENTERTAINMENT PROGRAMS ON TELEVISION

It is interesting to note that in the one study examining the content of TV entertainment, alcohol was specifically excluded from the category of drugs, which were defined as "any psychoactive or mood-modifying substance."[20] Had alcohol been included, no doubt the incidence of programs with thematic relevance to drug use would have been much higher than "one every nine days" which Charles Winick found. In addition, the sample was limited to entertainment programs and those appearing on the major networks. This excludes a good deal of syndicated entertainment, as well as local and network news and documentary programs on the

17. D. L. Kanter, "Some Aspects of the Broadcast Anti-Drug Program," *Public Opinion Quarterly* 35, no. 3 (Fall 1971), p. 459.
18. Kramer, "A Review."
19. M. T. O'Keefe, "The Anti-Smoking Commercials: A Study of Television's Impact on Behavior," *Public Opinion Quarterly* 35, no. 2 (Summer 1971), pp. 242–248.
20. Charles Winick, "A Content Analysis of Drug Related Network Entertainment Prime Time Programs, 1970–72," in National Commission on Marihuana and Drug Abuse, *Drug Use*, pp. 698–708.

topic. Thus, the total TV programs about drugs can be assumed to be much greater than Winick analyzed. No data are known to exist on the total attention given the topic on television.

Winick's study, on the whole, confirms what one would expect about the treatment of the subject. The TV industry code itself specifically prohibits the positive portrayal of narcotic addiction or illegal drugs. Winick concluded that "the consequences and effects of drug use are almost uniformly presented as being personally and socially undesirable," and details of the drug culture were presented as "uniformly ugly."[21]

The settings and situations in which the problem is dealt with, however, correspond to the basic nature of TV entertainment. In television entertainment, drugs are treated primarily as a law enforcement problem—in 38 out of 56 programs found. Drugs provided subject matter for several episodes in police-detective series such as "Adam-12," "Ironside," "Mod Squad" and "Mannix." There were other programs classified as "treatment-oriented." Occupational groups involved in illegal drug use are students, housewives, entertainers and prostitutes—in 26 of 38 programs in which occupation was identified. The programs concentrate on heavy users and abusers of drugs, and the drug most used is heroin. Most frequently, drug use occurs in unusual and exotic situations.

Although the TV dramatic portrayals may point to some extreme problems of drug abuse in society, the context in which they are presented may have little relevance for the viewing audience who identify neither with pushers and addicts, the supercops who chase them, nor the exotic situations in which the stories take place. Statistically, real-life experimenters and recreational users outnumber TV's heavy users and abusers by a wide margin. Undoubtedly, the use of marihuana, amphetamines and barbiturates exceeds the proportion of heroin users protrayed in TV drama. Also, the portrayal of drug use predominantly in a law enforcement context oversimplifies the problem considerably.

The point is simply that if the viewer does not identify a problem with his own situation, it is not likely that either learning or behavioral change will result.

In any event, we can learn only a limited amount by the examination of the manifest messages of television entertainment. The Dean Martin ("one more martini") syndrome, the characterization of the happy-go-lucky, successful and sociable drunk, could well be a much more insidious and effective device for the condoning of alcohol as an instrument of escape and relaxation than is TV drama. Latent messages, embodied in contexts, situations and characterizations—messages which are revealed through what characters do rather than what they say—may be more important. T. W. Adorno speaks about the "multilayered" structure of television and its latent messages:

Mass media are not simply the sum total of the actions they portray or the messages that radiate from these actions. Mass media also consist of various layers of meaning superimposed on one another, all of which contribute to the effect.

21. Ibid.

[The 'latent' message] . . . may be more important than the overt, since this hidden message will escape the controls of consciousness, will not be looked through, will not be warded off by sales resistance, but it is likely to sink into the spectator and mind.[22]

Thus, while it is not likely that a figure in the media would advocate the misuse of drugs (some song lyrics may be exceptions), the portrayal in a television series, a motion picture, or magazine story of a character who uses drugs but who is also apt to lead a very desirable and exciting life—who may be resisting authority or acting out problems with parents, teachers or others—may have latent meaning for those who identify with such problems.

MOTION PICTURES AND DRUGS

The substantial concern and evidence of influence of motion pictures on youth was documented more than 40 years ago in a series of studies supported by the Payne Fund.[23] Just as the new medium of television is the focus of most of our current attention, the motion picture received serious study in the 1930s and 1940s.[24]

Although the content, style, and audiences for film have changed with the changes in social issues of the day, the motion picture still remains a powerful medium, both reflecting and projecting those

issues—including the issue of drug use. The continuing concern about the effects of films is based to a large extent on the fact that the movie audience has traditionally been a young one; that is no less true today. Attendance statistics indicate that nearly seven out of 10 admissions are by people 12 to 29 years old.

The best current information on the contents of recent films dealing with drugs is provided by Winick.[25] Although films portraying drug use have been produced since the early days of motion pictures, it was not until the 1950s and 1960s that successful and popular films dealt openly with narcotic use and addiction. Examples include *The Man with the Golden Arm*, 1955; *A Hatful of Rain*, 1957; *Monkey on my Back*, 1957; and *Synanon*, 1966.

Recently, the frequency of drug-related films has increased substantially. In 1971, Winick found 89 of 231 feature film releases—38.5 percent—to have "some significant content related to drug use" in a preliminary screening, and 23—10 percent—in which the portrayal was an integral part of the film's plot.[26]

There seems to be a striking difference in film and TV portrayals. In contrast to two-thirds of TV dramas which treated drugs as primarily a law enforcement problem, only eight of the 23 films involved law enforcement officials extensively. Also, unlike TV drama, the act of taking drugs was depicted, and euphoria or other pleasant effects of drug use was sometimes shown. Winick notes

22. T. W. Adorno, "Television and the Patterns of Mass Culture," in *Mass Communication*, ed. W. Schramm (Urbana: University of Illinois Press, 1960), pp. 594–612.

23. W. W. Charters, *Motion Pictures and Youth* (New York: Macmillan Co., 1933).

24. Ruth A. Inglis, *Freedom of the Movies* (Chicago: University of Chicago Press, 1947); Hortense Powdermaker, *Hollywood: The Dream Factory* (New York: Little, Brown & Co., 1950).

25. Charles Winick, "A Content Analysis of Drug Related Films Released During 1971," National Commission on Marihuana and Drug Abuse, *Drug Use*, pp. 709–717.

26. Ibid.

several themes which might affect audience attitudes, hardly any of which were shown on television.

First, he noted in five films a "glamorous attitude about drug use." Second, he found that there is the connotation of drugs as aphrodisiacs in more than one-third of the films. A third theme relates to youth. Designated "anti-square films," they

. . . are primarily concerned with marihuana and hallucinogens, the use of which is related to personal liberation, a challenge to convention and self-expression on the part of young people, usually from middle-class backgrounds.[27]

Another theme dealt with the urban drug culture in a context of "helpless alienation," and a fifth dealt with what was called the "beautiful losers"—those who are doomed and withdraw from reality through drug use. Finally, there are the films dealing with hippie communes, the members of which use certain drugs to "recharge their emotional batteries."[28]

Thus, film entertainment reflects a much less stereotyped picture of drug use than does television drama. There are, of course, some obvious reasons for this difference, most of which are concerned with what is "permissible"—permissibility being defined in terms of the composition of the audience and the greater audience selectivity in choosing films.

Since TV viewing is assumed to be much less selective, the primary effect may be informational. The rather unreal TV world of drug situations, well removed from the life of the viewer, has already been described. There is considerably

more choice in motion picture viewing, however. There also seems to be a much closer connection to the life experiences of the viewer. The motion picture may serve much more as a reinforcing function for individuals who are more knowledgeable about drugs prior to viewing. This could be especially important in view of the fact that few of the films were found to propose any kind of solution to the problem. Winick's conclusions on this point are as follows:

It is noteworthy that few of these films propose any 'solution' to the society's drug problem. It is very significant that most of the films studied, although they have significant drug content, are not *primarily* concerned with drugs. Rather, the characters are shown participating in the drug interaction as a regular but not exclusive activity . . . in most of the films, the drug use is taken for granted.[29]

NEWSPAPER AND MAGAZINE COVERAGE

We could find no formal research studies on the coverage and treatment of drugs, drug users, or any related topics in either newspapers, magazines, or radio and television informational and news programs.

An interesting case study is provided by "Death of a Rock Star," described as a mini–case study of the death of Janis Joplin, 27-year-old rock star, in October 1970. This demonstrates the diversity of coverage given the event by two newspapers and three magazines.[30]

The *New York Times* carried a Reuters story, straight-forward in

27. Ibid., p. 715.
28. Ibid.

29. Ibid.
30. Francis H. Voelker and Ludmila A. Voelker, eds., "Death of a Rock Star," in *Mass Media: Forces in Our Society* (New York: Harcourt Brace Jovanovich, 1972), pp. 138–147.

approach, but which attempted to explain the death—which the coroner determined to be an overdose of heroin—through a personality profile derived from public statements of Ms. Joplin. Describing her as a misfit in her home town of Port Arthur, Texas, the newspaper quoted her as having said, "I read, I painted, I didn't hate niggers. . . . Man, those people back home hurt me." Presumably, then, to rid herself of the hurt, Ms. Joplin revealed, "When I get scared and worried . . . I tell myself 'Janis, just have a good time.' So I juice up real good and that's just what I have."[31]

Similarly, the *St. Cloud Daily Times* carried a UPI story, also pointing out that she had run away from home at age 17.

Newsweek and *Life* coverage both referred to "devils" or "demons" which possessed her. *Newsweek* described her as an "aggressively shy, coarsely sweet, belligerently vulnerable child-woman. . . ."

Janis Joplin sang the blues, a black man's music, even though she was white, because she was born with ready-made grief inside her. No matter how she tried, no matter what the anodyne, she could not quiet her devils.[32]

A *Life* article by Albert Goldman, entitled "Drugs and Death in the Run-Down World of Rock Music," compared Ms. Joplin's death with the death of Jimi Hendrix, another 27-year-old rock star who had died three weeks earlier in London from an overdose of sleeping pills. Hendrix' death was described as "an inevitable product of his life." But, according to the article, "Janis Joplin was possessed by a very different demon."[33]

Newsweek's coverage was the most sensational:

She never hesitated to sacrifice the beautiful tone for the raw power of emotion, for the animal sounds that accompanied the animal sensual grace of her passionate body . . .

Janis liked it when someone wrote how sexy her breasts were. 'She'd been called many things,' says a friend, 'but never desirable. Before, she was kind of a pig, never bathed or dressed. Now she was like a little girl playing dress up, crying out to be pretty, to be loved.'[34]

In contrast to the more popular press, *Rolling Stone* magazine carried a personal and empathetic story with considerably less analysis of motives and personal background, stereotypes and sensationalism, and considerably more detail on the circumstances of her death. Letters in sympathy from readers were published as well.

Although it is difficult to draw conclusions from one such single event, there may well be a reinforcing stereotype in the popular press about the causes and consequences of drug abuse. The stereotype of the lost and lonely child possessed by devils and demons, the exotic and sensational life styles, and the inevitability of death as an outcome of drug use would hardly appear to enlighten the public on the problems and causes of drug use in society.

Such newspaper and magazine coverage tends to link rock stars like Janis Joplin and Jimi Hendrix with both the drug and youth cul-

31. Ibid.
32. Ibid.
33. Ibid.
34. Ibid.

tures. In this fashion, rock music has become symbolic of youth today. The rock culture has become the drug culture in many ways, and the messages of song lyrics have been publicly criticized during the past few years.

POPULAR SONG LYRICS

A current contention is that popular song lyrics dramatize and encourage the drug experience. In 1971, the Federal Communications Commission (FCC) issued three opinions on the words used in popular music which "promote or glorify the use of illegal drugs." The FCC claimed that broadcasters have a responsibility to serve the public interest and that, as such, the playing of drug-oriented records was of questionable value. Laying aside the First Amendment debates, the issue from our perspective is whether drug-oriented lyrics reflect the drug culture or are responsible for promoting it.

Although opinions have been voiced on both sides, there does not seem to be a strong case for a causal link between song lyrics and drug use.

Despite the seemingly obvious references to drugs in such popular songs as "With a Little Help from My Friends," where the Beatles sing "I get high with a little help from my friends," the majority of lyrics taken from the "top 40" are subject to varying interpretations. Moreover, if one accepts popular music as an art form, its meaning becomes even more of an elusive and subjective experience. The above-mentioned Beatles' phrase, for example, has been interpreted as referring to:

1. a need for affection when alone;

2. the assistance Ringo seeks when he's out of tune; or

3. a friend providing marihuana.[35]

One study surveyed over 700 teenagers on their musical preferences. Not only did 70 percent of the subjects claim that the song's "sound" was more important than its "meaning," but less than one-third were able to decipher the lyrics or give an accurate interpretation of the meaning of the lyrics.[36]

Commenting on the relationship between rock lyrics and drug use, David Smith of the Haight-Ashbury Medical Center said:

Youth likes rock music. Drug-using youth likes rock music. Non-drug youth likes rock music. There is no causal relationship between the two . . . To say that contemporary music is causative in the current wave of drug abuse is a very questionable judgment . . . A person doesn't become an alcoholic because he hears a pro-alcohol song such as 'One for my baby,' and there are many others. The person with alcoholic tendencies hears the same pro-alcohol songs as does the social drinker, or the non-alcohol user. Whether a person becomes a drug user is not determined by the music he hears but primarily by personality characteristics.[37]

It is most likely that, although some song lyrics are expressions of the life styles of drug users and may be used as reinforcements of that life style, they are results rather than causes of drug use. The research evidence we gathered does not lead one to any stronger conclusion.

35. E. S. Schwartz et al., "Popular Music and Drug Lyrics: Analysis of a Scapegoat," in National Commission on Marihuana and Drug Abuse, *Drug Use*, pp. 718–746.
36. Ibid., p. 722
37. Ibid., p. 720.

ADVERTISING IN MEDICAL JOURNALS

The role of over-the-counter drug advertising and the effects of mass media advertising and program content on drug orientations in our society sometimes seem dwarfed by the influence which the medical profession wields over the use of drugs. Considering the complexity and greater health risks inherent in prescription drugs and their dispensing, it seems appropriate to analyse how the media affect the people who may have more influence on the social orientation to drugs as a solution to problems than they care to admit—the physicians who are bombarded with drug advertising through medical journals.

Senator Gaylord Nelson—Democrat, Wisconsin—who has been involved in studying various aspects of drug advertising for several years, has chastised the advertisers and producers of drugs. Nelson has claimed that $5,000 per doctor "is spent annually to persuade him to prescribe drugs."[38] Whether advertising, by its very nature, can provide unbiased information to physicians is questionable. It has been estimated that 25 percent of industry sales is spent on advertising, while only 6.2 percent of industry sales goes into research and development.[39]

A ten-year survey of medical and psychiatric journals by R. Seidenberg[40] revealed an increasing tendency of drug advertisements to suggest chemical solutions for nonmedical, nonpsychiatric problems—usually those associated with stress and tensions of everyday life.

The encouragement of this type of drug use was also explored in some detail by Henry Lennard et al. in an article published in Science:

In the context of current usage, drugs are medical agents whose function is the solution of medical problems. Only to the extent that interpersonal and other human problems can be construed as medical-psychiatric problems can they be considered appropriate targets for drug treatment.

It is apparent that the pharmaceutical industry is redefining and relabeling as medical problems calling for drug intervention a wide range of human behaviors which, in the past, have been viewed as falling within the bounds of the normal trials and tribulations of human existence. Much evidence for this position is to be found in the advertisements of drug companies, both in medical journals and in direct mailings to physicians.[41]

Several examples are given to illustrate this theme in medical journal advertising. An example is an ad showing a young woman with books in arm—a new college student. The captions surrounding her read, in part, as follows:

Exposure to new friends and other influences may force her to reevaluate herself and her goals . . . Her newly stimulated intellectual curiosity may make her more sensitive to and apprehensive about unstable national and world conditions.[42]

The text, suggesting that Librium "can help get her back on her feet," led the authors to conclude:

38. G. A. Nelson, "Is TV Selling Your Children on Drugs?" *Family Health* (June 1972), pp. 34ff.

39. *Chemical Marketing Reports,* vol. 202 (20 November 1972), p. 4.

40. R. Seidenberg, ed., "Advertising and Abuse of Drugs," *New England Journal of Medicine* 284, no. 14 (April 1971), pp. 789–790.

41. H. L. Lennard, et al., "Hazards Implicit in Prescribing Psychoactive Drugs," *Science* 19 (July 1970), pp. 438–441.

42. Ibid.

Thus, the normal problems and conflicts associated with the status change and personal growth that accompany the college experience are relabeled medical-psychiatric problems, and as such are subject to amelioration through Librium.[43]

A physician who follows the advice of these ads is doing more than prescribing a drug. He is also communicating an acceptable model to the patient for dealing with interpersonal relationships and personal anxieties.

CONCLUSIONS

Perhaps the greatest criticism that can be made of charges about the effects of mass media on drug use, as well as about the research deriving from these charges, is their simplicity in the formulation of the problem. The bulk of the research designs that we have noted assume that one can discover some basic cause and effect relationships between media content and audience behavior. This is analogous to the general pattern of advertising research which tries to discover simply whether an increase in sales has resulted from the advertising messages appearing in the media. The best current theories of mass communication research dispute this simple, direct, one-to-one relationship in assessing the effects of mass media.

A better explanation of media effects, although not the easiest to demonstrate, is a functional one. That is, the media alone are considered neither necessary nor sufficient causes of human behavioral changes. They work "as influences, working amid other influences, in a total situation."[44] These influences

43. Ibid.
44. J. T. Klapper, *The Effects of Mass Communication* (New York: Free Press, 1960).

include: (1) audience predispositions leading to selectivity of perceptions, exposure, and retention; (2) group influences and group norms; (3) interpersonal sources of information and communication; and (4) the credibility of opinion leaders and the mass media.

Further research addressed to the social consequences of mass media should be structured to include all media as part of a multifaceted environment operating in conjunction with personal and social factors which may determine the final consequences of media messages.

Almost all of the serious studies we have found of youthful drug use and abuse have pointed out non-media factors, such as the role of peer groups and their social norms, as important influences in the experimentation or use of drugs. Communication research has similarly pointed out that although the mass media may play a significant role as information sources— whether about products or ideas— decisions to adopt the ideas or use the information are generally determined by influences other than the media. The primary influences seem to be one's immediate acquaintances —friends, neighbors and work associates—who are sources of advice and who thus become the opinion leaders or influentials in decisions to act or behave in certain ways.

The media, then, are part of an environment which is composed of many factors leading to change. The media, by their very existence, perform certain functions in the society for the individual, for subgroups of the society, and for the culture as a whole. The media not only inform, but also provide alternative evaluations and advice. They transmit cultural values and norms through their activities of advertising, entertainment, information, and editorial positions.

The mass media legitimize the topic of drug use by the attention they give to the problem through news and information coverage, as well as through the views of life presented in their dramatic and fictional forms. This important role of mass media in our lives has been suggested in George Gerbner's analysis.[45]

In a real sense, the mass media are the "agenda-setters" of our culture. The selection of issues and the focus of attention that is given different aspects of the society establish priorities for social action. Gerbner lists four ways in which public communications define our reality. They tell us: (1) what is; (2) what or who is important; (3) what is right or wrong; and (4) what is related to what. Man's exposure to his immediate environment is necessarily limited. Thus, what he

45. George Gerbner, "Toward 'Cultural Indicators': The Analysis of Mass Mediated Public Message Systems," in G. Gerbner et al., eds., *The Analysis of Communication Content* (New York: John Wiley & Sons, 1969).

knows (what is) is determined to a large extent by the attention given to ideas, people and issues in the mass media. Also, by focusing on certain people, ideas or issues, the media strongly influence our knowledge of what and who is important. The media, through comment, slant, attention and interpretation, also teach us what is right and wrong. Finally, the juxtaposition of ideas and events inevitably forms a sense of relatedness, context and associations which teach us what is related to what.

We must conclude that, as part of the current environment, the mass media are a contributing factor in social change—including the changes we have witnessed in the social orientation to drug use. We feel that all contributing factors which can be identified must be treated as causal. There is a danger that too much attention given to mass media may divert us from recognizing other causes and solutions. Nevertheless, the media must be held accountable to the extent that they contribute to an orientation which may lead to dysfunctional forms of drug use.

Drug Abuse and the College Campus

By GERALD L. ROBINSON AND STEPHEN T. MILLER

ABSTRACT: Traditionally, American society has entrusted to its colleges and universities the authority to govern broad aspects of student life on campus; it has expected in return the mental, physical and moral well-being of the students in their charge. By the late 1960s, however, both the concept and practice of *in loco parentis* by educational institutions had come under increasing attack, with challenges most frequently being directed to the right of colleges and universities to control nonacademic aspects of student life and conduct, including the use of psychoactive drugs. Despite the concern voiced by parents and educators over the escalating use of psychoactive drugs by young people and the waves of drug use reaching the college campus, college administrators, with virtually no experience in this area, generally found themselves unprepared to cope with the problem. The intent of this paper is to examine the responses of college and university administrators to student drug use, to explore the manner in which drug policies have been formulated and implemented in response to the perceived problem, and to reflect on the impact and effectiveness of the policies which have emerged and which are currently in force at institutions of higher learning throughout the country.

Gerald L. Robinson is Executive Director of Personnel, University of Pennsylvania. Since 1957, he has served that same University as Vice Dean of Admissions, Director of Residence, Dean of Men and Dean of Residential Life. Mr. Robinson has also chaired several university committees, including the Administrative Assembly, the University Eligibility Committee, the Disciplinary Committee and the Committee on Drugs and Drug Abuse.

Stephen T. Miller is currently an Instructor in Business Law at the Wharton School of Business and Finance and has served, since 1969, as Director of Graduate Housing for the University of Pennsylvania. Mr. Miller also served, from 1965 to 1969, as Assistant Dean of Men for Dormitory Counseling and has been a member of University committees for residence staff training, emergencies and civil disorders.

HISTORICALLY, society's leaders have entrusted to college and university officials in the United States both the autonomy and the authority to regulate and govern broad aspects of student life on the campus. This power to act *in loco parentis* in virtually all matters concerning the mental, physical and moral well-being of the student was, until fairly recently, simply taken for granted and exercised as a matter of course; colleges and universities both accepted and were willing to play this role, and the families of students were grateful for the promise that the student's every need would be duly cared for by the institution.

The almost universal acceptance of the concept and practice of *in loco parentis* began to diminish, however, in the late 1950s, when veterans of the Korean War returned to collegiate life and began chipping away at its foundations. As family life underwent considerable change, and as young people became more assertive in the face of authority, negative reactions to the image projected by *in loco parentis* took the form of frequent challenges to the right of an educational institution to control the nonacademic aspects of student life and conduct.

This assault on colleges and universities as parent surrogates reached its zenith in the late 1960s, when substantial numbers of disenchanted students rose up, within the context of an emerging youth culture, and angrily rejected what they regarded as an unjustified and inappropriate relic of the past. This rejection often found expression in a kind of dramatic dismissal of the traditionally accepted social norms, rules of conduct and life styles, which were quickly replaced by often conspicuous and socially affronting modes of speech, dress and behavior. Much of the apparent rush to participate in the "new" sexual freedom and use of psychoactive drugs for "mind expansion" coincided with that emergence of the youth culture and its outward symbols.

The initial reactions of parents, educators and political leaders to what they perceived to be the impending demise of their society and its institutions were shock, anger, frustration and dismay. Slowly but surely, however, enlightened members of the older generation saw the need for reassessing its values and at least listening to what young people had to say. Only during this process of reevaluation and rebuilding did educational communities become alerted to the serious limitations they would inevitably face with respect to their ability to establish and enforce rather idealized concepts of social and moral conduct.

COLLEGE STUDENTS' DRUG USE

Of all the expressions of youthful alienation and rebellion, probably the most shattering and incomprehensible to the older generation has been the escalating use of psychoactive drugs by young people, for in many ways drug abuse has destroyed individuals and families and has seriously shaken our social and educational institutions.

When the first serious waves of drug abuse reached the college campuses in the mid-1960s, administrators, with virtually no experience in this area, found themselves unprepared to respond satisfactorily and appropriately to the students' drug-related problems, to the impact drug use had on the surrounding communities, and to public pressure for its elimination. Out of frustration, ignorance, confusion and lack of understanding, college administrators most often turned to the only procedure they knew for dealing with student behavioral problems: the disciplinary process. At the same time, however, these disciplinary measures were coming under increasing attack from students as being basically unfair and without due process. Thus, young people in trouble with drugs, and sometimes with the law, came to feel an even greater sense of anger, despair and perhaps even betrayal. Not until well after these early shock waves subsided did college communities begin to pull themselves together and to develop more rational policies and procedures for addressing the problem of drug abuse on the campus.

Part of this awareness led the more courageous administrators to question the basic assumptions underlying the demand for intervention, that is, that psychoactive drug use on campus was indeed a reality and that its nature and magnitude were sufficient to be defined as or to cause a problem requiring immediate and official intervention strategies. For these officials, the answers seemed to lie in anonymous responses of students to self-administered questionnaires, often completed in the classroom, regarding their drug use and its effects. So was born the college student drug survey. By 1973, hundreds of colleges and universities throughout the country had conducted student drug surveys. Because no serious effort has been made to perfect or to standardize questionnaires, interview schedules, sampling procedures, operational definitions, estimating techniques or reporting procedures, however, these survey results are severely limited in terms of comparability, reliability, validity and generalizations drawn. Nonetheless, they are useful as indicators of the current nature and dimensions and future trends of drug use among a substantial proportion of the college and university student population.[1]

During its two-year existence (1971 to 1973), the National Commission on Marihuana and Drug Abuse made a concerted effort to determine the nature, extent and patterns of drug use among secondary school and college students throughout the United States. Toward this end, more than 200 student surveys were collected and their data analyzed.[2] In addition, data pertaining to high school and college students were extrapolated from the results of the commission's national survey of youth and adults[3] and were presented in the commission's second year report.[4] Table 1 presents in summary form these survey data regarding the incidence (ever use) of, and percentage change in, college student drug use, by drug type, 1969 to 1972.

As indicated, these figures should not be treated as absolutes, but

1. For a discussion of student survey methodology, see, National Commission on Marihuana and Drug Abuse, Drug Use in America: Problem in Perspective (Washington, D.C.: Government Printing Office, 1973), pp. 71–73 (hereinafter referred to as Report).
2. Ibid.
3. Herbert Abelson et al., "Drug Experience, Attitudes and Related Behavior Among Adolescents and Adults," in National Commission of Marihuana and Drug Abuse, Drug Use in America: Problem in Perspective, Appendix, vol. 1 (Washington, D.C.: Government Printing Office, 1973), pp. 488–870 (hereinafter referred to as Appendix).
4. National Commission on Marihuana and Drug Abuse, Report, pp. 73–84. For a full discussion of the patterns of college student drug use, see, pp. 84–93.

TABLE 1

INCIDENCE (EVER USE) AND PERCENTAGE CHANGE IN COLLEGE STUDENT
DRUG USE BY DRUG TYPE, 1969–1972

DRUG TYPE	INCIDENCE BY YEAR OF SURVEY (FIGURES ARE MEAN PERCENTAGES)				PERCENT CHANGE	NCMDA 1972 NATIONAL SURVEY INCIDENCE FIGURES
	1969	1970	1971	1972	1969–1972	(PERCENT)
Tobacco	62	52	68	58	− 6	n.a.
Alcohol	90	86	86	83	− 7	98
Marihuana	32	36	45	50	+ 56	67
Hallucinogens	6	9	13	14	+133	27
Stimulants	22	17	21	24	+ 9	} 33*
Depressants	12	14	14	15	+ 17	
Opiates	5.1	4.3	3.4	6.0	+ 18	4.3

* For both medical and nonmedical reasons.

rather as indicators of the nature and magnitude of the problem. Used in this fashion, it is interesting to note how they compare with the estimates of college administrators relative to the percentage of students on their campuses they believed to have used these same psychoactive drugs. The data in table 2 clearly illustrate the extent to which college and university officials underestimated, relative to students' self-reports, the incidence of drug use among their student bodies.

It is important to keep these discrepancies and underestimates in mind when evaluating the degree to which they have formed the basis of, or have any bearing upon, the drug policies which have emerged to deal with psychoactive drug use on the college campus.

TABLE 2

COLLEGE STUDENTS' SELF-REPORTS AND COLLEGE ADMINISTRATORS' ESTIMATES
OF THE INCIDENCE OF DRUG USE, BY TYPE, 1972

DRUG TYPE	STUDENT SURVEY DATA (MEAN %)	NCMDA 1972 NATIONAL SURVEY	ADMINISTRATORS' ESTIMATES (PERCENTAGES)
Alcohol	83%	98%	33.3% thought 81–100% of students had used alcohol
Marihuana	50	67	23.4 thought 51 or more of students had used marihuana
Hallucinogens	14	27	13.2 thought 11–35 of students had used LSD
Stimulants	24	} 33	13.6 thought 21–35 of students had used amphetamines
Depressants	15		22.7 thought 11–35 of students had used barbiturates
Opiates	6	4	14.4 thought 3 or more of students had used heroin
Cocaine	n.a.	10.4	5.5 thought 6 or more of students had used cocaine

NOTE: For full range of administrators' responses, see, Robinson et al. (as cited in footnote 5), Table 3, p. 571.

DRUG POLICIES AND THEIR IMPLEMENTATION

During 1972, the National Association of Student Personnel Administrators' Committee on Drug Education conducted, under contract to the National Commission on Marihuana and Drug Abuse, a review of college and university drug policies and their implementation.[5] The sampling frame used in the study was composed of all accredited colleges and universities in the United States with a fall 1970 enrollment of at least 500 students. As stated in their report:

The researchers sought a set of selection criteria that would yield a large number of institutions of higher learning throughout the country, sufficiently diversified along a number of important dimensions to allow for inclusion of the broadest possible range of policies, procedures and regulations governing the use of drugs on campus.[6]

The sampling design ultimately employed produced a 50 percent stratified proportionate random sample of 1,035 institutions, or 50.6 percent of all accredited colleges and universities with the established minimal enrollment. The stratification variables were: (1) geographic distribution (state in which institution located); (2) type of control (public v. private); and (3) degree-granting program (associate level degree or above, but less than baccalaureate v. baccalaureate or higher).

In accordance with the objectives of the study, a precoded, 46-item self-administered questionnaire was developed, pretested and mailed to the institutions included in the sample. Of the 632 questionnaires returned, 531, or 51.3 percent, were considered complete enough to be usable. These represented 81.5 percent of the four-year public institutions; 38.3 percent of the two-year public institutions; 45.7 percent of the four-year private institutions; and 34.5 percent of the two-year private institutions.

As a follow-up to the written questionnaire, a 10 percent random sample of 50 institutions was contacted by telephone. The purpose of the inquiry was to obtain some greater sense of the extent to which colleges and universities follow in actual practice the provisions contained in their written policies. Additionally, the inquiry delved into administrative estimates of the number of drug cases they handled during the year and into their recommendations for assistance from the federal government.

The results of this survey clearly reveal the difficulties encountered by these institutions in their efforts to design and enforce drug policies which: (1) are appropriate to the nature and magnitude of the problem; (2) are acceptable to the various factions on the campus and in the surrounding community; (3) meet the existing federal, state and local legal requirements; and (4) do not force the institutions to acknowledge publicly the existence of a drug problem or to adopt specific and rigid methods of dealing with any drug problems which might surface.

The data show that the typical drug policy in force at the responding institutions was characteristically vague; made no distinctions between possession, sale or transfer

5. G. L. Robinson, L. R. Young, and M. E. Duffy, "Review of College and University Policies Concerning Illegal and Unprescribed Drugs and Narcotics," in National Commission on Marihuana and Drug Abuse, *Appendix*, vol. 2, pp. 548–581.

6. Ibid., p. 548.

of drugs; usually failed to differentiate among drug types; contained no specific mention of ethical pharmaceuticals or alcohol; covered on-campus violations only; and rarely stated what specific sanctions or penalties could or would be invoked for policy violations.

Essentially, all of this suggests the general tendency of college administrators to adopt a kind of avoidance technique for dealing with drug use on campus. It may perhaps best be viewed as an effort to avert the kind of direct confrontation that would be required under a more explicit policy—that kind of policy itself being generally perceived as tantamount to an admission, or at least an acknowledgment, of the existence of a problem. As the commission has noted:

Whatever the reason, there is an obviously strong tendency among university administrators to hide campus drug problems from public view.[7]

In their responses to questions pertaining to sanctions and penalties for drug law violations, administrators revealed a rather surprising inconsistency and unevenness in their application. In large part, the type and severity of the sanctions applied appeared to be a function of the range of options available, the detector of the violation, and the degree of public and official attention it attracted. Commenting on this point, the commission noted, for example, that:

Violators of campus drug policy are referred to counseling in 34% of the instances in which campus personnel detected the offense. By comparison, students arrested for or convicted of violating the drug laws were referred to counseling only 26% of the time.[8]

In an effort to determine the manner in which drug policies were formulated and developed, the researchers inquired into the role of students, faculty and staff. The results show that although most of the policies were clearly addressed to students, less than one-half of the sample secured student assistance in the formulation of campus drug policies and guidelines for their implementation. Rather:

Drug policy was a product of a committee with the administrators playing the leading role in formulating and interpreting. Most schools provided for student participation on these committees, but considered students as ancillary decision-makers regarding drug policy. Faculty and staff were similarly regarded.[9]

Both initially and finally, the formulation of drug policies, their interpretation and the application of sanctions and penalties for drug and alcohol violations are the prerogative of the administrator, with staff latitude in dealing with individual cases being restricted to policy guidelines.

The staff was . . . required to report all on-campus drug incidents, while relieved of this responsibility for off-campus violations. The usual scenario was for the administrator to receive the initial report and then to decide among alternatives: disciplinary board, counseling, other referrals or personal action. In considering the typical penalties imposed against first offenders, a drug violation was considered as quite serious, with an average of ⅓ of the students suspended upon conviction. Internal sanctions, particularly in denying academic awards, were used more sparingly.[10]

In an effort to determine where there was a deliberate or conscious

7. National Commission on Marihuana and Drug Abuse, *Report*, p. 388.
8. Ibid.

9. National Commission on Marihuana and Drug Abuse, *Appendix*, vol. 2, p. 558.
10. Ibid.

effort to seek out drug users on campus, administrators were queried about the provisions for searching residence halls. The data show that most schools—81.6 percent—had defined a policy on room search. Although college and university personnel—dean's staff, residence advisory staff and campus police, for example—were generally assigned to this task, civil and other authorities were occasionally permitted to search student residence halls for the presence of drugs. It should be noted that although some schools did require a lawful search warrant before permission to search was granted, the majority apparently engaged in or permitted such searches without legal sanction.

That students were often "kept in the dark" regarding the specific provisions of the drug policy in force, the actions which might be taken, and the penalties or sanctions which would be imposed for policy violations was a fact reinforced by the finding that the institution's drug policy, which most often was disseminated in student handbooks only, was usually couched in the most general and ambiguous terms, and referred only obliquely to the provisions of existing legislation. The data show that only about 30 percent of the responding institutions routinely informed their students of the federal, state and local laws which pertained to them or of the penalties for their violation. Rather, existing drug and alcohol laws were ordinarily disseminated to students only upon request.[11]

Nonetheless, most colleges and universities still appear to retain some vestiges of their former and traditional protective role when it comes to shielding student drug use from public view. Information obtained by counseling personnel was reported to be treated as confidential in 86 percent of the cases, and confidentiality was likewise extended to medical personnel and student affairs in more than 50 percent of the responding institutions. Parents and law enforcement authorities were notified of a student's drug problem or activity, subsequent to detection, in only about 25 percent of the cases; only 10 percent of the schools routinely (always) notified law enforcement authorities of drug policy violations. Similarly, the colleges and universities tend to respect the privacy of student records; substantiated information concerning student drug use was not generally conveyed to such outside agencies as the military services, credit bureaus or potential employers without the consent of the student concerned. The researchers conclude, however, that selective criteria seem to operate "regarding the extent of confidentiality and the right of certain outside agencies to share information about individual drug use."[12]

In all candor, however, it should be noted that the apparent efforts taken by colleges and universities to protect students from the consequences of detection and prosecution by law enforcement authorities are not entirely altruistic; they are, at the same time, designed and utilized to insulate the institution and to protect its public image.

EXISTING COLLEGE DRUG POLICIES

As indicated earlier, subjective estimates by college administrators

11. Ibid., p. 551.   12. Ibid., p. 554.

regarding the nature and magnitude of student drug experience bear little resemblance to what college students themselves have reported in various surveys. To the extent that administrators based their schools' drug policies on their own perceptions of student drug experience, these policies were often unrealistic and unproductive.

In cases where administrators attempted to develop policies based on survey data rather than on subjective judgments, the results were generally equally unproductive because: (1) in many instances the survey methods were inadequate, thus producing unreliable and invalid data bases; (2) the interpretations of the data that did exist were often flawed or less than objective, frequently reflecting the crisis conditions under which the interpretations were made; and (3) the policies deriving from these flawed interpretations were frequently tailored to meet political requirements, and thus more accurately represent judgments of convenience rather than rational and objective attempts at policy formulation.

In essence, the policies which have been reviewed may generally be characterized as ambiguous, nonspecific, noncomprehensive, inconsistent, poorly thought out and variously implemented. The effect of such policies is that none of the parties concerned, including the college or university, the student body, parents, the surrounding community and the alumni, has been well served. Furthermore, to the extent that these policies have not been well formulated, college and university administrators have increasingly found themselves "under siege" by students, parent groups, politicians, community leaders, alumni, law enforcement officials and others, demanding what each perceives to be a more rational and effective response to student drug use. It appears that the college and university administrator has become the new focal point for competing interests attempting to resolve what are essentially political issues, many of which are more properly the purview of legislative bodies. In the absence of legislative guidelines, however, college officials will be left in their current position of formulating on an ad hoc basis the drug policy provisions which will prevail.

RECENT TRENDS AND NEW DIRECTIONS

Recent survey data and on-campus observations suggest that the use of such dangerous drugs as heroin, LSD, cocaine and methedrine has substantially diminished on the college campus but that the recreational use of marihuana has continued at a fairly high level. Of particular concern has been the upsurge of multi-drug use involving ethical pharmaceuticals—tranquilizers, barbiturates and amphetamine compounds —both singly and in combination, frequently with alcohol. In addition, there is considerable evidence to suggest a significant increase in the use of alcoholic beverages of all types.

With respect to these recent changes, some parents seem almost to have breathed a sigh of relief upon seeing their youngsters consuming alcohol rather than shooting heroin or popping pills. Colleges and universities, too, have tended to adopt a more flexible attitude regarding the consumption of alcohol on campus. The survey data show, for example, that 31 percent of the schools permit the consumption of beer, wine and liquor in student residence halls and that 26 percent permit such consumption in fraternities and sororities. At the same time, however, the administrators reported that such consumption was indeed occurring in both the residence halls—57 percent—and the fraternities and sororities—40 percent. The data further show that penalties for violation of the alcohol policy tended to be considerably more lenient than for other drug offenses; 54 percent received

a reprimand or warning only.[13] As Bentley Glass has noted:

The real issues facing our universities and colleges are whether it is possible to enforce existing laws more restrictively on a campus than in the surrounding community, and whether it is proper and desirable for university authorities to attempt a police function.[14]

13. Ibid., pp. 550–551.
14. Cited in Sidney Cohen, *The Drug Dilemma* (New York: McGraw-Hill, 1969), p. 120.

Drugs and Public Health: Issues and Answers

By BERTRAM S. BROWN

ABSTRACT: Since shortly after the turn of the century, drug abuse in the United States has been defined and treated, at least in part, as a public health issue requiring the intervention and services of the federal government. Thus, over the years the government has developed a broad spectrum of specialized agencies and activities to deal with the drug problem. These range from the creation of a "Narcotics Farm" in 1935 to the establishment of the National Institute on Drug Abuse in 1973; from the study of marihuana use and its effects to the sponsorship of narcotic antagonist research; from the training of professional and paraprofessional treatment and rehabilitation personnel to the conduct of multi-modality field trials of heroin addict rehabilitation programs. Clearly, the principal weakness in the national public health approach to narcotic addiction and drug abuse lies in the area of primary prevention, particularly as it is directed to high risk adolescents. The intent of this paper is to highlight some of the drug abuse activities and accomplishments of the National Institute of Mental Health within the Public Health Service of the Department of Health, Education and Welfare; to examine some of the significant issues and demands of the national drug program in recent years; and to indicate the directions that have been pursued in an effort to find solutions to drug abuse problems.

Bertram S. Brown is Director of the National Institute of Mental Health, Department of Health, Education and Welfare, and Professor of Clinical Psychiatry at the George Washington University Medical School. He has been a member of the advisory board of Parents Without Partners since 1966 and special assistant to the Secretary of HEW for drug abuse prevention since 1970. He received an M.D. from Cornell in 1956 and an M.P.H. from Harvard in 1960.

DRUG problems have been defined as a public health issue in the United States since shortly after the turn of the century, when a Narcotics Division was established within the Public Health Service (PHS) in 1908. In fact, the National Institute of Mental Health itself, with its broad mandate to prevent mental illness and promote mental health through research, training, and services development and delivery, is a direct bureaucratic descendant of the Narcotics Division. In 1938 that unit became the Division of Mental Hygiene in PHS and, little more than a decade thereafter, was further transformed into the National Institute of Mental Health (NIMH).

Other important early dates in the federal response to drug problems include the opening in 1935 of a hospital—originally called a Narcotics Farm—in Lexington, Kentucky, to treat addicted persons convicted of federal crimes whom the courts deemed more suitable for treatment than imprisonment. Establishment of a second such hospital followed in 1938 in Fort Worth, Texas. In the same 1929 law which had authorized these special hospital facilities, Congress additionally directed PHS to undertake research in the cause, treatment and prevention of drug addiction. Thus, addiction was viewed as a public health problem on a national scale, with initial efforts set in motion to understand the drug problems of the day, and to offer modern, humane care and rehabilitation to addicted persons.

The chronology of most significant dates in the national public health response to drug abuse next jumps forward to the mid-sixties; drug abuse was burgeoning to an epidemic level in the United States. In 1966, a special Center for Studies of Narcotic and Drug Abuse was established within the National Institute of Mental Health to coalesce drug abuse activities and provide a central focus for projects and grants dealing with this growing problem. Two years later the center was made one component of a further intensified national drug abuse program administered by an NIMH Division of Narcotic Addiction and Drug Abuse. The new division also incorporated the Lexington and Fort Worth treatment facilities, now renamed Clinical Research Centers, and the Addiction Research Center at Lexington, which had become the responsible unit for carrying out the original congressional mandate to conduct research on drug dependence.

Finally, in the most recent development, a separate National Institute on Drug Abuse was established September 25, 1973 as a sister institute of NIMH in a newly formed Alcohol, Drug Abuse, and Mental Health Administration within PHS.

This last step accords with the congressional intent, expressed in the Special Office and Treatment Act of 1972, that such an independent drug program with the full breadth and resources of an institute be established no later than the end of 1974. By direction of Congress, the National Institute on Drug Abuse will ultimately replace the White House-level Special Action Office for Drug Abuse Prevention, which was set up in 1971 as a temporary coordination and policy making organization to guarantee that the full weight of all of the government's drug treatment, prevention, research and education programs would be exercised as swiftly and decisively as possible in reducing the impact of drug abuse on individuals and on American society.

Highlights of NIMH drug abuse activities and accomplishments discussed below portray in part the significant issues and demands facing the national drug program in recent years and indicate the directions that have been pursued to find solutions to drug abuse problems.

THE CONTEMPORARY PROBLEM

Compared to the present situation, in 1908, 1929 or even 1966, the number of narcotic addicts in the nation was small, although their numbers had been sufficient to bring them recognition over the years as a population in need of public health attention.

The situation in the United States in recent years poses a most striking contrast, with abuse of many varieties of dangerous drugs steadily on the increase. In gross estimates, a brief summary of today's drug scene would include: several hundred thousand persons addicted to narcotics, chiefly heroin; between 2 million and 2.5 million people chronically using barbiturates or other sedatives; as many as 5 million persons intermittently taking oral amphetamines obtained without prescriptions.

Furthermore, in a relatively new and potentially very destructive drug abuse phenomenon, a rise to unknown proportions has occurred in poly–drug use, with clearly escalated risks to the individuals who ingest random mixtures of drugs. This practice is one signal that, despite progress in recent years, the problems of drug abuse continue to increase in complexity. In part, this may be attributable to

the development each year of dozens of new therapeutic compounds, many with considerable abuse potential. As these become available on the market, the boundaries of the drug abuse area expand.

Another major factor which helps to make solution of the problem difficult is the classification of the drug abuser himself. While no one questions the applicability of the term *drug abuse* to the heroin addict, the "speed freak," or the chronic hallucinogenic cultist, there is continuing debate over classification of such individuals as the intermittent user of marihuana or the person who is chronically using various prescription drugs which enable him to cope with the stresses of everyday living.

Examined in this context, the drug problem becomes reflective of society's definition of the norm and of what constitutes acceptable behavior. The extent to which this definition changes over time determines the magnitude of the problem at any given period. Issues surrounding legalization of marihuana are one example of this dynamic. Another compounding difficulty is the problem of dealing with the economic and social conditions which are closely linked with the genesis of many manifestations of drug abuse.

There also has been some "good news." The use of hallucinogens, for example, while still a problem, has been on the decline, following a time a few years ago when the spread of "tripping" on LSD was a leading factor in prodding the reality of drug abuse in the country into the public consciousness. Also encouraging is preliminary evidence of a downward trend in rates of heroin addiction which officials of the White House Special Action Office for Drug Abuse Prevention recently perceived in examining data on various dimensions of the heroin problem. Indicators cited for this optimistic development are a decrease in narcotics-related deaths; a reduction in hepatitis serum cases traceable to use of contaminated heroin injection needles; and a drop in official crime statistics, including the type of crimes normally committed by addicts. These indicators signal "a likely reduction in the total addict population in the foreseeable future," according to Dr. Robert L. DuPont, Director of the Special Action Office.

RESEARCH: SEEKING ANSWERS

Ultimately, success in the national effort to reduce and prevent drug abuse depends on a continuing flow of new knowledge on all aspects of the problem. This requirement is being pursued through an intensive research program which includes supported projects in universities and research institutions and continuing laboratory and clinical investigations in intramural facilities such as the Addiction Research Center. Studies follow a spectrum ranging from work toward broadening understanding of the basic chemistry of abused substances to investigating psychological and epidemiological factors influencing drug use.

Because of the wide use of marihuana in our society, especially among the young but by no means limited to that group, a major marihuana research effort has been underway for several years. Detailed data on the extent of marihuana use and on its effects have been collected and summarized annually for three years in congressionally mandated reports on the status of knowledge of the health consequences of using this drug.

Selected highlights from the third annual *Marihuana and Health* report from the secretary of health, education, and welfare, dated January 1973, are:

— Marihuana use is highly age-related; to a lesser extent, it is also related to educational status. The highest rates of "ever used" are consistently found among college students. In 1972 this figure was 54 percent, an increase of 12 percent from 1971.
— The likelihood of genetic or neonatal abnormalities arising from cannabis use at present social levels of use is low. Animal research at substantially higher dosage levels than are likely to be employed by humans showed no evidence of hazard to fetal development. Nevertheless, there is no way of being certain that cannabis used in combination with other drugs might not have adverse reproductive consequences.
— Marihuana smokers characteristically use alcohol and tobacco prior to and concurrently with marihuana. This is contrary to the frequent suggestions that "the parents drink, and the kids smoke," and that marihuana use might for many people supplant alcohol use, thus reducing the severity of the alcohol problem in the United States.
— There is sufficient evidence to justify the warning that even social doses of marihuana may impair performance enough to lead potentially to motor vehicle accidents. In studies of the effects of alcohol and marihuana on driving-related visual

functions, it was found that marihuana interfered with peripheral and central vision to a greater extent and diminished performance more than did alcohol when subjects had to time responses accurately in order to respond correctly to some driving tasks.

—While there is little evidence to suggest that there are deleterious effects arising from a single episode of use, or from infrequent use, of marihuana—especially in the "well put together" individual who has no particularly difficulties in life—the issue of what effects may result from long term chronic use remains open until larger scale studies can be completed in populations which have been using cannabis for long periods of time.

The place of marihuana in our social structure has been fervently discussed in many public forums within the past few years. It is the business of the National Institute of Mental Health to contribute to that public debate by providing scientific information and to answer critical questions which otherwise may be discussed with emotional bias and an inadequate knowledge base.

In addition to widespread dissemination for scientific and general public use, findings on marihuana were made available to the National Commission on Marihuana and Drug Abuse, which was established by Congress in 1970 to conduct a two-year investigation of the impact of drugs in American society and to recommend legislative actions. The commission's recommendations, after analysis of data gathered from many sources inside and outside the federal government, generally were in the direction of decriminalization of private use of marihuana. Specifically, the first two recommendations by the commissioners for both federal and state levels were that:

1. Possession of marihuana for personal use would no longer be a federal or state offense, but marihuana possessed in public would remain contraband subject to summary seizure and forfeiture.
2. Casual distribution in private of small amounts of marihuana for remuneration, or insignificant remuneration not involving profit, would no longer be a federal or state offense.

Whether these and the many other recommendations of the commission will eventually be adopted on a broad scale depends on the future use of available knowledge and on thorough analysis and debate by the leadership of society and the public at large.

NARCOTIC ANTAGONIST RESEARCH

A further major component of the research program is an intensive effort to identify, evaluate and place into use as soon as possible one or more "narcotic antagonist drugs" in the treatment of heroin addiction. The usefulness of these compounds lies in their ability to block the "high" and other effects of heroin use and thereby help the addicted person overcome his need for heroin and rebuild his life along accepted patterns. Narcotic antagonists have the further characteristic of being nonaddictive, making them preferable to methadone, for instance, for use in the treatment of some patients. This is especially true for youngsters who have begun to experiment with heroin but who are not addicted. The use of a narcotic antagonist may prove to be a highly effective secondary prevention agent in this population.

At present, the most promising narcotic antagonist, naltrexone, is effective up to 48 hours when taken orally. This compound is now being tested in several clinical research centers to evaluate its efficacy further and to ascertain its safety for broad therapeutic use in human beings.

Other drug abuse research has also been underway on an expanded basis in the drug crisis years. In addition to pioneering work in the narcotic antagonist area, the Addiction Research Center has had a leading role in the assessment of the abuse potential of new compounds —in clinical studies of methadone, in investigations of the actions of various narcotics in the body, and in many other critical areas. The Center for Studies of Narcotic and Drug Abuse has pursued answers to biochemical and social questions important to understanding amphetamine and barbiturate abuse, and it supports research on such drugs as cocaine, which is becoming more widely used in this country. Efforts are also being expended to understand patterns of poly–drug use, factors influencing progression from one drug to others, and other topics of public health importance.

TREATMENT: EXPANSION AND IMPROVEMENT OF SERVICES

Of necessity, the foremost emphasis in the national drug abuse program to date has been on tertiary prevention, that is, treatment of addicted persons and drug abusers,

with the goal of removing or controlling their disabilities to a degree which permits them to be psychologically and socially rehabilitated. When the drug epidemic began, a sudden sharp increase in new heroin users, and growing numbers in serious trouble from other drug use, sorely taxed the limited existing national resources for treatment, prevention and control. As the drug abusing population grew each year, so did the waiting lists for treatment at an inadequate number of treatment programs.

Today, following a diligent federal effort to expand the nation's treatment capacity, enough resources are available that any person who wants to enter treatment is able to do so.

In terms of NIMH-supported community-based treatment and rehabilitation programs alone, a dramatic increase has occurred in the past three years. In 1971, NIMH supported 23 community-based treatment programs with a capacity of some 13,000 patients. At the end of 1973 there were 183 grant programs in operation, treating nearly 75,000 addicts and drug abusers of all types. The NIMH-funded programs account for approximately half of all of the federal treatment capacity. Other agencies providing or supporting treatment and rehabilitation programs include the Department of Defense; Veteran's Administration; Enforcement Assistance Administration and Bureau of Prisons in the Department of Housing and Urban Development; and the Job Corps in the Department of Labor. As noted above, coordination of these several programs has been the responsibility of the Special Action Office for Drug Abuse Prevention.

In addition to the community assistance programs to increase the availability of services, special grants have been made to support and evaluate certain treatment programs which may demonstrate new or more effective methods of delivery of services. One such project demonstrates ways of reintroducing heroin abusers who are already under treatment into the mainstream of the economy through work-support mechanisms which reduce or eliminate the need for welfare and the other correlates of unemployment. Another explores a new focus for delivering services under the auspices of a labor union. Several experimental projects call for monitoring the long term effects of methadone treatment upon body functions and performance. Other studies concentrate on special groups, such as teenage and female addicts or addicts with severe psychiatric disorders, in order to uncover better ways to adapt programs to the needs of these groups.

CIVIL COMMITMENT

The National Institute of Mental Health has also had responsibility for operating the national civil commitment program for narcotic addicts under Titles I and III of the Narcotic Addict Rehabilitation Act (NARA) of 1966. Recognizing addiction as a stubborn disease frequently characterized by relapse, Congress designed the NARA program to emphasize total care: hospitalization plus follow-up supervision and support aimed at maintaining an addict's motivation to rehabilitate himself upon return to an unchanged community—a community most likely including the same inducements to return to drugs that the addict had been unsuccessful in resisting earlier, namely poverty, criminality, violence, blocked op-

portunity, and drug-using friends.

More than 6,000 patients have been served under NARA. Initially the inpatient phase of this program was conducted at the Clinical Research Centers in Lexington and Fort Worth. Gradually, as local services expanded across the country, a shift occurred to the point where all services, including hospitalization, if necessary, and follow-up treatment and services, are provided in the cities where the addicts reside. This change has made it possible to transfer the two facilities —which have served nobly as a part of the Public Health Service's addict treatment program for more than 60 years—to the Bureau of Prisons for use once again in treating a prisoner addict population. The Fort Worth facility was transferred in 1971, and the Lexington facility in early 1974.

In all of its drug abuse treatment programs, NIMH has fostered a multi-modality approach, thus offering a variety of treatment methods from which the drug abuser may choose and among which he may move in the course of his treatment as his progress indicates. The multi-modality program approach takes the realistic view that no cure for heroin addiction currently exists, that no one method of treating any form of "soft" drug abuse is suitable for all problems, and that persons not succeeding in one form of treatment may find help in another. Thus, in the case of the addict, the individual who cannot maintain abstinence in drug-free therapy may shift to methadone treatment without interrupting rehabilitation or risking relapse while awaiting admission to a new program. In another example, methadone maintenance may be required for a new patient with acute abstinence problems, but detoxification and abstinence may be possible for him later on when group psychotherapy, family counseling and other rehabilitation techniques have helped him to restructure his life.

So far, there has been relatively little research on the efficacy of various treatment approaches to heroin addiction and, for all practical purposes, none in other areas of drug abuse. Defining appropriate evaluation criteria is a major problem. Current criteria for evaluating treatment vary almost as much as the treatment approaches themselves, and the few studies of present-day treatment which are now available reflect these differences. All programs have the problem of patients who relapse to drugs and drop out of treatment, and all experience difficulties in following up former patients. Furthermore, the few detailed evaluation studies have dealt only with persons still in treatment, and not those who have been discharged as "rehabilitated."

Although there is no consensus today which yields a single set of criteria for program effectiveness, generally, indices of success are abstention from illegal drugs, a halt in criminal behavior, and employment. The ability to keep patients in treatment is also an important criterion in evaluating a program as a whole.

A preliminary evaluation of the federal civil commitment program has been made in a study of a representative sample of more than 1,000 patients in drug-free aftercare over a one-year period. Of those patients, only 13 percent abstained completely from illegal drugs. However, among the patients who did use illegal drugs, narcotics—usually heroin or illicitly obtained methadone—were used on an average of no more than three or four days per month, and the use of drugs declined the longer the patients were in treatment. Seventy-one percent of the men and 86 percent of the women in aftercare were arrest-free, and full- or part-time jobs were held at some time during the year by 74 percent of the men and 42 percent of the women.

The effectiveness of methadone treatment and drug-free approaches has been compared in another year-long study of more than 1,000 opiate addicts in treatment in community facilities supported by NIMH. The majority of the patients studied were in methadone maintenance programs; these had an active retention rate of 65 percent. Drug-free outpatient therapy had a retention rate of 46 percent, while the modality with the lowest retention rate was the therapeutic community, with 29 percent. The performance of methadone patients with respect to days of gainful employment was notably superior to that of the patients in drug-free therapies, even when therapeutic community residents were excluded from comparison. However, the 33 percent unemployment rate among methadone patients was relatively high when compared to reports from other methadone maintenance programs. Generally, there was less abuse of narcotics and other drugs, including alcohol, among methadone patients over age 25 than among those aged 21 to 25. The highest percentage of patients who abstained from narcotics, did not abuse alcohol, and were free of arrests was found in the limited group who remained throughout the year in therapeutic communities.

These findings offer indicative, but in no sense definitive, information about different treatment approaches used with varied segments of the addict population. They are, at best, interim reports, since they deal almost exclusively with continuing treatment. They also refer to quite different groups of addicts, thus offering no firm basis for comparing different programs. As an illustration, when programs supported by NIMH were studied, addicts being treated under the civil commitment program were 60 percent white, with an average age in the late twenties, while community center patients were over two-thirds black or Chicano, in their early twenties. Moreover, the two groups were not equivalent in terms of employment history, arrest history or education.

Attempts to compare treatment methods are further complicated by the variations in criteria for admission and discharge set by different programs—criteria which can affect the degree of "success" achieved.

TRAINING AND EDUCATION

With an increased awareness and responsiveness to drug abuse throughout the nation, the concomitant need arises for training more professionals and paraprofessionals to staff the many new and expanding community treatment and prevention programs. The numbers of people needed are many—an estimated 20,000 in the immediate future—and desired qualifications vary. The full process of treatment and rehabilitation depends on the knowledge and talents of physicians, psychologists, social workers, teachers, probation officials, lawyers, criminologists, judges, the clergy, vocational counselors and job placement personnel, and many others.

A continuing and major contribution also is made by ex-addicts. Drug treatment centers perhaps rely more than any other type of rehabilitation program on the services of these former patients. As people who have "been there and made it back," ex-addicts are important role models for addicts struggling to make a lasting break with drugs. Many ex-addicts become skilled therapists by combining their own experience with on-the-job training.

The value of training in drug abuse prevention has also been recognized for other elements of the community. For instance, various community leaders and education administrators and teachers are in need of appropriate drug abuse knowledge and sensitization to the values and life styles of youth, who constitute the major body of drug users in the average American community.

To work toward removing the manpower deficiency, the National Institute of Mental Health opened six training centers in various regions of the country where skills and knowledge are upgraded or taught to a diversity of workers. Additionally, a new National Drug Abuse Training Center in Washington, D.C. has been organized in cooperation with the Special Action Office for Drug Abuse Prevention to deliver a broad spectrum of training courses of one-day to three-week duration and to develop, test, and teach improved methods of rehabilitation and prevention to workers in the field. Students attending the National Training Center are utilized to test particular training designs. Once validated, these designs are made available to the NIMH regional training centers, to seven regional centers sponsored by the United States Office of Education, and then to any drug abuse training program nationwide, regardless of its funding source. Another mission of the National

Training Center is to train decision makers and program administrators from all levels of government, as well as from the voluntary sector, who influence the type, availability and management of drug programs.

Altogether, several thousand persons have received training to date in the national and regional centers. In addition, more than 80 currently active grant-supported projects for training professionals and paraprofessionals contribute to increasing the availability of urgently needed personnel. Several large grants provide drug abuse training to health professionals of different kinds. Other projects include: a program for familiarizing clergymen with drug use and abuse, conducted at Washington Hospital in Jamaica Plain, Massachusetts; a program for counselors underway at George Washington University; and a comprehensive course at the University of Arkansas directed at career teachers, who are in an excellent position to further the prevention of drug abuse. In yet another special program, medical school faculty representatives receive one to three years of training in alcohol and drug abuse, the ultimate aim being that they develop a specific curriculum in these subjects in their training sequence for doctors, so that future doctors are introduced to current concepts in alcohol and drug treatment and prevention.

PRIMARY PREVENTION: THE ULTIMATE ARMAMENT

Finally, where do we stand with respect to primary prevention? All workers in the field of drug abuse would agree that the preferred first priority in drug abuse programs is to prevent, not to treat casualties after they occur. The fact of the matter is, however, that today our ability to conduct primary prevention is severely limited both by inadequate knowledge of the etiology of drug abuse and by the lack of prevention approaches with demonstrated effectiveness.

Although a highly regarded information dissemination program has been built in the National Clearinghouse for Drug Abuse Information to make factual materials and data broadly available, accurate information alone is clearly an insufficient weapon against the incentives which have led an increasing number of people to experiment with drugs and many thousands to continue their use. Information on the techniques, methods, and combinations which will prevent drug abuse is still missing.

Effective preventive education models are being sought in projects throughout the country, including numerous NIMH grant-supported programs and the Office of Education "Help Communities Help Themselves" program. In addition, the Special Action Office for Drug Abuse Prevention has initiated activities aimed at finding viable prevention models for widespread activation.

To date, however, primary prevention is admittedly the weak suit in the national public health approach to narcotic addiction and drug abuse. The chief prevention target in the future must logically be the nation's adolescents, for whom and with whom we must develop convincing drug abuse educational programs and alternative pursuits which are more appealing than the drug experience. Additional effort and resources must be given to this search.

SUPPLEMENT

The History of Russia and Eastern Europe: A Survey of Scholarly and Related Writings (1966–1970)

By David Hecht

THIS survey of studies on the history of Russia and Eastern Europe published during the half-decade 1966 to 1970 must be, at best, a summary. Hopefully, certain trends and tendencies will be indicated, as well as specific references to the most important writings which have appeared in the United States, the Soviet Union and elsewhere. The article is organized chronologically and topically within approximate historical time periods.

During the years under discussion, a tremendous amount of material has been published on Russia, much of it dealing with the revolutions of 1917 and the period afterwards. In some instances, the editorial quality of the works which have appeared in print does not match the soaring prices of books and magazines. Many reprints of older monographs have made their appearance. Great interest has been manifested in evaluating the Bolshevik Revolution a half-century after 1917. Perhaps as a consequence of détente in Soviet-American political relations, earlier American-Russian historical relations have been studied with renewed interest.

Of course, anything of an historical nature published officially or legally in the USSR must fall within the category of Marxist and Leninist interpretation. This framework of Marxism and Leninism may be flexible or inflexible, but it is always present.[1]

1. *See*, for example, two large-scale publications of the Institute of History of the Soviet Academy of Sciences which attest

---

David Hecht is Professor of History at Pace University. He received his A.B. magna cum laude from Brooklyn College, and his M.A. and Ph.D. from Harvard University. He is author of Russian Radicals Look to America *and has contributed to* Harvard Slavic Studies *and to numerous scholarly journals, including* The Annals.

I wish to thank the Scholarly Research Committee of Pace University for financial and other aid, and my wife, Anne Dahlgren Hecht, for her assistance.

As for Marxism in Eastern European countries under Soviet influence, the reader must be further cautioned that the virus of nationalism has certainly not been stamped out. Older nationalist attitudes reappear within the newer mold of Marxism-Leninism.

For detailed bibliographical listings the reader is urged to consult such reference guides as: (1) the United States Library of Congress, Slavic and Central European Division, *The USSR and Eastern Europe: Periodicals in Western Languages*, compiled by Paul L. Horecky and Robert G. Carlton, 3rd ed., revised and enlarged (Washington, D.C., 1967); or (2) the Library of Congress, *Monthly Index of Russian Accessions;* or (3) *The American Bibliography of Russian and East European Studies*, ed. Fritz T. Epstein, published by the Indiana University Press at Bloomington until 1966, and for immediately succeeding years, ed. Kenneth E. Naylor, published by Ohio State University, Columbus; or (4) the Library of Congress, Slavic and Central European Division, *Czechoslovakia, a Bibliographical Guide*, ed. Rudolf Sturm (Washington, D.C., 1968).

Other important bibliographical and reference aids are the two-volume *Half a Century of Soviet Serials, 1917–1968: A Bibliography and Union List of Serials Published in the USSR*, compiled by Rudolph Smits (Washington, D.C., Library of Congress, 1968); *Dictionary of*

Russian Historical Terms from the Eleventh Century to 1917, compiled by S. G. Pushkarev, ed. George Vernadsky and Ralph T. Fisher (New Haven and London: Yale University Press, 1970); and the two-volume *Bibliography of Russian Emigré Literature, 1918–1968*, edited and compiled by Ludmila Foster (Boston: G. K. Hall, 1970).

Geographical works helpful to the understanding of Russian history include Allen F. Chew's *An Atlas of Russian History: Eleven Centuries of Changing Borders* (New Haven: Yale University Press, 1967) and W. H. Parker's more ambitious, if flawed, *An Historical Geography of Russia* (Chicago: Aldine Publishing Co., 1969). Slightly off the beaten track is Harry J. Nerhood's comprehensive *To Russia and Return: An Annotated Bibliography of Travellers' English-Language Accounts of Russia from the Ninth Century to the Present* (Columbus: Ohio State University Press, 1969).

In terms of general histories of Russia, the republication in Moscow between 1965 and 1967 of M. N. Pokrovsky's *Izbrannie Proizvedeniia [Selected Works]* in several large volumes represents a certain rehabilitation in the Soviet Union of this classic Marxist historian and active participant in the Bolshevik Revolution who died in 1932.[2] As a kind of historical coincidence, we find during this same period the first full translation of Paul Miliukov's *Histoire de Russie (History of Russia*, Paul Miliukov et al., 3 vols., New York: Funk and Wagnalls, 1968–69). The late Professor

to this conclusion: *Istoriia i Istoriki: Istoriografiia Vseobshchei Istorii [History and Historians: Historiography of General History]* (Moscow, 1966) and *Ocherki Istorii Istoricheskoi Nauki v SSSR [Outlines of the History of Historical Science in the USSR]*, vol. 4, ed. M. V. Nechkina et al. (Moscow, 1966).

2. *See also*, M. N. Pokrovsky, *Russia in World History: Selected Essays*, trans. and ed. Roman and Mary Ann Szporluk (Ann Arbor: University of Michigan Press, 1970) for a little later revival of interest in Pokrovsky in the United States.

Miliukov, a contemporary of Pokrovsky, and apart from his eminence as an historian, was also a leader of the Constitutional Democratic (Kadet) Party of Russia.[3] In our own time and somewhat reminiscent of Miliukov's historical synthesis is James H. Billington's ambitious *The Icon and the Axe: An Interpretive History of Russian Culture* (New York: Knopf, 1966).

To turn to more specific works on early Russia, T. Sulimirski's *The Sarmatians* (New York: Praeger, 1970) is a history of these ancient peoples based principally on archeological sources. Sarmatia, of course, is a Roman name for the Russian plain. We also have Imre Boba's illuminating *Nomads, Northmen and Slavs: Eastern Europe in the Ninth Century* (The Hague, 1967) and the unusual, if tendentious, monograph on the foreign policy of ancient Rus by V.T. Pashuto: *Vnieshniaia Politika Drevnei Rusi* (Moscow, 1968).

Of historical importance is the second volume of the late Professor G. P. Fedotov's *The Russian Religious Mind*, this one (unlike the first which dealt with Kievan Christianity) concerned with *The Middle Ages: The Thirteenth to Fifteenth Centuries*, ed. J. Mayendorff (Harvard University Press, 1966). Quite another point of view on this subject is found in I. U. Budovnits' book, *Monastyri na Rusi i Borba s Nimi Krestian v XIV–XVI Vekakh* [*Monasteries in Russia and the Peasants' Struggle with Them during the*

14th–16th Centuries] (Moscow, 1966). Arthur Voyce's *The Art and Architecture of Medieval Russia* (Norman: University of Oklahoma Press, 1967) is a useful guide which ranges beyond what is promised in the title. Gerald R. Seaman's *History of Russian Music*, vol. 1, *From Its Origins to Dargomyzhsky* (New York: Praeger, 1968) contains much useful material on Russian folk music.

The rise of the Muscovite state is ably treated in John L. I. Fennell's *The Emergence of Moscow, 1304–1359* (Berkeley and Los Angeles: University of California Press, 1968) and in a new translation by A. E. Moorhouse of the older seminal work by Aleksandr E. Presniakov, *The Formation of the Great Russian State: A Study of Russian History in the Thirteenth to Fifteenth Centuries* (Chicago: Quadrangle Books, 1970). This version, however, lacks Presniakov's original footnotes. As a matter of fact, the above-mentioned monograph by Fennell leans in part on Presniakov's scholarship.[4]

A significant Soviet study concerned mainly with the times of Grand Prince Ivan III and his son Basil III is S. M. Kashtanov's *Sotsialno-Politicheskaia Istoriia Rossii Kontsa XV-Pervoi Poloviny XVI V.* [*A Socio-Political History of Russia from the End of the 15th through the First Half of the 16th Century*] (Moscow, 1967). S. B. Veselovskii's *Issledovaniia po Istorii Klassa Sluzhilykh Zemlevladeltseev* [*Researches on the History of the Class of Serving*

3. Two recent works in English (both of uneven quality) on Miliukov are the latter's *Political Memoirs, 1905–1917*, ed. and abr. Arthur P. Mendel, trans. Carl Goldberg (University of Michigan Press, 1967) and Thomas Riha's biography, *A Russian European: Paul Miliukov in Russian Politics* (University of Notre Dame Press, 1969).

4. Fennell also contributes a stimulating article on the origins of the Russian epic, *The Lay of the Host of Igor* [*Slovo o Polku Igoreve*] in *Oxford Slavonic Papers*, ed. R. Auty, J. L. I. Fennell and J. S. G. Simmons; New Series, vol. 1 (Oxford University Press, 1968).

Landowners] (Moscow, 1969) offers valuable insights into the relations of the boyars and the early Muscovite princes. An unusual contribution to medieval Russian history is found in *The Testaments of the Grand Princes of Moscow*, trans. and ed. Robert Craig Howes (Ithaca: Cornell University Press, 1967). A scholarly and lively history of the Cossacks from their 15th-century origins to this century is presented by Philip Longworth, *The Cossacks* (New York: Holt, Rinehart and Winston, 1970).

The penetrating observations by the well-known foreigners in 16th-century Russia—von Herberstein, von Staden, and Giles Fletcher—are treated in various recent works: *Beschreibung Moskaus, der Hauptstadt in Russland, Samt des Moskowitischen Gebietes, 1557*, by Sigmund Freiherr von Herberstein, ed. Bertold Picard (Graz, Austria, 1966); *The Land and Government of Muscovy: A Sixteenth Century Account* by Heinrich von Staden, trans. and ed. Thomas Esper (Stanford University Press, 1967); and two renderings of Fletcher's treatise, the first, *Of the Rus Commonwealth*, ed. A. J. Schmidt for the Folger Shakespeare Library (Cornell University Press, 1966) and the second, *Of the Russe Commonwealth*, facsimile edition with variants, ed. Richard Pipes and John V. A. Fine, Jr. (Harvard University Press, 1966).[5]

Undoubtedly the most important recent scholarly work in English on 16th- and 17th-century Russia is George Vernadsky's *The Tsardom of Moscow, 1547–1682* (New Haven: Yale University Press, 1969) in two parts, being volume 5 of the large-scale *A History of Russia* projected by Professor Vernadsky and his late colleague at Harvard, Michael Karpovich. The first four volumes have previously been completed and published by Professor Vernadsky. Professor Karpovich never found it possible to fulfill his commitments to the later periods of Russian history before his death in 1959.[6]

A new translation of a section of V. O. Kliuchevsky's detailed and distinguished *A Course in Russian History* is welcome. It is *The 17th Century*, trans. Natalie Duddington, introd. Alfred J. Rieber (Chicago: Quadrangle Books, 1968). The impact of this formidable pre-Revolutionary liberal Russian historian has tended to be lessened among English-speaking students in part because of mediocre translation.

An important primary, but here abridged, source of information for the pre-Petrine Muscovite state is *The Travels of Olearius in Seventeenth-Century Russia*, trans. and ed. Samuel H. Baron (Stanford University Press, 1967). Foreign trade relations of Muscovite Russia are treated in Walter Kirchner's book of essays (published separately at earlier dates), *Commercial Rela-*

---

5. For a supplement to these titles, the reader may profitably consult the volume edited by Lloyd E. Berry and Robert O. Crummey, *Rude and Barbarous Kingdom: Russia in the Accounts of Sixteenth-Century English Voyagers* (Madison: University of Wisconsin Press, 1968).

6. Four specialized works worth mentioning are: Carsten Goehrke's treatment of wastelands in Muscovite Russia, *Die Wüstungen in der Moskauer Rus* (Wiesbaden, 1968); A. N. Grobovsky's short study, *The "Chosen Council" of Ivan IV: A Reinterpretation* (Brooklyn, N.Y.: Theo. Gaus' Sons, 1969); Philip L. Barbour's *Dimitry, Called the Pretender: Tsar and Grand Prince of All Russia, 1605–1606* (Boston: Houghton Mifflin, 1966); and R. E. F. Smith's translated documents on *The Enserfment of the Russian Peasantry* (New York: Cambridge University Press, 1968).

tions Between Russia and Europe, 1400–1800 (Indiana University Press, 1966). Alexander Gerschenkron's *Europe in the Russian Mirror: Four Lectures in Economic History* deals in a stimulating way with 17th-century Russian mercantilism and later industrialization.[7]

New scholarly works on Peter the Great are scarce. The old and biased biography by K. Waliszewski, in its English translation from the French, has been reprinted (New York: Greenwood Press, 1968). The material on The Great Northern War in *The New Cambridge Modern History*, vol. 6, *The Rise of Great Britain and Russia, 1688–1715/25*, ed. J. S. Bromley (New York: Cambridge University Press, 1970) is disappointing.[8] L. Jay Oliva attempts a summation of this watershed age in his slender volume *Russia in the Era of Peter the Great* (Englewood Cliffs, N.J.: Prentice-Hall, 1969).

A truncated version of John Bell's *A Journey from St. Petersburg to Pekin, 1719–22* is edited by J. L. Stevenson (New York: Barnes and Noble, 1966). More satisfactory is Clifford M. Frost's *Muscovite and Mandarin: Russia's Trade with China and Its Setting, 1727–1805* (Chapel Hill: University of North Carolina Press, 1969).

The daughter of Peter the Great is the subject of a new but poor biography by Tamara Talbot Rice: *Elizabeth, Empress of Russia* (New York: Praeger, 1970).[9] A specialized study in war and diplomacy during Elizabeth's reign is Herbert H. Kaplan's *Russia and the Outbreak of the Seven Years' War* (Berkeley and Los Angeles: University of California Press, 1968).

---

7. Other important writings on internal Russian history of this time (some extending to more recent years) emphasize religious developments and social upheavals: Serge A. Zenkovsky's valuable *Russkoe Staroobriadchestvo: Dukhovnye Dvizheniia Semnadtsatogo Veka* [*Russia's Old Believers: Spiritual Movements of the Seventeenth Century*] (Munich, 1970); Robert O. Crummey's *The Old Believers and the World of Antichrist: The Vyg Community and the Russian State, 1694–1855* (Madison: University of Wisconsin Press, 1970); Hans-Heinrich Nolte's *Religöse Toleranz in Russland, 1600–1725* (Göttingen, 1969); I. I. Smirnov et al., *Krestianskie Voiny v Rossii XVII–XVIII VV.* [*Peasant Wars in Russia in the 17th and 18th Centuries*] (Moscow, 1966); and the anti-Marxist work of Roland Mousnier, *Fureurs Paysannes: Les Paysans dans les Révoltes du XVIIe Siècle* [*France, Russie, Chine*] (Paris, 1967).

Russian expansion eastward is covered in Vincent Chen's uneven *Sino-Russian Relations in the Seventeenth Century* (The Hague, 1966); James R. Gibson, *Feeding the Russian Fur Trade: Provisionment of the Okhotsk Seaboard and the Kamchatka Peninsula, 1639–1856* (Madison: University of Wisconsin Press, 1969); and Alton S. Donnelly's ground-breaking *The Russian Conquest of Bashkiria, 1552–1740* (New Haven: Yale University Press, 1968).

The reader's attention is also directed to René Grousset's *The Empire of the Steppes: A History of Central Asia*, trans. Naomi Walford (New Brunswick, N.J.: Rutgers University Press, 1970). This comprehensive work starts from ancient days and ends with the 18th century.

8. At this point we may include David Woodward's wide-ranging *The Russians at Sea: A History of the Russian Navy* (New York: Praeger, 1966), since Peter the Great is, of course, credited with the creation of the fleet. Erik Amburger's *Geschichte der Behördenorganisation Russlands von Peter dem Grossen bis 1917* (Leiden, 1966) is a kind of detailed reference work of institutions and government offices, both central and local, in imperial Russia.

9. Alexander V. Berkis' *The History of the Duchy of Courland (1561–1795)* (Towson, Md.: Paul M. Harrod Co., 1969) contains some valuable materials of the time of Duke Biron, the "favorite" of the empress Anna (1730–40). Marc Raeff, in *Plans for Political Reform in Imperial Russia, 1730–1905* (Englewood Cliffs, N.J.: Prentice-Hall, 1966) presents a number of important primary documants, translated into English, starting from the accession of the empress Anna.

We find a greater harvest when we come to the age of Catherine II. Works of intellectual, social, political and diplomatic history, as well as biographical studies of important figures, fall into this time. Marc Raeff's *Origins of the Russian Intelligentsia: The Eighteenth-Century Nobility* (New York: Harcourt, Brace and World, 1966) is provocative. The Soviet historian I. A. Fedosov's specialized study *Iz Istorii Russkoi Obshchestvennoi Mysli XVIII Stoletiia: M. M. Shcherbatov* [*From the History of Russian Social Thought in the 18th Century: M. M. Shcherbatov*] (Moscow, 1967) really fails to do justice to either the life or works of this erudite but undiscriminating conservative. Prince Shcherbatov's polemical pamphlet *On the Corruption of Morals in Russia* has been more than competently edited and translated by A. Lentin (London and New York: Cambridge University Press, 1969).

A short semi-popular account of Derzhavin the gifted court poet of Catherine the Great and "discoverer" of Pushkin, is found in the Soviet scholar I. Z. Serman's *Gavrila Romanovich Derzhavin* (Leningrad, 1967). Much inferior to the above is Jesse V. Clardy's *G. R. Derzhavin: A Political Biography* (The Hague, 1967). Two works on a notable literary, historical and political figure of the time of Catherine the Great and after are Henry M. Nebel, Jr.'s *N. M. Karamzin: A Russian Sentimentalist* (The Hague, 1967) and *Selected Prose of N. M. Karamzin*, trans. and introd. Nebel (Evanston: Northwestern University Press, 1969).

In *Catherine the Great and the Russian Nobility: A Study Based on the Materials of the Legislative Commission of 1767* (New York: Cambridge University Press, 1967),

Paul Dukes studies, somewhat dryly, the relations of Catherine II to the nobility against the background of the famous *Nakaz* Commission. John T. Alexander's *Autocratic Politics in a National Crisis: The Imperial Russian Government and Pugachev's Revolt/1773–1775* (Bloomington: Indiana University Press, 1969) adds to our understanding of these events so dangerous to Catherine's throne—although the shabbiness of the publisher's format leads one to wonder.

Suvorov, the outstanding military figure who served Catherine (and her successor Paul) is the subject of a noteworthy biography by Philip Longworth, *The Art of Victory: The Life and Achievements of Field-Marshal Suvorov, 1729–1800* (New York: Holt, Rinehart and Winston, 1966). Turkish-Russian relations, starting with Catherine's time, come under detailed scrutiny in M. S. Anderson's *The Eastern Question, 1774–1923: A Study in International Relations* (New York: St. Martin's Press, 1966).[10] Alan W. Fisher has used not only Russian but Turkish sources in his able, if short, *The Russian Annexation of the Crimea, 1772–1783* (New York: Cambridge University Press, 1970). We may conclude this section with notice of the colorful travel account of the resourceful young American: *John Ledyard's Journey Through Russia and Siberia, 1787–1788: The Journal and Selected Letters*, ed. and introd. Stephen D. Watrous (Madison: University of Wisconsin Press, 1966).

When we enter the 19th century we are already on the threshold of modern times. Professor Hugh

10. Of minor interest in this connection is Norman E. Saul's monograph, *Russia and the Mediterranean, 1797–1807* (Chicago: University of Chicago Press, 1970).

Seton-Watson details with clarity the course of Russian history, especially political history, from the reign of Alexander I to the fall of the empire in *The Russian Empire, 1801–1917* (Oxford: Clarendon Press, 1967).[11]

A popular, if unoriginal, biography of Alexander I is E. M. Almedingen's *The Emperor Alexander I* (New York: Vanguard Press, 1966). Patricia K. Grimsted has written in detail, sometimes in an oversimplified way, of the conduct of diplomacy during this reign in *The Foreign Ministers of Alexander I. Political Attitudes and the Conduct of Russian Diplomacy, 1801–1825* (Berkeley and Los Angeles: University of California Press, 1969).[12] The Napoleonic campaign of 1812 in Russia receives attention from various writers. Only one of these books is particularly outstanding and that is Carlo Zaghi's *Napoleone e l' Europa* (Naples, 1969).[13] Marc Raeff's *The Decembrist Movement* (Englewood Cliffs, N.J.: Prentice-Hall, 1966) offers the student some documents, translated into English,

with commentary, on this movement of revolt at the end of the reign of Alexander I.

American-Russian relations during this time are dealt with informatively in N. N. Bolkhovitinov's *Stanovlenie Russko-Amerikanskikh Otnoshenii, 1775–1815 [The Establishment of Russian-American Relations, 1775–1815]* (Moscow, 1966).[14]

The nineteenth century is certainly the great age of Russian literature and it is fitting to call attention to one or two works on Alexander Pushkin, regarded as the national poet, whether in tsarist or in Soviet times. Walter N. Vickery gives us a well-rounded appreciation of Pushkin as poet in a modest-sized volume, *Alexander Pushkin* (New York: Twayne Publishers, 1970).[15] David Magarshack's *Pushkin: A Biography* (New York: Grove Press, 1968), although longer, is less successful.

Russian economic development in the first half of the nineteenth century—with special emphasis on industrialization during the reign of Nicholas I—is ably treated in William L. Blackwell's *The Begin-*

11. *See also*, Sidney Harcave's somewhat parallel *Years of the Golden Cockerel: The Last Romanov Tsars, 1814–1917* (New York: Macmillan, 1968) and two rather unsatisfactory works, John D. Bergamini's *The Tragic Dynasty: A History of the Romanovs* (New York: G. P. Putnam's Sons, 1969) and Graham Stephenson's *Russia from 1812 to 1945. A History* (New York: Praeger, 1970).

12. *See also*, the far from definitive biography by Michael Jenkins of Alexander I's hated minister, *Arakcheev: Grand Vizier of the Russian Empire* (New York: Dial Press, 1969).

13. *See also*, P. A. Zhilin, *Gibel Napoleonovskoi Armii v Rossii [The Destruction of Napoleon's Army in Russia]* (Moscow, 1968); Alan Palmer, *Napoleon in Russia* (New York: Simon and Schuster, 1967); Daria Olivier, *The Burning of Moscow, 1812*, trans. Michael Heron (New York: Thomas Y. Crowell Co., 1966); and R. F. Delderfield, *The Retreat from Moscow* (New York: Atheneum, 1967).

14. *See also*, Dieter Boden, *Das Amerikabild im Russischen Schrifttum bis zum Ende des 19. Jahrhunderts* (Hamburg, 1968); David Hecht, *Russian Radicals Look to America, 1825–1894* (revised and reprinted, New York: Greenwood Press, 1968); and *Russian Studies of American Literature: A Bibliography*, compiled by V. A. Libman, trans. Robert V. Allen, ed. Clarence Gohdes (Chapel Hill: University of North Carolina Press, 1969).

15. *See also*, Vickery's controversial monograph on the demise of Pushkin, *Death of a Poet* (Bloomington: Indiana University Press, 1967).

16. *See also*, the comprehensive but ideologically blemished study by N. S. Kiniapina, *Politika Russkogo Samoderzhaviia v Oblasti Promyshlennosti (20–50e Gody XIX V.) [The Policy of the Russian Autocracy in the Area of Industry, the 1820's to the 1850's]* (Moscow, 1968).

ning of *Russian Industrialization,
1800–1860* (Princeton University
Press, 1968).[16] Less comprehensive
is Walter M. Pintner's *Russian
Economic Policy under Nicholas I*
(Ithaca: Cornell University Press,
1967).[17]

P. S. Squire's *The Third Department: The Establishment and Practices of the Political Police in the
Russia of Nicholas I* (London, Cambridge: Cambridge University
Press, 1968) is a somewhat repetitious treatment of this subject.

Several studies center on the
awakening intelligentsia within the
repressive era of Nicholas I. P. V.
Annenkov's memoir, *Zamechatelnoe Desiatiletie, 1838–1848* [*The
Extraordinary Decade*] has been
edited by Arthur P. Mendel and
translated by I. Titunik (Ann Arbor:
University of Michigan Press, 1968).
Edward J. Brown's *Stankevich and
his Moscow Circle, 1830–1840*
(Stanford University Press, 1966) is
a competent if slender work.[18]

Two treatises have appeared on
the unusual figure of Chaadaev, at
one point officially declared insane
for his controversial ideas: Raymond
T. McNally's useful *The Major
Works of Peter Chaadaev: A Translation and Commentary* (University
of Notre Dame Press, 1969) and, in
the wake of this first one, the trans-

lation by Mary-Barbara Zeldin of
Chaadaev's *Philosophical Letters*
and *Apology of a Madman* (Knoxville: University of Tennessee Press,
1970). Eberhard Mueller's *Russischer Intellekt in Europäischer
Krise: Ivan V. Kireevskij, 1806–
1856* (Cologne, 1966) is a close and
valuable analysis of the thought
of this leading Slavophile. It is not
inappropriate to round off this section by taking note of Jesse Zeldin's
pioneering translation into English
of Nikolai Gogol's *Selected Passages
from Correspondence with Friends*
(Nashville: Vanderbilt University
Press, 1969). It is these late essays
by the famous Russian satirist which
so shocked the critic Belinsky by
their reactionary attitudes.[19]

Diplomatic history revolving
around Russia of this time is the
subject of a handful of specialized
monographs. The most important
are Derek Hopwood's *The Russian
Presence in Syria and Palestine,
1843–1914: Church and Politics in
the Near East* (New York and London: Oxford University Press, 1969)
and Bernhard Unckel's *Osterreich
und der Krimkrieg: Studien zur
Politik der Donaumonarchie in
den Jahren 1852–1856* (Lübeck,
1969).

As we pass to the reign of Alexander II with its attempted reform
and modernization of Russia, it
seems cogent to write of the contemporary Russian peasantry and its
problems. A monumental work,
ranging far beyond the era of the
reforming tsar, is Lazar Volin's *A
Century of Russian Agriculture:
From Alexander II to Khrushchev*
(Cambridge, Mass.: Harvard University Press, 1970). Wayne S.

---

17. *See also*, Richard M. Haywood, *The
Beginning of Railway Development in
Russia in the Reign of Nicholas I, 1835–
1842* (Durham, N.C.: Duke University Press,
1969).

18. Another slender volume, Leonard
Schapiro's *Rationalism and Nationalism in
Russian Nineteenth-Century Political
Thought* (New Haven and London: Yale
University Press, 1967) deals a little with
this period. *See also*, O. V. Orlik's *Rossiia i
Frantsuzskaia Revoliutsiia 1830 Goda* [*Russia and the French Revolution of 1830*]
(Moscow, 1968) for a Soviet investigation
of the impact of that French revolution upon
the emerging Russian intelligentsia.

19. *See also*, *Letters of Nikolai Gogol*,
ed. Carl Proffer (Ann Arbor: University
of Michigan Press, 1967).

Vucinich has edited a collection of interesting, if uneven, articles, *The Peasant in Nineteenth-Century Russia* (Stanford University Press, 1968). One contributor to this symposium, Terence Emmons, has also written a full-length study, *The Russian Landed Gentry and the Peasant Emancipation of 1861* (Cambridge University Press, 1968). François-Xavier Coquin's *La Sibérie: Peuplement et Immigration Paysanne au XIXe Siècle* (Paris, 1969) is an impressive survey.

An informative work on Alexander II's outstanding and long-lived war minister is F. A. Miller's *Dmitrii Miliutin and the Reform Era in Russia* (Nashville: Vanderbilt University Press, 1968). Illuminating documentary insight into some phases of Alexander II's foreign and domestic policies is found in *The Politics of Autocracy: Letters of Alexander II to Prince A. I. Bariatinskii (1857–1864)*, ed. A. J. Rieber (The Hague, 1966). The rather amicable constitutional relations between Finland (as autonomous Grand Duchy) and the Russian Empire, from the time of Alexander I to that of Alexander II, are surveyed perceptively by Osmo Jussila in *Suomen Perustuslait: Venäläisten ja Suomalaisten Tulkintojen Mukaan, 1803–1863 [Finnish Fundamental Laws as Interpreted by Russia and Finland, 1803–1863]* (Helsinki, 1969). This monograph has a summary in English.

An important overall study of the history of Russian education which also contains much material on this period is Patrick L. Alston's *Education and the State in Tsarist Russia* (Stanford University Press, 1969).[20]

Despite certain weaknesses, Alexander Vucinich's *Science in Russian Culture, 1861–1917* (Stanford University Press, 1970) makes a significant contribution. It is the second in Professor Vucinich's projected three-volume investigation of the subject.

A number of conservative thinkers of Alexander II's reign and after are the subjects of biographical inquiry. Martin Katz, in *Mikhail N. Katkov: A Political Biography, 1818–1887* (The Hague, 1966), offers a few nuggets on the stridently reactionary journalist. Two ruminative works that deal respectively with two Panslav ideologists are Robert E. MacMaster's *Danilevsky: A Russian Totalitarian Philosopher* (Harvard University Press, 1967) and Stephen Lukashevich's *Konstantin Leontev (1831–1891): A Study in Russian "Heroic Vitalism"* (New York: Pageant Press, 1967). I must admit, in passing, that Panslav thought is not one of my favorite subjects.

No student of Russian culture should overlook the publication in English translation of the third volume of the late Thomas G. Masaryk's *The Spirit of Russia*, ed. George Gibian and trans. Robert Bass (New York: Barnes and Noble, 1967). This work by the noted Czech leader concentrates on Dostoevsky and Tolstoy and offers political and philosophical insights, though some readers may find them dated.[21]

---

20. *See also*, Sophie Satina's modest but informative *Education of Women in Pre-*

Revolutionary Russia, trans. A. F. Poustchine (New York: the author, 1966).

21. Further on Dostoevsky, *see*, the late Konstantin Mochulsky's detailed biography, *Dostoevsky: His Life and Work*, trans. Michael A. Minihan (Princeton University Press, 1967) and Thelwall Proctor's survey *Dostoevskij and the Belinskij School of Literary Criticism* (The Hague, 1969). On Tolstoy, *see*, R. F. Christian's mainly literary *Tolstoy: A Critical Introduction* (Cam-

The relation of Panslavism to a small area of Russian foreign policy is treated in David MacKenzie's *The Serbs and Russian Pan-Slavism, 1875–1878* (Ithaca: Cornell University Press, 1967).[22]

Various aspects of Russian expansion in Asia are considered in several interesting studies. Hélène Carrère d'Encausse's *Réforme et Révolution Chez les Musulmans de l'Empire Russe: Bukhara 1867–1924* (Paris, 1966) is an ambitious undertaking that spills over into Central Asia well beyond the emirate of Bukhara. Of parallel interest is Seymour Becker's *Russia's Protectorates in Central Asia: Bukhara and Khiva, 1865–1924* (Harvard University Press, 1968).[23]

R. K. I. Quested's *The Expansion of Russia in East Asia, 1857–1860* (Kuala Lumpur: University of Malaya Press, 1968) is a good account of Russia's acquisition of the Amur region and of the background of the 1860 Treaty of Peking. Professor Firuz Kazemzadeh has written expertly on *Russia and Britain in Persia, 1864–1914. A Study in Imperialism* (Yale University Press, 1968).[24]

The populist ("going to the people") peasant-socialist and terrorist movements, noteworthy during the latter part of the reign of Alexander II (the "tsar of freedom"), are a source of continuing interest to students of modern Russia. James F. Scanlan's pioneering translation into English of Peter Lavrov's *Historical Letters* (Berkeley and Los Angeles: University of California Press, 1967) makes readily available the ideas of a theorist who had marked influence upon the emerging Russian radical youth of a century ago. Andrzej Walicki's *The Controversy over Capitalism: Studies in the Social Philosophy of the Russian Populists* (London: Oxford University Press, 1969) is a stimulating exposition by a Marxist scholar of the Polish Academy of Sciences in Warsaw.[25]

Weg. Englands zum Russisch-Britischen Abkommen von 1907 (Opladen, West Germany, 1968); G. L. Bondarevski's *Angliskaia Politika i Mezhdunarodyne Otnosheniia v Basseine Persidskogo Zaliva (Konets XIX–Nachalo XX. V.)* [*England's Policies and International Relations in the Persian Gulf Basin at the End of the 19th and the Beginning of the 20th Centuries*] (Moscow, 1968); *Korea and Manchuria between Russia and Japan, 1895–1904: The Observations of Sir Ernest Satow, British Minister Plenipotentiary to Japan (1895–1900) and China (1900–1906)*, sel. and ed. George Alexander Lensen (Tallahassee, Fla.: Diplomatic Press, 1966); and also by Mr. Lensen and by the same publisher (1967), *The Russo-Chinese War*, which deals with Russia and the Boxer Rebellion.

25. *See also*, Richard Wortman's *The Crisis of Russian Populism* (New York: Cambridge University Press, 1967); S. S. Volk's *Narodnaia Volia, 1879–1882* [*The People's Will, 1879–1882*] (Moscow, 1966); and Albert L. Weeks' very uneven and somewhat misleadingly titled biography of Tkachev, the Russian revolutionary "Jacobin": *The First Bolshevik: A Political Biography of Peter Tkachev* (New York University Press, 1968).

---

bridge University Press, 1969). Sarla Mittal's *Tolstoy: Social and Political Ideas* (Meerut, India, 1966) leaves much to be desired.

22. *See also*, Thomas A. Meininger's *Ignatiev and the Establishment of the Bulgarian Exarchate, 1864–1872: A Study in Personal Diplomacy* (Madison: State Historical Society of Wisconsin for the Dept. of History, University of Wisconsin, 1970).

23. The 1844—before the Russian conquest—travel account, *A Mission to Bokhara* by Joseph Wolff, ed. and abr., with an introduction by Guy Wint (New York: Praeger, 1969) is fascinating.

24. Other worthwhile studies on Russian expanionist diplomacy in Asia include Horst Jaeckel's *Die Nordwestgrenze in der Verteidigung Indiens 1900–1908 und der*

Developing Russian industrialization during the later imperial period is treated ably by John P. McKay in *Pioneers for Profit: Foreign Entrepreneurship and Russian Industrialization, 1885–1913* (Chicago: University of Chicago Press, 1970).[26]

Robert F. Byrnes' *Pobedonostev: His Life and Thought* (Bloomington: Indiana University Press, 1968) is a new biography of the influential reactionary teacher, scholar and statesman of the reign of Alexander III and of the first half of that of Nicholas II.[27] A melancholy and knowledgeable account of the Jews in pre-Revolutionary Russia is *Russian Jewry (1860–1917)*, by Jacob Frumkin et al., trans. Mirra Ginsburg (New York: Thomas Yosellof, 1966). Ezra Mendelsohn's *Class Struggle in the Pale: The Formative Years of the Jewish Workers' Movement in Tsarist Russia* (New York: Cambridge University Press, 1970) basically fulfills the promise of its title. What has sometimes been called Russia's Dreyfus Affair is examined by Maurice Samuel in *Blood Accusation: The Strange History of the Beilis Case* (New York: Knopf, 1966). This is the notorious legal case of 1913 in which a Russian Jew was accused of ritual murder by Russian authorities and which became an international *cause célèbre*.

A revival of interest in Nicholas II and in the empress Alexandra—some of it sentimental—has been observable lately. Certainly the most well-known of recent biographies is Robert K. Massie's almost astonishingly sympathetic *Nicholas and Alexandra* (New York: Atheneum, 1967). Victor Alexandrov's *The End of the Romanovs*, trans. William Sutcliffe (Boston and Toronto: Little, Brown and Co., 1966) is dramatic but often of dubious historical value. *Russia under the Last Tsar*, ed Theofanis G. Stavrou (Minneapolis: University of Minnesota Press, 1969) is a collection of essays on various historical developments during the reign rather than a biography.

The reviving revolutionary and opposition movements of these times continue to produce an abundant literature. The nascent Russian Social Democracy is the subject of Allan K. Wildman's *The Making of a Workers' Revolution: Russian Social Democracy, 1891–1903* (University of Chicago Press, 1967). Complementing this work in part is David Lane's statistically interesting but somewhat bewildering *The Roots of Russian Communism: A Social and Historical Study of Russian Social Democracy, 1898–1907* (Assen, The Netherlands, 1969).

Richard Pipes' *Struve, Liberal on the Left, 1870–1905* (Harvard University Press, 1970) explores the thought of the young Struve—first Marxist, then veering to liberalism. It is the first volume of a projected two-volume biography. *Vladimir Akimov on the Dilemmas of Russian Marxism, 1895–1903*, ed. Jonathan Frankel (Cambridge: Cambridge University Press, 1969) is a

26. See also, Jurgen Nötzold's interesting *Wirtschaftliche Alternativen der Entwicklung Russlands in der Ära Witte und Stolypin* (Berlin, 1966). A. M. Anfimov's *Krupnoe Pomeshchiche Khoziaiztvo Evropeiskoi Rossii (Konets XIX–Nachala XX Veka)* [*Large-Scale Landlord Economy in European Russia (End of the 19th Century to the Beginning of the 20th Century)*] (Moscow, 1969) is dogmatic and uninspired.

27. See also, Gerhard Simon's *Konstantin Petrovič Pobedonoscev und die Kirchenpolitik des Heiligen Sinod 1880–1905* (Göttingen, 1969). Pobedonostsev was, of course, Procurator of the Holy Synod during these years.

far from unsuccessful attempt to vindicate the spokesman of "economism" within the Russian Social Democratic Party during the latter's formative years.

Israel Getzler's *Martov: A Political Biography of a Russian Social Democrat* (London and New York: Cambridge University Press, 1967) is an innovative, if somewhat idolizing, biography of the Menshevik leader. Eva Broido's *Memoirs of a Revolutionary* (New York: Oxford University Press, 1967) offers a rather sad autobiographical account of the life of a revolutionary woman who devoted much of her energies to the Menshevik cause. Three other autobiographical works by Menshevik leaders, each interesting in its own way, each with a preface by Leopold H. Haimson, are Noah Zhordania, *Moia Zhizn* [*My Life*], trans. from the Georgian by Ina Zhordania; Gregory Uratadze, *Vospominaniia Gruzinskogo Sotsial-Demokrata* [*Reminiscences of a Georgian Social Democrat*]; and Boris Dvinov's *Ot Legalnosti k Podpoliu (1921–1922)* [*From Legality to the Underground*]. These three works were all published in 1968 by the Hoover Institution, Stanford, California.[28]

Some new works on Lenin are worth recording. Bertram D. Wolfe's *The Bridge and the Abyss: The Troubled Friendship of Maxim Gorky and V. I. Lenin* (published for the Hoover Institution, New York: Praeger, 1967) makes sombre and fascinating reading.[29] Another volume, published under the same auspices and in the same year, is the collection of stimulating essays, ed. Leonard Schapiro and Peter Reddaway, *Lenin: The Man, The Theorist, The Leader. A Reappraisal.*[30]

A very negative and hostile picture is painted by Edward Ellis Smith in *The Young Stalin: The Early Years of an Elusive Revolutionary* (New York: Farrar, Straus and Giroux, 1967). Paul Avrich's widely ranging *The Russian Anarchists* (Princeton University Press, 1967) details this movement from Bakunin and Kropotkin through the Revolutions of 1905 and of 1917.

The Revolution of 1905, centering in the attitudes of Bolsheviks and Mensheviks to the developing events of this unsettled time, and favoring the Mensheviks, is the subject of Solomon M. Schwarz's *The Russian Revolution of 1905: The Workers' Movement and the Formation of Bolshevism and Menshevism* (University of Chicago Press, 1967). L. K. Erman's *Intelligentsiia v Pervoi Revoliutsii* [*The Intelligentsia in the First Revolution*] (Moscow, 1966) clearly favors

28. *See also*, on Menshevism, A. M. Bourguina, *Russian Social Democracy: The Menshevik Movement. A Bibliography*, preface by Leopold H. Haimson (Stanford: The Hoover Institution, 1969). Quite another type of bibliography, centering on the late 19th- and early 20th-century Russian revolutionary movement is *"The Okhrana": The Russian Department of Police. A Bibliography*, compiled by Edward Ellis Smith (Stanford, The Hoover Institution, 1967). Smith has also written a biography of the young Stalin, noted in the text, and based in part on this material.

29. Maxim Gorky's *Untimely Thoughts: Essays on Revolution, Culture, and the Bolsheviks, 1917–1918*, trans. Herman Ermolaev (New York: Paul S. Eriksson, 1968) are generally hostile and polemical criticisms of Lenin and his policies, set forth by Gorky in his newspaper *Novaia Zhizn* [*New Life*].

30. Of lesser importance is the slender volume, ed. Leonhard Haas, *Lenin: Unbekannte Briefe, 1912–1914* (Einsiedeln, Switzerland, 1967). These letters are from the Swiss Federal Archives. To be read with caution is the uneven *Lenin and the Russian Revolution* by Harold Shukman (New York: G. P. Putman's Sons, 1967).

the Bolsheviks during the 1905 Revolution.

A modern account of the Russian 1905 naval disaster at Tsushima during the war with Japan, and concentrating on the extraordinary voyage of the Baltic fleet, is found in J. N. Westwood's *Witnesses of Tsushima* (Tokyo, Sophia University Press in cooperation with the Diplomatic Press, Tallahassee, Fla., 1970). The role of President Theodore Roosevelt as mediator between Russia and Japan at war is stressed in Eugene P. Trani's *The Treaty of Portsmouth: An Adventure in American Diplomacy* (Lexington: University of Kentucky Press, 1969).[31]

In the aftermath of the 1905 Revolution we have a few works focusing on the Duma period. Despite many shortcomings, A. Ia. Avrekh's *Stolypin i Tretia Duma* [*Stolypin and the Third Duma*] (Moscow, 1968) is a book of more than passing interest.[32] Margarete Wolters studies the relation of the Fourth Duma to the conduct of foreign policy in *Aussenpolitische Fragen vor der Vierten Duma* (Hamburg, 1969).

Risto Ropponen is disappointingly diffuse in his attempts to evaluate Russian military strength before 1914.[33] K. F. Shatsillo's study

of the rebuilding of the Russian navy after 1905 has some value.[34]

The Revolution of February 1917, which at last brought down the Imperial regime, is the subject of at least two investigations of unusual and contrasting interest. E. N. Burdzhalov's *Vtoraia Russkaia Revoliutsiia: Vosstanie v Petrograde* [*The Second Russian Revolution: The Uprising in Petrograd*] (Moscow, 1967) offers many arresting points, not least of all his underplaying of the role of the Bolsheviks and stress upon the spontaneity of the February Revolution.[35] George Katkov in *Russia 1917: The February Revolution* (New York: Harper and Row, 1967) boldly ascribes this revolution to conspiratorial groups in Russia such as Freemasons, plus German agents. Such an interpretation is certainly unfashionable; at the same time, it is disturbing.[36] In this connection, I am reminded of the conversation concerning the origins of the American Civil War that William Dean Howells records he had with an Italian sea captain while traveling on a ship from

---

der Europäischen Grossmächte in der Zeit von 1905 bis 1914 die Kraft Russlands? (Helsinki, 1968).

34. See, *Russkii Imperializm i Razvitie Flota Nakanune Pervoi Mirovoi Voiny (1906–1914 GG.)* [*Russian Imperialism and the Development of the Fleet on the Eve of the First World War (1906–1914)*] (Moscow, 1968).

35. Many years ago, the late W. H. Chamberlin emphasized the spontaneous character of the February Revolution in his monumental *The Russian Revolution*, 2 vols. (New York: Macmillan Co., 1935; reprinted in paperback, New York: Universal Library, Grosset and Dunlap, 1965).

36. *Russia in Revolution, 1890–1918* by Lionel Kochan (New York: New American Library, 1966) offers few surprises or novelties. Of greater value is Stuart Ramsay Tompkins' *The Triumph of Bolshevism: Revolution or Reaction?* (Norman: University of Oklahoma Press, 1967).

---

31. An unusual and interesting study of Russian and Finnish attitudes toward the dissolution of the Swedish-Norwegian union in 1905 is Sune Jungar's *Ryssland och den Svensk-Norska Unionens Upplösning: Tsardiplomati och Ryskfinländsk Pressopinion kring Unionsupplösning från 1880 till 1905* (Åbo, Finland, 1969).

32. Zygmunt Lukawski analyzes the policies of the Polish Circle in the Russian State Duma during the years 1906–1909 in his monograph, *Koło Polskie w Rosyjskiej Dumie Państwowej w Latach 1906–1909* (Wrocław, 1967). This volume contains a summary in Russian.

33. *Die Kraft Russlands: Wie Beurteilte die Politische und Militärische Führung*

Genoa to Naples. To this fervent contemporary Italian believer in Garibaldi, the cause (over and beyond slavery) of the Civil War was simplicity itself: "In this world there is but one cause of mischief,— the Jesuits."[37]

The controversial July days of 1917 is the subject of Alexander Rabinowitch's monograph, *Prelude to Revolution: The Petrograd Bolsheviks and the July 1917 Uprising* (Bloomington: Indiana University Press, 1968). The author absolves Lenin of responsibility for this abortive rising against the Provisional Government. Rex A. Wade in *The Russian Search for Peace: February-October 1917* (Stanford University Press, 1969) skillfully explores the morass in which Russia floundered in its search for a "democratic" peace during the short life of the Provisional Government. V. S. Vasiukov's *Vnieshniaia Politika Vremennogo Pravitelstva [The Foreign Policy of the Provisional Government]* (Moscow, 1966) is a doctrinaire treatment and interpretation of a subject now considered relevant in the USSR.[38]

The Bolshevik Revolution of 1917 and the aftermath make the subject matter of numerous books from the USSR, especially in connection with commemorations of the fiftieth anniversary. Among these, one of the most disheartening, insofar as originality of insight, new views, and style of writing are concerned, is the ambitious miscellany dedicated to I. I. Mints, the eminent Soviet specialist in the subject, *Oktiabr i Grazhdanskaia Voina v SSSR [October and the Civil War in the USSR]* (Moscow, 1966). Mints' own bulky volumes on the Bolshevik Revolution are not much more advanced: *Istoriia Velikogo Oktiabra v Trekh Tomakh [The History of Great October in Three Volumes]*; vol. 1, *Sverzhenie Samoderzhaviia [The Overthrow of the Autocracy]* (Moscow, 1967); and vol. 2, *Sverzhenie Vremennogo Pravitelstva; Ustanovlenie Diktatury Proletariata [The Overthrow of the Provisional Government; The Establishment of the Dictatorship of the Proletariat]* (Moscow, 1968). I have not seen vol. 3.[39]

A more novel work stressing Soviet Russia's economic (not political) need to trade with the West is V. A. Shishkin's *Sovetskoe Gosudarstvo i Strany Zapada v 1917-1923 GG. [The Soviet State*

---

37. William Dean Howells, *Italian Journeys* (Boston and New York: Houghton Mifflin Co., 1867; rev. ed., 1901), pp. 58-59. The American writer was Abraham Lincoln's consul at Venice during the war years 1861-1865.

38. Louis de Robien's *Journal d'un Diplomate en Russie [1917-1918]* (Paris, 1967) is the anonymously edited, sometimes perceptive, memoirs of a minor figure attached to the French Embassy during those years. Albert Rhys Williams' *Journey into Revolution: Petrograd 1917-1918*, ed. L. S. Williams (Chicago: Quadrangle Books, 1969) reveals the viewpoint of a consistently dedicated American friend of the Bolsheviks.

39. *See also*, from Soviet writers the collection of essays edited by P. I. Sobolev et al., *Istoriia Velikoi Oktiabrskoi Sotsialisticheskoi Revoliutsii [History of the Great October Socialist Revolution]* (Moscow, 1967); L. M. Spirin, *Klassy i Partii v Grazhdanskoi Voine v Rossii (1917-1920 GG.) [Classes and Parties in the Civil War in Russia (1917-1920)]* (Moscow, 1968); O. F. Solovev, *Velikii Oktiabr i Ego Protivniki [Great October and Its Enemies]* (Moscow, 1968).

The reader may consult profitably two works on the development of Soviet historiography in the aftermath of the Revolution: G. D. Alekseeva, *Oktiabrskaia Revoliutsiia i Istoricheskaia Nauka v Rossii (1917-1923 GG.) [The October Revolution and Historical Science in Russia (1917-1923)]* (Moscow, 1968) and L. V. Ivanova, *U Istokov Sovetskoi Istoricheskoi Nauki [At the Sources of Soviet Historical Science]* (Moscow, 1968).

and the Countries of the West, 1917–1923] (Leningrad, 1969).

Some works of interest on this period from non-Soviet writers include Arno J. Mayer's controversial *Politics and Diplomacy of Peacemaking: Containment and Counterrevolution at Versailles, 1918–1919* (New York: Knopf, 1967); the more conventional *Russia, Bolshevism and the Versailles Peace* by John M. Thompson (Princeton University Press, 1966); Richard H. Ullman's illuminating second volume on the British intervention in Russia, *Britain and the Russian Civil War, November 1918–February 1920* (Princeton University Press, 1968); and George A. Brinkley's *The Volunteer Army and Allied Intervention in South Russia, 1917–1921* (University of Notre Dame Press, 1966). We may conclude this section by noting Paul Avrich's *Kronstadt 1921* (Princeton University Press, 1970), a monograph that deals with the famous mutiny against Soviet authority by the sailors at the naval base outside Leningrad.

Memoir materials of this period abound. Two such works of unusual interest are A. V. Lunacharsky's *Revolutionary Silhouettes*, trans. and ed. Michael Glenny (New York: Hill and Wang, 1968) and George Annenkov's *Dnevnik Moikh Vstrech* [*People and Portraits*] 2 vols. (New York: Inter-Language Literary Associates, 1966). Lunacharsky was the first Soviet Commissar of Education; Annenkov was in the avant-garde movements of the Revolutionary era and a friend of the poets Blok and Mayakovsky, among others.[40]

A great many appraisals and reappraisals of the Bolshevik Revolution from non–Soviet hands have appeared, occasioned by the fiftieth anniversary in 1967 of that Revolution. Isaac Deutscher's *The Unfinished Revolution: Russia, 1917–1967* (New York: Oxord University Press, 1967) is a series of lectures mixing pessimism and optimism from a Marxist viewpoint. Bertram D. Wolfe's *An Ideology in Power: Reflections on the Russian Revolution* (New York: Stein and Day, 1969) is a collection of articles, often stimulating, frequently gloomy, sometimes prolix. Walter Laqueur's *The Fate of the Revolution: Interpretations of Soviet History* (New York: The Macmillan Co., 1967) is an intelligent gathering together of differing opinions on such figures as Lenin and Stalin and topics such as "1917" or "Soviet historiography."

Two important symposia are *Revolutionary Russia*, ed. Richard Pipes (Harvard University Press, 1968) and *Fifty Years of Communism in Russia*, ed. Milorad M. Drachkovitch [Publication of the Hoover Institution] (Pennsylvania State University Press, 1968).[41]

Finally, one should not neglect the melancholy and devastating portraits of Soviet leaders by Stalin's daughter Svetlana Allilueva in *Only One Year*, trans. Paul Chavchavadze (New York: Harper and Row, 1969).

40. *See also*, Stephen P. Timoshenko, *As I Remember*, trans. Robert Addis (Princeton, N.J.: Van Nostrand, 1968) and Viktor Shklovsky, *A Sentimental Journey: Memoirs, 1917–1922*, trans. and ed. Richard Sheldon (Cornell University Press, 1970).

41. Similar collections include *The USSR after 50 Years: Promise and Reality*, ed. S. Hendel and R. L. Braham (New York: Alfred A. Knopf, 1967); *The Soviet Union: A Half-Century of Communism*, ed. Kurt London (Baltimore: Johns Hopkins Press, 1968); *The Impact of the Russian Revolution, 1917–1967: The Influence of Bolshevism on the World outside Russia*, ed. Jane Degras (New York: Oxford University Press, 1967); and E. H. Carr, *The October Revolution: Before and After* (New York: Alfred A. Knopf, 1969).

A vast amount continues to be published on most aspects, domestic and foreign, of Soviet Russia. I must omit most of this material, not only for reasons of space, but also because so much of it is ephemeral. However, some writings of more lasting value covering the different nationalities, regions and religions, as well as economic development, are noted here.[42]

A few works on Soviet political luminaries as well as the period of "purges" are worthy of mention. The revolutionary journalist Radek is the subject of a thoughtful biography by Warren Lerner, *Karl Radek: The Last. Internationalist* (Stanford University Press, 1970). A revival of interest in Bukharin, the "Old Bolshevik" who was executed in 1938, is visible in the reissuing of the latter's *Put k Sotsializmu v Rossii: Izbrannye Proizvedeniia* [*The Path to Socialism in Russia: Selected Works*], ed. Sidney Heitman (New York: Omicron Books, 1967).[43] George W.

42. On the Ukraine, *see,* the two vols. of documents from Austrian archives by Theophil Hornykiewicz, *Ereignisse in der Ukraine, 1914–1922* (Philadelphia: W. K. Lypynsky East European Research Institute, 1966, 1967), and Oleh S. Pidhainy, *The Formation of the Ukrainian Republic* (Toronto: New Review Books, 1966). On the Georgians, *see,* the work of the same name by the eminent scholar David M. Lang (London and New York: Praeger, 1966). Armenia is ably dealt with in *Armenia on the Road to Independence, 1918* by Richard G. Hovannisian (Berkeley and Los Angeles: University of California Press, 1967), and in *A Mandate for Armenia* by James B. Gidney (Kent, Ohio: Kent State University Press, 1967). On Siberia, *see,* the source book edited by N. Ia. Gushchin et al., *Istoriografiia Sovetskoi Sibiri (1917– 1945 GG.)* [*Historiography of Soviet Siberia (1917–1945)*] (Novosibirsk, 1968).

Islam in the Soviet Union by Alexandre Bennigsen and Chantal Lemercier-Quelquejay (New York: Praeger, 1967) ranges widely over the subject. *The Jews in Soviet Russia since 1917*, ed. Lionel Kochan (New York: Oxford University Press, 1970) is a praiseworthy, if gloomy, collection of essays by diverse authors. William B. Stroyen's *Communist Russia and the Russian Orthodox Church, 1943–1962* (Washington, D.C.: Catholic University of America Press, 1967) is a competent and bold work. *The Doukhobors* by George Woodcock and Ivan Avakumovic (Oxford University Press, 1968) is a fascinating study of one of the most renowned Russian sects—in both its Russian and Canadian environments. An original and sardonic analysis is Lowell Tillett's *The Great Friendship: Soviet Historians on the Non-Russian Nationalities* (Chapel Hill: University of North Carolina Press, 1969).

On economic development, Alec Nove's *An Economic History of the USSR* (London:

Allen Lane Press, 1969) fulfills a need, as does Anatole G. Mazour's earlier *Soviet Economic Development, Operation Outstrip: 1921–1965* (Princeton, N.J.: Van Nostrand, 1967). Antony C. Sutton's *Western Technology and Soviet Economic Development, 1917–1930* (Stanford: The Hoover Institution, 1968) is a revelation of the extent of foreign, such as German and American, assistance in the Soviet economic recovery of the 1920s. Violet Conolly's *Beyond the Urals: Economic Developments in Soviet Asia* (New York: Oxford University Press, 1967) delivers what the title promises. James Bunyan's *The Origin of Forced Labor in the Soviet State—1917–1921* (Baltimore: Johns Hopkins Press, 1967) discusses Soviet labor policy during the beginning years. *Women in the Soviet Economy* by Norton T. Dodge (Baltimore: Johns Hopkins Press, 1966) is a factual presentation of the subject. Illuminating, but to be read with caution, is I. A. Kurganov's *Zhenshchiny i Kommunizm* [*Women and Communism*] (Flushing, N.Y.: the author, 1968).

43. By the same editor there is the useful *Nikolai I. Bukharin: A Bibliography* (Stanford: The Hoover Institution, 1969). *See also,* Victor Serge, *Memoirs of a Revolutionary, 1901–1941,* trans. and ed. Peter Sedgwick (New York: Oxford University Press, 1967) for an account of Serge's troubles with Stalin. Robert Conquest's *The Great Terror: Stalin's Purge of the Thirties* (New York: Macmillan Co., 1968) and *Il Potere in Russia: Da Stalin a Brezhnev* by Arrigo Levi (Bologna, 1967) are significant studies "from outside."

Simmonds has edited a useful compendium of *Soviet Leaders* (New York: Thomas Y. Crowell Co., 1967) which is not limited to political figures. Edward Crankshaw's *Krushchev: A Career* (New York: Viking Press, 1966) has serious limitations, but it does supply a biographical need. Nikita Khrushchev's own memoirs have had wide publicity, but some have questioned their authenticity.[44]

Soviet military forces are the subject of several interesting and informed works from varying points of view.[45]

From the stream of writings on Soviet foreign policy, I should like to call attention to Adam B. Ulam's *Expansion and Coexistence: A History of Soviet Foreign Policy, 1917–1967* (New York: Praeger, 1968). This descriptive and analytic

survey is of high quality, although it does lack a bibliography.[46] George F. Kennan's *Memoirs, 1925–1950* (Boston: Little, Brown and Co., 1967) offers valuable views on Soviet foreign policy by the veteran American foreign officer and specialist on Russian affairs.[47]

Finally, notice is offered of a very few works on education, culture, the arts and science of the Soviet period.[48]

Also of interest are A. Avtorkhanov's *The Communist Party Apparatus* (Chicago: Henry Regnery Co., 1966) and *Political Terror in Communist Systems* by Alexander Dallin and G. W. Breslauer (Stanford University Press, 1970).

44. *Khrushchev Remembers*, with introduction, commentary and notes by Edward Crankshaw, trans. and ed. Strobe Talbott (Boston: Little, Brown and Co., 1970).

45. These include Michel Garder's *A History of the Soviet Army* (New York: Praeger, 1966), a study revised and expanded from the original French edition; Raymond L. Garthoff's *Soviet Military Policy: A Historic Analysis* (New York: Praeger, 1966), which also contains material published earlier; Malcom Mackintosh's comprehensive but uneven *Juggernaut: A History of the Soviet Armed Forces* (New York: Macmillan Co., 1967); Roman Kolkowicz's *The Soviet Military and the Communist Party* (Princeton University Press, 1967); and Robert W. Herrick's controversial *Soviet Naval Strategy: Fifty Years of Theory and Practice* (Annapolis: U.S. Naval Institute, 1968).

See also, Marshal Zhukov's *Greatest Battles* by Georgi K. Zhukov, ed. Harrison E. Salisbury and trans. Theodore Shabad (New York: Harper and Row, 1969).

46. For direct source material on foreign relations, the reader may consult such works as *Foreign Relations of the United States, 1946*, vol. 6, *Eastern Europe; The Soviet Union* (Washington, D.C.: Dept. of State, 1969) or the two volumes of documents on *Soviet Foreign Policy (1928–1934)*, ed. Xenia J. Eudin and Robert M. Slusser (published for the Hoover Institution, Pennsylvania State University Press, 1966 and 1967).

Such Soviet surveys of foreign affairs as those published in Moscow in 1967 by A. A. Akhtamzian, V. B. Ushakov, and I. A. Kirilin lose much of their value as a result of their tendentiousness.

47. *See also*, Beatrice Farnesworth's illuminating biography of William Bullitt, colorful American diplomat: *William C. Bullitt and the Soviet Union* (Bloomington: Indiana University Press, 1967). *The Comintern: Historical Highlights, Essays, Recollections, Documents*, ed. M. M. Drachkovitch and Branko Lazitch (published for the Hoover Institution, New York: Praeger, 1966) is a very mixed bag indeed on the Third International.

48. Sheila Fitzpatrick's *The Commissariat of Enlightenment. Soviet Organization of Education and the Arts under Lunacharsky* (London: Cambridge University Press, 1970) is a commendable study. Ilya Ehrenburg's sixth volume of his memoirs, *Post War Years: 1945–54*, trans. T. Shebunina (Cleveland: World Publishing Co., 1967) as always makes unusual literary and political reading, as does, in another connection, the memoir by Ilya Schneider, *Isadora Duncan: The Russian Years*, trans. David Magarshack (New York: Harcourt, Brace and World, 1968).

Two important works on Soviet science are *The Soviet Academy of Sciences and the Communist Party, 1917–1932* by Loren R. Graham (Princeton University Press, 1967) and *The Rise and Fall of T. D. Lysenko* by

EASTERN EUROPE

Again, as mentioned at the outset, there is no claim to completeness in this section. On the other hand, I hope I shall not be accused of too much arbitrariness of selection.

Broad general surveys are disappointingly few and, where they exist, are often flawed. Roger Portal's *The Slavs: A Cultural and Historical Survey of the Slavonic Peoples*, trans. from French by Patrick Evans (New York: Harper and Row, 1969) should hopefully have been a logical introduction to Eastern Europe, but it remains a rather elementary, if bulky, survey with perhaps a disproportionate number of pages devoted to the Russians. *Nationalism in Eastern Europe*, ed. Peter F. Sugar and Ivo J. Lederer (Seattle: University of Washington Press, 1969) offers national histories by various specialists, concentrating on the nineteenth century.[49] A broad survey of the peasants of Eastern Europe in recent times is found in *Soviet and East European Agriculture* (Berkeley and Los Angeles: University of California Press, 1967), ed. Jerzy F. Karcz.[50]

How parliamentary government worked in several states of Eastern and Central Europe (Poland, Es-

tonia, Latvia, Lithuania and Czechoslovakia, for example) in the period between the two world wars is the theme of a collection of frequently informative essays, ed. Hans-Erich Volkmann, *Die Krise des Parlamentarismus in Ostmitteleuropa zwischen den Beiden Weltkriegen* (Marburg, 1967).[51]

A first-rate book dealing with Finland is John H. Hodgson's *Communism in Finland, A History and Interpretation* (Princeton University Press, 1967). Several new works, none satisfactory, have appeared on Gustav Mannerheim, the Finnish national hero of modern times.[52] H. Peter Krosby's *Finland, Germany, and the Soviet Union, 1940-1941: The Petsamo Dispute* (Madison: University of Wisconsin Press, 1968) is a solid study concerned with Finnish nickel and Finland's pro-German orientation before the outbreak of war once more with the USSR.[53]

The three Baltic states, Estonia, Latvia and Lithuania, are the subject of a collection of papers read at the University of Maryland and edited by Ivar Ivask, *First Conference on Baltic Studies: Summary of Proceedings* (Tacoma, Wash.: The Association for the Advancement of Baltic Studies, 1969). *Lat-*

Zhores A. Medvedev, trans. I. M. Lerner (New York: Columbia University Press, 1969).

49. The Czech historian Miroslav Hroch grapples with the issues of national awakening among the Czechs, Lithuanians, Finns, and other small nationalities—not necessarily all Eastern European or Slavic—in a small but interesting study, *Die Vorkämpfer der Nationalen Bewegung bei den Kleinen Völkern Europas* (Prague, 1968).

50. George D. Jackson, Jr.'s *Comintern and Peasant in East Europe, 1919-1930* (New York: Columbia University Press, 1966) has some merit but is deficient in its use of linguistic source materials.

51. *Eastern Europe in Transition*, ed. Kurt London (Baltimore: Johns Hopkins Press, 1966) is a symposium, with few surprises, by Western European scholars, on nationalism and communism in this area during the comparatively recent past.

52. These include the third and fourth volumes of the biography by Stig Jägerskiöld on *Mannerheim, 1918* and *1919* (Helsinki, 1967, 1969). Oliver Warner's *Marshal Mannerheim and the Finns* (Helsinki, 1967) is in English.

53. *Three Days to Catastrophe* by Douglas Clark (London: Hammond, Hammond & Co., 1966) is a popularly written account of British and French reactions to the Winter War of 1939-1940.

via: Country and People, ed. J. Rutkis (Stockholm, 1967) is an informative compendium, written by *émigré* scholars, and aimed at the English-speaking reader. Alfred E. Senn's *The Great Powers, Lithuania and the Vilna Question, 1920–1928* (Leiden, 1966) deals competently with this issue so ruinous to Lithuanian-Polish relations during the interwar period.

Much interesting writing on Polish history has emerged in recent years. Kazimierz Ślaski's *Wątki Historyczne w Podaniach o Początkach Polski* (Poznań, 1968) analyzes carefully the historical elements in the legends surrounding the origins of Poland. A significant collection of studies on the history of the faculty of philosophy and history of the Jagellonian University in Cracow—Poland's oldest university—is *Studia z Dziejów Wydzialu Filozoficzno—Historycznego Uniwersytetu Jagiellońskiego*, ed. Sylwiusz Mikucki (Cracow, 1967).[54]

Two specialized studies make a contribution to Polish economic history of earlier centuries: Jan M. Malecki's *Związki Handlowe Miast Polskich z Gdańskiem w XVI i Pierwszej Polowie XVII Wieku* [*Commercial Relations of Polish Towns with Danzig in the 16th and First Half of the 17th Century*] (Cracow, 1968) and Henryk Zins' *Anglia a Baltyk w Drugiej Polowie XVI Wieku* [*England and the Baltic Sea in the Second Half of the 16th Century*] (Wroclaw, 1967).

For more recent times we have M. K. Dziewanowski's important, if poorly edited, study in English of a prime mover of Poland's rebirth, *Joseph Pilsudski: A European Federalist, 1918–1922* (Stanford: Hoover Institution Press, 1969).[55]

A fair amount has been written about Polish foreign relations as Poland emerged to independence and in the years thereafter. Piotr S. Wandycz's *Soviet-Polish Relations, 1917–1921* (Harvard University Press, 1969) is a highly competent account. Also worthwhile is the monograph by Anna M. Cienciala, *Poland and the Western Powers, 1938–1939* (Toronto: University of Toronto Press, 1968). *Documents on Polish-Soviet Relations, 1939–1945*, vol. 2, *1943–1945* [prepared by the General Sikorski Historical Institute] (London, 1967) makes for sombre reading.[56]

Nicholas Bethell's *Gomulka: His Poland, His Communism* (New York: Holt, Rinehart and Winston, 1969) offers insights on both Poland and Gomulka for the many years of the latter's sway, beginning in 1956.

Finally, the late Professor Waclaw Lednicki's *Russia, Poland and the West* (Port Washington, N.Y.: Kennikat Press, 1966) reveals the author's continuing and erudite interest in this subject.

The earlier history of Czechoslovakia is well represented by Howard Kaminsky's *A History of*

54. In commemoration of the six-hundredth anniversary in 1964 of the founding of the University of Cracow, we have a scholarly group of papers, *Les Universités Européenes du XIVe au XVIIIe Siècle: Aspects et Problèmes. Actes du Colloque International à l'Occasion du VIe Centenaire de l'Université Jagellone de Cracovie, 6–8 Mai 1964* (Geneva, 1967).

55. *See also*, Waclaw Jędrzejewicz, ed., *Diplomat in Paris, 1936–1939: Papers and Memoirs of Juliusz Lukasiewicz, Ambassador of Poland* (New York: Columbia University Press, 1970).

56. In the same melancholy vein, *see also*, the Vatican documents contained in *Le Saint Siège et la Situation Religieuse en Pologne et dans les Pays Baltes, 1939–1945* (Vatican City, 1967).

the Hussite Revolution (Berkeley and Los Angeles: University of California Press, 1967); Milada Blekastad's impressive work on the seventeenth-century Moravian scholar-educator *Comenius: Versuch eines Umrisses von Leben, Werk und Schicksal des Jan Amos Komenský* (Prague, 1969);[57] and William E. Wright's illuminating monograph concentrating on the policies of the enlightened Hapsburg, Joseph II, *Serf, Seigneur, and Sovereign: Agrarian Reform in Eighteenth-Century Bohemia* (Minneapolis: University of Minnesota Press, 1966).

A pioneering work in English, although biased and poorly written, is *The Czech Revolution of 1848* by Stanley Z. Pech (Chapel Hill: University of North Carolina Press, 1969). Perhaps more valuable is the *Festschrift*, ed. Peter Brock and H. Gordon Skilling, *The Czech Renascence of the Nineteenth Century: Essays Presented to Otakar Odložilik in Honour of His Seventieth Birthday* (Toronto: University of Toronto Press, 1970).

The history of the Czechoslovak republic after 1918 is represented by several works on vital internal matters such as Czech-Slovak relations.[58] A relatively small but objective survey embracing Poles, Czechs, and Slovaks is Frederick G. Heymann's *Poland and Czechoslovakia* (Englewood Cliffs, N.J.: Prentice-Hall, 1966).

George F. Kennan's *From Prague after Munich: Diplomatic Papers, 1938–1940* (Princeton University Press, 1968) offers valuable first-hand and painful reports.[59]

Hungarian history from the eighteenth century to the end of Hapsburg rule is enriched by several monographs. Béla K. Király's *Hungary in the Late Eighteenth Century: The Decline of Enlightened Despotism* (New York: Columbia University Press, 1969) is a solid and perceptive presentation.[60] An excellent work in English on a prominent Hungarian nationalist leader before Kossuth is Stephen Széchenyi *and the Awakening of Hungarian Nationalism, 1791–1841* by George Barany (Princeton University Press, 1968). István Barta's *A Fiatal Kossuth* [*The Young Kossuth*] (Budapest, 1966) is an important study of 20 years (1816–1836) of the life of the great Hungarian statesman, from a Marxist approach. An informative account of the development of the Social Democratic movement in Hungary prior to World War I

---

57. This biography was written in Norway and published simultaneously in Oslo.

58. *See*, for example, from Slovak Communist points of view, *Slovensko v 20. Storočí* [*Slovakia in the 20th Century*] by Lubomir Lipták (Bratislava, 1968) and *Slovenská Otázka v Československu* [*The Slovak Question in Czechoslovakia*] by Samo Faltan (Bratislava, 1968).

59. On foreign policy the reader may also consult three works from Marxist Czechoslovak historians: *ČSR a Středoevropská Politika Velmocí 1918–1938* [*The Czechoslovak Republic and the Central European Policy of the Great Powers 1918–1938*] by Alena Gajanová (Prague, 1967); *Nad Evropou Zataženo* [*Overcast*

over Europe] by Robert Kvaček (Prague, 1966); and *Mnichov a Edvard Beneš* [*Munich and Edvard Beneš*] by Míla Lvová (Prague, 1968). The first two of these volumes have summaries in English.

See also, Jörg K. Hoensch's somewhat narrowly conceived diplomatic history, *Der Ungarische Revisionismus und die Zerschlagung der Tschechoslowakei* (Tübingen, 1967).

60. *See also*, the biography by Éva H. Balázs, *Berzeviczy Gergely, a Reformpolitikus (1763–1795)* [*Gregory Berzeviczy, The Reform Politician (1763–1795)*] (Budapest, 1967). This work deals with the earlier years of the Hungarian "Jacobin" who died in 1822.

is Tibor Süle's *Sozialdemokratie in Ungarn: Zur Rolle der Intelligenz in der Arbeiterbewegung 1899–1910* (Cologne, 1967). *Hungarian-Jewish Studies*, ed. Randolph L. Braham (New York: World Federation of Hungarian Jews, 1966) is a collection of essays which surveys with unusual detachment the position of the Jews in Hungary from medieval to recent times.

Hungary's Way to World War II by Nandor A. F. Dreisziger (Astor Park, Fla.: Danubian Press, 1968) is a good, sometimes original, account in English of Hungarian revisionist foreign policy between the two world wars—including some kind words for Admiral Horthy.[61] Nicholas M. Nagy-Talavera's *The Green Shirts and the Others: A History of Fascism in Hungary and Rumania* (Stanford: Hoover Institution Press, 1970) ranges lucidly beyond Hungary, as its title indicates.

Various works of value on earlier Romanian history include *Romanii la Dunărea de Jos* [*The Romans on the Lower Danube*] by Radu Vulpe and Ion Barnea (Bucharest, 1968); Keith Hitchins' *The Rumanian National Movement in Transylvania, 1780–1849* (Harvard University Press, 1969); *Reforma Agrară din 1864* [*The Agrarian Reform in 1864*] by N. Adăniloaie and Dan Berindei (Bucharest, 1967); *Lupta Românilor pentru Unitatea Natională, 1834–1849* [*The Romanian Struggle for National Unity, 1834–1849*] by Cornelia Bodea (Bucharest, 1967); *Marea*

Răscoală a Țăranilor din 1907 [*The Great Peasant Revolt in 1907*] by Andrei Oțetea et al. (Bucharest, 1967); and the slender volume of essays by Miron Constantinescu and V. Liveanu, *Sur Quelques Problèmes d'Histoire* (Bucharest, 1966).

Stephen Fischer-Galați's *Twentieth-Century Rumania* (Columbia University Press, 1970) is a useful and balanced account. The volume of essays by *émigré* writers, *Aspects des Relations Russo-Roumaines* by George Cioranesco et al. (Paris, 1967) makes a case for Romania's regaining Bessarabia and northern Bucovina from the Soviet Union.

The history of the South Slavs as a unified Yugoslavia really begins, as is known, after World War I. Before that we have separate peoples living mostly under Hapsburg or Turkish rule. An important contribution by a Soviet scholar on the historical awakening of the Croat people in the nineteenth century is I. I. Leshchilovskaia's *Illirizm: K Istorii Khorvatskogo Natsionalnogo Vozrozhdeniia* [*Illyrism: A Contribution to the History of the Croat National Renaissance*] (Moscow, 1968).

Two interesting studies of Serbian society and culture are *La Vie Quotidienne en Serbie au Seuil de l'Indépendance, 1815–1839* by Georges Castellan (Paris, 1967) and *La Culture Serbe au Seuil de l'Indépendance (1800–1840)* by Yvonne Castellan (Paris, 1967).

The Road to Sarajevo by Vladimir Dedijer (New York: Simon and Schuster, 1966) is a controversial treatment by a prominent modern Yugoslav political figure of the assassination of the Austrian Archduke Francis Ferdinand.

A Short History of Yugoslavia: From Early Times to 1966, by H. C. Darby et al. and ed. Stephen

61. See also, the documents contained in *Allianz Hitler-Horthy-Mussolini: Dokumente zur Ungarischen Aussenpolitik (1933–1944)*, (Introductory study and preparation of the acts for publication by Magda Ádám et al.), ed. Lajos Kerekes (Budapest, 1966).

Clissold (New York: Cambridge University Press, 1966) is a comprehensive anthology worthy of mention. Traian Stoianovich ranges beyond both Yugoslavia and history in his interdisciplinary *A Study in Balkan Civilization* (New York: Alfred A. Knopf, 1967).[62]

Paul Shoup's *Communism and the Yugoslav National Question* (New York: Columbia University Press, 1968) deals dispassionately with these two vital matters.[63]

The vexed issue of Trieste and its environs, in dispute between Yugoslavia and Italy after World War II, and now presumably settled, is the subject of a judicious and detailed monograph by Bogdan C. Novak, himself of Slovenian background: *Trieste, 1941–1954: The Ethnic, Political and Ideological Struggle* (University of Chicago Press, 1970). To be read in connection with the above is an earlier study of more than topical interest: *Le Conflit de Trieste, 1943–1954* by Jean-Baptiste Duroselle (Brussels, 1966). An able volume concerned with Balkan, and especially

Yugoslav, diplomacy during the 1950s is *Balkan Triangle: Birth and Decline of an Alliance across Ideological Boundaries* by John O. Iatrides (The Hague, 1968).

Three works centering on the Bulgarian anti-Turkish and national movement of the 1860s and 1870s, all from contemporary Bulgaria, are Ivan N. Undzhiev's *Vasil Levski: Biografiia* (Sofia, 1967); Simeon Damianov's *Frantsiia i Bulgarskata Natsionalna Revoliutsiia* [*France and the Bulgarian National Revolution*] (Sofia, 1968); and Khristo Khristov's *Osvobozhdenieto na Bulgariia i Politikata na Zapadnite Durzhavi 1876–1878* [*The Liberations of Bulgaria and the Policy of the Western Powers 1876–78*] (Sofia, 1968).

Stavro Skendi's *The Albanian National Awakening, 1878–1912* (Princeton University Press, 1967) is informed and detailed, but marred among other things, by overzealous nationalism.

In conclusion, I am noting the deaths during this half-decade of a very few figures prominently connected with Russian history: Boris I. Nicolaevsky (1966); William Henry Chamberlin (1969); N. S. Timasheff (1970); and Alexander F. Kerensky (1970).

---

62. *See also*, Nikolaj Todorov, ed., *La Ville Balkanique, XVe-XIXe Ss.* (Sofia, 1970).

63. *See also*, Jozo Tomasevich et al., *Contemporary Yugoslavia*, ed. Wayne S. Vucinich (Berkeley and Los Angeles: University of California Press, 1969).

142

War and Revolution in Yugoslavia, 1941-1945
The Chetniks

Jozo Tomasevich. Formed in 1941 by officers of the defeated Yugoslav army under the leadership of General Draza Mihailovic, the
Chetniks were hailed as the first guerrilla movement in the European
occupied areas. By 1945, however, their forces had suffered total
destruction. In this definitive work, the author provides a detailed
history of the social, political, and economic conditions surrounding
the dramatic rise and fall of the movement, and includes an appraisal of General Mihailovic and the reasons for his defeat. $20.00

Ancestor Worship
in Contemporary Japan

Robert J. Smith. This first comprehensive study of Japanese ancestor
worship in a Western language—the result of fifteen years of research and intensive fieldwork—traces the historical evolution of
ancestor worship from its putative beginnings as an indigenous
tradition to the fundamental changes of the modern period, especially of the past thirty years. Included is the author's analysis of
his unique census of memorial tablets found in some 600 rural and
urban Japanese households. Illustrated. $12.50

Religion and Ritual
in Chinese Society

Arthur P. Wolf. Fourteen papers on various aspects of Chinese
religion focus on the beliefs and practices of the peasant and the ritual
specialists who serve him, rather than on the historical and philosophical doctrines of Taoism, Buddhism, and Confucianism. These
beliefs and practices are placed in the context of Chinese society,
affording a guide to the problem of studying religion in a complex
society and a new approach to the study of kinship and political
cultures. *Studies in Chinese Society*. $15.00

 Stanford University Press

Book Department

INTERNATIONAL RELATIONS

LEON GOURE, FOY D. KOHLER and MOSE L. HARVEY. *The Role of Nuclear Forces in Current Soviet Strategy.* Pp. iii, 148. Coral Gables, Fla.: University of Miami, 1974. No price.

This short but admirably succinct study begins with the assumption that the words of Soviet leaders—of party or army, in journals, papers, or speeches—do indeed reflect their developing strategy; and conversely that (for example) the warm toast of a trade delegation will assure only the naive of Societ good intentions. The chief assertion, which unites the separate essays, is that vast changes occurred in Soviet attitudes toward the role of nuclear forces in their strategy, between the inception of their nuclear program and recent times, but that, in the past two years, even more significant changes in their thinking have taken place. Soviet leaders, finding the "correlation of forces"—military, psychological, political, economic—moving in their favor, can now see great advantage in boldness. Hence the once frequently expressed assertion that there is "no victor in nuclear war" is now often re-

jected: with the massive increase in Soviet strategic forces it has gone out of style. It is, in one Soviet writer's views, one of the "disorienting claims of bourgeois ideologies" (p. 60). The Soviets, for their part, "seldom use the term *détente* in reference to the new relationship, and do so exclusively in pronouncements and communications aimed at Western targets" (p. xxi). This flows from the new position of superiority that they see themselves moving into, as the "correlation of forces" moves in their favor—or so these authors see it.

Americans, on the other hand, while decreasing their role internationally, have developed a school of thought, a whole philosophy, of détente. It has been a common Western assumption that the Soviet leadership went through the same learning process as Americans in defusing the Cold War and building a new relationship; this is dangerously ingenuous, the authors argue. Indeed, their learning process, if one follows to its logical conclusion the argument of Ambassador Kohler and Messieurs Gouré and Harvey, has been the exact reverse—that is, while Americans learned the language of détente, the Soviets probably, from about 1969 on, learned a new language of toughness and one in which they have great faith. Nor, the authors assert, is there evidence that the Moscow and Washington Summits of 1972 and 1973, or SALT I or SALT II, have had any discernible impact on Soviet positions.

To agree with these authors is to accept a very gloomy view indeed of the prospects for the West. The book was completed in early 1974, since which time "double-digit inflation" and the worst economic mess since the great depression have seemingly paralyzed the West, making the position still worse. The authors are convinced that a lag exists in American perceptions of what the Soviet leadership is thinking about, and of how the Soviets are thinking. To accept this position involves accepting the view that America has built its foreign policy in the past five years on illusions and wishful thinking, that the architects of this course, and those supporting them, have been hopelessly naive. The book is devoid of logical flaws, and the evidence as they marshal it is convincing. This may be an extremely important book from a policy point of view.

W. SCOTT THOMPSON
Tufts University
Medford
Massachusetts

MORTON H. HALPERIN. *Bureaucratic Politics and Foreign Policy.* Pp. ix, 340. Washington, D.C.: The Brookings Institution, 1974. $8.95.

For analysts of American foreign policy, this is an interesting, insightful, but incomplete book. It is interesting because of the many anecdotes and tidbits of information that Halperin has culled from the memoirs of those one hundred participants who were involved in making and implementing American foreign policy since 1945 and who chose to write about their experiences. It is insightful because of Halperin's obvious understanding of what it takes to be an enterprising (read effective) bureaucrat in the Washington foreign affairs bureaucracy and because of his ability to communicate to us what it

"feels like" to operate in that environment. But in spite of the information imparted and the arguments marshalled, the book remains incomplete because we are left at the end still wondering exactly how much effect the bureaucratic process that takes place in the executive branch affects the substance of policy.

The book is divided into three parts. In the first part, Halperin tells us who are the major participants in the foreign affairs bureaucracy, what their interests and perspectives are, why these must differ among the participants, and why we should pay attention to the differences. In the second part, he tells us how the pulling and hauling among the various players result in a Presidential decision. I found chapters eight and nine ("Information and Arguments" and "Maneuvers to Affect Information") among the most intriguing and original that I have ever encountered because of the way in which they show how the environment that bureaucrats operate in structures the types of arguments these players can make. In the third part, Halperin covers an area that he rightly states has been largely neglected in the foreign policy literature: implementation, or what it means to implement decisions and why the analyst must distinguish between a Presidential decision and a governmental action.

My source of dissatisfaction with the book stems from the fact that I am both a practitioner and a critic of bureaucratic politics. In trying to assess the effects that the bureaucratic process has on policy, these are the key questions that must be asked and answered: (1) Is there significant slippage between Presidential intent and governmental action on those issues Presidents care most about? (2) Does a President's awareness of the difficulty of implementing a given decision cause him to change his mind when making the decison? (3) Has bureaucratic politics made a significant difference in the substance of policy for those fifteen or twenty pivotal decisions of the post-1945 era? And (4) is Presidential anticipation of Congressional and public reaction to contemplated decisions much more significant than bureaucratic politics in explaining why we get the policy we get? Halperin deals with some but not all of these questions, and he treats none of them definitively. The result of his efforts, however, is a much more systematic and provocative treatment of the effects of process on content than we have had for a long time.

ROBERT J. ART

Brandeis University
Waltham
Massachusetts

TOWNSEND HOOPES. *The Devil and John Foster Dulles*. Pp. xii, 562. Boston, Mass.: Little, Brown, 1973. $15.00.

If, as is likely, an attempt is made at the end of this century to evaluate and rank the American Secretaries of State, the more intensive debate among historians as to the position on that list of a certain individual will probably focus on the tenure of John Foster Dulles. When that poll is taken it is perhaps correct to assume that considerable influence on the judgment of those scholars assessing the performance of the Secretaries of State will stem from such biographies as this one.

The book's title, *The Devil and John Foster Dulles*, prompts some bewilderment initially, especially so in view of the general knowledge that the late Secretary of State was solidly attached to, and motivated by, Christian and humanitarian principles. On closer reading, however, one discovers the correctness of the author's choice, and recognizes the basic tragedy of the Dulles tenure which the title suggests: that for all of his high motives, his genuine commitment to America's national interests, and his deep and abiding concern for the welfare of mankind, John Foster Dulles was consistently, indeed persistently, shackled by his own "theological baggage," as Thomas E. Dewey observed. His self-righteous, moralistic approach to foreign policy, coupled with an uncompromising an-

tipathy to Communism, militated against pragmatic assessment, tainted objective analysis and ultimately derailed rational thought. Disarmed frequently through ambiguity, his policies suffered from a lack of substance which not even a popular belligerence in his methodology could redeem. His legacy has become that of "massive retaliation," "rollback," and "brinksmanship," phrases considered nebulous at the time of their enunciation and still awaiting a satisfactory historical definition.

The author has drawn upon a mass of manuscript and documentary materials, oral history collections and interviews in the preparation of this biography. Moreover, he has delved deeply into the letters and statements of Dulles himself in order to delineate the development of those strong convictions of mission and purpose which dominated the Secretary's attitude on this nation's role in the post-World War II diplomatic arena. This device, while occasionally overdone, illuminates quite well those aspects of the man's character which contributed so significantly to his professional posture as a statesman. Of particular interest are those chapters detailing Dulles's formulation of the nuclear deterrent thesis, with those entitled "Policy Beginnings," "Massive Retaliation and the New Look," "A Gathering Immobility" and "Berlin—The Last Crisis" deserving both special praise and careful study.

A book of this dimension adds much to the history of the middle years of the Cold War, and clarifies in particular the thoughts and actions of the leading Cold War "Warrior"—John Foster Dulles. It is absorbing, sometimes humorous, and rarely dull. It should change some views; if not immediately, then in due time.

CALVIN WARNER HINES

Stephen F. Austin State University
Nacogdoches
Texas

STEPHEN E. PELZ. *Race to Pearl Harbor: The Failure of the Second London Naval Conference and the Onset of World War II.* Pp. xi, 268. Cambridge, Mass.: Harvard University Press, 1974. $17.50.

Drawing effectively on interviews and archival resources in Japanese and English, Stephen Pelz represents the fine breed of young American scholars with good connections abroad and substantial support at home, whose approach to international study has outdistanced old uni-dimensional techniques. The journalistic title of his book is misleading, however, for it implies that the Japanese Navy prepared the Hawaii attack as early as 1936; Admiral Yamamoto invented the assault scheme only after the 1940 maneuvers. The "race" mentioned in the appropriate subtitle means Japanese naval arming, one-sided until America stirred. While the publishers exaggerate in claiming that historians have slighted the naval race of the 1930s, the author—an assistant professor at the University of Massachusetts/Amherst—performs a scholarly service by exploring the internal and external ramifications affecting all three Great Powers most concerned: Japan, the United States, and Britain.

The nine-page bibliography lacks annotations but supplies indigenous renderings for Japanese citations, and is comprehensive, although one misses Bradford Lee's fine *Britain and the Sino-Japanese War* (Stanford, 1973). Otherwise valuable but distant end notes, consuming twenty-three pages, refer unnecessarily to an American college textbook and rely excessively on a U.S. Naval Academy history. The style is monographic, enlivened by flashes of felicity ("The Royal Navy resembled an aging concubine," p. 179) but marred by clumsiness (Takahashi became "a government financial expert after failing in business," p. 12). Track charts (pp. 37–38) are superfluous. The translations from Japanese are generally satisfactory, one exception being the odd use of "strategy section" to describe a general staff echelon. Experts will resist the gossipy allegation that Japanese imperial princes were keen to unseat the Emperor during the turbulent 1930s (p. 10).

Pelz's study is useful not only for unraveling the tangle of prewar Far Eastern navalism (extending to Mahan's influence on Japanese thinking, and the role of public opinion), but also for deepening our understanding of delicate postwar efforts to achieve arms limitation. Particularly chilling today, especially for critics of the alleged resurgence of Japanese militarism, is Pelz's observation that "Japan's continued economic advance and the United States' financial collapse made a naval race seem feasible" in the thirties (p. 40). While the inability to restrain naval ambitions conferred transient benefit upon Nippon—obsessed by pressures of time and of technological advantage—in the larger sense the derailment of naval negotiations in 1936 foretold the catastrophe which would eventually befall Japanese sea power and nation.

ALVIN D. COOX
San Diego State University
California

CHARLES PENTLAND. *International Theory and European Integration.* Pp. 283. New York: The Free Press, 1973. $9.95.

In an area that has both suffered and benefited from the incessant social science penchant to theorize, Charles Pentland has written a refreshing book that offers no overarching conceptual scheme for analyzing the state of the literature about European political integration. His well written volume attempts to identify the areas of compatibility and the points of difference among the major approaches to integration theory. In this he is successful; the book is a solid and useful overview of the major approaches to European political integration.

Pentland identifies four distinctive approaches to the problems of international political integration—the pluralist approach, functionalism, neofunctionalism, and federalism.

In a separate chapter for each approach, the author reviews the major writers in that area and applies their insights to three levels of analysis—the System, the States, and the Individual. Each of the four chapters closes with Pentland's analysis of the operational features of each approach in the context of the European postwar experience. Avoiding a descriptive-historical framework, the author traces the relationships between the development of each approach and the eventual outcome when applied to Western Europe.

The second part of the volume illustrates the complementary aspects of all four approaches and the author nicely illustrates his thesis by taking a number of the explanatory propositions from the literature and placing them in a framework that utilizes the three levels of analysis. The principal theoretical concerns of the integration theorists emerge and the author ably supports his argument that a review of the major approaches and issues in the field will yield dividends in allowing the reader to examine, compare, and contrast the major contributions to the integration literature. Pentland argues that this is not the time to impose a general paradigm or theory on the field; exploration and debate can make vital contributions to the research priorities in the study of integration.

The author argues, in closing, that the process of political integration can best be viewed as four distinct but interrelated processes; integration is best viewed as a condition of the international system as a whole. As important, the dynamic relationship between system change and state behavior requires greater consideration. A division between foreign and domestic policy is untenable in the analysis of integration. Pentland argues, finally, for an emphasis on social-psychological research at the individual level, an approach overlooked by most of the major theorists in the field and one that might provide fresh and rewarding insights into the political integration process.

RIORDAN ROETT
The Johns Hopkins University
Washington, D.C.

RAYMOND VERNON, ed. *Big Business and the State: Changing Relations in Western Europe.* Pp. ix, 310. Cambridge, Mass.: Harvard University Press, 1974. $12.50.

MILTON S. HOCHMUTH. *Organizing the Transnational: The Experience with Transnational Enterprise in Advanced Technology.* Pp. xiv, 211. Leiden, The Netherlands: A. W. Sijthoff, 1974. No price.

In the important book, *Big Business and the State*, edited by Raymond Vernon, Director of the Harvard University Center for International Affairs, a dozen contributors explore the connections between enterprises and national governments in western Europe in the post-World War II years. Professor Vernon's opening essay is thoughtful and stimulating. In it, he seeks to isolate unique national elements and also common characteristics of government-business links in the 1950s and to demonstrate how in the 1960s and early 1970s changes occurred. Looking at current events, he perceives a disenchantment with the intense public sector activity of the recent past and by the late 1960s in France and elsewhere "a rediscovery of the power of the market. . . ." Vernon shows clearly the dichotomy between national planning and the foreign trade-investment that accompanied European integration. He demonstrates how in industries that depend on high technology and scale production, strictly national policies conflict with industrial and organizational realities. The time may be here, Vernon suggests, when European governments can no longer make policy without taking into account interrelationships between European firms and enterprises headquartered outside Europe.

In the second essay, Stuart Holland focuses on Europe's public enterprises. The immediate postwar nationalizations, he argues, were based primarily on socialist economic policy, the salvage of ailing enterprises, and the punishment of collaborators. By the 1960s and 1970s, some governments were using public enterprises as policy instruments to offset the negative national effects of EEC trade liberalization, to reverse recessionary trends, to supply employment in less developed areas, to take on high risk ventures, to maintain competition, and to cope with problems created by multinational enterprise. But Holland reports that "No serious attempts appear to have been made to relate the aims of new public enterprise at a national level with [European Economic] community policy." Regrettably, Holland's piece gives the reader little feel for the criteria for successful or unsuccessful public enterprise or for the future of public enterprise measured by such criteria.

After these "syntheses," part II offers rich details on public policies in Italy (by Romano Prodi), Germany (by Georg H. Küster), Britain (Trevor Smith), France (Charles-Albert Michaelet), and Sweden (Göran Ohlin). The reader becomes aware of immense variations: no all-European public policy exists. Nonetheless, one is struck by how often countries followed one another's lead. Vernon emphasizes the lead of France; Stuart Holland, the lead of Italy; but this reviewer was impressed by the interactions. Thus, a German memo might be inspired by French experience with indicative planning; the French "Nora report" (1967) advocated a central holding organization along the lines of Italy's Istituto per la Ricostruzione (IRI); the 1971 Italian Gestioni e Partecipazione Industriale (GEPI) was originally inspired by Britain's Industrial Reorganisation Corporation (IRC). It all involved a learning process—the shuttling of information, comparisons, and alternative strategies between and among nations. What is revealed is fascinating.

Part III of this skillfully organized collection turns to specific industries: aluminum (Zuhayr Mikadashi), computers (Nicolas Jequier), automobiles (Louis T. Wells), steel (J.E.S. Hayward), and aerospace (M.S. Hochmuth). Wells is particularly interesting on the interconnections between European automobile makers. And don't miss Jequier's gem of an article.

Hochmuth's own book, *Organizing the Transnational*, includes much of the data in his article in the Vernon volume (sometimes there is almost word for word repetition). But Hochmuth's book should not be judged by his article. It is far from a mere enlargement of the shorter piece. Rather his volume provides an in-depth look at six cases where governments have engaged in multinational ventures in high technology products—in weapons, space systems, and aircraft. Hochmuth's book meshes beautifully with the overall Vernon theme, that is, it indicates the enormous variety and complexity in big business-state interrelationships. Hochmuth was himself a participant in the NATO Hawk air missile defense project and the U.S.-West German tank development (MBT-70). His volume reveals the successes and failures in the management structures of such projects. With "insider"-type knowledge, insight, and perception, Hochmuth has penetrated the intricate mysteries of the organizations of these transnational government enterprises, including their relations with private firms. His conclusions should provide guidance to future participants (governmental bodies and private companies) in transnational projects.

MIRA WILKINS
Florida International University
Miami

ASIA AND AFRICA

LUDWIG W. ADAMEC. *Afghanistan's Foreign Affairs to the Mid-Twentieth Century: Relations with the USSR, Germany and Britain.* Pp. 324. Tucson: University of Arizona Press, 1974. $13.00. Paperbound, $7.95.

Ludwig Adamec is one of a small but increasing number of American scholars who have turned their attention to the study of Afghanistan. The output of this group has also been increasing, and the present writer has reviewed for the

Annals works by Richard Newell and Leon Poullada in the past two years. Newell provided a general overview of the constitutional changes of King Zahir Shah in his book, and Poullada concentrated on an important aspect of history in analyzing the reforms and overthrow of King Amanullah. Adamec here covers a longer period of time from, roughly, the turn of the century to the end of the second World War and looks specifically at the relationship between Afghanistan and its two powerful neighbors, the Soviet Union and Great Britain (through India), and its attempt to find a balance through closer relations with Germany. In doing so he builds on and, to an extent, overlaps with, the material presented in his earlier work, *Afghanistan 1900–1923: A Diplomatic History.*

Arnold Toynbee once wrote that the two key cities of Asia were Antioch and Herat, as it was through and past these two that great movements of history took place. The latter, in western Afghanistan, displays the geographic importance of the country astride the mountains that separate the steppes of Central Asia from the Indo-Gangetic plains and the Iranian plateau to the south and emphasizes the role played as guardians of the passes through the ranges. Adamec describes briefly the "Great Game" between Russia and Britain (unfortunately in a literary style far removed from Kipling!) as a prelude to his detailed presentation of the developments within his time frame.

There is no doubt from the reading of the book that an unusual amount of effort has gone into the research which serves as the basis of the study. He has used source material in Kabul, New Delhi, and London and has had access to Soviet and German documents. The last have been skillfully used in looking at the period preceding and during World War II when German influence in Iraq, Iran, and Turkey as well as Afghanistan was worrisome to the Allies. One is all but overwhelmed with the mass of documentary material—the notes covering the sources, unfortunately, are relegated to the back of the book, leaving the reader the choice of ignoring them or fumbling to locate them.

The lack of the book is analysis. We are told in great detail what happened but are rarely presented with a clear explanation of the forces at work in Afghanistan or the powers outside which led to the actions taken by the government in Kabul. For example, what were the reasons for the British "hands off" policy during the troubles which followed the downfall of Amanullah and culminated in the enthroning of Nadir Shah? The author misses a chance to stand back from the documents and to reflect on the forces which led to the behavior described.

There are some problems which could be overcome by careful editing and which will cause difficulty for the reader not closely familiar with Afghan history. For example, names are spelled in different ways from chapter to chapter. The tables in the appendices which give office holders are helpful but can also be confusing, as names are sometimes excluded. An example: George Merrell was *not* American Ambassador from 1951 to 1959.

Nonetheless, Adamec has done an admirable job in chronicling the international relations of a state which has struggled to preserve its identity against the expansion of two empires and which continues to maintain a balance among outside powers. One hopes that a similar study of the postwar period will follow.

CRAIG BAXTER

Accra
Ghana

JAMES BARBER. *South Africa's Foreign Policy: 1945–1970.* Pp. viii, 325. New York: Oxford University Press, 1973. $14.50.

Mr. Barber can be counted on to write sound, reliable, worthwhile texts on Southern Africa and this book can be recommended to all readers and students who want a straight-forward account of the central elements in the foreign policy of those in control of the government of South Africa. The book is concisely and well written, and is based on a thorough, careful and scrupulous analysis of the main published official sources.

In his introduction the author explains the approach and method which he chose to adopt, not least the limits which he set himself, and he frankly acknowledges that he has had opportunity to examine only a portion of the evidence which is available for the twenty-five-year period. Nevertheless he conducted many valuable interviews in South Africa, thus supplementing his selection of printed material. Divided into four parts entitled "The Aftermath of War (1945–1948)," "The Early Years of National Party Rule (1948–1959)," "The Years of Crisis and Doubt (1960–1966)" and "The Years of Confidence (1966–1970)," there are twenty chapters, each with a significant and helpful title.

If a reviewer were to choose to attack the author for what he did not set out to do, or for his political standpoint, it would not be difficult to enlarge on his omissions or to erect a variety of strawmen for demolition. Certainly the book could have given more space to Africa, Colored and Indian organizations in South Africa and their relations with the world outside South Africa. It could also have been more critical of Britain and her exercise of crucial British responsibilities towards South Africa throughout the Twentieth Century since the Anglo-Boer War. In the years before 1948, when Smuts was defeated by Malan and the Afrikaner-Nationalists took over, and even before 1961, when South Africa left the Commonwealth and the new Republican regime settled into the saddle, more constructive and firmer pressure might have been exerted by imperial or metropolitan Britain.

However, even within the author's own framework, and granted the general soundness of his work within that framework, there are some questionable assertions, and errors, which might usefully be pointed out to the non-specialist reader. Thus the very first sentence of the book is misleading in its confident assertion that "at the end of the Second World War the South African Government had no suspicion that in the years ahead it would face persistent and increasing international hostility." A quotation from Jan Hofmeyr, Deputy Prime Minister, at the United Nations meeting in May 1945 is cited in support of this statement. But what else could a representative of his country, and a deputy for his Prime Minister, General Smuts, have said on such an occasion other than that the evil of war had brought an enhancement of the "prestige and honor of our country amongst the nations of the world." Inside South Africa and speaking to fellow South Africans of all races in 1943 and 1944, the enlightened Hofmeyr had spoken very differently. He had been emphatic about the danger that South Africa, despite its opposition to Germany, Italy and Japan, might itself succumb to the evils of Nazism and extreme racism.

The author's lack of an intimate knowledge of South Africa also comes out in other contexts, for example his use of the word "ironically" when he refers to the tradition of Afrikaner leadership continuing in the United Party (page 48), or to the new vocabulary of "White South Africa" of "the late 1950s" in which the word "natives" was replaced by "Bantu" (p. 115). The English speaking minority among White South Africans were long resigned to the necessity of Afrikaner leadership in any strong anti-Afrikaner-nationalist party if they were to have significant Afrikaner companionship. As for the introduction of "Bantu" into official as well as political nomenclature, the reference should be to the late 1940s rather than 1950s: already in the early 1950s there was important legislation bearing the label "Bantu" (for example, the Bantu Authorities Act, 1951, and the Bantu Education Act, 1953).

But such omissions and errors apart, together with a few oversights in the bibliography, this book makes a valuable contribution.

KENNETH KIRKWOOD
Oxford University
Great Britain

CHARLES A. JOINER. *The Politics of Massacre: Political Processes in South Vietnam.* Pp. vii, 346. Philadelphia, Pa.: Temple University, 1974. No price.

The Politics of Massacre, substantially a collection of analyses of Vietnamese politics written during the 1960s, is a morgue of articles about toppled regimes and abandoned counterinsurgency programs. Only the title is new and exciting. The articles, on such topics as administration in the Diem regime (still in present tense) and the brilliance of Douglas Pike's book *Viet Cong*, add nothing to present day knowledge of Vietnam. They make dull reading, too.

The author's plea in the preface is that the South Vietnamese be left alone. He insists, despite the fact that North and South Vietnamese share one of the most cohesive national histories in human experience, that they are, and should remain, two nations. Vietnamese do not take this matter lightly: the first article of the Paris Peace Accords states that Vietnam is one nation.

This outdated portfolio may best be treated as a historical document. It is obvious that there was somethimg terribly wrong with much of the thinking of political scientists about Vietnam in the 1960s. Nothing is more important to the discipline than is an evaluation of why so many predictions and prescriptions about Vietnam went so sour. In Joiner's work can be found many of the weaknesses common to the "nation-building" and "counterinsurgency" studies about Vietnam.

It is taken for granted that the NLF, as a revolutionary force, must be defeated. There is an obsessive focus on organizational structure, of both NLF and the various Saigon regimes. Conflicts in the structures of economic class and landholding are virtually ignored. Most importantly, Vietnamese nationalist struggle against foreign— American—domination is not mentioned as even a minor political factor in Vietnam. It is as though the fact that Saigon-based governments from the Diem regime onward have been almost wholly financed by the United States is of no political significance.

JOHN LEWALLEN
Oakland
California

ELLIS S. KRAUSS. *Japanese Radicals Revisited: Student Protest in Postwar Japan.* Pp. xiv, 192. Berkeley: University of California Press, 1974. $11.00.

This is a superb blend of modern political socialization theory and field surveys among Japanese university students in 1962 and 1970. One would go far to find a Ph.D. thesis so beautifully designed to test rival theories of socialization and provide insights for both the specialist in Japan and political scientist interested in how radical students either outgrow their radicalism or retain it in adulthood. Japanese students are an especially good example because of their role in the 1960 riots against Premier Kishi and the U.S.-Japan Security Treaty and their later occupation of college campuses in 1968–1969. In brief, anyone—either Asian specialist or youth expert—will find this a fascinating study.

Krauss had the advantage of his Stanford mentors and a Sophia University professor's 1962 survey of 100 students who had been either leaders or followers in the 1960 demonstrations. Sophia also provided him with help in relocating those students in 1970 (he found 53 in major cities), and it is clear that he prepared himself well by mastering the literature on student politicization and student/adult socialization before going to Japan for a year's language study followed by a year's research. He begins with a survey of the literature, including the rival theories of "maturation" versus "generational continuity": either radicals outgrowing their student activism or persisting in belief if not behavior. Then he discusses the influence of family, to find it minimal on Japanese students compared with the effect of peer-group opinion in universities. The small sample limits the applicability of Krauss' research to the entire Japanese university student population, but he brings in other relevant studies and makes tentative conclusions that impress this writer who has studied political attitude change in Japan since 1952. Teachers were evidently influential on the radicals, but peers were the key group as activists and non-activists associated with like types.

The key question of what happened to the ideas and behavior of the 1960 students ten years later shows that the former leaders and activists in student radicalism generally retained their beliefs, if not their enthusiasm for Marxism as a system, while not engaging in organizational opposition to the regime. They tended to work in professions rather than business firms, or small businesses if the latter, and to continue very active political discussion and individual acts of opposition to the conservative regime. On the other hand, those who had been intermittent activists as students or inactive lost much more ideological Marxism and seldom discussed or behaved in a political sense. This suggests the loss of ideology, as the Japan Socialist Party suffered in the 1960s and the Japan Communist Party switched to pragmatic programs of law, order, and prices. Voting fell off, however, as both the conservative ex-students and radicals lost faith in the political process and the competing parties which all seemed to be selfish and unresponsive to public needs. The latter sense was clearly evident to this writer during the summer 1974 Diet election campaign observed in Tokyo, but in what advanced country hasn't the public lost faith in its leadership to solve economic problems?

Krauss concludes his excellent study with the implications of his ex-student survey for the Japanese political system, and he includes 20 tables to illustrate the 1960 and 1970 research, including in-depth interviews with a few of the sample in 1970.

DOUGLAS H. MENDEL, JR.
University of Wisconsin
Milwaukee

LINCOLN LANDIS. *Politics and Oil: Moscow in the Middle East.* Pp. iv, 201. Cambridge, Mass.: University Press, 1974. $12.95.

Shortly after the Second World War, developments in the Middle East afforded the Soviet Union a good opportunity to penetrate the Middle East and seek to extend Moscow's political as well as economic domination over the area. In this book, the author discusses the various aspects of the Soviet penetration in the Middle East and analyzes in a special way the Russian tactics which tend to manipulate oil and politics towards achieving the Soviet main objective of enhancing the course of international communism.

The first chapter of the book deals mainly with the roots of Soviet oil interest in the Middle East, tracing it back to the British petroleum explorations in the area as early as 1901. In the succeeding chapters, the author discusses the development of Soviet economic policies and tactics in the area during the various eras of Lenin, Stalin, Krushchev, and Brezhnev-Kosygin. The main thrust of these chapters is to show how the Soviet national interest, as conceived and interpreted by these various leaders, was the chief factor behind the development and shaping of Moscow's political approaches to the various countries of the Middle East.

The author concludes that the Soviet political and economic policies in the area are directed towards three main objectives: (1) undermining whatever friendship and trust there is between certain Middle Eastern countries and the West; (2) importing Middle Eastern petroleum on a barter basis with Soviet arms and industrial goods which these countries need, and (3) controlling a vast pool of Middle Eastern and Soviet oil for the purpose of using it as an effective means to strengthen the cause of international communism. Some scholars of international studies might deem such objectives as fanciful and unrealistic. However, what the author did not emphasize in this book is the fact that the Arab-Israeli conflict, since it started, has continued to give Moscow the opportunity it seeks in achieving exactly these goals and objectives. As long as the Arab-Israeli conflict remains unsolved, it becomes increasingly fair to assume that the fanciful could very well become true.

Needless to say, the book is very enjoyable and rewarding to read. Moreover, it is replete with primary source materials quoted directly from various Soviet publications. The author is to be complimented, therefore, for his clear insight and perceptive analysis of such a difficult and complex subject.

WILSON B. BISHAI
Harvard University
Cambridge
Massachusetts

CHARLES MILLER. *Battle for the Bundu: The First World War in East Africa.* Pp. x, 353. New York: Macmillan, 1974. $9.95.

The East African Campaign is a fascinating footnote to the First World War. Not only were the Germans undefeated at the time of the Armistice, they were in a position to continue the campaign. The chief interest of this campaign for a contemporary reader lies in how this was accomplished. The German army was largely composed of Black Africans recruited in a Colonial territory which had been administered rather harshly and for only a relatively few years by a Germany late on the imperial scene. The most marked characteristics of German African policy were several major shifts in its direction and the rather frequent turnover in Governors.

The commander of German troops in the field was Colonel Paul von Lettow-Vorbeck, a career officer of high intellect who fully grasped the point of his small war: to cause the Allies to commit more and more troops in what was a by-way to the main conflict and to keep those troops engaged for as long as possible.

Miller understands the crucial importance of von Lettow's brilliant use of African troops and makes clear his ability to fight a successful guerrilla war in territory several thousand miles from home country. Locally recruited, these troops were fully integrated with the regular German soldiers and settler volunteers. The whole army was virtually unsupplied from Germany throughout the campaign. The local knowledge, partial immunity to tropical illnesses and bravery of the African troops were vital to German success. Unfortunately, Miller has been unable to find African voices to aid in the chronicle of events. His major sources are all European.

Despite this lack, Miller has produced a continuously interesting narrative. Embellished from time to time with brief conjectures of conversation, sometimes in terrible Swahili, the account is largely factual and quite accurate. Although Miller has clearly traveled widely in East Africa, his descriptions of the countryside are sometimes slightly overdrawn and his style is quite informal.

This is not a scholar's study of the First World War in East Africa. There are no footnotes, the bibliography is good, but by no means exhaustive, and the brief account of German settlement and administration in East Africa is defective. Nevertheless, the account of the campaign is very engrossing, quite accurate and drawn from published primary sources and correspondence. Miller uses very well the published diaries of the British Colonel, Richard Meinertzhagen; the autobiographical works of General von Lettow-Vorbeck and Vizeadmiral Max Loof; the letters of General Jan Smuts and the reminiscences of Admiral King-Hall. He also has combed such journals as *Tanganyike Notes and Records* and the official histories compiled by the several governments involved following the end of hostilities.

The skill with which he has marshalled these sources to recreate a most remarkable war is admirable. This is good informal history.

EDGAR V. WINANS
University of Washington
Seattle

ALABA OGUNSANWO. *China's Policy in Africa: 1958–1971.* Pp. ix, 310. New York: Cambridge University Press, 1974. $19.50.

The period covered by this book has seen significant changes in African politics. Generally, there has been no dearth of writings on developments during this period. There have been many studies of individual countries, processes and institutions, and leaders in Africa. Comparatively little of this published material has been devoted specifically to the emergence of the People's Republic of China as a factor in African development.

This book therefore fills an obvious gap in describing and analyzing Chinese activities and policies from the time that Africa began to receive serious attention from the Peking regime, until three years ago. It is a valuable contribution to an understanding of the contemporary impact on Africa of a world communist power.

The author, lecturer in International Relations at the University of Ife has produced a thorough, detailed, and comprehensive treatment of his subject. Based on meticulous research, his well-written book reflects a painstaking examination of a wide range of sources, including such recognized periodicals as the *Peking Review* and the *China Quarterly* and reports of the New China News Agency (Hsinhua), as well as discussions with officials in England and Africa.

Dr. Ogunsanwo combines perceptive analysis of Chinese ideological goals with a frank discussion of China's pragmatic approach in the applications of these goals to various African countries. He sees China's policy in Africa as a reflection of two influences: her relations as a communist power with the capitalist world, and the internal conflict within world communism resulting from the bitter mutual hostility between herself and Russia.

The contradiction between Chinese ideological commitment to revolution, and her actual support of conventional, conservative, and even reactionary governments is brought out in detailed discussion of such examples as the importation of grain to the value of several million dollars from South Africa, readiness to establish diplomatic relations with the 1963 government in Zanzibar headed by a Sultan, and siding with the aristocratic minority Tutsi against the Hutu peasant majority in Rwanda. A valuable record of China's actual economic involvement in Africa is provided by a description—country by country—of the development of trade, and various projects concerned with financial and technical aid.

In a final chapter the author offers pertinent observations on possible future trends in China's policy in Africa. This chapter would have been improved by a discussion of China's bid for recognition as leader of the third world (comprising 76 nations in Asia and Latin America as well as Africa) as an international force poised against the two superpowers, the United States and Russia. But this is a minor criticism, and does not detract from the value of an excellent addition to available studies of the politics of Africa.

LESLIE RUBIN

Howard University
Washington, D.C.

K. OKOCHI, B. KARSH and S. B. LEVINE, eds. *Workers and Employers in Japan.* Pp. 538. Princeton, N.J.: Princeton University Press, 1974. $20.00.

This volume presents the results of a joint study by two scholars from Princeton and eleven from Tokyo. The imprint *Princeton akamonde* (Princeton through the "Red Gate," that is, Tokyo University) is here justified by a well organized, expert and searching explanation of labor relations in Japan, affording insights into the nature and working of the Japanese society and economy in general.

Japan's current image (from 1950 to the present) is the "economic miracle": 10 percent annual rise in GNP, 15 percent in manufacturing (lately reduced, since troubled oil was poured on this floodtide, to about half those percentages). Japan's previous history is usually explained in terms of a peculiarly complex social psychology (national-solidarist, traditional-paternalist, military-fascist) with a brutally direct resultant: the workers' subordination in low-wage slavery. This book presents a much wider and deeper investigation, amply tracing the basic social dynamics, distinguishing the varying stages and factors in the process.

Even before Japan's capitalist industrialization—which now dates back almost a century—traditional social solidarism, expressed in "lifetime employment" ("tenure" for the worker) conflicted with "merit criteria," at different times, in different ways, as labor supply and market conditions varied. Dichotomy is a chronic feature of Japan. Two sets of values have persisted: a samurai Confucian rationalism and a popular secular kinship system. The Japanese proletariat was formed from poor samurai on the one hand, peasants on the other—with craftsmen pertaining either to the one group or the other. It still reflects these social outlooks.

Training has been by imitation; hence, the stress on "wage and grade" norms for remuneration and promotion. However, the combination of Oriental ethics with Western technology, which has throughout been Modern Japan's special achievement, involving recurrent cruxes of adaptation demanding entrepreneurial innovation, often made personal ability the decisive criterion.

Trade-unionism was not originated by MacArthur; in 1897 a Mr. Takano from California was appointed A.F. of L. Organizer for Japan. Eight American-type craft unions followed, featuring benefit-schemes and initially stressing "social status," but proceeding to "more practical" demands—which led to "harsh suppression." Good education in Japan has contributed to widening wage-differentials, especially between workers in large and small firms: the higher-educated going largely to the former. This is also evident between males and females; utilization of the latter greatly rein-

forced the "dormitory" system and paternalism. By World War I, dichotomy was marked between "craft and industrial" unions (syndicalist, increasingly radical) and "company" unions ("vertically" organized). Militarist Japan fostered the latter.

The American occupation authorities, in the next stage of the dialectical process, freed the radicals and upheld their demands (though not their ideology). Waves of unionization and politicalization followed. Given wide American ignorance of Japanese conditions (p. 50), from the beginning the horses mostly had control over the riders. Zaibatsu and kanbatsu (the so-called financial and bureaucratic cliques) became powerful again, as well as the labor movement, so latterly we have some situation of "countervailing power."

This is a bare summary of matters fully and factually pursued in this book, but it may serve to show the coverage, probingness and topical cogency of this excellent study of the social dynamics of modern Japan.

E. STUART KIRBY
Asian Institute of Technology
Bangkok

SCOTT R. PEARSON and JOHN COWNIE. *Commodity Exports and African Economic Development*. Pp. vii, 285. Lexington, Mass.: Lexington Books, 1974. $17.50.

This book offers three principal contributions to students of commodity exports and economic development. First, the invited authors bring together considerable background material on the principal commodities of several African countries: timber, coffee, and cocoa (Ivory Coast); cocoa and timber (Ghana); coffee (Ethiopia); cotton (Uganda); oil (Nigeria); copper (Zambia); copper (Zaire); and diamonds (Sierra Leone). Second, in their opening and concluding chapters, the principal authors introduce a comparative framework for measuring net social gain from commodity exports. Third, the chapter on Sierra Leone (by Killick) offers some intriguing insights into the comparison of labor-intensive with capital-intensive methods of production, which indicate that *even in mining*, it may be profitable for less developed countries to rely more on labor relatively to machines.

I will not devote much space to the descriptive materials, although they dominate in the number of pages. In all chapters, they are clearly written and comprehensive. To analytical economists, the work of the two principal authors on methodology will be of special interest and controversy. These chapters introduce a concept of net social gain (NSG), measured by the receipts minus expenditures in foreign exchange, less domestic resource costs, and plus externalities (other benefits to the nation, through linkages, employment, and the like). Shadow prices are used in calculating NSG.

It is especially in the use of shadow prices that controversy will arise. First, there is the perennial question of how the shadow prices were arrived at, and whether or not they are sensible. The invited authors are not equally clear on this point. But in addition, there is the question of whether NSG is (or should be) measured in a "value added" sense (the net accounting contribution of commodity exports to the gross domestic product), or whether it represents the difference between what *is* with the commodity exports, and what *would be*, if commodity exports had never been undertaken. The authors note early (p. 4) that if one assumes "that the domestic resource cost of producing a net unit of foreign exchange is exactly equal to the real worth to the economy of that unit, as reflected in its shadow price," then "net social gain to the economy is zero." One wonders whether the test of appropriate shadow price should not be that it does indeed bring equality between cost and worth of foreign exchange, and therefore *always* bring NSG to zero. Any other solution raises questions about the appropriateness of the shadow prices selected, yet to use the definition here proposed would be to wipe out the concept of NSG, which is also nonsense. The best theoretical

answer might be to use those shadow prices which would bring to zero the NSG of all *other* export activities (in the absence of the commodity being analyzed). Then the NSG for the commodity would truly represent the difference between the "is" and "would be" situations. The difficulties of estimating such a "might-have-been" are, of course, enormous.

In sum, the authors have rejected the "value added" concept of net social gain and have moved toward a comparison between the situation with commodity exports and the alternative without. Their methodology is worthy of understanding; they admit the problems of shadow prices (and make all their conclusions contingent upon this problem); but I believe they misjudge the enormity of the risk. The result is that such judgments as (p. 258) that Zaire has a comparative advantage over Zambia in copper production appear very tenuous.

By definition, NSG has three parts: (1) an economic rent, (2) an adjustment for shadow prices, and (3) externalities. But once it has been calculated, it may be differently divided into an efficiency factor and a foreign exchange factor. The coefficient for the former is 1 minus the domestic resource costs divided by the shadow price of foreign exchange. This measures the leverage possessed by a unit of domestic resources in creating foreign exchange. The coefficient for the latter is 1 minus the imported goods, services, and earnings of foreign companies divided by the foreign exchange receipts of the exporters. This reflects the volume of foreign exchange becoming available to the country. The product of these two coefficients equals the net gain coefficient, which is NSG divided by the value of foreign exchange receipts adjusted for the shadow price of foreign exchange. *Provided* that one accepts the definition of NSG (including the shadow prices), these two coefficients supply an interesting method of breaking it down into significant components, possibly for comparisons among commodities and/or countries.

With one exception, the chapters by

invited authors follow a set pattern: first descriptive, then the calculation of NSG. In the final chapter, the principal authors summarize information on NSG by countries and make some comparisons, such as that economic rent varies over an enormous range, with mineral activities high and agriculture and silviculture middling or low; and that external effects (mainly linkages— forward, backward, technological, final demand and fiscal) also differ by commodities—example: final demand linkages are high where domestic factors are intensively used, and low where foreign factors predominate.

The one exception is an outstanding chapter on Sierra Leone by Tony Killick, in which diamond mining is divided into two sectors: the now nationalized mining company, and the Alluvial Diamond Scheme (ADS), which consists of small producers using rudimentary tools. What may surprise many people is that ADS turns out to have both a higher efficiency coefficient and a higher foreign exchange factor than large-scale, capital intensive methods. This raises the fascinating question of whether less developed countries, with severe unemployment, ought not to do their mining through small-scale enterprises widely diffused. This question, which would both challenge the conventional wisdom and offer new ways of approaching unemployment, no doubt yields different answers with different minerals. But it is certainly worthy of much more study than it has received.

JOHN P. POWELSON
University of Colorado
Boulder

ARIEH SHARON. *Planning Jerusalem: The Master Plan for the Old City of Jerusalem and its Environs.* Pp. 211. New York: McGraw-Hill, 1973. $25.00.

Mr. Sharon is a distinguished architect, a member of the "planning team" for "the old city of Jerusalem and its environs." He has been writing about planning in Israel for more than twenty years. This is a sumptuous book, sponsored by the Israeli Ministry of the Interior and the Municipality of Jerusalem. With 71 full-color maps, 175 photographs, 27 plans and 28 reproductions of old maps, this beautiful book traces "the plan in the context of history," it deals with the several walls and gates, with the structure and architecture of the old city. Since the old city came under Israeli control after the Six Day War, it has been the purpose of the Prime Minister to open it up to Jewish occupancy, replacing shabby Arab tenements with modern housing, replacing narrow alleys with broader streets.

Changing the grades of the medieval alleys to permit the introduction of gravity-flow piped water and sewage disposal has left some of these Arab buildings so far above the new street grade that their foundations crumble. The Western ("Wailing") Wall, now freely open to access by Jews, is the scene of jurisdictional disputes among sects, each of which claims its "turf."

The man in charge of the new plan— like myself, lawyer-administrator, not architect—gave me an hour and a half to explain his difficulties to a sympathetic fellow-professional. Every time he has plans ready for a block of twenty flats (some ear-marked for high Israeli officials) the archaeologists suddenly intervene. Not here, part of the wall of Herod is on this site! The act of a young Australian Christian in setting fire to the Mosque of Omar, which honors the stone from which Mohammed ascended to heaven—the third most sacred Moslem shrine—forced Israel to deny public access to the Mosque as too hazardous.

The ridge above the Mount of Olives, one of Christianity's most sacred shrines, is still in Jordanian territory. Its crest is now crowned by one of an American world chain of hotels. These seem to me some political realities that render the planning team's work unrealistic—a basic conflict between the "long-term" plan and the "short-term" concerns of politicians that few planners seem ready to try to resolve.

CHARLES S. ASCHER
Institute of Public Administration
New York

LEONARD WELLER. *Sociology in Israel.* Pp. v, 315. Westport, Conn.: Greenwood Press, 1974. No price.

The State of Israel represents an anomaly in modern political life. It is a developing nation located in a "third-world" region with a European-educated, Western-oriented social structure. This complexity is compounded by ethnic diversity and a powerful religious establishment. It is therefore a perfect setting for social research dealing with inter-group relations and culture conflict, criminology and family life. This book is a comprehensive survey of the impressive body of sociological research executed by Israeli sociologists since the founding of the State in 1948.

Professor Weller, chairman of the Department of Sociology at Bar Ilan University, has done a considerable job compiling and categorizing the literature and organizing it into a comprehensible whole. Among the topics included are the traditional areas of social class, criminology and the family. In addition, subjects of particular concern to the young state, such as religion, immigration and absorption, education and the unique Israeli communal farm, the Kibbutz, occupy chapters in this volume. Further, the disparities and difficulties resulting from the confrontation of oriental Jewish settlers with the dominant Western value system are implicit in much of the material, reflecting a salient cleavage in Israeli life.

The book is not without weaknesses, however. Although it is primarily a survey text one assumes that it might have been organized more imaginatively. Often as not one is merely presented with a series of names, research descriptions and tables with little originality or insight. Even the most cursory survey is incomplete without integration and analysis. This allows the reader to assimilate the heart of the material described and leaves him with provocative concepts which may lead him to search out the original literature. Such effort is often absent in Weller's volume.

Also evident in this work are glaring errors of omission. There is, for example, no mention of divorce or its ramifications. Clearly, in a full chapter dealing with family relations, some time should have been spent on this topic.

Equally conspicuous for its absence is the entire sub-field of political sociology. Little is to be found in relation to voting habits, political attitudes, interest and participation levels and authority patterns. One must question the wisdom of Weller's decision to limit the scope of his study almost exclusively to the work of sociologists (p. 6). Doubtless the political-sociological work of such analysts as Shlomo Avineri and Yehezkel Dror might have better balanced this volume.

Sociology in Israel is an important survey and reference work. It neatly presents the results of twenty-five years of native self-research. Despite its weaknesses it stands as a valuable contribution to international and comparative sociology.

DAVID J. SCHNALL
Staten Island Community College
New York

World Bank Economic Report. *Nigeria: Options for Long-Term Development.* Pp. xi, 256. Baltimore, Md.: The Johns Hopkins University Press, 1974. $12.00. Paperbound, $6.00.

In 1971, the World Bank sent an economic mission to Nigeria under the leadership of Mr. Wouter Tims, presently Director of the World Bank Economic Analysis and Projections Department. This book presents the results of that mission, and it also utilizes material drawn from the findings of 1971 reports of three other similar missions: the World Bank Agricultural Sector Review Mission, a World Bank Transport Sector Review Mission, and a UNESCO Project Identification Mission. The members of the World Bank economic mission, like Mr. Tims, are experienced and knowledgeable economists, population and water supply specialists, loan officers, and statisticians. As suggested by their names—T. K. Osgood, C. Wilkinson, E. Lim, D. C. Rao, B. H. Decaux, V. P. Gandhi, M. Leiserson, P. W. Whitford, R. Rajagopalan, D. Pearce, and C. D. Papavassilov—they come from varying countries and regions of the world.

In his "Forward" to the volume, Hollis B. Chenery, the World Bank Vice President for Development Policy, addresses it to a sophisticated audience—"scholars and practitioners in the field of economics and social development." This reviewer agrees that it is mostly this audience that would be able to appreciate the intricate technicalities which fill the 256 pages. Some administrators with very strong economic, mathematical, and/or statistical background may also find the book useful, clearly not as a regular handbook but as a guide to economic planning.

The entire book, which presents an optimistic appraisal of Nigerian economy, contains a general summary followed by thirteen chapters sequentially titled: "Economic Trends and Development Policies," "Employment and Income Distribution," "Investment Programs and Policies," "Fiscal and Monetary Trends and Prospects," "The Balance of Payments and Aid Requirements," "Petroleum," "Agriculture, Manufacturing, Education and Infrastructure," "Options and Implications for Long-Term Development," "Long-Term Projection Model of the Economy," "Agriculture," "Fiscal Trends and Prospects," "Education and Training," and "Transportation and Power." A very loaded discussion of the subject of each chapter is interspersed with illustrative statistical tables, and there are altogether some eighty-two of these tables in the main text. In addition, charts and maps are used to make some points clearer in several of the chapters. A "Statistical Annex" containing fifty additional tables also appears at the end of the book. This is particularly useful, and for these tables, one-page presentations of "Sources" of data and some explanation

"Notes" are provided. The tables themselves contain data that include population, employment, public debt, crude oil production, and the like.

In sum, the book is very analytical. Up-to-date statistical data are utilized, and there are some keen future projections on Nigerian economy. To researchers and others interested in the assessment of aspects of the economy, it is an invaluable contribution as a source book.

JULIUS EMEKA OKOLO
Howard University
Washington, D.C.

EUROPE

BERNARD E. BROWN. *Protest in Paris: Anatomy of a Revolt.* Pp. vii, 240. Morristown, N.J.: General Learning Press, 1974. $8.95.

The historian tends to be uneasy with the presentation of an event of contemporary history, such as Bernard Brown's study of the events of May 1968 in France, when it is declared to be "in the tradition of the critical essay based on historical materials" and to provide "building blocks for a theory of revolution." Are these historical materials sufficiently weighty to carry the mass of analytical conclusions that are to rest upon them? Does the escape into theory add to our understanding of the events themselves? And can a study devoted largely to an analysis of actors in one short historical drama in one country add much to the theory of revolution in modern industrial society?

The opening chapter adds no new details to existing descriptions of the student and worker revolt, but does provide a good, brief synopsis of the major events. Anecdote and synthesis combine to give a readable account of the dramatic two months of barricades in the Latin Quarter and of the general strike in the rest of France. A highly critical summation of the views of Aron, Touraine, and Crozier dismisses the abstractions of several of France's leading sociologists, and leads into a first-class account, "Red Flags, Black Flags," of the principal revolutionary groups among the student leadership. Here Brown provides a devastating demonstration of the fragmentation that condemned the revolt to failure. These failings are examined at greater length in a later chapter when Brown convincingly shows that the main reason for the students' failure was the refusal of the French Communist party to indulge in any alliance with "adventurists" to its left or to use the revolt for any other purpose than immediate economic concessions. Here however Brown invalidates his own earlier statement that the revolt "came close to the seizure of power" (p. vii). The student revolt demonstrated that a government unwilling to use the full force at its disposal can be compelled to tolerate, for a short period, large-scale disorder in one area of its capital city; but the lack of an alliance of students and workers, or rather the refusal of the workers to put their genuine power at the disposal of the revolutionary student leadership, made the seizure of power impossible.

For this reason the events of May 1968 are not central to a theory of revolution in a society strained by the process of modernization. As Brown himself states, "the lesson of revolutionary uprisings in the modern era is that power is seized not against the state, but through the state." Talk of takeover of power was restricted to revolutionary student leaders whose ephemeral ascendance was due mainly to widespread dissatisfaction with specific conditions of university life. The theorizing of the extremists lies either on the historical fringes of revolutionary Marxism or, as Brown usefully shows, in the peculiarly French, or even Left Bank, phenomenon of the linking of art and politics that the "situationists" inherited from the surrealist followers of André Breton. Thus the value and fascination of this book rest in the dissection of the political aspects of a distinctively French student revolt rather than in its contribution to an understanding of the general nature of modern revolutions.

F. ROY WILLIS
University of California
Davis

SYLVIA KOWITT CROSBIE. A *Tacit Alliance: France and Israel from Suez to the Six Day War*. Pp. ix, 280. Princeton, N.J.: Princeton University Press, 1974. $13.50.

Almost from its beginning in 1948, the State of Israel effected with the French government—or, more accurately, with various of the French ministries and segments of the defense industries of France—an extraordinary degree of military and scientific-technologial cooperation. Indeed, during the Fourth Republic and as long as David Ben Gurion was Prime Minister of Israel, the hard core relationships between the two countries were conducted through the ministries of defense. Since Ben Gurion was also Israel's Minister of Defense and he had a De Gaullean view as to how a country should be led, he conducted Israel's part of these relationships outside the Israeli diplomatic establishment, which was neither consulted nor generally advised of what was going on. All it knew was that, somehow, Israel was getting from France the military equipment essential to its survival and the technological-scientific cooperation needed to lay the groundwork for defense industries of its own. On the French side, until De Gaulle took charge at the end of the 1950s, the weakness of the French executive branch, resting upon fragile coalitions, with ministers pursuing their own interests, policies, inclinations and even careers, and with cabinet solidarity virtually non-existent, the Israeli defense negotiators had extraordinary room for maneuver and a corresponding success.

This subtle alliance relationship has never been depicted so meticulously as by Mrs. Crosbie. She began with the advantage of having served in the Israeli Ministry for Foreign Affairs and while that Ministry was excluded from the "tacit alliance" during Ben Gurion's career, his successor, Levi Eshkol, had more orthodox ideas of how foreign affairs should be conducted and clued it in. Intrigued by what went on, how and with what effects, Mrs. Crosbie has painstakingly combed through memoirs of participants, studies of Franco-Israeli relations by non-participants, and periodicals, supplementing these with interviews with forty-two French and twenty-three Israeli government officials, generals, diplomats and knowledgeable private citizens. This painstaking exploration of a shadowy relationship has been executed with objectivity, instinctual understanding, and economy of words which make it an extremely illuminating addition to the literature of Franco-Israeli relations, Middle East politics, French politics before and under De Gaulle, international defense and intelligence relationships; and some of the problems which diplomatic establishments have when chiefs of state and prime ministers distrust them and shrewdly perceive opportunities for action outside the limits of conventional diplomacy. All in all, this painstaking study is both perceptive and compact.

SMITH SIMPSON
Georgetown University
Washington, D.C.

RONA M. FIELDS. *A Society on the Run: A Psychology of Northern Ireland.* Pp. 216. Baltimore, Md.: Penguin Books, 1973. $2.15.

ROSEMARY HARRIS. *Prejudice and Tolerance in Ulster: A Study of Neighbours and Strangers in a Border Community.* Pp. vii, 234. Totowa, N.J.: Rowman and Littlefield, 1972. $10.00.

Violence in Northern Ireland continues to attract social scientists who, perhaps, otherwise would have no interest in the Irish. The increased attention generally has benefited Irish studies, accomplishing field work and presenting new perspectives to complement the more traditional research of historians, demographers, and social anthropologists. *A Society on the Run* is such a book, written after the author had spent only about six months total time in Ireland in the course of three separate visits.

Rona M. Fields' primary concern is a description of the consequences for the individual of living in a society which is "on the run." By this she does not mean having too much to do in too little time. Instead she means a constant fear,

a dread, through which "everything else is perceived in a skewed perspective, because the constant need for self protection makes various details magnified or diminished."

Using what she calls "tools of the psychologist's trade," such as personality tests, and counseling and clinical interviewing techniques, she discusses what "being on the run" means to some: members of the British army in Northern Ireland; men behind wires in internment camps; children growing up under conditions of violence; women living in a male dominated society; and political leaders. The author writes in a lively style, and does indeed provide interesting insights into the social-psychological conditions of several persons living in Northern Ireland.

The book is mistitled, however, in that it is about various individuals and not about the society as such. The author makes little use of systematic quantitative techniques, and instead, in her own words, walks "a methodological tightrope, the strands of which are history, journalism and sociology." As a result, there is no indication in the book of the degree to which her informants and test subjects represent anyone except themselves. The basic question of the prevalence of the "on the run" syndrome among the Northern Irish remains unanswered.

Prejudice and Tolerance in Ulster, on the other hand, is aptly titled. Working in the tradition of participant observation, Rosemary Harris presents a richly detailed account of the daily lives of several households in a small Northern Irish village and in its surrounding rural area. As a social anthropologist, her main theoretical interest is in understanding the persistent stereotypes which separate persons who know each other well. She argues that the Northern Irish are well suited for such a study because, unlike societies divided by race or language, both Catholics and Protestants in her village to a large extent shared a common culture. Many of these neighbors, furthermore, had close and friendly relationships across religious lines. In spite of this, hostile religious stereotypes remained and determined much of everyday life, especially the important matter of marriage and kinship.

Harris approaches her task in a straightforward manner. Her opening chapters describe the physical setting of the area under study; then come chapters on the family system, household networks, and kinship ties. With this background, she discusses what values and attitudes Protestants and Catholics shared in common before delineating the social separation of the two groups. After examining religious stereotyping in the village, she devotes three chapters to the influence on Protestant prejudice of denominationalism, of income and geographic location of residence, and of "class" structure. In a concluding chapter she considers the relevance of her findings to a better understanding of the general situation in Northern Ireland.

Neither Harris nor Fields provides a "solution" to the strife in Northern Ireland. In fact, in spite of their quite different approaches, one is impressed with their common conclusion that the religious dichotomy existing in that nation is as important a social reality as is age or sex. Both books are useful as supplementary reading on the Northern Irish question.

ROBERT E. KENNEDY, JR.
University of Minnesota
Minneapolis

STEPHEN KOSS, ed. *The Pro-Boers: The Anatomy of an Antiwar Movement.* Pp. v, 280. Chicago, Ill.: University of Chicago Press, 1973. $12.00.

A. J. ANTHONY MORRIS. *Radicalism Against War, 1906–1914: The Advocacy of Peace and Retrenchment.* Totowa, N.J.: Rowman and Littlefield, 1974. Pp. 448. $17.50.

The outbreak of the Boer War in 1899, when the British Empire was at its zenith, brought forth not only intense patriotic fervor but also an impassioned attack on the imperialistic mentality. Ebullient Jingoism, inspired by Cecil Rhodes's dramatic activities and by the first fighting in the Transvaal,

effectively drowned out the voice of those protesting the war; yet these voices were eloquent.

Stephen Koss, professor of history at Columbia, has judiciously selected some 120 speeches and articles from 1899 to 1902 opposing, on moral or economic or political grounds, the imperialistic mentality and the attempt to crush the handful of South African farmers. The protestants were a diverse lot: pacifists, idealists, "little Englanders," sentimentalists who considered the sturdy Boers wholly admirable and the British as bullies, humanitarians who were shocked by the horrors of concentration camps and the burning of Boer farms. (Parallels with America's involvement in Vietnam are striking.)

Indiscriminately dubbed "pro-Boers," ridiculed by the press, their meetings harassed by mobs, the opponents of war were too individualistic and disparate to launch a united political campaign. Their strongest arguments fell on deaf ears — for example, that the government could not say what the nation was fighting *for,* that the war was turning most of the world against Britain, that it was adventurism by Rhodes and not any important issue that was at stake, that thousands of young men were being uselessly killed and wounded, that Britain's reputation for justice and tolerance was being seriously undermined. The "khaki election" of 1900, with Joseph Chamberlain's assurance to Parliament that the war was "effectively over," was the answer to the dissidents. Yet the war dragged on until 1902; Boer commandos and guerrilla fighting continued to reveal the antiquated methods of the army, and the tiny Boer forces stood off the imperial army for thirty months.

The aftermath of the war saw the peace movement gain impressive strength. In 1906, after a decade of Conservatism, the Liberals swept into power (401 Liberals to 157 Tory Unionists) with a strong show of idealism. Many Liberals were "Radicals"—that is, anti-imperialists, advocates of universal disarmament, of friendly relations with all countries, of open diplomacy, of settlement of international disputes by arbitration. The Radical cause was often aided by those who, like Lloyd George and Churchill, were "economists," as Morris calls those who desired a curb on expenditures for dreadnoughts and armies so that money might be available for domestic reform.

Anthomy Morris, senior research officer at the London School of Economics, has made an exhaustive study of the parliamentary scene from 1906 to 1914 as it relates to the advocacy of peace and retrenchment. One is led through the intricacies of international diplomacy, the negotiation of ententes with France and Russia, the effects of Balkan and other crises, and the perennial suspicion of German expansion and the Kaiser's truculence. Morris has apparently examined every single speech in the House of Commons and every article in important newspapers and journals bearing on the political expression of idealism during the eight years of his study.

His book teems with footnotes, hundreds of them not merely citing sources but containing informative sidelights. He assumes thorough knowledge of British political institutions on the part of his readers, and also of many historical events that provide background for parliamentary debates. Because he concentrates so completely on the struggle for peace and disarmament, one must remind himself of other weighty issues (such as curbing the House of Lords or instituting social reform) that concerned Parliament at the time.

Koss's 25-page Introduction (curiously printed with irregular margins) and his brief prefaces to the selected speeches and articles by and about the pro-Boers are admirable in their concision; they tell the reader precisely what he needs to know without overwhelming him with detail. Morris, on the other hand, is concerned to tell the full story. He omits little that bears on the parliamentary struggle for disarmament and peace. His scholarly book is well worth the time and concentrated

attention it requires. Only its price is inhibiting.

JAMES G. LEYBURN
Washington and Lee University
Lexington
Virginia

GREGORY J. MASSELL. *The Surrogate Proletariat.* Pp. vii, 448. Princeton, N.J.: Princeton University Press, 1974. $18.50.

The "Surrogate Proletariat" is a term used by the author to describe the Moslem women Soviet officials tried to use as a lever to undermine the strong solidarity of the family and kinship systems of the tribal peoples living in a remote area of Central Asia during the early years of the Soviet revolution (1919–29). Coercive methods having failed, the officials tried other ways of reorganizing the area along the new revolutionary lines. One of them was to use the native women, who appeared exploited and degraded by their own group, as a sort of "deprived proletariat" who could be induced to help break up the traditional family systems. However, contrary to the picture presented to the outside world, these women did, in fact, have a great deal of power "behind the throne" in their respective groups, and although the Soviets used them successfully to undermine male authority, they failed to develop new goals and institutions which would substantiate the women's new positions of power. In the end, this experiment was not successful enough to be used as a model for further attempts to force change on unwilling peoples.

Those who are aware of the great gaps in our knowledge of human behavior will welcome this insightful reconstruction of an obscure epoch in history. For it is a reconstruction that will be useful even today to many countries which are struggling to initiate change in traditional and isolated societies. In the case of the Soviets it was a matter of transforming a "feudal-patriarchal mode of life" directly into "modern" socialism. The actors in the scene were a fascinating lot, such as the tragic Native Central Asian officials who acted as middlemen between the native peoples and the Soviet officials, but were never trusted by the new regime and eventually painfully liquidated; the newly recruited field organizers sent to change the lives of people who lived in a completely different world in terms of ethnicity, religion and way of life; and the members of the Moslem Surrogate Proletariat who were recruited to assist in the transformation—marginal women such as orphans and young widows whose lives did not follow the normal tribal family pattern.

Historical data never tell the whole story, especially when the writer is dealing with such a remote area of the world, and, in this case, an area which until recently had been closed to scholars. The author acknowledges that he has reconstructed this dramatic period of history "as much on inference as on evidence." He has used official publications of the Soviet government and Communist Party, the works of historians, ethnographers, sociologists and lawyers, and as many eye-witness reports as could be found. The result is a brilliant description of the events, so logically and carefully presented that the reader feels that the author's major assumptions must be correct.

The extensive bibliography contains references to many Soviet documents never before listed in a publication of the Western World.

AILEEN D. ROSS

McGill University
Montreal
Canada

BEN-CION PINCHUK. *The Octobrists in the Third Duma, 1907–1912.* Pp. vii, 232. Seattle: University of Washington, 1974. $10.50.

Will Rogers was fond of saying that he was a member of no organized political party, that he was a Democrat. The same observation could have been made by an Octobrist in respect to his own political affiliation. Professor Pin-

chuk notes in this work that although the Octobrists chose to call themselves the Union of October 17, they were unified only in their general commitment to work within the framework of the October Manifesto. Attempts to define more specific goals or to develop any coherent organizational structure proved sterile. In the Third Duma, the Octobrists tended to accept the leadership of A. I. Gunchkov whose qualities of leadership probably outweighed ideology in giving direction and purpose to the actions of the party.

The Octobrists generally cooperated with the government and served as the fulcrum on which P. A. Stolypin anchored the shifting coalitions he employed to enact his programs. The marriage with the government was a union without love, and the Emperor (the author unhappily employs the terms tsar and tsarism) himself maintained a consistent distaste for the leaders of the party. Stolypin pursued his goals, sometimes with a legislative mandate and sometimes without. He operated in between the Emperor and the court camarilla on the one hand and the Duma on the other, frustrating the aspirations of the constitutionalists while forcing the unreconstructed representatives of the old order to allow the Duma more latitude than they were willing to concede. In the end, Professor Pinchuk finds the Octobrists disillusioned and sees in their disillusionment the basis for the Octobrist leaders playing prominent roles in the February, 1917, revolution.

This present work suffers from several defects. The first third of the book especially is poorly organized, making it both repetitive and difficult to follow. While he is concerned with the Octobrists, nowhere does the author systematically analyze the composition of the Octobrist membership of the Third Duma nor does he acquaint the reader with any of the cast of characters. Professor Pinchuk identifies individual Octobrist deputies only as they appear to play some role in the narrative rather than delineating in any systematic way the qualities, outlook, and relative importance of even the leading figures. Even Guchkov, who occupies so much of the author's attention and is nearly always at center stage, is not the subject of any comprehensive profile that might provide the reader with a greater understanding of his leadership role.

The book itself is poorly produced. The type is much too fine and makes sustained reading tiring. Moreover, type is badly set with some words separated and others run together, compounding the reading difficulty. The decision to hide footnotes away at the end of the text is always to be regretted. Even so, the general reader will find the book useful, although the specialist may wish to wait for a more definitive study.

FORREST A. MILLER
Vanderbilt University
Nashville
Tennessee

JOHN ROSSELLI. *Lord William Bentinck: The Making of a Liberal Imperialist, 1774–1839.* Pp. 384. Berkeley: University of California, 1974. $15.00.

John Rosselli has undertaken a study of the fascinating career of the somewhat eccentric Lord William Cavendish Bentinck. We follow Bentinck's development in his numerous posts, from Madras to Sicily and finally to the Governor-Generalship of India. The author has traced for us the major ideological influences on Bentinck—early nineteenth-century liberalism, Evangelicalism, and very limited doses of utilitarianism. Furthermore, Rosselli endeavors to delineate Bentinck's attempts to implement his firmly-held beliefs.

One of the major sections of Rosselli's study deals with Bentinck's role in the development of "Empire and Nationality." Lord William's reforming liberalism led him, as Governor-General of India, to hope "that Indians should become so 'civilized'—which to him had come to mean that they should adopt Western ways, industrialize their country, and perhaps turn Christian— as to ensure a final parting the least

hurtful possible" (p. 111). To effect this end Bentinck was willing to rely upon what Rosselli terms "benevolent interference" (p. 44) enforced by "British despotic rule" (p. 127). During Bentinck's gubernatorial tenure in Bengal, among other acts, he abolished *sati*, the self-immolation of widows, and decreed that English would henceforth be the language of administration. Thus, "Europeanization," for Bentinck, provided the key to India's "development."

Rosselli's sympathetic study of Bentinck seems weakest and most defensive when it approaches this discussion of the issue of "Europeanization" and modernization. Bentinck did not seem to draw a distinction between "Europeanization" and modernization, and Roselli does not examine the differences inherent in these concepts. The means used in attaining a given goal, however, cannot but affect the final form that goal will take. By opting for "Europeanization" and ignoring indigenous attempts at modernization, Bentinck alienated many of the leaders of Bengali society. As David Kopf has forcefully argued in his *British Orientalism and the Bengal Renaissance* (University of California Press, 1969), "Europeanization," as a means of modernizing Bengal, contributed to a repudiation of the Indian cultural heritage. Thus, when examined from the vantage point of Indian cultural history, many of Bentinck's well-intentioned actions, such as the abolition of *sati*, may be viewed as culturally disruptive. Rosselli's work suffers for it presents a less than complete picture of the Bengali milieu in which Lord William worked.

This may be one result of the format Rosselli has chosen to use. The study is not a straightforward narrative biography. Instead, after a brief analysis of Bentinck's development up to his governor-generalship, Rosselli devotes the remaining two-thirds of his work to a "series of essays on historical problems . . . which . . . this one man's career illuminates" (p. 12). The long essay on "Empire and Nationality" is followed by essays dealing with Bentinck's agrarian and judicial reforms, his attempts to aid in British Indian economic development, his role as an administrator, and his years as the Parliamentary representative of "radical" Glasgow. Rosselli acknowledges that the method used provides "coherence of argument" (p. 12). A concomitant risk involved in such an approach is the oversimplification of issues which Bentinck faced. One cannot help but feel that the series of essays presented provides a less than complete picture of the complexities of the societies in which Bentinck lived and ruled.

These flaws may be a result of the limitations imposed, in part, by the format selected for Rosselli's study. Keeping this in mind, however, the book remains a well-written and useful analysis recommended to scholars interested in the era.

DIANA TONSICH
University of Pennsylvania
Philadelphia

EZRA N. SULEIMAN. *Politics, Power, and Bureaucracy in France: The Administrative Elite.* Pp. viii, 439. Princeton, N.J.: Princeton University Press, 1974. $20.00.

Professor Suleiman has produced an impressive volume in three major areas. He conceived, researched, organized and wrote a detailed exploration and analysis of the French higher civil service as an integral part of the politico-administrative system of contemporary France which updates the Walter Sharp version of 1931. Furthermore, he has successfully (this reviewer believes) punctured the "stalemated society" and/or *la societé bloquée* theses, especially in the version of Michel Crozier. Most importantly, this study of interaction of the highest officials and *fonctionnaires* with the elected politicians demonstrates rather conclusively that the modern French governmental bureaucracy is neither totally subservient nor totally autonomous, but an institution that functions with most other societal institutions in a unique dynamic and non-Anglo-Saxon fashion.

The empirical examination of Suleiman makes extensive use of survey data concerning the background and behavior of the bureaucracy, but it is based on a wide range of recent studies which are interestingly linked to illustrate the nature, scope and role of the centralized and powerful higher civil servants. The author relies heavily on the monographic works of J. Meynaud, A. Girard, J. Siwek-Pouydesseau, C. Debbasch and J. C. Thoenig-E. Friedberg in addition to theoretical constructions of sociologists and political scientists on both sides of the Atlantic. Yet, Suleiman has put together a noteworthy contribution which has its own distinctive qualities. For example, the move from the Fourth Republic's "institutionalization of crises" approach is carefully drawn without resorting to clichés or myths, but emphasizing the reality of reform within a state of flux in relationships and policies. Important as they are, the ministerial-civil servant conflicts are not emphasized as the only framework for inspecting the bureaucracy's power in the political system. Suleiman moves from Paris to the provinces, depicting the relationship of local prefects, mayors and regional representatives of the central administration to those central authorities. By focusing on the responsiveness and autonomy questions in the national-local spheres, the author not only draws a more complete portrait of bureaucracy but also gives an insight into the paramount role of the ministerial cabinet not vividly exposed before in the English language. The foremost value for many students may emerge in the sections on the role perceptions of *hauts fonctionnaires* and the conflicts and means of their resolution within the Gaullist era politico-administrative hierarchy.

The recent publication of John Armstrong's comparative and historical picture of administrative elites did a commendable job in the French parts, but Suleiman goes deeper into the why and hows of the recruitment process, education, social class and primarily, the core institutional mechanisms of the central elite. Furthermore, Suleiman is more aware of recent developments and studies. The two works do more than fill the large gap in our knowledge; they define the specific aspects of change and continuity in the Gaullist era in terms of political power and decision-making in the higher civil service.

Suleiman's major conclusions need to be considered by all serious students. They include the fact that the administrative corps is not representative of society yet can be responsive to it; that conflict between politicians and civil servants continues but is diminished substantially by new role perceptions which bring political chiefs closer to their workers; that cooperation between ministers and bureaucrats in public service often results in conflict between different departments and their respective civil servants no matter what type of regime or the degree of ministerial stability or instability; and that transformation in the Fifth Republic with its majority party, greater coherence and continuity in governmental policies and the increased collaboration among ministers have all had a perceptible impact on bureaucracy. The central question is therefore whether such a technocratic, unrepresentative, homogeneous elite is responsible for France's backwardness. The question of technocracy and the popular "stalemate" theses are demonstrated as defective in Suleiman's last chapter.

There are limitations to the study, but all are evident to the reader and considered by the author. The perspective is overwhelmingly from the administrators' side, not the deputy, or President or rural farmer. The book treats only the bureaucrats in the highest positions of the national level and in the regional structure, neglecting a comparable depth (and perhaps illustrating differences) of middle-level or lower echelon servants. Also, there is no consideration of interaction between the public and private elites in France, but this appears to be the subject of the next Suleiman effort. Despite these points, the work is a highly concen-

trated view of modern French politics in which the recent years appear to present a novel situation for France in which the governmental institutions and bureaucracy are used by a relatively cohesive political force in the formation of public policy.

PIERRE-HENRI LAURENT
Tufts University
Medford
Massachusetts

F. O. SHYLLON. *Black Slaves in Britain.* Pp. xi, 252. London: Oxford University Press, 1974. $14.50.

Through a careful examination of the facts, this work systematically destroys the myth that Chief Justice Mansfield's 1772 decision in the case of James Somerset made slavery illegal in England. In point of fact his ruling was much narrower and stipulated only that black slaves could not be forcibly removed from the country. Shyllon delineates the activities of a powerful interest group who had solid economic reasons for advocating perpetuation of the institution and who rightly reckoned that even the slightest legal breakthrough by advocates of abolition was an ominous portent for the future. Likewise, the endeavors of Granville Sharp and other devoted humanitarians are analyzed in considerable detail. Both sides in the controversy readily resorted to the law for support, and the central theme of *Black Slaves in Britain* in large measure follows a legalistic path.

The work is solidly grounded in both manuscript and printed sources, chief among which are Sharp's voluminous writings and his papers at Hardwicke Court, Gloucester. Furthermore, the most important of Shyllon's interpretations are convincing. He clearly demonstrates that attitudinal change among Britons towards the institution of slavery was a slower and less pervasive development than historians have traditionally believed. Indeed, moral suasion, while an omnipresent feature on the British political scene of the late eighteenth and early nineteenth centuries thanks to the efforts of Sharp and others, was not the decisive factor in the demise of slavery. Changing economic attitudes and conditions resulted in pressures, almost totally divorced from those exerted by humanitarian interests, which ultimately ended slavery in Britain as well as throughout the Empire.

The latter consideration focuses attention on what this reviewer considers the book's principal weakness: insufficient discussion of the correlation between opposition to slavery within Britain and that which led to the parliamentary decisions of 1807 and 1833 ending first the slave trade and then slavery throughout the far-flung reaches of Britain's splendid imperial edifice. Certainly the developments were closely related. Another shortcoming, albeit an understandable one, is the fact that the author, an African, occasionally allows his personal sentiments too much scope. For example, Shyllon's statement that "British historians have used too much imagination and too little sympathy when writing about Africa, Africans, and people of African ancestry" (p. xi) unjustly lumps all British students of the African past in a single category. These considerations having been duly noted, the overall importance of the study remains undeniable. Shyllon has given us a revisionist account of the forces which coalesced to end slavery in Britain, and future students of the subject in its manifold ramifications will be indebted to him.

JAMES A. CASADA

Winthrop College
Rock Hill
South Carolina

M. J. SYDENHAM. *The First French Republic, 1792–1804.* Pp. 378. Berkeley: The University of California Press, 1974. $13.00.

Here is a solid, informing study of France from the ending of the monarchy to the establishment of the Empire. The focus is on French politics as they responded to the interplay of proponents for differing regimes. Through all this, Sydenham avers, "the most general and the most enduring desire of the men of the Revolution" was for "the rule of law and the end of arbitrary government" (p. 9). He holds further that rather than ending the Revolution, Thermidor made it necessary to start again the revolutionary task of founding a widely accepted constitutional republic. Not surprisingly then, he allots over a third of this book to the Directory, a topic that too many authors pass by or shirk.

Although the political events from 1792–1804 form a convoluted and often obscure story, Sydenham narrates it with clarity, but in dealing with crises he packs little tension into his muscular prose. He is alert for battles that influence policy but he shows little concern for sociological and quantitative history. Without trafficking in scandal he enriches his writing with interesting sidelights and personal descriptions. He narrates and describes men's actions rather than judging them; he is no Whig. Sydenham reflects the influences of Albert Soboul and Georges Lefebvre and shows preference for the memoirs of A. F. Milo, Comte de Melito, Pierre Louis Roederer, the Marquis de Caulincourt, and Antoine Thibaudeau as sources.

Aside from a competent, detailed, and valuable narration of twelve troubled and significant years, what does one get from this book? A reader finds a narrative much concerned with the continuing efforts to establish a constitutional Republic; even in Brumaire some sought such a regime. One finds the author's view that the Directory suffered from inadequate constitutional structure, lack of confidence, and the inability to form a great center party. A reader finds Sydenham's judgment that the coup d'etat of 18 Fructidor made the executive independent of the legislative power, led to the breaking off of Anglo-French negotiations and to the Peace of Leoben, and indirectly improved the position of Napoleon. A reader further finds how the coup of 22 Floreal seemingly benefited the Directory but in fact began its decline. These two coups had effectively stifled moderation and compromise.

The usefulness of this competent and careful book is enhanced by its extensive chronology, its annotated bibliography, and its collection of biographical sketches. It is a creditable addition to the literature of the French Revolution.

GARLAND DOWNUM
Northern Arizona University
Flagstaff

ROBERT G. WESSON. *The Russian Dilemma: A Political and Geopolitical View.* Pp. vi, 228. New Brunswick, N.J.: Rutgers University Press, 1974. $12.50.

The title of this volume so accurately suggests its contents that the review will proceed by analyzing the elements of the title. Wesson writes about Russia rather than the Soviet Union, even though his account, in considerable part an historical one, comes up to the present time. He looks upon the Soviet Union as a Russian Empire, and even at times includes socialist East Europe as part of the empire. The "Russian Dilemma," as he sees it, largely involves the strains on this empire caused by a number of factors, political and geopolitical, that are impinging upon Russia at the end of the Twentieth Century.

There are really two themes that are played and replayed throughout the book. The first is the geopolitical one, and Wesson states it at the outset when he asserts that his purpose is "to relate Russia's development more closely to the geographic situation in which its people found themselves at the end of medieval times." The second theme, which is implied in the last sentence and in what was said above, is the familiar one of historical persistence, the more it changes the more it remains the same: the Twentieth Century Russian Empire is a good deal more a direct descendent of the Nineteenth Century one than most analysts (in Russia or out) have indicated. This theme eventually overwhelms the first and becomes the major message of the book.

Neither major theme is novel, of course. This suggests, on the one hand, that Wesson is talking about matters that numerous other people also consider important, and, on the other, that he will be hard put to find very much to say that

is new. The first half of the book has very little that is unfamiliar. It is basically a good synthesis of well-known theories about Russian historical development, which relies heavily on the standard sources. Chapter four, "The Leninist Resynthesis," firmly establishes the idea of "Autocracy Restored" (one of the chapter's subtitles). A particularly good section of the chapter discusses Lenin's borrowing of the terminology and forms of Western systems. But in this, says Wesson, he was "only following the secular Russian pattern of using Western tools and ideas for the strength of a non-Western Empire." Concludes the author, "the Leninist renewal brought little that was truly new."

The last half of the book includes a good deal more new material. Chapter five is the crucial chapter of the book, but in many ways it is the most disappointing. Entitled "Soviet Ambivalence," Wesson here writes of a number of contradictions in behavior and outlook that have characterized Russian and Soviet history, and between which Russia has vacillated. This is an eminently reasonable rubric under which to generalize about Soviet behavior, and Wesson has introduced a great deal of relevant information to support the concept. In spite of this, the chapter lacks the necessary focus. The author does not indicate from the outset what he is aiming to demonstrate. This the reader must gradually pull out himself by careful reading combined with reflection on the hint given in the chapter title, only to find in the last long paragraph of the chapter the kind of focus that would have helped so much at the beginning. This circuitous way of getting to the point is most evident in chapter five, but is found throughout the volume. It is the kind of flaw that probably could have been corrected, at least in part, by tighter editing.

Wesson draws his picture of Russian political development with extremely broad strokes, making dubious his suggestion (p. ix) that the analysis "may have predictive value." If the author has in mind the deterministic view that certain great patterns in Russian and

Soviet history keep being repeated, perhaps one can talk of prediction. But this is hardly the kind of prediction, based on rigorous data analysis, that current social scientists have in mind.

These problems should not detract from the positive features of the book. Wesson's study is facilely written and demonstrates erudition and a broad grasp of relevant materials. He seeks and achieves a high level of generalization, and has the ability to turn a good phrase. The problems he anticipates for the Soviet Union after the present phase of "Leninism Decadent" are stimulating to consider.

DONALD D. BARRY
Lehigh University
Bethlehem
Pennsylvania

C. ANNE WILSON. *Food and Drink in Britain*. Pp. 472. New York: Barnes & Noble, 1974. $17.50.

C. Anne Wilson has used the evidence of archaeological finds (bones, shells, utensils), records of later commerce in foodstuffs, and many other scattered sources of information, but especially cookbooks (*anglice* "cookery books"). Indeed, the whole subject is treated somewhat like a cookbook. Each general classification of food has a chapter to itself and each chapter has its own chronological organization beginning with the Stone Age. This may offend the historian but perhaps no other arrangement would have been much better. As the author says, "This is a history book, but it is also a recipe book."

The recipes, however, are the sticking point. Anyone who has seriously considered the present day proliferation of cookbooks and the culinary pages of newspapers and magazines must be convinced that many of them owe more to the free-wheeling imaginations of the writers than to sober practice; and most people will find it hard to believe that some of the recipes given in this book are not open to the same objection. The author herself finds it necessary to cast doubt on one or two recipes on just this count. It is also doubtful that cooks, even in upper-class families, could then usually read the cookbooks anyway.

What it comes to is that recipes can be misleading evidence because it is difficult to assess the extent of their use. No doubt the upper classes benefited from them more than others did. Naturally we do not read much about the diet of the poor, but various observations suggest that they did better generally (times of famine excepted) than is usually supposed.

The biggest problems were the coarseness of much of the available food in the Middle Ages, the necessity of preserving food for times of scarcity, and the immense role played by flavorings. The old goat had to be baited to death and then pounded to a pulp to make him edible; stockfish, imported as early as the ninth century, would last forever but it had to be soaked and pounded before use. Salt, spices, honey, sugar (often six or eight kinds of flavorings to a single dish) made food acceptable, at first from necessity, later from habit. Beginning with the dairy chapter, especially the section on cheeses, the work gets away somewhat from the cookbook motif. On the whole the book presents us with an immense store of significant, esoteric, and entertaining information.

CHESTER H. KIRBY
Brown University
Providence
Rhode Island

LATIN AMERICA

CHARLES D. AMERINGER. *The Democratic Left in Exile: The Antidictatorial Struggle in the Caribbean, 1945–1959*. Pp. 352. Coral Gables, Fla.: University of Miami Press, 1974. $19.95.

During the late 1940s and most of the 1950s, when dictatorship was the common form of government in the Caribbean, "a unique generation of men from a number of Caribbean countries collaborated for the realization of the democratic ideal" (p. 298). Known collectively as "the Democratic Left," their ranks included Romulo Betancourt of Venezuela, Jose Figueres of Costa Rica and Grau San Martin of Cuba. Their respective movements were considered democratic because of their commitment to democratic values, while their concern with nationalism, agrarian reform, social welfare and economic planning placed them, in the context of their time, on the left. In *The Democratic Left in Exile*, Charles D. Ameringer chronicles the anti-dictatorial struggle of these men and their followers, focusing on "who fought, how they fought, and where and why they fought" (p. 298).

In many ways, the book can be considered a study in frustration. Forced into exile, few truly effective tactics were available for the overthrow of the Caribbean dictators. Initially the movement was able to launch a series of unsuccessful invasions from the few countries briefly governed by its supporters. With the advent of Batista and Perez Jimenez in Cuba and Venezuela respectively, however, and the hardening of the Cold War which increased non-interventionist pressures from the United States, the Democratic Left had to resort to less dramatic tactics. These mainly consisted of attempts to arouse public opinion against the dictators and extensive collaboration with organizations dedicated to the promotion of human rights and freedoms such as the Inter-American Association for Democracy and Freedom. In the end, the dictators fell, but "this generation of leaders was unable to seize the opportunity which their opposition had made" (p. 298).

The reasons for this turn of events were the length of the struggle and the triumph of Fidel Castro. The combination of the two made the Democratic Left's concern with the issue of dictatorship versus democracy obsolete and its proposed solutions for the problems of Latin America inadequate. As Ameringer puts it, "After devoting their political careers to the struggle against reactionary forces, the leaders of the Democratic Left found their revolutionary credentials challenged. In contrast to Fidel Castro, they seemed to move too slowly and to be willing to compromise too readily" (p. 298).

Although clearly sympathetic toward the Democratic Left, Ameringer considers the results of its struggle "inconclusive" (p. 298). While the movement's failures are unambiguous, its successes involve intangibles that are considerably more difficult to assess. Nevertheless, the author argues that the Democratic Left "ultimately broke the power of the dictators, not merely by overcoming them physically but by helping to create the atmosphere which made them obsolete" (p. 298).

For those interested in Caribbean politics in the postwar period, *The Democratic Left in Exile* offers a fresh perspective, a scholarly compilation of relevant materials as well as new data gathered during personal interviews. The book also contributes to the growing literature on Latin American political thought, although this is not its primary focus.

SUSAN KAUFMAN PURCELL
University of California
Los Angeles

PETER L. EISENBERG. *The Sugar Industry in Pernambuco, 1840–1910: Modernization Without Change.* Pp. 307. Berkeley: University of California Press, 1974. $15.00.

Here is a book, complete with the paraphernalia of quantification, that deals, as the author says, "primarily with economic modernization and change" in a traditional sugar-growing area of Brazil, one with a history of sugar that goes back to the sixteenth century. The text is divided into two sections. The first, "The Economic Crisis," tells of the shrinking of markets and the process of technological innovation that this eventually provoked. The second concerns itself with "The Social Crisis," that is, land and the abolition of slavery. (I particularly enjoyed the discussion of the land system and of slavery.)

In a concluding chapter, the author summarizes his findings. Change, "in terms of a new distribution of power and income," did not take place. Modernization in Pernambuco preserved the ancient structures. "The only alternatives to stagnation for Pernambuco entailed recolonization or radical structural reforms, in both cases the costs would have been borne by the planters." Land reform would not have salvaged the private economy. The Pernambuco planters were able "to convert from slave to free labor with a minimum of inconvenience. . . ." The gradual abolition of slavery in Pernambuco was economically motivated. The planters transferred the losses suffered in export markets to the work force in the form of depressed wages and poor working conditions. The lack of jobs and the unattractiveness of free labor conditions on plantations led to vagabondage. The importation of European immigrants "to improve the quality of rural labor" was not feasible. Cuban sugar planters, by way of contrast, had the advantage of proximity to the American market, superior soil conditions, and an abundance of capital. (What is happening today to the sugar of Pernambuco, now that the price has soared to levels beyond the wildest expectations of Fidel Castro?)

The study is long on facts and figures, short on the purely human and humane, a fault, as I believe, of this kind of economic and social history. A sharper human dimension would have enlivened the charts, given added meaning to tables, brought the subject down to the level of people. I would have welcomed a fuller airing of the planter class. After all, isn't the book substantially about planters?

Dr. Eisenberg's conclusions are on the whole well taken, but since his book is an historical exercise, they should have been based on a broader documentation. I may be spoiled by the ponderous research of the scholars of the École des Hautes Études, but the insatiable thoroughness of the French was required here, if only to have laid the subject to rest for the foreseeable future.

The sugar industry of Pernambuco is not exactly my dish of tea, even though it is, of course, a proper subject for the historian. The trouble with the author's treatment is that after a while the reader loses sight of anything significant, and doesn't understand why Dr. Eisenberg has used a special situation to try to prove universals. There is a certain amount of social science model building that doesn't quite come off. There is also the feeling that Dr. Eisenberg's expanded doctoral dissertation would have profited from the sensitivity that surely would have resulted from added years of thinking and living.

On the pedestrian level, the book was badly proofread, the indexing of Brazilian family names is at times confusing, and there is a needless mixing of modern and old orthography. Finally, a handsomer title page would have been more in keeping with the quality of the printing.

Despite its limitations, the book is a good and admirably honest addition to the growing library of American writings on Brazil.

MANOEL CARDOZO
The Catholic University of
America
Washington, D.C.

CHARLES T. GOODSELL. *American Corporations and Peruvian Politics.* Pp. xi, 272. Cambridge, Mass.: Harvard University Press, 1974. $14.00.

Given the extensive literature on the role of the United States corporations in Latin American political-economic development, most readers of *American Corporations and Peruvian Politics* will be somewhat familiar with the respective roles of multinational corporations, the United States government and the host country and will have some feelings about the relevance of the arguments concerning economic imperialism. Professor Goodsell recognizes that there are preconceptions and polarized views on these subjects and finds that frequently they are not based on serious research. By examining the capacity of corporations to affect Peruvian politics, actual corporate behavior and the effects of this behavior within the framework of specific hypotheses, he attempts to narrow the gap between assertion and fact.

Six of the nine chapters are designed to assess the applicability of two conflicting viewpoints on imperialism. Based on personal interviews, questionnaires, observation, and library research, evidence is provided to evaluate both the "economic imperialism" and "corporate good citizen" hypotheses. While the reader is warned not to expect either hypothesis to be supported completely, it is suggested that several aspects of both hypotheses can be substantiated. Professor Goodsell finds that American corporations frequently act like imperialists—employing in Peru such means as direct lobbying, pressure groups, and a variety of bargaining techniques and prevailing upon the United States government for assistance—but often do not achieve their desired results. American firms have affected the political behavior, but have not exercised a great deal of control. A final plea is made for corporations to be evaluated on their own records rather than on the basis of general stereotypes.

A chapter is devoted to each of two less significant hypotheses regarding the impact of company towns on local political life and the role of foreign transportation projects and rural industrial investments on cultural assimilation. Although there are more important aspects of corporate power to discuss and while the findings were not particularly startling, some fascinating descriptions of Peruvian history and politics are included in these chapters.

Upon completing the book, most readers will have learned a great deal about Peru as well as about the research hypotheses. The author's objectivity and his aversion to overstatement will be appreciated. I recommend the book enthusiastically to both specialists and laymen with an interest in the political impact of United States corporations or with a desire to learn more about Peru. It is thoroughly researched and reads easily; to the author's credit,

the abundant footnotes do not become cumbersome. *American Corporations and Peruvian Politics* is one of the most enjoyable books on any subject that I have read in the past several years.

FRED MILLER

Salem
Oregon

E. V. NIEMEYER, JR. *Revolution at Querétaro: The Mexican Constitutional Convention of 1916–1917.* Pp. xi, 297. Austin: University of Texas Press, 1974. $10.00.

Several years ago, the late historian Charles C. Cumberland observed that "The convention which produced the [Mexican] Constitution of 1917 has unfortunately escaped the attention of serious scholars even though it was one of the most dramatic and most important assemblies in the 20th century" (Cumberland, Mexico: *The Struggle for Modernity*, 1968, p. 357). The recent study by E. V. Niemeyer, Jr. has corrected this deficiency. What is more, Niemeyer has given us a remarkably interesting treatment of this potentially dry, though important, subject.

The author's approach is direct and effective. After two short sections outlining the pertinent aspects of the historical background and events leading to the convention, Niemeyer organizes his book into chapters concerning the important issues confronted by the delegates at Querétaro. These included such major questions as how best to control and restrain the much-abused powers of the Church, how to protect and uplift the exploited laboring masses, and how to break the stranglehold on the national economy enjoyed by vested interests such as big agriculture and foreign capital. In addition, there is an interesting chapter entitled "The Prevailing Winds of Reform" which describes how issues championed by international reform movements of that era—prohibition, women's suffrage and the abolition of the death penalty—were also considered though not favorably acted upon. Finally, there is a concluding section which contains not only the author's evaluation of the work of the convention but also various appraisals made by the delegates themselves.

The book offers no startling new theses. Niemeyer observes—as others before him—that the election which produced the constituent assembly was essentially rigged to prevent the inclusion of elements hostile to the "First Chief" of the Revolution, Venustiano Carranza. He also shows—as others have claimed—that the delegates did not, in the long run, act as simple Carrancista rubber stamps, but rather went beyond their chief's draft proposal to include radically progressive provisions such as those concerning labor welfare and agrarian reform designed to help the common Mexican citizen. And he concludes what almost no one would deny: that the convention was a landmark in Mexican history and that the constitution which it produced has become the "foundation for the greatest transformation experienced by the Mexican people since the Conquest" (p. xi).

In sum, this book is of merit in that it fleshes out and breathes life into a chapter of Mexican history which has long been ignored. As such, it is recommended not only for specialists but also for any individual interested in Mexican history.

THOMAS W. WALKER
Ohio University
Athens

A. N. R. ROBINSON. *The Mechanics of Independence: Patterns of Political and Economic Transformation in Trinidad and Tobago*. Pp. ix, 200. Cambridge, Mass.: M.I.T. Press, 1971. $8.95.

This is an easy book to read, but it is by no means a happy book to review. However much one may sympathize with the intentions, the fact remains that the book represents a job too poorly done.

As I read I recalled time and time again a statement of the author's that

though events in Trinidad and Tobago had taken a dramatic turn in the year or so preceding publication, nothing about the book had had to be changed. More is the pity since the work is substantially defective and there is much about it that could and should have been seriously modified.

Principally the book lacks direction. It is not an autobiography. It is not a defense of programs and policies adopted in the teeth of unremitting criticism. It is not a general critique of societies with the post-independence experiences common to countries like Trinidad and Tobago. Nor is it, seriously, an analysis of Trinidad and Tobago and of its problems in the period of independence, and of prescriptions for resolving them. It is rather a patchy, rambling recollection of varied experiences by a politician who, one must often strive to remember, was at the center or near the center of the events of which he speaks.

At no time does the author identify and discuss the real problems of economic development in Trinidad and Tobago or in societies like it. Indeed at no time does the author really say what he is interested in. Snippets of history, snippets of economics, snippets of philosophy, snippets of politics, snippets of everything. But about anything or everything, substantially nothing.

The nearest the book comes to purposeful discussion is in its last two chapters entitled respectively "The Politics of Transformation" and "The Future of the Caribbean." But the analysis and the prescriptions contained therein beggar belief.

For example, the politics of transformation requires six major prerequisites, as follows: (1) A spirit of self-reliance; (2) development "through patience and good will" of "techniques of cooperation among neighboring countries, whatever the differences they may have"; (3) "the establishment of channels of communication with government, business, and intellectual centers in all major industrialized countries of the world. Not only must nationals at home and abroad be fully informed of the objectives, problems, and strategy of the national government, but representatives of potentially sympathetic foreign governments should be kept equally informed of them"; (4) "the need for people to identify with the political and economic objectives of the government"; (5) freedom of discussion; and (6) "the political will to transform the society, and both leadership and the people must have it."

As well it requires equality of opportunity, economic diversification, and the domestication of foreign firms by which is meant the attempt to induce the foreign firm "to accept the same obligations as a domestic owner."

In addition, there is one "single most essential requirement," and that is the political union of the Caribbean.

In all of this there is nothing new, and there is much that is merely middle of the road. As a practicing politician of some importance in Trinidad and Tobago, Mr. Robinson's status depends upon the presumption that he has much to offer in respect of the future development of his country; it is tragic that his book merely confirms that he does not.

Nothing written suggests that he disagrees with the current and past strategies that have landed Trinidad and Tobago in the mess in which it is today. His preoccupation with the subjective factors of political degeneration traps him into believing that all would be well if only men were honest, possessed goodwill, regularly communicated with the people and were committed to achieving the political union of the Caribbean. Nothing could be further from the truth. We could have all these things and unemployment, too; as well as, for that matter, continuing economic dependence, dispossession and rampant inequality. And having them we will be driven inevitably to the treadmill of objectless manipulation which Williams now walks, and which apparently Mr. Robinson is also prepared to walk.

But then what is to be expected of an author who believes, as Mr. Robinson

believes, that the Prime Minister's Better Village program—one of the crowning manifestations of uninspired political gymnastics of the last fifteen years—is an example of great potential achievement presumably to be emulated by a future political leadership?

JAMES MILLETTE
The University of the West Indies
St. Augustine
Trinidad

UNITED STATES

EDMUND BERKELEY and DOROTHY SMITH BERKELEY. *John Beckley: Zealous Partisan in a Nation Divided.* Pp. xvi, 312. Philadelphia, Pa.: American Philosophical Society, 1973. $6.00.

Until after World War II the significance of John Beckley's political operations was not generally known. Since then Philip Marsh, Joseph Charles, and Noble Cunningham have given us some acquaintance with this "mystery man." Now the Berkeleys have written a full-length, but somewhat disappointing biography.

English-born Beckley migrated to Virginia in his youth. By dint of hard work and studious effort he quickly established a reputation as a first-rate clerk. He played a small but not unimportant role in Virginia's struggle for independence, and he served as Richmond's second mayor. Because of his wide experience as a clerk and his acquaintance with Jefferson, Madison, and the leading Virginia politicians he was elected the first clerk of the United States House of Representatives in 1789, a post he held until the Federalists ousted him in 1797. He later regained the post and also became the first Librarian of Congress.

Beckley's most significant work, however, was that of political organizer, manager, and pamphleteer. His work was all-important in Pennsylvania in the elections of 1796 and 1800. Above all, he was a fanatical and sometimes vindictive partisan of the Republicans and a deadly enemy of the Federalists. In a valuable summary of Beckley's career the Berkeleys estimate his "as having been an able and highly dedicated Republican who, in spite of the handicaps of limited education, miserable health, and constantly strained finances, exerted a profound influence on the political trends of the critical times in which he lived, and upon the generation which came after him. He was as responsible as any one man for the overthrow of the Federalist domination of the government and all it stood for, and for the destruction of Hamilton's ambition to be a presidential candidate" (p. 285).

The authors give a lively account of the party warfare during the early years of the Republic, but at times they deal at length with events in which Beckley played little or no part. They fail to bring him to life; he is not fleshed out; his political maneuvers are still not well known. Too often the authors are forced to say Beckley "probably" did such and such, and on occasion they attribute to him views which more likely belonged to others. But in justice to the authors it must be noted that they searched the sources well. Perhaps the extant documents would yield no clearer picture of this important party manager.

ERNEST M. LANDER, JR.
Clemson University
South Carolina

RANDALL W. BLAND. *Private Pressure on Public Law: The Legal Career of Justice Thurgood Marshall.* Pp. xi, 206. Port Washington, N.Y.: Kennikat Press, 1973. $9.95. Paperbound, $3.95.

This first book on Thurgood Marshall, an extension of the author's Ph.D. thesis completed at Notre Dame, certainly will be followed by others that illuminate Marshall in a fuller and richer context.

Although Bland suggests that variables such as different backgrounds, motivations, experiences and beliefs can often be used to explain the be-

havior of a particular jurist (p. ix), he concentrates instead primarily on a description and analysis of all the cases that Marshall dealt with, first as NAACP Special Counsel, and from 1940 on for twenty-one years, as Director-Counsel for the NAACP Legal Defense Fund. These are followed by commentary on cases inportant in Marshall's legal career after he became, in turn, an Appellate Court judge, the U.S. Solicitor General and, in 1967, Associate Justice of the Supreme Court. While Bland attempted to flesh out this account with secondary sources and personal interviews, unfortunately, he was not able to secure any with Marshall himself. Partly as a result, this first black to be appointed to the Supreme Court comes through as a flat, distant, almost cardboard figure.

The seven-chapter book, including appendices listing several different categories of court cases, starts with a sketchy account of Marshall's early life in Baltimore through his Howard University Law School years in the early 1930s. The central chapters deal with Marshall's NAACP association, starting full-time in 1936, with stress on his role in helping to devise and personally direct implementation of the relatively conservative, coherent, long-range strategy of utilizing the only political institution to which the NAACP had access in order to push the varying Supreme Court majorities into a vastly expanded interpretation of the equal protection clause in the interests of fellow blacks. Over these years, the small staff headed by Marshall compiled the remarkable record of thirty-six wins out of forty-one cases, twenty-seven of the wins having been orally argued by Marshall, the single most effective advocate for racial equality in the country.

This would be a much more satisfactory book if the author had dealt more directly with the vast political and social changes during those two crucial decades that helped make the Marshall strategy so seasonably relevant, or had at least made Marshall come alive. Bland does, however, serve a useful

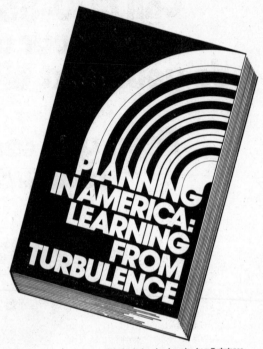

purpose in tracing Marshall's singular impact on the Court's expanded application of equal protection into such diverse areas as voting, interstate transportation, criminal due process, housing, recreational facilities and even military justice, in addition to Marshall's crowning achievement in the unanimous *Brown* decision.

THOMAS V. GILPATRICK
Sweet Briar College
Virginia

LINCOLN P. BLOOMFIELD. *In Search of American Foreign Policy: The Humane Use of Power.* Pp. 182. New York: Oxford University Press, 1974. $6.95. Paperbound, $1.95.

RONALD J. CARIDI. *20th Century American Foreign Policy: Security and Self-Interest.* Pp. iii, 388. Englewood Cliffs, N.J.: Prentice-Hall, 1974. $10.50. Paperbound, $5.95.

The postwar era in American foreign policy has come to an end and with it more than twenty years of consensus on American objectives and strategies in the world. Lincoln Bloomfield and Ronald J. Caridi agree on this, but otherwise their basic underlying assumptions could not be further apart. Bloomfield is a liberal realist driven to conclude that power is an immutable force in international politics but tirelessly searching for its more humane and rational forms. Caridi, while not an uncritical follower of "revisionist" history, is yet overwhelmingly persuaded that economic ambitions link up with aggressive and imperialistic American policies far more than past diplomatic historians have acknowledged. From the Spanish American war to the cold war with the Soviet Union, we have as often been an imperialist as a status quo power and this thread has been one which "revisionists" trace to the drive for economic expansion. Their "operative assumption . . . is that the policies, actions and attitudes of the United States, and not of the Soviet Union, led

to the polarization which followed [World War II]" (Caridi, p. 231).

Bloomfield is both more comprehensive and more sympathetic to the failures and successes of American foreign policy. He states "The facts of American investments abroad do not . . . confirm the 'imperialist theory' " (Bloomfield, p. 37). U.S. exports are only four percent of the total GNP and two-thirds of this goes not to weak dependencies but high income economic competitors. Private overseas capital investment is about $110 billion—a fraction of the two trillion dollor total of U.S. investment—and low income countries receive less than a third of this amount. On the income side, overseas investment income of $8 billion compares with $80 billion from domestic investment with one half deriving from developing countries and 63 percent of this from petroleum. Most important, "American policy has changed considerably from the bad old days when private investments were defended with power and blood" (Bloomfield, p. 38).

However, Bloomfield's analysis of "the crumbling consensus" and "where did we go wrong" is at least as devastating and agonizing as Caridi's. He is deeply concerned about the inherited class background of the foreign policy establishment, but sees their talents being called into play because of the urgencies of postwar problems as they were enlisted twenty years earlier by the New Deal. Parenthetically, neither Bloomfield nor Philip Quigg, whom he quotes ("No country in the world lends itself so poorly to the Establishment concept. . . ." *Ibid.*, p. 54) has said the last word on this issue. Nor does Bloomfield link the readiness of this group to seize the mantle of free world leadership with rather too uncompromising a sense of righteous zeal with their inbred social snobbery which has a basis in social class and personal psychology. (The Reinhold Niebuhrs, let alone the Norman Thomases, of our society are seldom if ever trustees of the Council on Foreign Relations nor are they likely to publish in *Foreign Affairs*.) It remains for someone else to connect the "embarrassing self-righteousness" and "catastrophic optimism" about which Bloomfield writes (p. 63) with the factor of deep-seated social and intellectual attitudes which all too often dominate our public-policy approaches. We need realists such as Hans Morgenthau and George Kennan, journals such as *Foreign Policy* and *The Review of Politics*, and the more intelligent revisionists such as Caridi to remind us of these perennial tendencies and temptations.

Nevertheless, I personally find Bloomfield's little volume more helpful because I sense the same painful Hobson's choice with which he grapples: "to go with the center and disregard the painful truths about justice and equality . . . or to go with the radicals and shut our eyes to the most elementary facts of the real world" (Bloomfield, p. 73). I see too the intellectual and spiritual confusion with which he struggles between "the ideology of political freedom and private property, the two institutions that define the innate U.S. antipathy to tyranny and to Communism" and "the operation of national interest which determines day-to-day strategy and tactics of any state engaged in international relations" (*Ibid.*, p. 75). He finds a resolution of this dilemma in the reuniting of Realpolitik with the humanistic traditions of Jefferson and Lincoln. (The skeptical reviewer asks what about the Louisiana Purchase and Lincoln's suspending of *habeas corpus*?) Still, he asks the right questions: Do we confuse tactics and values? Do we make the worldwide goal of stability an all-encompassing end in itself because of fear of nuclear war and overseas investments? Do we "embrace virtually any other totalitarians so long as they [are] not Communists?" Is it true in our postwar policies that "idealism continued to define the nation's purposes, while the means used became increasingly expedient" (*Ibid.*, p. 82)? And finally that "Vietnam represented a combination of doctrinaire

anti-Communism plus the political idealism . . . of Wilsonian self-determination and U.N. Charter strictures against aggression" and in the end got "the worst of both pragmatism and idealism" (*Ibid.*, pp. 82–83)? Through it all has the Government "discouraged long-range planning, ridiculed theorizing and avoided philosophy" (*Ibid.*)?

Bloomfield answers all these questions in the affirmative and his reason "is not conscious imperialism . . . [but] rather a form of high level incompetence" based on "an unstated belief that American omnipotence carried with it a kind of omniscience" (*Ibid.*). "Its error was to regard U.S. leadership—indispensable when other nations were flat on their backs—as permanent and inherent" (*Ibid.*, pp. 83–84). We acquired "a frank taste of power" and who among us can say we have lost the appetite? Surely not Bloomfield for whom "Cambridge friends as Special Assistants to Presidents [were] acting like the grand viziers of the Sultan—haughty, infected with power, suddenly incapable of the humanistic reasoning that previously distinguished them" (*Ibid.*, p. 88).

Strong words—perhaps uncompromisingly so—but seldom heard from someone with Bloomfield's breadth of experience, as are his words on lying in public life (pre-Watergate) and the dominance of the military. They offer a basis, however, for another and more meaningful Great Debate—not only with revisionists (whose thinking Bloomfield acknowledges) but also with policy-makers. I wish him well—without agreement on all his propositions. For example, surely the problem of human nature is not exclusively the struggle of virtuous human nature with a reverence for life with "organization, management, and system." What about the ambitious and power-lusting side of man's nature bound up with his unending quest for identity and security? Having written with such verve and courage, Bloomfield owes us a continuing output of thinking elaborating the ten premises for a better foreign policy which he promises will bring "light at the end of the tunnel."

Caridi's study poses opposing viewpoints on almost all the issues that Bloomfield raises, but offers fewer policy prescriptions. On questions from an American foreign policy establishment to the economic and imperialistic determinants of policy, he locates the source of our difficulties not in incompetence and social snobbery but the economic interests of dominant groups. These issues deserve discussion and study but touch the conduct of foreign policy less directly and immediately than some of the questions Bloomfield has raised. Nevertheless, there is a "revisionist" alternative explanation for every criticism students of foreign policy raise and if the Great Debate is to deal fairly and fully with the problems, it cannot escape the provocative issues that Caridi's important book has raised.

KENNETH W. THOMPSON
International Council
for Educational Development
New York

J. RONALD FOX. *Arming America: How the U.S. Buys Weapons.* Pp. viii, 484. Cambridge, Mass.: Harvard University, 1974. $15.00.

This is a very important book, superbly researched and written by an author whose experience includes both sides of weapons procurement as well as academic pursuit of the topic. Fox vividly describes the wasteful system that is a root cause of what President Ford calls "domestic enemy number one": inflation. The text varies from simple overview to complex detail, but there is a guide to the less technical chapters for the general reader.

Fox depicts defense industry as a sick giant, unable to generate reliable profits, overstocked with idle workers, and far more concerned with keeping projects going than with fulfilling contracts. Since it is the industry's only important customer, the Department of Defense (DOD) could demand high competence at low cost. But it does not, because military watchdogs are inexperienced and civil servants are illtrained; because friendships between DOD project managers and their civilian counterparts preclude real control by the former over the latter; and because of major misconceptions about defense "urgency," the patriotism of preserving certain firms, and the fear of government intervention in a misnamed "free enterprise." Most of Fox's evidence is from 1970–71, but separate reports in August 1974 by Bethlehem Steel and an Army materiel acquisition board support his view in more recent contexts.

Fox denies that the system "is run by dishonest and greedy men," but his own study suggests otherwise. An Academy graduate learns that "duty, honor, country" does not prevent superiors from ordering him to "misrepresent the facts." DOD officials play "games," a euphemism for lying, both among themselves and with Congress. And a manual for industry negotiators admits the frequent use of "outright lies."

The possibility of real reform in this never-never land seems remote, but Fox's recommendations demand consideration. He proposes better training and rewards for DOD cost control personnel, who would themselves analyze the contractor's operations to determine what the project "should cost," rather than depend on the firm's own inflated estimates. Senior DOD officials should penalize support subordinates who report deficiencies, and penalize firms that fail contract obligations. Competition between prototypes should decide which company wins a contract. Congressional committees must be more efficiently staffed, and taxpayers more alert to where their money is going.

Can defense spending be less wasteful? Fox shows that "should-cost" analysis alone can save the government "25 percent or more" of its over $10 billion research and development expenditures. If President Ford really means it about inflation, he should have his assistants read *Arming America* as soon as they finish *Twilight of the Presidency*.

W. T. GENEROUS, JR.
The Choate School
Wallingford
Connecticut

ROBERT A. MCCAUGHEY. *Josiah Quincy, 1772–1864: The Last Federalist.* Pp. vii, 264. Lawrence, Mass.: Harvard University, 1974. $12.00.

Josiah Quincy was a very important man in American history in many respects, yet he remains a little-known figure to most beginning students. In fact this is only the second full-length biography of the man, the first being the *Life of Josiah Quincy*, written by Edmund Quincy, published over 100 years ago. McCaughey still had to rely on this version for some of his research, for after Quincy published his work in 1867 he gave a trunk full of papers relating to Josiah to the then president of Harvard, James Walker. Walker burned much of this material, through carelessness or deliberate action. Yet what is important about this biography is McCaughey's twentieth-century historical interpretation of the life of Quincy. Seen over a perspective of a century, Quincy's most important contribution to our history was not, as Edmund Quincy emphasized, his eight years in Congress, but rather his role as one of the country's first municipal mayors (1823–1828), the fifteenth president of Harvard (1829–1845) and as an abolitionist in the 1850s. While mayor of Boston he modernized the machinery of government (for his day) and as president of Harvard he helped to transform the school into a college. For example, twenty-six cases of venereal disease were reported among Harvard students in 1821 alone, certainly lending credence to the charge that before Quincy's administration the school was known for its lack of scholarship, undergraduate indolence and dissipation. As an abolitionist Josiah aligned himself with his son Edmund and contributed important anti-slavery publications which hastened the demise of the

Whig party. Quincy's eight years in Congress were spent as "a member of a hopeless minority in a period of sharp ideological conflict," as a member of the Federalist Party, representing the elite of the New England area, and especially Boston. Thus Quincy has been regarded, quite properly, as a sectional leader, one of importance but one who did not capture national laurels or have a national outlook. Relegated to regional importance, he could be overlooked by historians writing about national history, for the War of 1812 ended his national career, yet he went on being a Federalist. McCaughey compares Quincy with John Quincy Adams' flexibility and national outlook—"the man of my whole country," which would take him to the presidency. Yet there is historical importance in negativism, too, and the reasons why Quincy remained a sectional leader have meaning to us today as well as to *chapters* in history. For forty-five years Quincy was in the political arena, directly or indirectly (beginning in 1796) and stood for elective office twenty-seven times. Indeed, one must question here the idea that to be of *sectional* importance must reduce one's national significance. McCaughey answers this question at the beginning of his book, actually in his preface, when he compares Quincy's role in American history to other sectionalists or provincials such as DeWitt Clinton of New York, John C. Calhoun of South Carolina and Thomas Hart Benton of Missouri, stating that one can discern from their lives "clues to a more comprehensive understanding of the many-threaded history of antebellum America."

There is other merit in this book. Quincy was from *the* aristocracy of Boston; he could stay in politics because of his family status and economic well-being. He purchased real estate, which required little of his time, and he did extremely well. Realty values in Boston tripled every twenty years between 1800 and 1860 and Quincy almost had to do well. McCaughey relates effectively what it meant to be *in* the aristocracy and portrays the life of the aristocracy as well. So this book should be read for a better understanding of the aims, aspirations. assumptions and conservative outlook on life of that group.

McCaughey, who teaches history at Barnard College, Columbia University, has presented us with a well-written and basically objective biography of this distinguished sectional leader. Highly recommended.

HENRY S. MARKS
Huntsville
Alabama

JAMES N. ROSENAU. *Citizenship Between Elections: An Inquiry into the Mobilizable American*. Pp. viii, 526. New York: The Free Press, 1974. $14.95.

Over several decades, social scientists have utilized increasingly sophisticated methodologies to advance knowledge about the public's participation in political life. Electoral behavior has been the most thoroughly researched area.

In this work, Professor Rosenau concentrates on a less well-researched aspect of participation. In essence, he has produced a lengthy theoretical and analytical exploratory study of some features of the behavior of the attentive public between elections, especially that small portion of which he labels as "mobilizable." In the specialized vocabulary he uses, Rosenau defines the attentive public as people "who communicate, with some regularity, ideas about public affairs to persons with whom they are closely associated (but not to persons whom they do not know)" (p. 103). The small mobilizable segment of this minority displays the additional quality of "within a reasonable time after they have been urged to do so by actors seeking to mobilize their support, act in a manner that corresponds with the request to establish first-hand contacts with some aspect of public affairs" (p. 106).

The writer concludes that a slow, steady growth is occurring in the size of the attentive public. His principal new hard data to confirm this judgment consist of the changes over time in the number of letters received by the White House, a U.S. Senator, and two newspapers.

The heart of the book consists of the presentation and testing of thirty-six major hypotheses about the many variables that are related to attentiveness and especially to mobilizability. What, for instance, are the similarities and differences between those simply attentive and the mobilized?

His data for this exercise were derived from responses to a mail questionnaire by samples of the membership of the Americans for Democratic Action (A.D.A.). In brief, one sample (the mobilizables) was composed of people who had returned a postcard to A.D.A. saying that they had written the President, their Senators, and Representative in support of its position on the 1963 Test Ban Treaty or the 1964 Civil Rights bill. Another sample (unmobilized attentives) was drawn from the A.D.A. members who had received appeals but did not return a postcard. The combined total of the samples was 3,362. Only forty-two of these labeled themselves as Republicans.

As the writer anticipated, some of the hypotheses were confirmed, some needed to be modified, and some were not verified. He concludes the analysis on "a cautious and tentative note." Among other things, he observes that "we have affirmed the existence of mobilizability as a characteristic of some active citizens, but we have failed to uncover its main source" (p. 469).

The book mainly will be of interest to those concerned about methodology and the development of theories for the study of participation. Despite the attractive title, it would be only of casual interest to others.

HOLBERT N. CARROLL
University of Pittsburgh
Pennsylvania

SANDY VOGELGESANG. *The Long Dark Night of the Soul: The American Intellectual Left and the Vietnam*

War. Pp. 249. New York: Harper & Row, 1974. $8.95.

JOHN HELMER. *Bringing the War Home: The American Soldier in Vietnam and After.* Pp. xv, 346, New York: The Free Press, 1974. $12.95.

The Long Dark Night of the Soul critically examines the response of "the American Intellectual Left" to the war in Vietnam. It has two elemental flaws: (1) there was in the 1960s no semblance of what the book is all about, *an* "Intellectual Left"; (2) there was indeed such a thing as a war in Vietnam, a fact the author ingeniously ignores.

This is a book about a *"them."* Sandy Vogelgesang corrals a number of intellectuals with nothing more discernible in common than their opposition to the Vietnamese War, an opposition which, she assumes, was theirs alone; inserts scattered quotations from their writings into a pseudo-psychological thesis (too convoluted to summarize here); and concludes where she started, that they acted like a herd of steers, veering in cadence, this way and that. Her analysis is unhelpful, as accusations of *thems* always are.

Miss Vogelgesang notes three social characteristics of intellectuals in our culture: "the exercise of moral conscience, obsession with their identity as intellectuals, and their relationship to power" (p. 16). She ignores an equally valid fourth, that intellectuals in at least the United States have been anarchically individualistic, jealous to the point of absurdity at times of their identities as individuals. So, she yokes together as subjects of group analysis such ill-matched figures as Norman Mailer and Hans Morgenthau, Walter Lippman and Hal Draper, TRB and Herbert Marcuse, I. F. Stone and Robert Lowell, Mary McCarthy and John Kenneth Galbraith. And this promiscuous round-up comes down in many cases to holding "the American Intellectual Left" collectively accountable for the blatherings of Susan Sontag, Miss Vogelgesang's favorite resort for a punchline in making a point. This is not good manners, let alone intellectual history.

Nor, in the end, is it commonly decent. For Miss Vogelgesang's explanation of anti-war sentiment among the intellectuals is almost purely internal. It is as if we are reading about a pathetic ménage of neurotics and psychotics, isolated hermetically in an exclusive Swiss asylum, their agonized minds spinning delusions out of filtered alpine air. In conclusion, Miss Vogelgesang writes that "the fault lay neither in the 'system' nor in the proverbial stars but largely within themselves" (p. 166). There is, in *Long Dark Night,* no such thing as an external, objective reality, no *social* psychology: no innumerable dead Vietnamese nor ruined Vietnamese society; no 57,000 dead American soldiers; no 3,000,000 veterans of the campaign; no political history of (at best) blunders and stubborn stupidity in the governing counsels of the nation; no embittered, divided nation; no social anxiety. There are only figments of "Intellectual Left's" imaginations: *"what was alleged to be* pro forma negotiations in 1966" (p. 104); "intellectuals' *suspicions* about the Administration's real resolve to end the war peaceably" (p. 105); the *belief* of "many intellectuals . . . that the Johnson Administration was isolating itself more and more from criticism, hardening its positions, and confusing or alienating the nation through contradictory statements and news management" (p. 108); the *belief* of "many leftist intellectuals" that the war was causing anxiety (p. 113); their *feeling* that no other country "came close [in Vietnam] to supplying the 500,000 troops and $30 billion per year provided by the United States" (p. 119); and so on. "To some extent," Miss Vogelgesang writes, "American intellectuals have always felt that darkness was about to fall. Miraculously or mysteriously, it never has done so" (p. 156). Vietnam was apparently a summer Sunday afternoon at the State Department (the author's regular place of employment).

Goodness knows that many intellectuals of the sixties, even a collective intelligentsia, merit a thrashing with a stout stick. And, in due time, someone will doubtless administer it. But *Long Dark Night* is not even a step towards understanding what happened. Written with the unattractive snideness of the cocktail party doyenne (form following substance), its insights are few and unoriginal, the best of them cadged unsportingly from the writings of Miss Vogelgesang's targets. Ronald Berman's *American in the Sixties: An Intellectual History* (1968), listed in the bibliography here but uncited in the text, remains the best hostile interpretation to date of what, how, and why the era thought.

John Helmer reminds us that there was a war. His study of the Vietnam Veteran, however, is also with its weakness. The bulk of the book (five of six chapters, 170 of 187 statistical tables) is based on a survey of 90 veterans resident in the Boston area. The reviewer is not conversant with current standards in quantitative analysis but will venture that a sample of 90 is an inadequate base from which to generalize about some 3,000,000 men who passed through Vietnam.

The most important part of the book is its first chapter, "The Wasting War." It is an admirable synthesis of several dozens of sociological studies about the nature of the armed forces in Vietnam. Professor Helmer reveals the chilling extent to which that army was an army of the working class and poor—by design; that (Attention: Miss Vogelgesang) this was the class which comprised "by far the largest part of the anti-war public" (p. 12); that this lower-class and unwilling infantry's function was to serve as expendable bait; that, for instance, American casualties were not considered in a fighting unit's performance rating and confrontations in which American forces took the initiative numbered only 14.3 percent of total armed encounters.

This chapter is a crisply and coolly written essay, a model in the exposition of statistical data, reflecting the confidence of genuinely scientific social analysis. Form following substance here too, however, Professor Helmer's prose goes polemical in Chapter Two ("Design of the Study") and outright trendy by Chapter Three ("Preparing For the War"), as if the flimsiness of the study's foundations will be thereby obscured. Until, by page 220, the four letter word appears (not in quotation), as out of place in serious social analysis as a graph of "Body Temperatures During Intercourse" would be in a pornographic film.

But the excellence of Professor Helmer's introductory chapter indicates what the contribution of his Boston study may eventually be. When a scholar with his abilities of theoretical synthesis correlates his statistics with the many others one hopes are being gathered, we shall come to an understanding of those men who had no choice but to stay awake during what was—no apologies—a long dark night of our nation's soul.

JOSEPH R. CONLIN
California State University
Chico

ALLEN YARNELL. *Democrats and Progressives: The 1948 Presidential Election as a Test of Postwar Liberalism.* Pp. x, 155. Berkeley: University of California Press, 1974. $8.95.

In a sensible monograph, unusually well documented from primary sources, Allen Yarnell of the faculty in history at the University of California, Los Angeles, concludes (p. 110) that Henry Wallace's Progressive party "aided Truman in his victory" in the presidential campaign of 1948. He adds, moreover (pp. 110–111), that the Progressives "did not precipitate any shift in domestic or foreign policy."

The argument over the impact of the Progressives has been a long one, and Yarnell's contribution to it is impressive and persuasive. Writers such as Rexford Tugwell, David A. Shannon, Jules Abels, Karl Schmidt, and Curtis MacDougall have supported or leaned toward the view that the Democratic party campaign became more liberal because of the influence of the Progressives. The focus of the Wallaceites in 1948 was toward a shift in foreign policy, one which today would be called a détente with the Soviet Union.

Yarnell demonstrates effectively that

Democratic campaign strategies and pronouncements did not move toward Wallace's positions. Analysis of the president's campaign plans, heavily influenced by a synthesizing memorandum in 1947 from the influential Clark Clifford, is an important chapter. More questionable is Yarnell's view (p. 114) that "Truman's election in 1948 was not a victory for liberalism," since a judgment must take into account alternatives genuinely available.

Wallace's own estimate of the policy impact of the Progressive campaign (pp. 109–113) gradually became more moderate, culminating in a 1953 letter to Curtis MacDougall conceding that "Communists had a strong influence in the party, especially after the 1948 election." He had broken with the short-lived party in 1950.

Seekers of statistical data will not find Yarnell's book a major source, but all scholars will find helpful the extensive bibliography and numerous footnotes citing documents in more than a dozen major repositories.

FRANKLIN L. BURDETTE
University of Maryland
College Park

GOVERNMENT AND POLITICS

FRANCIS A. ALLEN. *The Crimes of Politics: Political Dimensions of Criminal Justice.* Pp. vii, 105. Cambridge, Mass.: Harvard University Press, 1974. $6.95.

Published lectures rarely make compulsive reading, and this book is not much of an exception. It seems a pity that the present book of this author, who is a truly learned scholar, leaves much too much unexamined, and that although some of his contentions are clear, many of them remain shadowy. In three loosely interrelated essays, actually a series of his lectures delivered in March 1973, presented here in a small book on a big theme, he attempts to address himself to the politicizing features of our criminal justice system as they have been demonstrated in the last fifteen years or

so. The title has its attraction but, regrettably, it may create confusion by the apparent contradiction between the main title and the subtitle: the author does not seem to treat in his essays "political" dimensions which would involve a definite policy or ideological system of distributing justice; rather he treats "politics" which means the use of strategy or intrigue or maneuvers in current public affairs. As it reads, the book is a short tale which dramatizes the growing problem of the criminal justice system's engagement in the topical trends of ordinary daily politics.

The first essay, "Of Scholars, Crime, and Politics," indicates the author's assumption that political thoughts were more overtly expressed in the 1960s than before. The second, "Misadventures of a Concept," perhaps the most important section of the book, urges the adaptation of the political offense concept in the United States to the purposes of domestic penal law. Although the author suggests here that this "remains an interesting question for speculation" (p. 31), he does not offer his considerations and, apparently, he keeps himself far away from the speculation over the possible roots of this problem. The third essay, "Reflections on the Trials of Our Time," represents an exemplification of criminal cases to show how some of our criminal courts have been engaged in politicizing justice. All this is presented in a very civilized way, with some distinctly valuable scholarly thoughts. This is particularly so when the reader meets the author's unspoken thesis which seems to be that man is becoming more and more of a political being who is increasingly interested in and informed about the "politics" of his social environment. The author, thus, is correct in contending that "people are highly receptive to political analyses" (p. 2), yet at this point it might have been in order to shed some light on the sources and forces from where these analyses are directed to the intellect of ordinary people.

There seem to be some lapses in the book. One of them is the author's belief that criminology has fallen into the arena of political polemics, that "new tendencies in criminological thought" (p. 15) have emerged, and that a few radically oriented criminological works may have influenced judicial decision-makings by ignoring or distorting important aspects of criminal justice. Such ideas are so lacking in historical and social perspective that the reader may genuinely misunderstand what criminology and its scientific inquiries were and are about. Apart from the fact that criminology, quite unfortunately, does not seem to be too successful (at least not in our time) in guiding the operations of the criminal justice system, the author's interest in this book is restricted to the last decade only. It is in error to think that "rapid changes" (p. 9) and "new trends" (p. 11) developed only in the 1960s: Napoleone Colajanni, Enrico Ferri, Willem Adriaan Bonger, and a number of others in the last 150 years represented the same "new" trends (and they represented them in a scholarly fashion quite often superior to that of our modern radicals); virtually nothing is said today which was not already written in criminology a century ago. If the developments of particular intellectual ideas are worth writing about, as they are, they need to be based on more thorough spade-work than is in evidence in this book.

Another possible misunderstanding may arise out of the author's commenting on "the trials of our time," where the politicizing inclinations of some judges are again not new, and, clearly, not the products only of our age. The case of Jean Calas in 1762 is just one example of very many in the last centuries in which the courts ventured excursions from the administering of objective justice or ideologically political justice to the justice of "politics." As it took many years for Voltaire to reveal the truth behind the "crime" of Jean Calas, it may take another long time for the writers of history to judge Daniel Ellsberg, Father Berrigan, "The Chicago Seven," cited by the author, or even John Ehrlichman and others.

The reason why the author seems to be moving on somewhat weak ground in explaining these most publicized modern trials which he claims are "political," might be that he approached them without offering us his thoughts about the relationship between any given power structure and the criminal justice system, and that between the prevailing value system and the accused individuals, let alone the absence of his idea of who a political criminal really is. A few glimpses on these most important issues are enough only to recognize the author's admirable sense of academic impartiality that leads him to acknowledge or recognize rather than philosophize over these problems.

If not everything the author says is persuasive, it is due to the fact that the book leaves him with gaps he did not bridge and with theoretical spaces to fill in. Perhaps, however, these are not the qualities on which the three essays either aspire or deserve to be judged. Maybe, what the author simply wanted to demonstrate is his claim for describing or defining the concept of political crimes or political criminals. If so, the book's principal strength lies in this point. Indeed, an understanding of political criminality might be able to assist in the assessment of his cited criminal cases and the question whether these cases should be referred to the arena of political crimes or simply and ordinarily only to the sphere of crimes of "politics."

STEPHEN SCHAFER
Northeastern University
Boston
Massachusetts

KENNETH J. ARROW. *The Limits of Organization.* Pp. 86. New York: W.W. Norton, 1974. $4.95. Paperbound, $1.95.

The great bulk of economic theory has, until recently, been directed at dissecting one particular institution or "organization": the price system. The price system is simply a mediator among competing claims on society's scarce resources whose great virtue lies in the fact that it apparently captures the gains to cooperation (that is, efficient resource allocation) through the purely selfish acts of individuals and with a minimum of information. With the notable exception of the government, most other institutions are ignored or taken as data to the market.

In this slim volume, Professor Arrow's major contribution, especially for non-economists, is in directing attention to the role, the functioning and, particularly, the importance of other organizations in complementing the price system. Moreover, he develops a broad framework in which *all* organizations—defined to include the invisible institutions of moral and ethical principles as well as the more standard government, corporation, church, and others—can be analyzed. Not incidentally, he also summarizes, for the non-specialist, much of the recent technical literature in the area of the economics of information.

Arrow argues that the price system, with its well-known drawbacks in terms of both efficiency and distributive justice, can not (and, inevitably, will not) remain the sole arbiter of social life. Other organizations exist to achieve—through non-market methods—the benefits of collective action in situations where the market fails and, for Arrow, their very existence is evidence of the market's inefficiency. Ultimately, the major drawback of the market is seen as its inability (in practice, not formally) to provide sufficient information to permit rational decisions in the face of uncertainty and the interdependence of individual decisions. The well-known role of the government in "internalizing externalities," to use the economist's jargon, is a case in point. Arrow examines, generally, the characteristics of information, the costs of information channels and, ultimately, the superiority of organizations, over the impersonal market, in the acquisition, processing and retrieval of information. Also examined are the implications of information-gathering for the process and outcome of organizational decision-making as well as some considerations in the design of organiza-

tions and the optimal choice of internal communications structures. Finally, he argues, extensively, the value and need for authority (obedience to orders) in achieving an organization's goals while, at the same time, exploring the possibilities for increasing the "accountability" of authority in large organizations.

On the surface, this book is simply a highly-readable statement of Professor Arrow's views, both philosophic and economic, on the role of nonmarket organizations in efficiently allocating resources. Bubbling beneath the surface, however, are numerous important, interesting and difficult questions bearing on the organization of all aspects of society. For example, while it may be obvious to anthropologists, Arrow's analysis of the invisible institutions of moral and ethical principles may explain many of the failures of Western-devised development strategies for emerging nations. The nature of information, per se, and the design of optimal internal communications channels, as Arrow notes, underlie many of the great controversies in the economics of socialism. The discussion of the value and need for both authority and accountability bears directly on the U.S. social upheavals of the 1960s as well, I suspect, as on the widespread view that there has been a world-wide erosion of authority in all institutions, from government and families to universities and churches. Finally, free marketeers and Galbraithians, alike, will be interested in the view that the choice between private and public organizations is not necessarily a choice between market and non-market methods of resource allocation.

Arrow raises these questions in a very broad manner so as to avoid, intentionally, the very difficult analytical problems involved. While he naturally takes the view of an economist, the broad principles he discusses are equally applicable to political or social as to economic decision-making. I highly recommend this book to economists and non-economists alike. It can easily be read in an hour but one may spend several years to fully understand it.

JON HARKNESS
Northwestern University
Evanston
Illinois

JOHN DEARLOVE. *The Politics of Policy in Local Government.* Pp. 287. New York: Cambridge University Press, 1973. $12.50.

John Dearlove suggests that traditional approaches to policy-making overemphasize the impact of the environment, thus portraying governments as weak, open and responsive to environmental influences. Dearlove disagrees, finding governments strong, closed and unresponsive, able to avoid and resist demands for change and innovation. The evidence for this conclusion is drawn from interviews with 47 of the 66 Conservative Councillors on the 70-man Council for the Borough of Kensington and Chelsea. Although the councillors are part-timers and face the usual local government skill and time handicaps, they do benefit from accumulated expertise on the council, since the Borough is a safe conservative district. The committee system has norms much like Fenno describes in *The Power of the Purse:* chairmen are most powerful, new members are to be silent, attend meetings, do their homework, specialize, exhibit party loyalty and can expect to advance to a position of power with seniority. But regardless of councillor expertise, administrators reporting to the council are by far the council's most important information sources. Next are the senior committee chairmen. The bulk of the council relies on these sources for decision cues. Dearlove observes that these are sources internal to the council and they have a vested interest in choosing program continuation over program change. Senior councillors pass on information consonant with existing policy while administrators refrain from passing on information which challenges existing council policies, the ideology of its senior members or the value of the programs they themselves administer. Government becomes closed, powerful, and resistant to change. Dearlove's argument hinges on participants' perceptions. He tested no policy outputs for change or stability. Rather, he extrapolates council behavior from individual perceptions about information cues. Since he was unable to interview the borough administrators he was thus unable to benefit from their perceptions about policy persistence or change. Thirdly Dearlove chose a stable conservative borough for his model. Outcomes might well have been different had he chosen a borough where seats were more hotly contested. As it is, Dearlove's data tend to support another thesis which he begins by contesting that British local government focuses on administration, not policy-making, due to the highly centralized nature of the system.

Dearlove's book is provocative in demonstrating the connection between organization theory and theories of public policy formation. If the evidence is inconclusive, the insights are interesting and the book well written. It will be useful to students of local government, the legislative process and incremental decision-making.

JERRY MCCAFFERY
The University of Georgia
Athens

HUGH HECLO. *Modern Social Politics in Britain and Sweden: From Relief to Income Maintenance.* Pp. ix, 349. New Haven, Conn.: Yale University Press, 1974. $15.00.

A large number of social scientists and laymen with a progressive outlook toward politics have had a special interest in Great Britain and Sweden. The stable democratic political settings for rapid social change and the evolutionary nature of the movement toward social democracy in the two nations have been viewed as welcome alternatives to the modern authoritarian models. Readers with a special interest in British and Swedish social democracy as well as students of social policy will find Hugh Heclo's book worthwhile.

Tracing social policy development from the Nineteenth Century poor laws to contemporary debates about social inequality, Heclo singles out three major policy areas for case study treatment. These three income maintenance policies are unemployment benefits, old age pensions and superannuation. The last mentioned is the most interesting of the three cases because of its contemporary nature and its innovative characteristics. Utilizing a traditional approach to social history, the author gives detailed treatment to the forces, the men and the events which contributed to the development of social policies in Britain and Sweden. While eschewing the use of a rigid methodology, Heclo skillfully describes and interprets the evolution of social politics in the two nations. Fortunately, he constantly emphasizes comparison, and hence, while theory is lacking, some general conclusions do emerge.

Rejecting any notion of single or simple multiple causation, Heclo successfully traces the activities of and the relationship among the various elements in social policy development. In dealing with the complex social policy process, the author painstakingly treats demands of the masses, electoral pressures, party and interest group input, individual social reformer's efforts and governmental activity. The special roles in each nation of experts in the civil service, investigating committees and leadership forces are described. All are treated within the context of political culture. One example where technical knowledge and traditional belief come together was the narrow dedication to classical economic ideas among leaders who identified with widely differing political positions.

A concluding chapter is useful as a summary presentation. In this chapter a discussion of learning theory and social policy is presented, but it seems to be almost an afterthought. Had the author set out some of his arguments in this area in the beginning of the book and systematically dealt with them in the various contexts with which he deals, they would have been more creditable.

This well-written volume is dedicated to the noted British professor of social administration, Richard Titmuss; and this fact obviously tells something about the author's point of view. However, this point of view does not change this good social history which contributes significantly to understanding political involvement in the making of social policy.

STEPHEN P. KOFF

Syracuse University
New York

M. KENT JENNINGS and RICHARD G. NIEMI. *The Political Character of Adolescence: The Influence of Families and Schools.* Pp. xvi, 357. Princeton, N.J.: Princeton University Press, 1974. $12.50.

The extension of the franchise to eighteen-year-olds, by adoption of the Twenty-sixth Amendment in 1971, has heightened the relevance of such questions as: How are the new enfranchised cohorts of young voters going to cast their ballots? What are their attitudes toward political issues and candidates? How intense is their interest in political participation? What influences determine the political views of older adolescents?

A wealth of empirical data bearing on such questions is to be found in *The Political Character of Adolescence*, the most comprehensive contribution to the literature of political socialization that has so far appeared in print. The findings of the study focus most directly on the ways by which older teenagers are influenced by such agents as families, schools, and media of communication and by such factors as sex, race, social class, and current events.

Raw data for the investigation were gathered in the spring of 1965 by the Survey Research Center of the University of Michigan, where the senior author, Jennings, is professor of political science. His collaborator, Niemi, is associate professor of political science at the University of Rochester.

Staff members of the study visited 97 secondary schools in all parts of the United States and interviewed 1,669 seniors. (The interviews averaged one hour each.) They also interviewed 1,992 parents of the students in the sample and 317 of their teachers. The selection of schools and interviewees was carefully planned with a view to making the samples as representative as possible.

Questions asked dealt, *inter alia*, with political party preferences, candidate preferences (in the 1964 Presidential election), opinions on public policy issues (such as prayer in public schools, racial integration, free speech, the United Nations), political knowledge, concepts of "good citizenship," trust in political leaders, and the specific issue of lowering the voting age.

Correlations between students and their parents in the total sample were all positive. Coefficients of correlation were relatively high with respect to party preferences ($r = .47$) and candidate preferences ($r = .59$) and relatively low on policy issues (from $r = .08$ to $r = .34$). The investigators disclosed an interesting sidelight when they discovered that students' preferences and opinions were closer to what they *thought to be* the preferences and opinions of their parents than to what the parents actually reported for themselves, because a considerable minority of students made incorrect judgments as to the political views of their parents. This "lack of perceptual accuracy" on the part of adolescents is interpreted by the investigators as underscoring the "casual, sometimes completely absent efforts of parents to mold their children politically" (p. 330).

With respect to political information, the high school students were more knowledgeable than their parents about governmental structure and operation, but the parents knew more about current affairs and recent history.

One finding that seems to contradict the conventional wisdom is that on several counts mothers appear to have more influence than fathers on the political orientation of their offspring. Hundreds of other specific findings will engage the interest of the reader.

If the reader is a high school teacher, he may be disheartened to learn that neither the curriculum nor the teachers appeared to have any significant influence on the political socialization of students about to receive their high school diplomas. After reviewing their findings, the authors conclude, "Most disturbing from a policy standpoint were the feeble consequences of formal instruction" (p. 319).

With respect to the conclusion just quoted, the present reviewer would enter a caveat. To assess the noncongruence of political views between high school students and their social studies teachers as evidence of instructional failure or ineffectiveness is, at least, open to question. It may well be that this evidence testifies to the *success* of teachers who have deliberately refrained from imposing their personal political opinions and have tried to teach their students to think for themselves.

Professors Jennings and Niemi have scrupulously avoided the seductive trap of trying to select or arrange their evidence to support either simplistic explanations or predetermined conclusions. All too often such tendencies have marred monographic reports of earlier research in the field of political socialization. When the authors are baffled by apparent inconsistencies or inexplicable paradoxes, they frankly say so. Generalizations offered in their concluding chapter attest to their awareness of the inconclusiveness of much of their data and the multidimensional complexities of the problem that they had so painstakingly examined. Thus,

If there is one uncontested and unequivocal result from our work it is that the articulation between socializer and socializee varies markedly according to the orientation being considered. Such variation is most transparent in the case of students and their parents, where the correlations linking generations go from around .05 to .60. This span alone demonstrates that blanket, all-encompassing statements about *the* political socialization process are ill-founded (pp. 319, 321).

Since the primary data were collected in 1965, during the atypical political situation that followed in the wake of the Johnson-Goldwater campaign and before the period of most intense political activism by youth in the late 'sixties, one wonders if the findings might not have yielded significantly different results had they been obtained more recently. The authors do cite evidence from other sources to illuminate some changes noted during 1966–72. The next order of business for research workers in the field of political socialization might well be a comparable study of the *post-Watergate* political character of adolescents.

WILBUR F. MURRA
Southern Colorado State College
Pueblo

JAMES B. RULE. *Private Lives and Public Surveillance: Social Control in the Computer Age.* Pp. 382. New York: Shocken Books, 1974. $10.00.

The aim of Dr. Rule's book is to examine the power conferred on large organizations by the use of modern information gathering methods, as well as the impact of this power on private persons. The study was motivated, in great part, by his reflections on Orwell's *1984* in which life is totally robbed of personal privacy by a monolithic, authoritarian state. (Aptly enought the fictitious credit card depicted on the jacket design is issued to a Mr. Joseph K.)

The book consists of three generalized chapters on surveillance and control and five empirical studies of British governmental agencies and private American systems of credit control. Considerable attention is given to the use of documentation and computerization in modern societies.

Some of the author's observations are well worth underlining: his criticism of flights of fancy of those who contend that we are already in 1984; his point that those who most vehemently oppose surveillance and control are usually the same people who want the state to play an increased role in the economy; and his stress on the costs of control systems which might well bankrupt any political system which goes to excesses.

Among the more provocative subjects treated are the problem of identification of the "clientele" (a tattoed number on some conspicuous part of the body?) and the possibility of applying surveillance and control to the problem of human reproduction, a prospect long since warned against by Pope Paul in his encyclical *Humanae Vitae.*

The author concludes that a balance must be struck between freedom and privacy and social control. He accepts such systems while warning against their dangers. While the systems he has studied may be moving in the direction of total surveillance and control they are far from reaching that point at present. Nor, he contends, are centralization and computerization necessarily inconsistent with privacy. Control and surveillance are by no means new and, he points out, are perhaps less oppressive in a modern society than in former small communities where people never possessed any real privacy. Nathaniel Hawthorne long since anticipated Dr. Rule's preoccupation with tattooing.

The chapters which deal with general observations are the most stimulating and provocative and like the remainder of the book are written in a clear style free of jargon. The choice of systems studied is somewhat arbitrary; it would have been more meaningful to have compared similar systems in diverse countries or to have concentrated on such 1984-ish organizations as the Internal Revenue Service or nations employing identity cards.

Whether, however, in the Anglo-Saxon countries, we are living in 1984 or not is more a question of attitude than of objective reality. A paranoiac will see things differently from a lifelong inhabitant of a country where the Napoleonic Code prevails.

Finally, I am reminded of an anecdote involving my mother-in-law who has generally managed to defy all systems. In order to obtain an overdraft at the bank, Señora M. was compelled to submit a detailed inventory of her farm assets. Among other items she noted: Forty cows. In typical bureaucratic fashion, the bank agent informed her that he could not approve the loan until he had checked in person to see that the cows (representing approximately one percent of her assets) actually existed. Pressed for funds and determined not to be defeated by "the system," my mother-in-law hastily explained: Cross out the cows. They all died last night!

DAVID M. BILLIKOPF
New Canaan
Connecticut

ROLAND L. WARREN, STEPHEN M. ROSE, and ANN F. BERGUNER. *The Structure of Urban Reform.* Pp. 220. Lexington, Mass.: D. C. Heath, 1974. $14.00.

LORD REDCLIFFE-MAUD and BRUCE WOOD. *English Local Government Reformed.* Pp. 186. London: Oxford University Press, 1974. No price.

The Structure of Urban Reform is the end product of the Interorganizational Study Project, funded by the National Institute of Mental Health, housed at Brandeis University from 1965–1972. The focus of the study explores the similarities and differences within and among six community decision organizations, ranging from community action agencies to mental health councils, in nine cities and the modes of interaction in which community decision organizations engage each other at the local level.

In a very real sense, this work confirms the pluralistic nature of the local public sector. The authors found that each community decision organization enjoys a rather monopoly position in its own domain; and, although local interorganizational relationships can hardly be described as chaotic, there is relatively little interaction between community decision agencies.

One of the real strengths of this work is that the authors carefully defined the operational concepts examined. For instance, they note there is a significant difference between citizen involvement and citizen action. Whereas citizen involvement is citizen participation conducive or organizational maintenance, citizen action is directed toward the establishment of a new set of organizational and power relationships.

Most interesting is the chapter devoted to the former community action agency of Oakland, that is, the Oakland Economic Development Council.

Rather than seeking to be merely a purveyor of services, the Oakland agency set about gaining political power for the poor. Its quest for a redistribution of political power, however, ultimately was the source of its destruction.

The limitations of this work are several. One wishes that the authors had devoted more attention to the political environments in which community decision organizations function. Little stress was given to external political influences which certainly have a bearing upon interorganizational relationships. Further, some of the evaluative attitudes advanced (for instance, the authors repeatedly assert that the urban reforms of the sixties ended in failure) have little to do with the study undertaken. And for the sake of clarity, less employment should have been made of social science jargon.

This volume is a welcome addition to the fund of knowledge on urban politics and change. It breaks new ground. We need to devote more attention to the various micro aspects of urban politics.

Local government reform has proved to be largely a failure in the United States. In contrast, as a result of acts passed by Parliament in 1963 and 1972 English local government has been streamlined with the result that the whole of England, with the exception of the seven large urban areas, is covered by thirty-nine county councils.

Supplementing these county councils are 296 district councils.

The restructuring of English local government was primarily due to the recommendations advanced by two study commissions: the Royal Commission on Local Government in Greater London, which met from 1957–1960, familiarly known as the Herbert Commission, and the Royal Commission on Local Government in England, chaired by one of the co-authors of this work, Lord Redcliffe-Maud, from 1966–69. The excellence of this work is no doubt due to Lord Redcliffe-Maud's own immediate involvement in restructuring local government.

As the authors substantiate, reforming local government in England was needed simply because the prior antiquated structure was made for inefficient and unresponsive government. Most importantly, reforming local government in England was politically possible, unlike in the United States, due to the unitary nature of the political system and because of the absence of opposition to reform by most of the political elite.

In addition, there have been a number of changes *within* each unit of local government. Administrative power has been centralized in the office of the Chief Executive. New emphasis has been planned on "corporate planning" and "management by objectives." English citizens now have the benefit of an ombudsman in helping them redress unfair administrative actions.

Notwithstanding the massive reforms implemented, there are still problems associated with local government in England. Citizen knowledge and citizen involvement in local government and politics are minimal. The average electoral turnout in English local elections hovers around thirty-five percent. English local government is financially restricted because of its undue dependence on the rate (property) tax.

This volume presents a good brief introduction to English local government. One wishes, though, that the authors had devoted somewhat more attention to the behavioral aspects of local politics.

NELSON WIKSTROM
Virginia Commonwealth University
Richmond

SOCIOLOGY

ERIC ASHBY. *Adapting Universities to a Technological Society.* Pp. vii, 158. San Francisco, Calif.: Jossey-Bass, 1974. $8.75.

Eric Ashby views the university from the standpoint of what he calls "social biology," that is, he views the university as an organic system maintaining equilibrium by interaction with its environment. Changes in the environment must produce corresponding changes in the system if the system is to continue to maintain itself. Ashby's thesis is that the current university system is a hybrid holdover from the nineteenth century, and that the rapid expansion of technology in the twentieth century must occasion some change in the university system itself. Universities have become very expensive to run and are therefore more dependent on the patronage of outside forces, particularly the state; this financial dependence leads naturally to increasing pressure on what the university should teach and on whom they should admit. If the university is to preserve its traditional function as a haven of intellectual freedom and repository of humanistic values, it must adapt itself to these demands. Unfortunately, universities have not yet "devised any built-in mechanisms for change" (p. 15).

Rather than being the force for dehumanization which its detractors accuse it of, technology is a potential force for assisting in the preservation of these traditional values. For example, cost-efficiency analyses can reduce the financial burdens of the university. Expanded use of technological teaching aids can free teachers from rote work and allow time for the more valuable one-to-one relation of teacher to student. Finally, by fully integrating scientific training into the traditional humanistic teachings of the university, the university can acquire some of the internationalism, humility and rigor which belong to contemporary science.

Ashby is not, however, advocating any rehashed version of the now familiar technocratic vision of the world—that is, that good engineering is a sufficient condition for the good life of society. He is at least moderately aware of the dangers of such a technocratic world view, and very clearly aware of the fact that the question of ends is as important as that of means. He continually stresses the need for and value of traditional humanistic education. What he views as dangerous is the growing tide of anti-science. In opposition to this, he argues for the potentially liberating effects of an application of science to humanistic concerns. Those who look in Ashby's book for any tired old positivistic view of the world will be mostly disappointed.

Ashby's arguments move quite lithely from the general to the concrete, details enriching general argument. Still, one would want him to entertain in greater depth some of the anti-technological arguments of, for example, the Frankfurt school, which claim that technology is not neutral but has an implicit "logic of domination" built into it. Nor does he treat in detail what is becoming of growing concern—the glut of trained people on the market today and the corresponding decline in demand for university training. Still, Ashby's book is timely, well argued and provocative. It is at the least a helpful prolegomenon to a discussion of the future of the university.

TERRY PINKARD
Vanderbilt University
Nashville
Tennessee

JEREMY BOISSEVAIN. *Friends of Friends: Networks, Manipulators and Coalitions.* Pp. 285. Oxford, England: Basil Blackwell, 1974. No price.

Friends of Friends is two books rather than one; or perhaps more accurately, a book and a pamphlet. The book (Chapters 2 to 8) is an introductory manual on network analysis and is intelligent and useful. The pamphlet (Chapter 1 and scattered comments throughout) is a polemic against "the so-called structural-functional view of social behavior and society," and is, in my view, confused and irresponsible. I shall begin with the pamphlet and then go on to the book.

Boissevain argues that the "so-called structural-functional view" does not accord with social reality, and that we must shift our attention from formal institutions and corporate groups to individuals and networks and informal organization, from conformity to norms and social sanctions to individual manipulation of norms and striving after interest-defined goals, and from social integration, equilibrium and continuity to conflict and change. Such a polemical formulation might have been excusable fifteen years ago, but given the development of social anthropology in the last three decades, this tedious iconoclasm is long out of date. And it is positively harmful, for it makes what should be a set of *empirical questions* into an ideological pronouncement. Surely the degree to which formal institutions, corporate groups, personal networks, and informal coalitions are important in particular social settings is a matter *to be investigated* rather than asserted *a priori*. And likewise with conflict and consensus, stability and change, conformity to norms and manipulation of them. (In fact, Boissevain's theoretical overemphasis on networks and self-interest derives partly from his research experience in Mediterranean cultures in urban and suburban settings; he mistakenly assumes that all the world is like "his people.")

It is noteworthy that when Boissevain turns to actually explaining something (the ongoing strength of structural-functionalism) in a non-Mediterranean setting (England), his arguments sound very structural-functional: "It was the ongoing structural form of British universities, in which professors with old fashioned views had all the power, that inhibited intellectual innovation" (pp. 20–22). Furthermore, "the simultaneous rise of fascism and structural-functionalism are reactions to the shift in the balance of power away from the industrial agrarian, bureaucratic and military bourgeoisie in favor of the workers, native peoples and other subjugated persons" (p. 13). And the new student power "is helping to dislodge obsolete theories" and "may well bring about . . . a more rapid development of scientific theory" (p. 23). Aside from being historically questionable (and rather nasty), these arguments seem to have a lot to say about ongoing structures and functional interrelations between ideas and social forms, and not much about networks, entrepreneurs and choice-making. While condemning his strawman structural-functionalism, Boissevain seems to feel free, when it suits his purposes, to make use of arguments that could not be called anything other than structural-functional.

The bulk of *Friends of Friends* is a good introduction to networks, network analysis, and coalitions. Primarily it is an elaborated conceptual scheme with illustrative examples; its usefulness derives from the clarity of the concepts and the lively detail of the examples (mostly from Boissevain's research on Malta), both of which are enhanced by a pleasant, easy writing style. Interactional and structural criteria for analyzing networks, and the biological, physical, ideological and social factors that influence networks, are discussed at length. There is an extended examination (50 pages) of two personal networks. Brokers and varieties of coalitions are examined in detail. Finally, a Maltese case of "conflict as process" is viewed from a macro-sociological perspective. Much emphasis is placed upon social manipulation in the cause of personal goals.

When Boissevain is discussing and analyzing networks and coalitions, he is on fairly solid ground, but in moving to larger contexts and broader events, he is forced to bring structural factors in through the back door while denying

them—for example, the structure of the church within which the partiti struggled (p. 224) and "the long term processes" (p. 231) which are in fact the larger structural framework.

I have characterized this book as an introduction rather than a synthesis because there are few substantive hypotheses or theories about specified variables of networks of coalitions and their causes, correlates or consequences. And those that are set forth are not developed and in any case seem dubious, namely, that coalitions arise in fragmented, heterogeneous and insecure social settings and that corporate groups arise in well integrated, homogeneous and secure social settings (p. 203). Insofar as this is not tautological (for example, that "integration" is defined independently of the nature of groupings), it seems highly questionable in the light of Middle Eastern, West African, and East Asian data; for lineages, guilds, wards, quarters and religious orders were widespread corporate forms providing shelter for individuals in heterogeneous and insecure social settings.

Friends of Friends is thus a very mixed bag in terms of substance and value. I would not care to expose unsophisticated and uncritical students to it without considerable commentary.

PHILIP CARL SALZMAN
McGill University
Montreal
Quebec
Canada

NORMAN I. FAINSTEIN and SUSAN S. FAINSTEIN. *Urban Political Movements.* Pp. iii, 271. Englewood Cliffs, N.J.: Prentice-Hall, 1974. No price.

The book's subtitle, *The Search for Power by Minority Groups in American Cities,* more accurately discloses the contents of the publication. It is a rather general review of some of the ways in which Negroes and Spanish-speaking Americans have striven to influence governmental policy-making and administration in various large-sized communities. A brief treatment of the social and economic factors which exclude these minorities from the customary political processes of modern urban communities (poverty, segregation, and racism) is followed by detailing the unresponsiveness of those processes to minorities' demands. Alternative forms of political action which these minorities have tried to adapt to their needs constitute the book's core and its most lengthy portion. The other kinds of political action considered include community action programs; the provisions of the model cities legislation for target-area residents to participate in policy-making; community control of schools and health facilities; oppositionist groups; tenant movements; and service-oriented organizations. A few rather detailed case studies, drawing largely upon New York City and environs, are the basis for pertinent analyses and conclusions. Not all of the alternative forms of political action mentioned, however, receive anything like equal treatment this way. Nor do the writers draw anything like hard conclusions regarding the adaptability of the alternative instruments mentioned (model cities, for example) to the political ends and means most available to these socioeconomic groups.

The principal concern is with portraying aspects of political participation and consciousness among the poor. They use various case studies both to illustrate distinctive features of that participation and to impart some of the fine points of the situations in which the poor struggled. One case study examines why a political effort undertaken by some of New York City's urban poor failed; another seeks to explain the success of a similar movement (in both instances, the quest for community school control). A third case study focuses on the transmogrifying experiences of an effort to develop neighborhood health, educational, and economic services in Paterson, New Jersey. The resources and power available to these kinds of political movements among the urban poor, and their capacities to mobilize the same, rela-

tively assessed, round out the book's treatment of the subject. An appendix is attached, treating certain problems of definition and the historical perspective of political movements of this type.

Using the case studies, the writers attempt to derive certain explanations for the outcomes indicated. The failure of the New York City school reform, which sought to effect a high measure of responsiveness, if not dominance over a community school district, is attributed to difficulty among the poor in mobilizing what resources they had (mainly sympathizers) for the length of time needed. A scarcity of leadership (political and functional) and the difficulty of gaining access to the power centers with city-wide bases, through which change could be accomplished, proved additional burdens. Where desired school reform was successful, leadership and clientele support and legal facilitation were favorable, and equal to the end desired. The transformation of the initial effort in Patterson from one which could benefit the poor into something from which a broader range of interests would benefit derived mainly from a co-opting effort by non-poor groups. These conclusions point up both the strength and the weakness inherent in the case methods—plausible answers deriving from a few in-depth analyses which do not admit of broad generalizations capable of explaining the behavior of the much larger universe characterizing a particular phenomenon. Some other findings are noteworthy.

Involvement by individuals in the political movements studied is attributed less to personal ambition in politics, or the prospect of gaining or wielding power, than to a belief in the desirability of improving schools. To some, the schools were a cause to be active in; to others, their improvement was an end in itself—an ideology of sorts. This holds true irrespective of the race or sex of those involved, by and large, although the political skills and consciousness of some were more developed. More women than men were found to be involved, and more Negroes than Caucasians; Negroes predominated in the population of the school areas concerned. The socio-economic characteristics of involved individuals were rather similar to the area populations. This finding is similar to data cited in a number of other studies. Regarding resources, protesters have had to rely mainly on numbers, creating disturbances, and the professional organizer to achieve desired changes. The conclusion is that the protest movements studied had mixed results. They are adjudged successful in that they usually changed local bureaucratic behavior, that is, how to deal with a problem. Little lasting impact was noted on the underlying conditions which gave rise to the public dissatisfactions—in the instances studied, to perceived school inadequacies vis-à-vis the poor and the minorities.

The book is readable, but uneven in its treatment. A few case studies undergirding a rather general treatment of much fugitive literature on the subject give a somewhat fuller understanding. But more analyses, possibly building on the case method, are needed. The vital requirement now is information sufficient to allow firmer, more inclusive generalizations. This book is a useful beginning. Its merit lies in this fact, not in its recurring susceptibility to claiming more for the data than they will support. A good stool does not stand well on one leg.

HARRY W. REYNOLDS, JR.
University of Nebraska
Omaha

LLOYD A. FALLERS. *Inequality: Social Stratification Reconsidered.* Pp. xi, 330. Chicago, Ill.: University of Chicago Press, 1974. $12.50.

Fallers is a professor of anthropology and sociology at the University of Chicago; this book reflects the influence of both disciplines. The introduction is newly written and the rest of the book is a collection of previously published essays, all of which deal with some aspect of social stratification. The emphasis is on stratification in Africa, particularly Buganda (now part of Uganda).

The major theme of the introductory essay is that the term "social stratification" should be replaced with the term "inequality" because the latter is less loaded with cultural bias. He argues that the model of social stratification based on "a hierarchy of pansocietal horizontal layers" is not appropriate for the analysis of the system of stratification in many non-Western societies, particularly African societies. In Buganda, stratification is based on "dyadic interpersonal relations of superiority and inferiority." Authority roles are highly valued and more important than wealth and income as determinants of social status. A weakness of Fallers' argument is that he is rejecting an overly simplified (straw man) conception of "social stratification."

The second chapter deals with the "trickle effect" in American society. He argues that "status symbolic consumption goods trickle down, thus giving the illusion of success to those who fail to achieve differential success in the opportunity and status pyramid." The next four chapters deal with social stratification in Africa. One discusses the role conflicts for the modern chief in Uganda who works in a fully equipped modern office building one day and is out meeting with clan mates in a thatched hut discussing the wishes of ancestors the next. Another chapter considers the appropriateness of the term "peasant" when referring to African cultivators.

A theme repeated in several of the essays is that social inequality is a "moral phenomenon"; that is, "all human communities have values in terms of this." This is used to argue that social stratification is not an essentially economic phenomenon. The argument is consistent with Parsonian pluralism and inconsistent with a Marxist perspective. The three chapters that make up the second half of the book are all drawn from the author's previous work, *The Kings Men.* They deal with stratification and social mobility

BOOK DEPARTMENT

JOHN B. WILLIAMSON
Boston College
Chestnut Hill
Massachusetts

JEFFREY K. HADDEN and CHARLES F. LONGINO, JR. *Gideon's Gang: A Case Study of the Church in Social Action.* Pp. 245. Philadelphia, Pa.: Pilgrim Press, 1974. $6.95.

Responding to the racial crisis of the nation in the spring of 1968, the Ohio Synod of the United Presbyterian Church in the U.S.A. authorized three experimental congregations with a special focus on racial reconciliation. This book tells the story of the "Congregation for Reconciliation" in Dayton, a city-wide, nonresidential group recruited explicitly for the purpose of countering injustice. By early 1972, the future of the controversial Dayton mission was at stake, and its members, committed to continuation but fearing extermination, sought outside evaluation. Thus the authors, sociologists at the University of Virginia, became involved in the field work that led to this study.

Gideon's gang (the biblical allusion seems to be the authors' invention) averaged only some thirty members, but it took the offensive against injustice from the start. Not only did it confront local agencies and corporations, it also initiated the nationally-visible boycott of Gulf Oil, in protest of their policies in Angola. With a keen eye for the uses of the media, the pastor, the Reverend Richard Righter, led his volunteer troops in a most unconventional series of forays. This aroused intense controversy and evoked severe criticism from among the established churches that had launched the experiment.

The authors compare the Dayton group with a congregation in Cincinnati that emerged from the same denominational emphasis. While the Dayton church was immediately effective in community social and political action, it

failed to communicate successfully with sister congregations, thus defaulting on one of the stated goals of the project. The Cincinnati mission, unable to achieve much in direct action, did play an important role in interpreting social justice issues to the presbytery. The authors explain the trade-offs among goals by discussing varying pastoral styles, recruitment emphases, and environmental factors.

Central chapters analyze major congregational campaigns and examine membership self-understanding, strategies for conflict, and organizational dynamics. Dispensing with the customary sociological jargon, statistical data, and graphs, the authors have chosen rather to illuminate the struggle of the Congregation for Reconciliation vis-à-vis its environment in a narrative fashion, augmented by occasional theoretical insights. They adapt a dramaturgical framework from Kenneth Burke and H. D. Duncan to interpret the confrontation strategy of Righter's mission and refer to other social science perspectives in the footnotes. One chapter, seemingly out of step with the rest of the book, sharply criticizes the major claims in Dean M. Kelley's *Why Conservative Churches Are Growing,* arguing from the very limited empirical base of the present study.

The authors address themselves to the churches rather than to the academic community. They claim no theoretical advancement or startling empirical discoveries, but they do argue that their case study, with its insight into the consequences of manipulating social forces, has implications for policy decisions by liberal Protestant leadership. Their report provides critical perspective on the churches' role in society that seems particularly relevant in the present period of decline in institutional religiosity.

J. R. BURKHOLDER
Goshen College
Indiana

DAVID G. MANDELBAUM. *Human Fertility in India: Social Components and Policy Perspectives.* Pp. 144.

Berkeley: University of California Press, 1974. $6.00.

Most readers will pick up this book with high hopes: it is one of the first books dealing with social components of Indian fertility and highlighting policy perspectives by an eminent social anthropologist. In the preface, however, appears this important proviso: "The available data on some of the subjects considered are less than satisfactory. I have indicated some of the problems on which further research is particularly needed but have not tried to give here detailed evaluations of the research projects from which data are cited" (p. ix). Therein lies a big disappointment. Studies of unequal merit when cited without critical assessment are given uniform legitimacy and many questionable findings become accepted knowledge for the unsuspecting reader.

Throughout the book Professor Mandelbaum argues persuasively that to understand Indian fertility we must first understand Indian culture and Indian society. He explains that personal motivations and cultural considerations that promote large families have been imperfectly understood and generally ignored in the implementation of Indian Family Planning Programs. The points, while not all new, are well made and well taken.

The discussion centers on the circumstances under which the Indians have in the past limited their fertility, the traditional methods of birth control, and the major social and cultural differences that have a bearing on fertility behavior. In the first category, motivations include the desire to space births and, more importantly, the "pregnant grandmother complex," that is, a woman's shame in continuing childbearing after her daughter has begun doing so. The methods used include abstinence, withdrawal and abortion. Interestingly, Professor Mandelbaum makes no mention at all of infanticide or female child neglect which results in low rates of female survival and has been so noticeable in parts of India for many decades. The social and cultural differences include social and economic status: ". . . lower and poorer groups tend to bear more children . . ." (p. 42); religion ". . . may be of some significance, but more as a background variable than as a direct influence" (p. 57); joint family "quite irrelevant" (p. 57); urban residence and education (higher income and education are "the critical factors in lowering fertility in cities and towns as well as in the villages" [pp. 57–58]). Because educational opportunities, health and family planning services are more available and effective in urban areas the shift to patterns of lower fertility will come sooner (p. 58). There is no discussion of regional differences. It is true that sociological literature on India has often stressed the theme of unity in diversity, but while unity is paramount in considerations of overall Indian planning policies, the diversity needs to be stressed in discussion of plan implementations because regionalism is an important social as well as political reality.

The coverage of policy perspectives leaves most to be desired. Professor Mandelbaum sees proposals about how best to limit fertility as characterized by three motifs in which the main emphasis is on political decisions, birth-control technology, or economic change (p. vii). There is another motif: emphasis on the health and welfare of infant and mother. The thesis of the health perspective is that family planning services must be made an integral part of maternal and child health care if they are to succeed in countries where infant mortality is high, and where parents need to be assured that their live-born will survive to adulthood before they will undertake to limit births. While this child-survival hypothesis is mentioned in consideration of motivational factors, it is ignored in consideration of policy. Yet what could be more relevant to what Professor Mandelbaum himself calls "the contradiction between private interest and public welfare" which presents a "formidable obstacle in the way of effective reduction of the birth rate" (p. 13). The health theme in family planning now has wide acceptance not only in India but in large portions of the third world.

NARINDAR UBEROI KELLY
University of Pennsylvania
Philadelphia

ALBERT MEHRABIAN and SHELDON KSIONZKY. *A Theory of Affiliation.* Pp. v, 212. Lexington, Mass.: Lexington Books, 1974. $15.00.

A Theory of Affiliation is a report by two psychologists of a series of experiments designed to explore the factors involved in positive social behavior.

On the basis of studies by other psychologists and a certain amount of common sense, Mehrabian and Ksionzky reason that affiliation is affected by an individual's inclination or disinclination (R_1 and R_2) to associate with another and that the other's positive or negative reactions (r_1 and r_2) to an approach have much to do with its continuation.

Because of early training and past experience, every individual is assumed to have developed a positive or negative disposition to affiliate. The researchers undertook to isolate such an affiliative disposition from closely related dispositions, such as to conform, to ingratiate, to be dependent upon and to empathize. For experimental purposes they sought to operationalize measures of affiliative tendency, sensitivity to rejection and empathic tendency (pp. 164, 165, and 169). They also undertook to isolate behavioral clues permitting the standardization and rating of affiliation, ingratiation, indexes to dominance or status in social situations (relaxation) and properties of tension in social situations (intimate position and distress). Since these were the operational specifications by which their variables were "measured" in experimental situations, some of them are worth noting:

Affiliation = Declarative Statement Rate + Positive Verbal Content (p. 136).

Ingratiation = Positive vocal expressions − Negative Verbal Contents + Question Rate + Verbal Reenforcement Rate (p. 137).

Relaxation
(seated) = Arm Position Asymmetry + Body Lean Sideways + Leg Position Asymmetry − Body Lean Forward (p. 137).

Intimate
Position = Shoulder Orientation Away From the Other − Distance From the Other (p. 137).

Distress = Percent Duration of Walking + Rate of Object Manipulation (p. 138).

After a series of experiments in which such operational specifications were employed to determine the comparative effect on affiliative behavior of the factors assumed to determine it, the experimenters summarized their arguments in the form of logico-mathematical equations, concluding that affiliation, conceived as positive social action, varies with the positive and negative affiliative tendencies of the actor, the positive and negative response of the social object as estimated by the actor, the pleasantness and unpleasantness of the situation in which affiliation occurs and, finally, the positive and negative factors of social behavior.

It is rather unfair to evaluate Mehrabian's and Ksionzky's monograph in a context such as a review in *The Annals* which is concerned with the needs of the general intelligent reader. The monograph is embedded in and expresses the preoccupations with a tradition of experimental social psychology. It is a respectable addition to this tradition. The average reader will find it baffling and jargon ridden. Affiliation is not even defined until page 136 and then defined operationally as declarative statement rate plus positive verbal content. And should the average reader take the extraordinary amount of time required to pin down the meaning of the arguments, he will normally end up with propositions he took for granted from common sense. Perhaps one could hazard the stylistic law that holds in this literature: the use of unintelligible jargon in the literature of experimental social psychology increases monotonically with the triviality of the subject matter.

In assessing the clinical implications of their study, Mehrabian and Ksionzky suggest that in view of the paraprofessional movement in therapy their measures of affiliative tendency and sensitivity to rejection could be an effective tool for selecting persons able to maximize their effectiveness with clients and to skillfully establish rapport with strangers. Mehrabian and Ksionzky may at last have found a substitute for Dale Carnegie's How to Win Friends and Influence People.

DON MARTINDALE
University of Minnesota
Minneapolis

HAROLD E. QUINLEY. The Prophetic Clergy: Social Activism Among Protestant Ministers. Pp. ix, 369. New York: John Wiley & Sons, 1974. $14.00.

Not a single surprise will greet the informed reader of Harold E. Quinley's finely-detailed sociological portrait of the effects of the clergy's controversial intrusions into the public realm in the 1960s. From Jeffrey Hadden's work he or she would already have known about the gulf between pulpit and pew caused by such wanderings across the border between public and private in religion. From Dean Kelley's more popular accounting it could have been common knowledge not only that strict churches had grown during those years, but that the more open ones had also suffered relatively. Charles Y. Glock and Rodney Stark had already projected the expense to religious prosperity that would result from the churches' new ethical involvements.

The fact that nothing is surprising and everything is predictable does not detract from the value of Quinley's questionnaire-based survey. To have documentation where there had often been only generalization is useful; and to have this documentation applied so specifically to so many dimensions of the issue is even more valuable. Those who want to understand dynamics of American society will be better off than before; planners and prophets in religion will learn more of the assets and liabilities of playing it safe and taking risks in the light of a theological or humane vision.

After the religious revivals of the 1950s, when institutions of all sorts prospered, the more open churches (Quinley speaks of their clergy as "modernist," a term he defines well but one that can lead people to confusion because of a dated and different theological movement of the same name), facing the egregious violations of order and justice in America, began to address them. They used pulpits, pronouncements, and—most controversially—actions.

Unfortunately Quinley relies only on data from a California sample; northern California is atypical religiously, so far as the American spectrum is concerned. For that reason the book might have been titled more modestly, to preserve the regional nuance. But this concentration makes it possible for him to texture his findings better. One other criticism: all we hear from the laity is based on clerical perceptions. These could be skewed; for example, a certain kind of pastorally-incompetent cleric might go into social activism to compensate. In the process, he might be resentful of his laity. Other clerics were simply poor communicators, and did not read well or lead well those lay people who might have stepped further.

The data are from 1968; Quinley knows and says that the world has moved on. There is less polarization today. He might have added that a new prophecy is rising from the once-quiescent strict churches, and that his "modernists," chastened, have not buried all their social dreams but are more attentive to local realities of power and prejudice. His is a valuable contribution to understanding one of the most tense stages in an unfolding history of the politics of pulpit and pew.

MARTIN E. MARTY
The University of Chicago
Illinois

A. I. RABIN and BERTHA HAZAN. *Collective Education in the Kibbutz.* Pp. iii, 184. New York: Springer, 1974. $6.95.

The appearance and development of the Kibbutz system of society have engendered a great deal of excitement, curiosity and anticipation both within the system itself as well as by many onlookers from the outside. Some looked upon it as the panacea for many social ills. Others feared it because of its suspected leftist orientation. Some social scientists described it as a "community of purpose" as contrasted to a "community of persons," making it what sociologists call a "primary group" rather than a "secondary group." In its ideal form it started in Israel to be a realization of the concept of "total sharing." It developed into a relatively mature system of collective settlements which point to a number of accomplishments. Professor Rabin of Michigan State University and Bertha Rabin, an editor of works in psychology and education, have teamed up to collect, organize and present a series of articles ostensibly geared to an evaluation and an examination of the educational phase of this type of society. Nine other experts have offered their work in a series of eleven articles, all culled from their understanding in the fields of sociology, education and psychology.

The first series of articles seems to present rather a rosy picture of accomplishment in the field of the education and adjustment of children to society. An attempt seems to be displayed to balance the child's involvement both with his family and with the social group as a whole. While strong emphasis is made that the Kibbutz type of orientation is the key to this balanced adjustment, one often fails to see why the orientation could not as well be applied in any urban society. It is finally in Moni Alon's description of "the Youth Society" that one sees a balanced picture of achievements on one hand and problems and challenges on the other. In this article the education of the Kibbutz is defined as "ideological education" with the goal of reaching a "conscious identification with the national and socialist tasks espoused by the movement." Here the author points to both the disadvantages as well as the advantages. A degree of "social orientation" is reached which is good. However, the author honestly notes a degree of skepticism towards political parties and organized politics in general, thus presenting a picture of inner oriented society with a suspicious look to the outside. Since the present Kibbutzim are comprised of second or third generation participants, the secondary generations are deprived of the pioneering spirit that stimulated the founders. This same author also points up the skeptical attitude towards socialist ideology in this new generation who will not accept a position at face value. On the other hand, this author points to the glaring difference between the socialist achievements of the Kibbutz society and the "inequality oppression and other wrongs" in many other types of society. There are indeed dynamic changes going on in the Kibbutz society which involve technology and administration and are in nature demographic, economic, social and ideological. There are practically no events of juvenile delinquency in the schools. Boredom and lack of interest do not prevail. There are few cases of homosexuality, perversion and other deviations. He defines the overall approach in three fundamental dimensions — "identification with the values of the Kibbutz society, the guidance and demands of the educators, and the positive relations between parents and children." While he recognizes the need for changes in the educational patterns — and indeed there have been some changes — he argues for the need of stability within the overall picture so that the changes do not turn out to be passing "fads."

Indeed the Kibbutz system has not been a panacea. Yet, it has offered many recognizable values, some of which can be adopted to other forms of society. This writer regrets that the survey of Kibbutz education failed to include the contributions and nuances made in the religious Kibbutz which the editors and authors for some reason practically ignore. Nor have some of the shifting norms been adequately enunciated— for example, children being reassigned to parental homes in some Kibbutzim. All in all, however, the work deserves to be read and studied by those who are interested in examining various forms of society and education in our quickly changing world.

SAMUEL J. FOX

Merrimack College
Andover
Massachusetts

PAMELA ROBY, ed. *The Poverty Establishment.* Pp. 217. Englewood Cliffs, N.J.: Prentice-Hall, 1974. $7.95.

This collection of essays represents a radical departure from much of the poverty literature of the sixties. As the title suggests, the focus is upon the system and not upon the poor. A majority of the essays direct their attention toward the economic system which is viewed as the major source of the poverty problem. Attention is also given to ways in which the political system interlocks with the economic system, as well as the effects of the intervention by the political system to ameliorate the poverty problem, both in its repressive manifestations and in its liberal manifestations.

The tone of the volume is set by excerpts from two well known books: *Blaming the Victim* by William Ryan and *Regulating the Poor* by Frances Fox Piven and Richard A. Cloward. Other articles extend the analysis by providing a detailed examination of how the economic system, including government intervention in the economy, works (1) to create jobs which pay poverty wages (Barry Bluestone); (2) to create and maintain an unequal distribution of income in spite of the presumed impact of the welfare state and "progressive" Federal tax laws (Howard M. Wachtel and Larry Sawers); and (3) to benefit the capitalists via increasing profits while the poor pay via high prices, low wages and unemployment (Howard Sherman).

Programs to eliminate or ameliorate poverty are examined closely in other selections. Sol Stern shows how one of our oldest solutions to the poverty problem—"welfare"—is becoming more repressive and dehumanizing with the new "reforms" such as the separation of cash from services, the identification of the "employable," the reduction of grant amounts and the systems approach. David Wellman describes the irony of "Manpower training for low wage work" and training for non-existent jobs. David Horowitz and Reese Erlich examine the process by which the Job Corps became metamorphosed into a profit-making, people-processing concern serving the ideology and the pocketbooks of the capitalist contractors. According to another article by Barry Bluestone, one popular solution to the problems of the black ghetto, black capitalism, even at its best—in the form of small scale retail cooperatives and black owned production plants—is only going to provide a few more jobs and a little more pride for ghetto blacks who will still be dependent upon a white-owned economic system. In addition, our major tax-exempt "charitable" institutions, most notably the Ford Foundation and the Rockefeller Foundation, dispense not charity for the poor but influence and power to maintain the status quo for corporate America according to the analysis by David Horowitz and David Kolodney.

In the editor's introduction, Pamela Roby presents an overview of "How the establishment keeps the poor, poor, and the rich, rich." Later on in the volume Howard M. Wachtel argues that it is the characteristics of the capitalist system rather than the characteristics of the poor which cause poverty. In his analysis he makes clear why no government program, either liberal or conservative, would seriously attempt to eliminate poverty. In conclusion Frances Fox Piven indicates what social scientists should do: stay away from government; the critical perspective can only come from those outside the system.

SALLY BOULD VAN TIL
University of Delaware
Newark

MILDRED A. SCHWARTZ. *Politics and Territory: The Sociology of Regional Persistence in Canada.* Pp. 338. Quebec, Canada: McGill-Queen's Press, 1974. $14.75.

Regional cleavage has long been a preoccupation of the social sciences in Canada, and while a lot of speculative and impressionistic pieces have been written about the phenomenon, Mildred Schwartz's most recent book is the first to be constructed on a base of hard empirical data. All in all, the verdict on this volume will have to be very favorable, for it fills a significant gap in the literature in a manner which combines academic rigor and literary elegance. By integrating data gathered in a 1965 survey of the Canadian electorate with aggregate statistics, Professor Schwartz describes faithfully the basic dimensions of political regionalism and concludes with some stimulating interpretations of the future of regionalism in Canada.

As with many good academic works, *Politics and Territory* is as significant for what it *is not* as for what it *is*. In the first place, the nature of the survey data at her disposal forced Mildred Schwartz into virtually equating "politics" with "political parties and elections." While the author herself recognizes this shortcoming, the reader is left wondering whether there is any connection between the regional patterns of mass behavior and the actual outputs of the Canadian political system. Unless parties and elections are proven to be significant determinants of public policy, the connections between regionalism and partisan support are but interesting social artifacts.

Where the emphasis on mass attitudes and electoral behavior becomes most puzzling is in chapter three, where Professor Schwartz uses popular vote, seats in the House of Commons, and Cabinet representation as indicators of regional or provincial *power*. Despite her caveats it is a gross distortion of Canadian political reality to suggest that the power of a particular province is significantly enhanced by the number of government members it has elected to the House of Commons. The basic strength of the province of Ontario, for instance, lies not in mass attitudes to federal political parties, but in a large and lucrative tax base, and in an articulate and self-assured set of provincial elites who can bargain as equals with the federal government in any number of interjurisdictional arenas. The data in chapter three are interesting but they do not say much— if anything—about provincial power.

A further weakness of the book, which is related to the former, is that it looks only at the attitudes and behavior of the mass to the neglect of the political elites. Surely the spate of recent literature in Canadian political science—most notably, works by Richard Simeon, Ken McRae, Donald Smiley and Robert Presthus—forces one to the conclusion that any analysis of mass phenomena is only significant within the context of the dominant value system and behavior patterns of national and provincial elites.

To conclude, when reviewing a book about which one feels basically benevolent, it is an easy tactic to criticize the author for what he or she has not done; to point to the gaps in the analysis rather than to address one's comment to the analysis itself. Taken as a whole, *Politics and Territory* is brimming over with data and insight and it is as important for the hypothesizing it stimulates as it is for the hypotheses it tests; it is a must for any serious student of Canadian politics or political sociology.

MIKE WHITTINGTON
Carleton University
Ottawa

HARRY H. VORRATH and LARRY K. BRENDTRO. *Positive Peer Culture.* Pp. vi, 158. Chicago, Ill.: Aldine, 1974. $7.50.

The subtitle *Charting a New Course for Education and Training with Contemporary Youth* is testimony to the challenge of PPC, *positive peer culture.* The training is *with* contemporary youth, not *of* them.

As most readers will know, PPC is a formal method in which nine youths (or *youth,* as the authors refer to the group, thus denying the individuality of each member) engage in group discussions of their behavioral problems under a group leader, with the overriding principle at issue that *giving* is more important than *receiving.* The youths have to learn to relate to one another and not to depend on adults; they learn to recognize lack of concern for "self and others." Rather than demand obedience, PPC "demands that young people become the mature and productive human beings they can be." The problems are packaged—*"low self-image, inconsiderate of others, inconsiderate of self, authority problem, easily misled, aggravates others, easily angered, stealing, lying, fronting."* The method for their resolution consists of the group leaders *inspiring* the youth, of turning problems back to them for their own solutions, with some guidance of course from leaders. The book is didactic, compendium in form. It begins with a letter from "One Delinquent to Another." A brief two pages then tell us what PPC is, and isn't. It departs decisively from traditional approaches—for example, therapeutic approaches. Its purpose is to build positive youth *subcultures.* Though developed first for delinquent youth, PPC "is now being

employed in . . . schools, community programs, juvenile courts, group homes and other childcare facilities." The senior author's devotion and long experience are everywhere evident in advice given in the brief chapters on "Issues," "Identifying Problems," "Staff Roles and Responsibilities," "The Group Session," and "Cultivating a Positive Culture." The junior author complements the advice with supportive, psychological references, with which few would cavil. If anyone wants to run a group, in any circumstance, every bit of excellent advice is here for the taking. Had an advertising expert thought up something of the kind for selling soap, he would have charged $175 for the slim volume, and been highly regarded for his expertise.

One wishes the method well, and happily remembers reflections of it in earlier days—in India, for example, where peer group formations of the kind were built by the British Army into the training of officer cadets from diverse cults and regions, with at least gratifying short-term results.

The method stands or falls, however, with the caliber of the group advisers. But if all were Vorraths, what would the outcome be?

It is here that doubts arise: the authors, one would suggest, have not looked far enough into youth, or culture, to see that good intentions are not enough. The Boy Scout movement is full of such. What is missing is a grasp of the basic assumptions upon which PPC rests. Each young person has to learn, not only respect for "self and others" but to be sparked by something akin to traditional loyalties.

This can be found, perhaps, in Jeffersonian principles: there is a surprising congruity between the basic motivation of a Jefferson in the early days of the founding of this nation and what PPC needs at its core. Jefferson knew where he was going in the pursuit of life, liberty and *happiness*; PPC has no inkling of anything of the kind. Yet it could have. One would suggest that Brendtro, at least, look into the mind of the greatest of Americans, Thomas Jefferson, for a fundamental purpose for the warm, human intentions of PPC.

WILLIAM STEPHENSON
University of Missouri
Columbia

ELIZABETH ANN WEINBERG. *The Development of Sociology in the Soviet Union.* Pp. xv, 173. Boston, Mass.: Routledge & Kegan Paul, 1974. $14.00.

Elizabeth Ann Weinberg, a graduate of Vassar, took her Master's degree at Harvard with the late Merle Fainsod on public opinion research in the Soviet Union, and her doctorate with Leonard Schapiro at the London School of Economics, where she is currently a member of the Department of Sociology. The book at hand, whose title accurately indicates its content, is an expansion of her dissertation. She calls it "a case study in the institutionalization of a discipline in a particular society."

The particular society, of course, is one in which inquiry in general has suffered certain constraints. Before the Revolution, a period to which the author intentionally devotes only two pages, Russian sociology was subject to the same influences that characterized sociology in the rest of Europe and in the United States. It concerned itself with such themes as the philosophy of history, the history of civilization, the idea of progress, political philosophy, and the nature of sociology itself. After the Revolution sociology became, by official decree, historical materialism, although such subjects as biosociology (the relationship between organic and social forces) and criminology were temporarily tolerated, especially at the Psycho-Neurological Institute and the University of Petrograd, where Sorokin, an opponent of Marxism, held a professorial appointment until he was forbidden to teach in 1921. (The author's suggestion that Sorokin may have lectured by candle-light because he was "scared" rather than because of the absence of electric power is gratuitous. Sorokin was fearless, and the au-

thorities would have had no difficulty finding him at the University, even in the dark.) Later on, after Sorokin was comdemned to death, sociology came to be considered a "bourgeois" discipline; from the mid-thirties to the mid-fifties it was replaced by courses in Marxism-Leninism-Stalinism; and the word itself was prohibited.

Ms. Weinberg, however, is much more interested in the revival of sociology, with the necessary official sanction, after the Party Congress of 1966. She accordingly describes the sociological research now conducted in the Soviet Union—research on time budgets, labor, stratification, marriage and the family, urban problems, criminology, religion and atheism, and public opinion. Her book is not a serious study in the sociology of knowledge but rather a report of the state of the discipline as it now obtains in that country. For those of us for whom the Russian language is a barrier to intercourse, it is a welcome and useful kind of information.

ROBERT BIERSTEDT
University of Virginia
Charlottesville

ECONOMICS

PHILIP S. BAGWELL. *The Transport Revolution from 1770.* Pp. 460. New York: Barnes & Noble, 1974. $17.50.

This book is in the admirable tradition of British economic history which embraces social as well as accounting costs and gains. It is unaffected by the recent fashion, in America, of straining out all but the strictly commercial considerations. That is like telling me that I have all sorts of furious viruses in my system without mentioning my antibodies that keep most of the bodies under control. Professor Bagwell is as much aware as any practitioner of the "new economic history" of the desirability of efficiency, but he is always conscious of cultural impingements. His thesis is that all forms of British domestic transport require to be integrated, operated in the black as a system, but deliberately incurring financial losses here and there in the interest of preserving quality of life.

The experiment in the United States in railway rehabilitation may take heart from the advice of this author for his own country, though the facts are discouraging. "If investment had been made in main line electrification in the 'cheap money' years (1932–9), British railways would have been in an exceptionally strong position to provide fast, reliable, and inexpensive freight and passenger services in postwar Britain. The present nonsensical situation of an under-utilized railway system existing alongside a grossly overcrowded road network need not have arisen." The policy of the Transport Commission of 1947 (Attlee labor government) of "optimum allocation of transport resources" was followed in 1952 by the conservatives' philosophy "of the 'unseen hand' of private interest." This alternative is not recommended by "the 40-ton trucks roaring through the roads of Kentish villages or the growth of urban ghettos in the shadow of motorway viaducts." The imminent choice for Britain, Bagwell insists, is "either a blinckered policy of trying to make the railways pay in the narrow sense by constantly pruning back 'unprofitable' services, or a large expansion of investment in a thoroughly modern railway system based on the conviction that in the long run on both economic and social grounds this is an absolute necessity for civilized living."

This thorough study, descriptive and analytical, is also entertaining. In 1898 the conference of Municipal Engineers recommended to the public authorities that the extended use of motor vehicles would "contribute to the general improvement of the sanitary condition of our streets and towns." The sanitarians were agreeing with Dr. Bruce Porter, a contemporary motor user, that "the amount of irritation to the nose, throat and eyes in London from dried horse manure" was "something awful."

The excellence of this volume is enhanced by full bibliography, index, maps, charts, and tables. A particular treatment of coastwise travel and shipment is a feature of the book. In telling the story of transport much besides in British economic history is attractively revealed.

BROADUS MITCHELL
New York City

DAVID DONNISON and DAVID EVERSLEY, eds. *London: Urban Patterns, Problems, and Policies.* Pp. vi, 452. Beverly Hills, Calif.: Sage, 1973. $25.00.

PETER HALL et al., eds. *The Containment of Urban England.* Vol. I. Pp. 648. Beverly Hills, Calif.: Sage, 1973. $35.00.

PETER HALL et al., eds. *The Containment of Urban England.* Vol. II. Pp. 464. Beverly Hills, Calif.: Sage, 1973. $25.00.

The British New Towns, greenbelts, public housing estates, decentralization of industry and jobs, and the policies which brought these about have received world-wide praise. For those who seek to follow this model, these books will come as a shock. All is not well in utopia.

Nineteen urbanologists wrote essays for the London volume, concentrating not so much on solutions to the city's problems as on the need for better research and understanding of causes of the ailments before remedies are prescribed. Because it is limited to London's housing, employment, and education, the work will be of limited value to the general reader. Social science researchers may find herein some useful comparisons with U.S. research on social class, and reading achievement by mixed ethnic groups, for example, but this reviewer has the impression that much U.S. research in both methodology and analysis has gone well beyond what is presented here.

No such reservations are held with respect to the two volumes by Peter Hall and his associates. They give us the results of a five-year (1966–71) study which critically evaluates the achievements of the British planning system launched with the passage of the 1947 Town and Country Planning Act. This study, in fact, parallels the study of the U.S. Northeastern Urban Complex directed by Marion Clawson.

Most readers will find volume two to be the most informative, but many chapters of volume one should be examined and some read with care. Two vital portions are chapter three, tracing the evolution of British Planning, and chapter 13, which traces changes in postwar Britain, "for which the planning system, set up to deal with a simpler, more static world, was ill prepared."

Volume two would be a useful text for planning and urban studies. It describes and evaluates how the planning process dealt with the growth phenomenon whose documentation makes up most of volume one. What were the planning goals? The planning machinery? Who were the participants and how did they interact and with what results? Finally, what have been the impacts of postwar planning on housing, industrial location, population decentralization, and transportation facilities and use?

American readers will find the concluding chapters most interesting. Here are presented the end results of the planning activity and the conclusions are surprising. Urban England has indeed been contained, but at what cost? (At the cost of skyrocketing land prices.) Social balance has not been achieved in the New Towns although some have become virtually self-contained. Housing needs of the poor have not been met although the social and economic costs of the failure have, as always, fallen most heavily on the lower income people.

These analyses and conclusions are massively supported by data from the 100 metropolitan areas in which 75 percent of the English and Welsh live (but which occupy only one-third of the land) by housing figures, industrial data and a host of other quantitative measurements. In this respect the work is a marked departure from the usual social science generalizations, unsupported by quantification, which characterize so much of the writing on urban affairs. An attempt has also been made to give precision to such loosely used and imprecise terms as "urbanization," "megalopolis," and "conurbation."

If the authors are correct in their conclusions, what then happened to the bold visions of Ebenezer Howard, Raymond Unwin, Patrick Abercrombie and the other founding fathers of British planning? Curiously, Howard's model of urbanization based on rapid, constant growth would more likely have met the rapidly changing conditions after World War II than would Abercrombie's model based on slow, controlled growth. But the 1947 planning system, which evolved from the ideas of the founders was not, according to the authors, a system at all.

"The critical point . . . is that the so-called 1947 planning system—the central theme of this book—is really two systems. One was the system as imagined in theory, and as given legislative expression in the 1947 Act. The other was a very different system, as actually operated in the 1950s and the 1960s. . . . In particular, the elementary but important fact about this actual system is that it depends basically upon an interaction between the private developer and the public planners." In other words, the system is basically a market system resulting in the *control* of land use rather than the *development* of land use as envisioned by the founding fathers as the pure planning ideal.

In the concluding chapter are presented some policy alternatives to the present system. One alternative in land control is government ownership of all urban or potential urban land. Hall and his associates would perform a useful service by giving us some in-depth comparisons between British planning and planning in Stockholm where most of the available urban land is owned by the city.

JAMES R. BELL
California State University
Sacramento

JOHN FAYERWEATHER. *Foreign Investment In Canada: Prospects For National Policy.* Pp. 200. Toronto: Oxford University Press, 1974. $2.95.

John Fayerweather, in his role as Professor of International Business in New York University's Graduate School of Business, brings a fresh, informed view from the outside on a problem which has been a Canadian political and economic issue since the Royal Commission on Canada's Economic Prospects in 1957: More Canadian industry is owned by non-residents than in any other industrial country (over 60 percent in total with several sectors much higher—chemicals 78 percent, rubber 97 percent, electrical apparatus 77 percent—by 1963 figures).

The question is what effect does this situation have on a country's sovereignty, economic development, regional development, social policies, trading policies, and the like? As such this book will be of interest not only to political scientists but also economists interested in the role of the multinationals. It is in many ways a case study of the extreme in international flows of ideas, capital and technology. The author backs up his conclusions with several surveys including some which he has conducted himself. He also draws on written and spoken opinions of various leaders in different sectors. He concludes that "one of the few clear-cut facts in the current Canadian picture is the strong trend in recent years towards less favorable views of foreign investment," a reasonable statement in view of the growth in visibility of this issue. But this is a curious issue which fluctuates in public opinion and is openly distorted in discussions. He feels that one of the chief reasons for the differences in views on foreign ownership is the difficulty which Canadians have in defining the goals of their nationalism. Dimensions of the attitudes which are dealt with are regional, socioeconomic, opinion groups and political parties.

Although Fayerweather concludes that the capacity for national action is restricted by the dominant role of federal provincial relations in the public sector and the limited role of government acting independently of the business community, the prediction is made that substantially more restrictive government policy will appear within the decade. Presumably this will happen regardless of changes in public opinion.

In his analysis of the various issues he does not seem to grasp the full significance of extraterritoriality. The economic effects are dealt with lightly while the emotional effect is almost ignored. He fails to discuss the refusal of the U.S. government to even negotiate such matters as trading with the enemy by national firms bought out by U.S. multinationals.

The small errors due to writing about a foreign country are there but are few and quite inconsequential; Fayerweather has done a fine job in this respect. The analysis of political events over the last decade in view of foreign ownership is quite sound although he would probably wish to reassess the 1972 election as a result of the 1974 election. Time will be well spent on this book by those interested in the place of multinationals in a national economy. John Fayerweather has presented an informed scholarly case study free from the biases of a multinational spokesman and free from the forest which would envelop writers in a society under examination.

GORDON DOWSLEY

Toronto
Canada

ANTONY FISHER. *Must History Repeat Itself?* Pp. v, 155. Levittown, N.Y.: Transatlantic Arts, 1974. $6.00.

At best the answer is "maybe"; at worst it is "yes"—that is, if one accepts the basic premise of the slim volume under review. For, what we have here essentially is a personal statement of belief in the virtues of unhindered competition and the evils of government intervention in economic affairs, combined with a sincere, though unconvincing, effort to document the repeated failures of governments and politicians to grasp and act upon the proper principles of economic behavior. The author—a former RAF pilot, turned successful chicken farmer and dairyman, *and* a self-professed admirer of the words of Adam Smith and the works of Hayek, Röpke and Friedman, among others—sets the tone at the very beginning. He asserts that the key to growth and prosperity lies in maximized choice for the individual, but that as government powers increase, individual freedom of choice diminishes. Hence, it is governments or, more correctly, governmental policies—based as they are on mistaken notions or, worst, "on ignorance" (p. 20)—that serve to stifle progress and growth.

The chief villains in the plot are: (1) taxation, (2) government expenditures, and (3) inflation—the last being aided and abetted by government actions and lack of understanding of cause-and-effect relationships. And while in discussing these matters the author addresses himself mainly to his own British countrymen, he draws on experience elsewhere to make his case. Thus, we are led through a series of historical episodes (the first being the Diocletian Edict of A.D. 301), from which we can purportedly learn a lesson as to what is the right and what is the wrong course of economic decision-making. It is interesting, though perhaps not entirely surprising, to note the author's conclusion at the end of this journey—namely, that "Maximum individual choice in economic decisions can achieve wonders even when there is little or no freedom to vote" (p. 61).

This particular exercise in historical interpretation is followed by a more detailed examination of the economic policies of post-World War II British governments. From agricultural subsidies, through social welfare programs, to government spending and inflation, the story is the same: Government intervention minimizes individual choice and reduces economic well-being—even, mind you, the wellbeing of the poor who, if given the choice, may not have chosen to pay the taxes in exchange for receiving public services. Add to this the "evils" of joining the EEC and abiding by its rules, and you have a very dismal future indeed.

Not so, however, if you are willing to accept the author's program for economic reform, offered "with the conviction that there [does] exist a distinctive positive policy to escape the clutches of a syndrome that appears to be leading toward increasing economic and political chaos . . ." (p. 124). Applied to Britain, this ten-year program features drastic reduction in taxation and public expenditures. Every single item in the British budget—save one—is marked for reduction: Health, education, housing, unemployment compensation, sickness and industrial injuries, roads, and others. Curiously enough, the only item singled out for an actual increase is defense. But, then, didn't the venerable Adam Smith himself concede that "defense is of much more importance than opulence?"

IMANUEL WEXLER
University of Connecticut
Storrs

PHILIP J. FUNIGIELLO. *Toward a National Power Policy: The New Deal and The Electric Utility Industry, 1933–1941.* Pp. 271. Pittsburgh, Pa.: University of Pittsburgh Press, 1973. $12.95.

The fly-leaf of this book characterizes it quite well when it describes it as a comprehensive and readable analysis of the conflict between Franklin D. Roosevelt's New Deal and the electric utility industry. The book ties together the scattered events and conflicting personalities involved in the attempts to develop a national power policy.

Beginning with a survey of the factors contributing to the origins and evolution of the privately owned electrical industry and the growth of the antimonopoly opposition in the 1920s, the author then covers in detail the major areas of conflict: the Public Utility Holding Company Act, the Rural

Electrification Administration, the Bonneville Power Administration, and the various efforts to plan for the power needs of the Second World War. He brings out the complexities of top-level policy-making and the vast network of interpersonal relationships that led to conflict and compromise, and that in the end resulted in no real power policy at all.

The book is a thoroughly documented research study, which should serve as a valuable source of references for scholars interested in this area of history, and is therefore an important contribution to a better understanding of the New Deal. It has, however, in the opinion of this reviewer three faults, which, while by no means fatal to the mission of the book, do detract somewhat from its overall effectiveness.

The first the author himself admits in his preface. As an economist, this reviewer noted with some disappointment the omission from the book of any analysis of the economic aspects of the utility industry during the period. He concentrates solely on the political aspects of his history, which while they are important and valuable, do leave somewhat of a vacuum.

The second criticism is one of dates. The author lists in his subtitle to the book that he is covering the period from 1933–1941. Yet he really covers the decade of the 1920s quite thoroughly as well, so that his title is a bit misleading. More important perhaps is the fact that the book does not move along strictly chronologically, in that each chapter usually starts with the 1920s and moves forward from there. The author is of course analyzing in detail the particular aspects of the area of concentration of that chapter and thus goes back to the early origins of the problem each time, but carrying the history from 1920 to 1942 with each topic, and then going back in the next chapter again to the 1920s does cause some chronological confusion in the mind of the reader.

Finally, the title of the book is rather misleading to another aspect. It is called *Toward a National Power Policy* and leads one to believe that it is leading up to a power policy which will emerge at the conclusion of the book. It is rather disappointing for the reader, who may not be otherwise aware of it, that one discovers only in the final few pages, and indeed only learns for certain in the very last sentence, that no national power policy ever did develop. The work might better have had a title which indicates that it brings out why no national power policy ever was formulated in that period.

It is indeed a compliment to the author of the study that this reviewer can find only such minor nits upon which to pick. On the whole it represents a valuable addition to the history of this interesting subject.

SIDNEY I. SIMON

Rutgers University
New Brunswick
New Jersey

ALAN GARTNER and FRANK RIESSMAN. *The Service Society and the Consumer Vanguard.* Pp. 266. New York: Harper & Row, 1974. $8.95.

This book concerns itself with the tremendous increase in the production and consumption of human services since World War II, the potential for consumer power resulting from this growth, and how it should be steered for maximum social benefits.

The large increase in service—most obvious in the fields of health, education, welfare and government employment—is accompanied by a second major characteristic: production depends on consumer involvement. An example is a patient's willingness to contribute his medical history and follow a prescribed medical regimen in order to produce good health. How to use and design a consumer-based system of productivity constitutes the book's major thrust.

In a consumer-based system, the consumer is more likely to recognize the inappropriateness of such traditional industrial values as hierarchy and competition. Writers see those who have been largely kept out of industry—women, youth, minorities—as vanguard forces for change. They are the deprived and disadvantaged consumers who reject old values and traditional structures. The fact that all three groups are already concentrated in service fields explains their potential.

The first six chapters describe the service society and the many contradictions stemming from our profit-oriented economy. The remaining five chapters discuss the conflict between the professional and the consumer, consumer characteristics, training and management for consumer-oriented practices, and essentials for the new vanguard to achieve a genuine egalitarian society.

Always optimistic in their analysis of consumer power, both emerging and potential, the writers, nevertheless, are not dreamers. They predict "the peculiar, uneven, incomplete, side-by-side development of the industrial and service sectors" (p. 254).

The book is an important contribution to the literature on consumerism. Using a variety of important statistical data, it points out trends and places in perspective a number of theoretical and operational issues in our always uncertain and complex society. The discussion on the delivery of human services in China, for example, and on evaluation as a management issue are of special relevance to present-day problems of service accessibility and accountability. The authors never deviate from the central theme—namely, that consumers are gradually becoming a new force of production and that their economic significance is likely to have important political repercussions as well. However, because of its convoluted analysis and style, this book is unlikely to attract for long many of the vanguard groups across the land, who inspired its writing and could benefit in many ways from reading about themselves and their emerging power as perceived by the authors.

GAËTANE M. LAROCQUE
Ohio Department of Health
Columbus

BENNETT HARRISON. *Urban Economic Development: Suburbanization, Minority Opportunity, and the Condition of the Central City.* Pp. v, 220. Washington, D.C.: Urban Institute, 1974. $4.50.

The author, an economist at M.I.T., has challenged the conventional wisdom that dispersal of blacks to suburbs improves their economic condition and that the central city is not economically viable. Harrison argues, to the contrary, that ghetto redevelopment is feasible if certain institutional changes are made: a reorganization of urban government and public control of land use. Past and present efforts to crack the hard core of poverty and unemployment, such as Urban Renewal, certain programs of federal support (for example, the Kennedy Plan), Model Cities and "black capitalism" have failed, for all are variously subsidizations of established business interests, often controlled from the outside, and not aimed at the total needs of the community. Harrison advocates community-wide development through the vehicle of the Community Development Corporation. Harrison suggests we wrench around our thinking about the efficacy of market mechanisms and private enterprise to solve social problems and try something truly innovative.

But in making a strong case for what is probably good policy, Harrison inadvertently opens his proposal to serious sociological criticism. He believes that the process of suburbanization of people and jobs is explainable primarily in economic terms and does not reflect any moral malaise or "pathology" of the city and is not a reaction to "race *per se.*" His economic analysis, I suspect, is impeccable, but there are questionable policy implications for acceding to the present and growing race-class polarization and trying to alleviate the problem primarily with ghetto redevelopment. Harrison does not mention the fact that massive and intractable housing segregation is at the root of the school segregation problem or that large ghetto concentrations themselves compound many social problems. Economic redevelopment alone to the point of meaningfully alleviating these problems would be intolerably long in coming.

Blacks and some white ethnic groups are increasingly interested in enclave living and economic development with community control, but that is not the same as their wanting central city, ghetto living. A recent Gallup Poll showed that four-fifths of central-city residents prefer to live outside the present city. This is pan-ethnic and does not preclude a desire for enclave living in the suburbs or elsewhere in the city. An exclusively economic argument for accepting and redeveloping large ghettos could be turned into a rationalization of the status quo and against Harrison's liberal goals of social change.

Harrison gives no credence to the fact that anti-urban ideology, a dislike of pluralism and, more recently, a fear of crime are also important factors behind the suburban migration of people *and jobs;* technology and economic incentives are often only facilitating mechanisms. While it would be difficult to link the suburban trend to "race *per se*," it certainly reflects institutional or structural racism, which is a more difficult notion but nonetheless a real factor. Central cities, the ghetto in particular, do need redevelopment, but not to the neglect of a coupled effort to open up the suburbs. But with this caveat, Harrison's proposal deserves a wide hearing.

IRVING LEWIS ALLEN
University of Connecticut
Storrs

ROBIN MARRIS, ed. *The Corporate Society.* Pp. vii, 403. New York: Halsted Press, 1974. $23.50.

Ten sociologists, economists and organization theorists attempt, in this volume, to explain what has gone wrong with modern industrial society. Three of the authors focus attention on "the society," three concentrate on "the

corporations," and three center on "the public sector." The tenth, the editor, strives (unsuccessfully) to synthesize the contributions of his colleagues.

The main theme that emerges from these essays is the increasing significance of external costs and benefits, the inability of the market system to cope with them, and the consequent necessity of public or governmental action.

This theme is distilled from these ideas. These externalities are the consequence of uncontrolled population and economic growth, technological advance and urban interdependence. They tend to demean work, to worsen racial tensions, threaten physical well being, and cause civil disorder. A lack of information as to the impact, causes, possible remedies and how to assess the costs of curbing these externalities creates confusion and resentment.

In each society there is a growing demand that smog, pollution and urban decay be eliminated, crime curbed and the alienation of workers ameliorated. This demand intensifies long standing tensions as to the relation of the individual and the society.

That demand tends to focus blame for many or most of these externalities on the corporations. Particularly the largest and most dominating among them are charged with efforts to control market and consumer behavior, and to influence the government to serve their selfish interests.

In Part II a sociologist, an organization theorist and a Nobel Laureate economist assess the "effects of transformation from small business to giant corporations." They point to great human benefits effected by corporations and simultaneously to widespread suspicion and distaste they have engendered. They stress the need for "processes," "strategies" and individuals which "mediate between the aspirations of the corporation and its environment," for reward systems within our corporations that associate career advancement "with the stakes of society," and for governmental institutions that place externalities "on the agendae of corporations" by identifying them, establishing their social costs, and assessing the costs in individual cases.

The first of three economists whose views are presented in Part III is concerned with "allocative efficiency," that is, how much of each good (for example, urban transport) or service (police protection) government shall provide. The second author writes of the efficiency of governmental operations and the difficulties faced in rendering public services because of the impossibility of measuring costs and benefits. The third author is concerned with disamenities—air craft noise or stream pollution—and how the costs of curbing or eliminating such disamenities shall be distributed among producer, consumer and the public.

All in all this is a stimulating, but not easily read, book. It treats of problems of social policy that are still being defined. It makes clear that traditional economic concepts and mechanisms, particularly the corporation, limited liability and the market, may have to be supplemented to cope with these new social problems. That supplementation may mean, the editor suggests, that "the days of the stockholder corporation must be numbered."

JOHN J. CORSON
Arlington
Virginia

ARTHUR P. SOLOMON. *Housing the Urban Poor: A Critical Evaluation of Federal Housing Policy.* Pp. viii, 227. Cambridge, Mass.: MIT Press, 1974. $12.00.

For several reasons this recent book is likely to be influential in public discussions about the role of government in housing over the next few years. It is, first of all, directed to the issue which now emerges as central—whether cash subsidies to families in need of improved housing are preferable to subsidized construction of new dwellings. This issue is developed by comparing costs and other monetary impacts of only six subsidy programs in actual use, to represent the unmanageable variety of programs in existence or proposed. While the factual data come primarily from housing agencies in Boston, the book is defined and organized with considerable clarity so that potential implications for other urban areas can be worked out without much difficulty. Finally, the book is an enterprise, and might easily be interpreted as a policy statement of the Joint Center for Urban Studies of Harvard University and MIT—if places like that have policies.

The "benchmark" programs which Solomon uses to make his case are three new construction programs— conventional public housing, leased new housing and Section 236 rent supplement new housing—two rehabilitation options, under the leasing program and under Section 236—and finally the leasing program applied to existing units without rehabilitation. He compares these on the basis of "housing consumption benefits" (defined as the difference between the market rental value of the subsidized unit and the rent paid by the occupant), "horizontal equity" (a measure of the amount of subsidy enjoyed by equally needy households under several simultaneously available housing subsidy programs), "vertical equity" (a measure of the proportion of the subsidy dollar which goes to investors or administrators rather than to improvement in household welfare), the property tax effect allowing for the fact that some programs remove housing from local tax rolls while others add new construction or new tax-paying ability to those rolls, employment-stimulus effects—that is, jobs created, particularly for minorities—Federal budgetary effect allowing for reduction in taxes paid by developers of subsidized housing under some programs, the annual resource cost, and several non-monetary benefits such as "consumer sovereignty" and "racial and economic dispersion." Several of these measures may strike particular readers as inappropriate or too narrowly defined; the indirect effects of programs which Solomon builds into his comparisons—for example, the impact that subsidized new construction may have on the rent of standard existing units in a local market—get short shrift. It is at least quite clear what has been included, and that is commendable.

Solomon concludes that housing allowances in some form—particularly through the leasing of existing private units for subleasing to families at such rent as they can afford to pay—ought to be the Federal government's principal, if not exclusive, approach to providing the nation's poor with better housing. The per-unit cost of newly constructed or even rehabilitated dwellings is so high that a given aggregate subsidy amount will result in many fewer families being moved from substandard to standard housing, in comparison with subsidized leasing of existing dwellings. To abbreviate his comparisons still further, he estimates that one million dollars of resource cost expended on conventional public housing would provide this degree of assistance to 387 families, while the same amount used to lease existing (non-rehabilitated) housing would produce the equivalent benefit for 608 families (p. 153). This is Solomon's measure of "cost-effectiveness."

The issue thus clearly laid out is not new. The merits and demerits of "rent certificates" have been debated by housing economists and policy-makers for decades, and though he is cognizant of counter-arguments Solomon does not do justice to them. The strongest objection to housing allowances has been the fear that an insufficient supply of adequate low-rent dwellings in the private inventory would cause those allowances to drive up the market price of that part of the housing inventory, affecting adversely not only the number of potential beneficiaries but also other households above the subsidy level who must compete for the same units. The subsidy would be transformed into a windfall for certain property owners and multiplied several times.

Whether this happens depends on the elasticity of housing supply, the rate at which the inventory of standard housing expands in response to augmented purchasing power. Solomon simply assumes (p. 62) that this will not be a problem. If he were happily correct in this assumption, the housing allowances program would merely be a particular form of subsidized "filtering" —inducing households higher on the income ladder to move up to something better while releasing older dwellings to families on the income rungs below. That in turn raises a far broader question than Solomon attempts to discuss— whether it is generally preferable to speed up the filtering process by pushing from below or pulling from above.

For as long as the United States has had a national housing policy its effect has been concentrated on expansion of the supply of middle to upper-middle income dwellings, and it has done this primarily through unsubsidized reforms in mortgage credit institutions and by "tax expenditure" measures. There is room for substantial further improvement in these areas, but this nation's recent housing history strongly suggests that it has been those efforts which have earned gold stars for "cost effectiveness" as Solomon uses that term.

This brings us back to the title of Solomon's book and his opening discussion of the book's purpose. He assumes that Federal housing policy is solely concerned with the urban poor, and should therefore be designed and evaluated on that basis. He sees no sense in programs or goals that keep pushing for higher and higher levels of aggregate production of new housing units, ultimately because he believes newly constructed low-rent housing to be cost-ineffective as a means of helping poor families out of substandard dwellings. He is insensitive to the concern for better housing that the whole population shares, a concern that has persuaded the Federal government to restructure mortgage credit institutions and adjust tax provisions thereby improving access to better—and therefore more newly built—housing for the great preponderance of households, both renters and owners. The poor are a special case; but their housing needs, too, ultimately can be satisfied only by an expanding and improving inventory.

WALLACE F. SMITH
University of California
Berkeley

ARTHUR L. STINCHCOMBE. *Creating Efficient Industrial Administrations.* Pp. vii, 208, New York: Academic Press, 1974. $9.50.

Professor Stinchcombe's new book is a collection of three studies in the industrial administration of steel mills in three South American Countries: Chile, Argentina and Venezuela. They serve as a vehicle to establish his ideas about the relevance of sociology in understanding economic development and the function of industrial management.

Where Professor David C. McClelland of Harvard identifies the primary key to the economic development of underindustrialized countries in the development of an individual achievement motive within the minds of a select number of its citizens, Professor Stinchcombe attributes economic lag to the development of the social conditions necessary for industrial efficiency. Where Professor McClelland emphasizes individual psychology, Professor Stinchcombe emphasizes the individual's role as shaped by the social structure.

His study consists of the collection of data on how people behave in and how they are oriented to their roles as industrial administrators in three different Latin American cultures in the steel industry. By explaining the individual role behavior of industrial administrators he hopes to identify the impact of social influence bearing on individuals in their behavior within the industrial organization and thereby correlate such behavior with effective organizational performance

Stinchcombe uses Max Weber's "Economy and Society" as his basic paradigm. He explains his use of the model as follows: Bureaucracy increases the degree of discipline in organizations. Then the structural variables of bureaucracy such as the differentiation of work status from kinship status among others become the dependent variable in the study of effective industrial administration.

Stinchcombe goes on to contrast two forms of bureaucratic behavior within Venezuela, the impossible, irrational Venezuelan traffic control bureaucracy and the rational administrator bureaucracy in charge of the pipe rolling mill in the Venezuelan steel mill, all within the same country!

Then in a series of chapters on written and oral social systems, he describes the contrast between cosmopolitan oriented executives and locally oriented government bureaucrats, the relationship between bureaucratic structure and innovative behavior and the social sources of individual rationality, thereby completing his theory.

The remaining chapters on the motivation of economic activity and the politics of economic development are interesting but hardly unique.

The quintessence of the industrial administrator's behavior was defined by Chester Barnard as "decision making." Professor Herbert Simon strained this idea to include all of an administrator's behavior, though how useful this concept was has remained an open question. A concept that includes within its range a soldier on K.P. asking himself what potato he ought to peel next and a head of state making up his mind whether or not to launch a nuclear war encompasses a terribly broad range. A concept that includes everything and excludes nothing ultimately explains nothing.

Professor Sayles eschewed decision making and portrayed the manager as an expediter making deals here and there to keep information and materials moving through his station. Stinchcombe elevates the administrator to the status of an innovator who is involved in continuous problem solving, a concept that falls somewhere between Sayles' thinking and Simon's.

Stinchcombe concludes that industrial administration is routinization of innovation. He dismisses McClelland's achievement motive by stating that people innovate not by putting more energy into their work but more thought into their work.

The contrast between achieving man and thinking man was perhaps best put by an English worker. The British Labor Party was holding its annual conference in Blackpoole, England in the late 1940s. A debate was scheduled between Ernest Bevin, the Labor Party's foreign expert, and foreign minister within the government, and Richard Crossland, the eminent socialist-theorist on the Palestine issue. The American Labor Attaché, Sam Berger, attempting to sound out the delegates' reaction asked a British rank and file delegate whom he thought would dominate in the debate.

The British worker, taking his pipe out from between his teeth, muttered "Ernie'll smear him." When Mr. Berger noted the brilliance of Crossland, the worker went on, "Look, Sam, intellectuals like you and these other fellows like Crossland, you get more ideas in a day than fellows like Ernie and me get in a lifetime, but ya see, fellows like Ernie and me, we got to do something about them ideas."

This is about as succinct a contrast between man acting and man thinking as has been expressed, social research jargon to the contrary notwithstanding. The reviewer for one looks upon this debate between McClelland and Stinchcombe as a sterile "War of Words."

Professor Stinchcombe brings many unique and thoughtful insights to industrial administration that make the book worthwhile reading despite the reviewer's challenge to some of them.

WILLIAM GOMBERG
University of Pennsylvania
Philadelphia

OTHER BOOKS

ABEDIN, NAJMUL. *Local Administration and Politics in Modernizing Societies: Bangladesh and Pakistan.* Pp. viii, 458. New York: Oxford University Press, 1974. $14.00.

ALLMAN, JOE and WALT ANDERSON. *Evaluating Democracy.* Pp. v, 339. Pacific Palisades, Calif.: Goodyear, 1974. No price.

BANFIELD, EDWARD C. *The Unheavenly City Revisited.* Pp. viii, 358. Boston, Mass.: Little, Brown, 1974. $8.95.

BARTHOLOMEW, PAUL C. *Summaries of Leading Cases on the Constitution.* 9th ed. Pp. v, 407. Totowa, N.J.: Littlefield, Adams, 1974. $3.50. Paperbound.

BEALS, ALAN R. *Village Life in South India: Cultural Design and Environmental Variation.* Pp. 189. Chicago, Ill.: Aldine, 1974. $7.50. Paperbound, $2.95.

BELL, J. BOWYER. *The Horn of Africa: Strategic Magnet in the Seventies.* Pp. v, 55. New York: Crane, Russak, 1974. $4.95.

BENT, ALAN EDWARD. *The Politics of Law Enforcement.* Pp. v, 203. Lexington, Mass.: Lexington Books, 1974. $12.50.

BERRINGTON, HUGH. *Backbench Opinion in the House of Commons, 1945–55.* Pp. vii, 265. New York: Pergamon Press, 1974. $19.50.

BETTELHEIM, CHARLES. *Cultural Revolution and Industrial Organization in China: Changes in Management and the Division of Labor.* Pp. 128. New York: Monthly Review, 1974, $6.95.

BHATIA, KRISHAN. *Indira: A Biography of Prime Minister Gandhi.* Pp. ix, 290. New York: Praeger, 1974. $10.00.

BLECHMAN, BARRY M., EDWARD M. GRAMLICH and ROBERT W. HARTMAN. *Setting National Priorities: The 1975 Budget.* Pp. vii, 268. Washington, D.C.: The Brookings Institution, 1974. $2.95. Paperbound.

BLOS, PETER. *The Young Adolescent.* Pp. vi, 252. New York: The Free Press, 1974. $3.95. Paperbound.

BONSIGNORE, JOHN J. et al. *Before the Law: An Introduction to the Legal Process.* Pp. ix, 388. Boston, Mass.: Houghton Mifflin, 1974. No price.

The Book of the States, 1974–75. Vol. XX. Pp. 608. Lexington, Ky.: The Council of State Governments, 1974. $14.50.

BORNSTEIN, MORRIS and DANIEL R. FUSFELD, eds. *The Soviet Economy: A Book of Readings.* 4th ed. Pp. vii, 543. Homewood, Ill.: Richard D. Irwin, 1974. $7.95. Paperbound.

BOSSARD, JAMES H. S. and ELEANOR S. BOLL. *Adolescents in Wartime: Children and Youth. Social Problems and Social Policy.* Pp. 168. New York: Arno Press, 1974. No price.

BOWERS, WILLIAM J. *Executions in America.* Pp. v, 489. Lexington, Mass.: Lexington Books, 1974. $20.00.

BRINKMAN, GEORGE, ed. *The Development of Rural America.* Pp. v, 140. Lawrence: University of Kansas, 1974. $8.50.

BRYDEN, KENNETH. *Old Age Pensions and Policy-Making in Canada.* Pp. x, 264. Montreal, Ca.: McGill-Queen's University, 1974. $5.00.

BURCHETT, WILFRED. *My War with the CIA: The Memoirs of Prince Norodom Sihanouk.* Pp. 281. Balitmore, Md.: Penguin Books, 1974. $1.95. Paperbound.

BURNETT, JACQUETTA H. *Anthropology and Education: An Annotated Bibliographic Guide.* Pp. viii, 159. New Haven, Conn.: HRAF Press, 1974. $8.00. Paperbound, $3.50.

CARROLL, JOHN. *Break-Out from the Crystal Palace: The Anarch-Psychological Critique: Stirner, Nietzsche, Dostoevsky.* Pp. 188. Boston, Mass.: Routledge & Kegan Paul, 1974. $15.00.

CAVE, WILLIAM M. and MARK A. CHESLER. *Sociology of Education: An Anthology of Issues and Problems.* Pp. iii, 552. New York: Macmillan, 1974. $6.95. Paperbound.

CICOUREL, AARON V. *Cognitive Sociology: Language and Meaning in Social Interaction.* Pp. 189. New York: The Free Press, 1974. $7.95. Paperbound, $2.50.

CLARKE, PETER, ed. *New Models for Mass Communication Research.* Vol. II. Sage Annual Reviews of Communication Research. Pp. 320. Beverly Hills, Calif.: Sage, 1974. $15.00.

CLAUSEN, AAGE R. *How Congressmen Decide: A Policy Focus.* Pp. vii, 243. New York: St. Martin's, 1973. $9.95. Paperbound, $4.50.

COLLINS, W. P., ed. *Perspectives on State and Local Politics.* Pp. v, 303. Englewood Cliffs, N.J.: Prentice-Hall, 1974. No price.

COCHRAN, CHARLES L., ed. *Civil-Military Relations.* Pp. v, 366. New York: Free Press, 1974. $10.95.

CONLIN, JOSEPH ROBERT, ed. *The American Radical Press, 1880–1960.* Vol. I. Pp. 720. Westport, Conn.: Greenwood, 1974. $29.95.

CONLIN, JOSEPH ROBERT, ed. *The American Radical Press, 1880–1960.* Vol. II. Pp. 720. Westport, Conn.: Greenwood, 1974. $29.95.

COPLIN, WILLIAM D. *Introduction to International Politics: A Theoretical Overview.* 2nd ed. Pp. ix, 460. Chicago, Ill.: Rand McNally, 1974. $8.95.

COTLER, JULIO and RICHARD R. FAGEN, eds. *Latin America & the United States: The Changing Political Realities.* Pp. x, 417.

Stanford, Calif.: Stanford University Press, 1974. $17.50. Paperbound, $4.95.

CZAPLICKA, M. A. *The Turks of Central Asia in History and at the Present Day.* Pp. 242. New York: Barnes & Noble, 1974. $10.00.

DAVIS, GARY A. and THOMAS F. WARREN, eds. *Psychology of Education: New Looks.* Pp. 514. Lexington, Mass.: D. C. Heath, 1974. No price.

DAVIS, MOSHE, ed. *The Yom Kippur War: Israel and the Jewish People.* Pp. vii, 362. New York: Arno Press, 1974. $9.00.

DENENBERG, HERBERT S. *Getting Your Money's Worth: Guidelines About Insurance Policies, Health Protection, Pensions and Professional Services.* Pp. 183. Washington, D.C.: Public Affairs Press, 1974. $4.50. Paperbound.

DENISON, EDWARD F. *Accounting for United States Economic Growth: 1929–1969.* Pp. vii, 355. Washington, D.C.: The Brookings Institution, 1974. $12.95. Paperbound, $5.50.

DICKINSON, H. T., ed. *Politics and Literature in the Eighteenth Century.* Pp. v, 234. Totowa, N.J.: Rowman and Littlefield, 1974. $7.75. Paperbound, $4.00.

DiRENZO, GORDON J. *Personality and Politics.* Pp. 560. New York: Doubleday, 1974. $3.50. Paperbound.

DORSON, RICHARD M. *America in Legend: Folklore from the Colonial Period to the Present.* Pp. vii, 336. New York: Pantheon, 1974. $5.95. Paperbound.

DRESSLER, DAVID and DONALD CARNS. *Sociology: The Study of Human Interaction.* 2nd ed. Pp. vii, 636. New York: Alfred A. Knopf, 1973. No price.

EZER, EHUD BEN. *Unease in Zion.* Pp. 352. New York: Quadrangle, 1974. $12.50.

FERNBACH, DAVID, ed. *Karl Marx: The Revolutions of 1848, Political Writings.* Vol. I. Pp. 365. New York: Random House, 1974. $10.00. Paperbound, $2.45.

FERNBACH, DAVID, ed. *Karl Marx: Surveys from Exile.* Vol. II. Pp. 375. New York: Random House, 1974. $10.00. Paperbound, $2.45.

FIRTH, CHARLES HARDING. *The House of Lords During the Civil War.* Pp. vi, 309. Totowa, N.J.: Rowman and Littlefield, 1974. $13.50.

FLOWER, J.E., ed. *France Today: Introductory Studies.* 2nd ed. Pp. vi, 211. New York: Barnes & Noble, 1974. $8.50. Paperbound, $4.25.

FOSS, MICHAEL. *Tudor Portraits: Success and Failure of an Age.* Pp. 239. New York: Barnes & Noble, 1974. $8.50.

FOSTER, RICHARD B., ANDRE BEAUFRE, and

WYNFRED JOSHUA, eds. *Strategy for the West: American-Allied Relations in Transition.* Pp. vii, 258. New York: Crane, Russak, 1974. $11.00.

FRODSHAM, J. D. *The First Chinese Embassy to the West.* Pp. viii, 222. New York: Oxford University Press, 1974. $13.00.

GARDINER, JOHN A. and DAVID J. OLSON, eds. *Theft of the City: Readings on Corruption in Urban America.* Pp. vi, 432. Bloomington: Indiana University Press, 1974. $15.00. Paperbound, $4.95.

GARNETT, JOHN C., ed. *The Defence of Western Europe.* Pp. viii, 134. New York: St. Martin's Press, 1974. $12.95.

GEIST, HAROLD, ed. *From Eminently Disadvantaged to Eminence.* Pp. vii, 109. St. Louis, Mo.: Warren H. Green, 1973. $8.50.

GORKY, MAXIM. *On Literature.* Pp. 396. Seattle: University of Washington Press, 1974. $10.00.

GROSS, FELIKS. *The Revolutionary Party: Essays in the Sociology of Politics.* Pp. xix, 280. Westport, Conn.: Greenwood Press, 1974. $13.95.

HADDEN, JEFFREY K., ed. *Religion in Radical Transition.* Pp. 166. New York: E. P. Dutton, 1974. $7.95. Paperbound, $2.95.

HASKELL, MARTIN R. and LEWIS YABLONSKY. *Criminology: Crime and Criminality.* Pp. v, 620. Chicago, Ill.: Rand McNally, 1974. $6.95. Paperbound.

HAUPT, GEORGES and JEAN-JACQUES MARIE. *Makers of the Russian Revolution: Biographies of Bolshevik Leaders.* Pp. 452. Ithaca, N.Y.: Cornell University Press, 1974. $15.00.

HAWLEY, WILLIS D. and DAVID ROGERS, eds. *Improving the Quality of Urban Management.* Urban Affairs Annual Reviews. Vol. 8. Pp. 640. Beverly Hills, Calif.: Sage, 1974. $20.00.

HAYEK, F. A. *Law, Legislation and Liberty: Rules and Order.* Vol. I. Pp. vii, 184. Chicago, Ill.: University of Chicago, 1973. $7.95.

HEAD, SYDNEY W., ed. *Broadcasting in Africa.* Pp. vi, 453. Philadelphia, Pa.: Temple University Press, 1974. $20.00.

HELD, VIRGINIA, SIDNEY MORGENBESSER, and THOMAS NAGEL, eds. *Philosophy, Morality, and International Affairs.* Pp. vii, 338. New York: Oxford University Press, 1974. $3.95. Paperbound.

HENDERSON, PHILIP. *Swinburne: Portrait of a Poet.* Pp. xi, 304. New York: Macmillan, 1974. $10.95.

HOLDER, ANGELA RODDEY. *The Meaning of the Constitution.* Pp. 120. Woodbury, N.J.: Barron's Educational Series, 1974. $2.25. Paperbound.

HUOPANIEMI, JUKKA. *Parliaments and European Rapprochement.* Pp. v, 138. Groningen, The Netherlands: Sijthoff, 1973. No price.

ICSSD *International Bibliography of the Social Sciences: Economics.* Vol. XXI. Pp. ix, 460. Chicago. Ill.: Aldine-Atherton, 1974. $25.00.

ICSSD *International Bibliography of the Social Sciences: Political Science.* Vol. XXI. Pp. vii, 292. Chicago, Ill.: Aldine-Atherton, 1974. $25.00.

ICSSD *International Bibliography of the Social Sciences: Sociology.* Vol. XXII. Pp. ix, 322, Chicago, Ill.: Aldine-Atherton, 1974. $25.00.

INCIARDI, JAMES A. and CARL D. CHAMBERS, eds. *Drugs and the Criminal Justice System.* Vol. II. Sage Criminal Justice System Annuals. Pp. 249. Beverly Hills, Calif.: Sage, 1974. $15.00.

JANSIEWICZ, DONALD R. *The New Alexandria Simulation: A Serious Game of State and Local Politics.* Pp. v, 98. San Francisco, Calif.: Canfield, 1973. $4.95. Paperbound.

JAROS, DEAN and LAWRENCE V. GRANT. *Political Behavior: Choice and Perspectives.* Pp. 366. New York: St. Martin's Press, 1974. $12.95. Paperbound, $6.95.

JOHNSON, SAMUEL A. *Essentials of Political Parties: Their Relation to American Government.* Pp. iv, 202. Woodbury, N.Y.: Barron's Educational Series, 1974. $1.95. Paperbound.

JONES, A. H. M. *The Roman Economy: Studies in Ancient Economic and Administrative History.* Edited by P. A. Brunt. Pp. v, 450. Totowa, N.J.: Rowman and Littlefield, 1974. $22.50.

KEEBLER, ROBERT S. *A Political Testament: Guidelines to National Greatness.* Pp. 256. New York: Vantage, 1974. $6.95.

KLEBANOFF, SHOSHANA. *Middle East Oil and U.S. Foreign Policy: With Special Reference to the U.S. Energy Crisis.* Pp. v, 288. New York: Praeger, 1974. $16.50.

LAQUEUR, WALTER, ed. *A Dictionary of Politics.* Revised edition. Pp. 565. New York: The Free Press, 1974. $14.95.

LAWRENCE, RICHARD D. and JEFFREY RECORD. *U.S. Force Structure in NATO: An Alternative.* Pp. vii, 136. Washington, D.C.: The Brookings Institution, 1974. $2.50. Paperbound.

LEE, ALFRED McCLUNG. *Toward Humanist Sociology.* Pp. v, 224. Englewood Cliffs, N.J.: Prentice-Hall, 1974. $3.95. Paperbound.

LEAVITT, HAROLD, LAWRENCE PINFIELD, and EUGENE WEBB, eds. *Organizations of* the Future: Interaction with the External Environment. Pp. v, 198. New York: Praeger, 1974. $16.50.

LESTER, RICHARD A. Antibias Regulation of Universities: Faculty Problems and Their Solutions. Pp. xiii, 167. New York: McGraw-Hill, 1974. $4.95. Paperbound.

LOGAN, R. M. Canada, the United States, and the Third Law of the Sea Conference. Pp. iii, 122. Washington, D.C.: National Planning Association, 1974. $3.00. Paperbound.

LORA, RONALD, ed. America in the '60s: Cultural Authorities in Transition. Pp. vii, 447. New York: John Wiley & Sons, 1974. $9.95.

MANSFIELD, EDWIN, ed. Economics: Readings, Issues, and Cases. Pp. vii, 440. New York: W. W. Norton, 1974. $5.95. Paperbound.

MARCZEWSKI, JAN. Crisis in Socialist Planning: Eastern Europe and the USSR. Pp. v, 245. New York: Praeger, 1974. $18.50.

MARK, MAX. Modern Ideologies. Pp. 248. New York: St. Martin's Press, 1973. $9.95. Paperbound, $3.95.

MASARYK, TOMAS G. The Meaning of Czech History. Edited by Rene Wellek, translated by Peter Kussi. Pp. vii, 169. Chapel Hill: North Carolina Press, 1974. $9.95.

MCLANE, CHARLES B. Soviet-Asian Relations. Soviet-Third World Relations, Vol. II. Pp. 150. New York: Columbia University Press, 1974. $15.00.

MCLELLAN, DAVID S., WILLIAM C. OLSON, and FRED A. SONDERMANN, eds. The Theory and Practice of International Relations. 4th ed. Pp. v, 492. Englewood Cliffs, N.J.: Prentice-Hall, 1974. No price.

MCNALL, SCOTT G. The Sociological Perspective: Introductory Readings. 3rd ed. Pp. vii, 660. Boston, Mass.: Little, Brown, 1974. $6.50. Paperbound.

MCNALL, SCOTT G. The Sociological Experience: A Modern Introduction to Sociology. 3rd ed. Pp. ix, 377. Boston, Mass.: Little, Brown, 1974. $5.95. Paperbound.

MESSINGER, SHELDON L. et al., eds. The Aldine Crime & Justice Annual: 1973. Pp. v, 535. Chicago, Ill.: Aldine-Atherton, 1974. $20.00.

MILLER, NEAL E. et al., eds. Biofeedback and Self-Control: 1973. An Aldine Annual on the Regulation of Bodily Processes and Consciousness. Pp. v, 539. Chicago, Ill.: Aldine, 1974. $20.00.

MINEAR, RICHARD H., ed. Through Japanese Eyes: The Past. Vol. I. Pp. 147. New York: Praeger, 1974. $7.50. Paperbound, $2.75.

MODELSKI, GEORGE, ed. Multinational Corporations and World Order. Sage Contemporary Social Science Issues, no. 2. Pp. 160. Beverly Hills, Calif.: Sage, 1972. $3.95. Paperbound.

MORGAN, LAEL. And the Land Provides: Alaskan Natives in a Year of Transition. Pp. 352. New York: Doubleday, 1974. $10.00.

MORGAN, ROBERT J. A Whig Embattled: The Presidency under John Tyler. Pp. xi, 199. Hamden, Conn.: Archon Books, 1974. $10.00.

MOSLEY, LEONARD. Power Play: Oil in the Middle East. Pp. ix, 463. Baltimore, Md.: Penguin, 1974. $2.95. Paperbound.

MORRILL, J. S. Cheshire, 1630–1660: County Government and Society during the "English Revolution." Oxford Historical Monographs. Pp. 357. New York: Oxford University Press, 1974. $17.75.

MORRISON, DENTON E., KENNETH E. HORNBACK, and W. KEITH WARNER. Environment: A Bibliography of Social Studies Series EPA-600/5-74-011. Pp. 860. Springfield, Va.: National Technical Information Service, 1974. $7.45.

NAJITA, TETSUO. Japan: The Modern Nations in Historical Perspective. Pp. v, 152. Englewood Cliffs, N.J.: Prentice-Hall, 1974. No price.

NATHAN, HARRIET and STANLEY SCOTT, eds. Emerging Issues in Public Policy: Research Reports and Essays, 1960–1965. Institute of Governmental Studies. Pp. vii, 1968. Berkeley: University of California, 1973. No price.

NATHAN, HARRIET and STANLEY SCOTT, eds. Emerging Issues in Public Policy: Research Reports and Essays, 1966–1972. Institute of Governmental Studies. Pp. vii, 200. Berkeley: University of California, 1973. No price.

NEEDHAM, RODNEY. Remarks and Inventions: Skeptical Essays about Kinship. Pp. 181. New York: Barnes & Noble, 1974. $11.75.

NELSON, JACK. Captive Voices: The Report of the Commission of Inquiry into High School Journalism. Pp. 288. New York: Schocken Books, 1974. $10.95. Paperbound, $1.45.

NIETHAMMER, CAROLYN. American Indian Food and Lore. Pp. vii, 191. New York: Macmillan, 1974. $4.95. Paperbound.

NIMMO, DAN D. Popular Images of Politics. Pp. iii, 184. Englewood Cliffs, N.J.: Prentice-Hall, 1974. $7.95. Paperbound, $3.50.

PAREKH, BHIKHU, ed. Jeremy Bentham: Ten Critical Essays. Pp. v, 204. Portland, Ore.:

International Scholarly Book Services, 1974. $15.00.

PATERSON, WILLIAM E. and IAN CAMPBELL. *Social Democracy in Post-War Europe.* Pp. vii, 82. New York: St. Martin's Press, 1974. $6.95.

POLSBY, NELSON W. *Political Promises: Essays and Commentary on American Politics.* Pp. vii, 279. New York: Oxford University Press, 1974. $9.95.

The Position of the French Language in Quebec. No. I. Pp. ii, 362. Portland, Ore.: University of Quebec, 1974. $3.95. Paperbound.

The Position of the French Language in Quebec. No. 2. Pp. iii, 484. Portland, Ore.: University of Quebec, 1974. $3.95. Paperbound.

The Position of the French Language in Quebec. No. 3. Pp. iii, 557. Portland, Ore.: University of Quebec, 1974. $3.95. Paperbound.

RAMER, LEONARD V. *Your Sexual Bill of Rights: An Analysis of the Harmful Effects of Sexual Prohibitions.* Pp. 126. New York: Exposition, 1974. $5.00.

REDMAN, ERIC. *The Dance of Legislation.* Pp. 319. New York: Simon and Schuster, 1973. $2.95. Paperbound.

REYNOLDS, LLOYD G., STANLEY H. MASTERS, and COLLETE MOSER, eds. *Readings in Labor Economics and Labor Relations.* Pp. v, 459. Englewood Cliffs, N.J.: Prentice-Hall, 1974. No price.

ROBBINS, HORACE H. *Fictive Capital and Fictive Profit: The Welfare-Military State. A Political Economy Based on Economic Fictions.* Pp. 417. New York: Philosophical Library, 1974. No price.

ROBERTSON, MARIAN. *Diamond Fever: 1866–1869.* Pp. 250. New York: Oxford University Press, 1974. $22.00.

ROCHE, KENNEDY F. *Rousseau: Stoic and Romantic.* Pp. ix, 177. New York: Barnes & Noble, 1974. $11.00.

ROCK, PAUL and MARY McINTOSH. *Deviance and Social Control.* Pp. viii, 322. New York: Barnes & Noble, 1974. $17.50. Paperbound, $7.50.

RODINSON, MAXIME. *Islam and Capitalism.* Pp. viii, 308. New York: Random House, 1974. $10.00.

ROGERS, GEORGE C., JR. et al., eds. *The Papers of Henry Laurens: Volume Four: Sept. 1, 1763–Aug. 31, 1765.* Pp. 722. Columbia: University of South Carolina Press, 1974. $25.00.

ROSE, JERRY D. *Introduction to Sociology.* 2nd ed. Pp. vii, 560. Chicago, Ill.: Rand McNally, 1974. $5.95. Paperbound.

ROSENTHAL, ALAN. *Legislative Performance in the States: Explorations of Committee Behavior.* Pp. v, 215. New York: The Free Press, 1974. $8.95.

RUBIN, LESTER, WILLIAM S. SWIFT, and HERBERT R. NORTHRUP. *Negro Employment in the Maritime Industries.* Vol. VII. The Racial Policies of American Industry. Pp. v, 204. Philadelphia: University of Pennsylvania, 1974. $12.00.

SÁNCHEZ-ALBORNOZ, NICOLÁS. *The Population of Latin America: A History.* Pp. vii, 299. Berkeley: University of California, 1974. $17.50.

SANDHU, HARJIT S. *Modern Corrections: The Offenders, Therapies and Community Reintegration.* Pp. vii, 342. Springfield, Ill.: Charles C. Thomas, 1974. $10.95. Paperbound, $8.95.

SAYLES, GEORGE O. *The King's Parliament of England.* Pp. 164. New York: W. W. Norton, 1974. $7.95. Paperbound, $2.95.

SCHACHT, JOSEPH and C. E. BOSWORTH, eds. *The Legacy of Islam.* Pp. vi, 530. Oxford, England: Clarendon Press, 1974. No price.

SCHNAPPER, M.B., ed. *Presidential Impeachment: A Documentary Overview.* Pp. iii, 144. Washington, D.C.: Public Affairs Press, 1974. $4.50. Paperbound.

SEGAL, DAVID R. *Society and Politics: Uniformity and Diversity in Modern Democracy.* Introduction to Modern Society Series. Pp. 206. Glenview, Ill.: Scott, Foresman, 1974. $2.50. Paperbound.

SEITZ, FREDERICK and RODNEY W. NICHOLS. *Research and Development and the Prospects for International Security.* Pp. vii, 74. New York: Crane, Russak, 1974. $4.95.

SHEIKH, AHMED. *International Law and National Behavior: A Behavioral Interpretation of Contemporary International Law and Politics.* Pp. vii, 352. New York: John Wiley & Sons, 1974. $11.95.

SHERMAN, LAWRENCE W., ed. *Police Corruption: A Sociological Perspective.* Pp. 360. New York: Doubleday, 1974. $2.95. Paperbound.

SHONFIELD, ANDREW. *Europe: Journey to an Unknown Destination.* Pp. 98. White Plains, N.Y.: International Arts and Sciences, 1974. $6.00.

SILLERY, ANTHONY. *Botswana: A Short Political History.* Studies in African History, no. 8. Pp. viii, 219. New York: Barnes & Noble, 1974. $8.75. Paperbound, $5.50.

SILVER, ISIDORE, ed. *The Crime-Control Establishment.* The American Establishment series. Pp. 149. Englewood Cliffs, N.J.: Prentice-Hall, 1974. $6.95. Paperbound, $2.45.

SMELSER, NEIL J. and GABRIEL ALMOND, eds. *Public Higher Education in California.* Pp. 318. Berkeley: University of California, 1974. $12.50.

SMITH, ROGER M., ed. *Southeast Asia: Documents of Political Development and Change.* Pp. 608. Ithaca, N.Y.: Cornell University Press, 1974. $19.50.

SMULKSTYS, JULIUS. *Karl Marx.* TWAS Series, no. 296. Pp. 151. New York: Twayne, 1974. $6.95.

SPERBER, MURRAY A., ed. *And I Remember Spain: A Spanish Civil War Anthology.* Pp. viii, 337. New York: Macmillan, 1974. $7.95. Paperbound, $3.95.

SOLERI, PAOLO. *Arcology: The City in the Image of Man.* Pp. 121. Cambridge, Mass.: MIT Press, 1973. Paperbound, $7.95.

SORKIN, ALAN L. *Education, Unemployment, and Economic Growth.* Pp. v, 186. Lexington, Mass.: Lexington Books, 1974. $12.50.

SPIEGEL, STEVEN L., ed. *At Issue: Politics in the World Arena.* Pp. 326. New York: St. Martin's, 1973. $4.50. Paperbound.

STEIN, DONALD G. and JEFFREY J. ROSEN. *Learning and Memory.* Pp. vii, 208. New York: Macmillan, 1974. $4.25. Paperbound.

STRICKLAND, D. A. *The March Up Country: Deciding to Bomb Hanoi.* Pp. viii, 51. Wilmette, Ill.: Medina University Press International, 1973. $2.00. Paperbound.

STRUPP, HANS H. et al., eds. *Psychotherapy and Behavior Change: 1973.* An Aldine Annual on Practice and Research. Pp. vi, 543. Chicago, Ill.: Aldine, 1974. $20.00.

TOMKIN, A. E. *Signed and Posted: A Collection of Public Letters.* 2nd ed. Pp. vii, 124. New York: Philosophical Library, 1974. $5.00.

TUCHMAN, GAYE, ed. *The TV Establishment: Programming for Power and Profit.* Pp. v, 186. Englewood Cliffs, N.J.: Prentice-Hall, 1974. $6.95.

Tuition: A Supplemental Statement to the Report of the Carnegie Commission on Higher Education on "Who Pays? Who Benefits? Who Should Pay?" Pp. 87. Hightstown, N.J.: McGraw-Hill, 1974. $2.50. Paperbound.

UHLAN, EDWARD. *The Rogue of Publishers' Row.* Pp. 254. Jericho, N.Y.: Exposition, 1974. $2.95. Paperbound.

VAN CLEVE, RUTH G. *The Office of Territorial Affairs.* Pp. ix, 228. New York: Praeger, 1974. $10.00.

VON DER MEHDEN, FRED R. *South-East Asia, 1930–1970: The Legacy of Colonialism and Nationalism.* Library of World Civilization Series. New York: W. W. Norton, 1974. $7.95. Paperbound, $3.45.

VON HERTZEN, HEIKKI and PAUL D. SPREIREGEN. *Building a New Town.* Pp. 233. Cambridge, Mass.: The MIT Press, 1973. $5.95. Paperbound.

WADDINGTON, LAWRENCE C. *Arrest, Search, and Seizure.* Glenco Press Criminal Justice Series. Pp. 227. Beverly Hills, Calif.: Glenco Press, 1974. $8.95.

WERTHEIM, W. F. *Evolution and Revolution: The Rising Waves of Emancipation.* Pp. 416. Baltimore, Md.: Penguin Books, 1974. $2.75. Paperbound.

WHITRIDGE, ARNOLD. *Rochambeau: America's Neglected Founding Father.* Pp. 340. New York: Collier, 1974. $3.95. Paperbound.

WHITTEN, N. E., JR. *Black Frontiersmen: A South American Case.* Pp. vii, 221. New York: Halsted Press, 1974. $11.25. Paperbound, $5.50.

WICKLUND, ROBERT A. *Freedom and Reactance.* Pp. 205. New York: Halsted Press, 1974. $10.95.

WILCOX, FRANCIS O., ed. *China and the Great Powers: Relations with the United States, the Soviet Union, and Japan.* Pp. v, 103. New York: Praeger, 1974. $10.00.

WILLIAMS, ROBERT L. *Educational Alternatives for Colonized People: Models for Liberation.* Edited by Anne M. St. Pierre. Pp. vii, 130. Cambridge, Mass.: Dunellen, 1974. $8.95.

WILLRICH, MASON and THEODORE B. TAYLOR. *Nuclear Theft: Risks and Safeguards.* Pp. v, 252. Cambridge, Mass.: Ballinger, 1974. No price.

WINDER, ALVIN E. *Adolescence: Contemporary Studies.* 2nd ed. Pp. ix, 427. New York: D. Van Nostrand, 1974. No price.

WINSLOW, ROBERT W. and VIRGINIA WINSLOW. *Deviant Reality: Alternative World Views.* Pp. vi, 335. Boston, Mass.: Allyn and Bacon, 1974. $4.95. Paperbound.

WYNN, DANIEL W. *The Black Protest Movement.* Pp. 258. New York: Philosophical Library, 1974. $7.50.

ZOLL, DONALD ATWELL. *Twentieth Century Political Philosophy.* Pp. vii, 190. Englewood Cliffs, N.J.: Prentice-Hall, 1974. $4.95. Paperbound.

INDEX

THE AAPSS

Number
of Copies

P | C

The Satellites in Eastern Europe   P
A Crowding Hemisphere: Population Change in the Americas   P
Recreation in the Automation Age   P & C
The Future of the Western Alliance   P & C
Current Issues in International Labor Relations   P & C
Disasters and Disaster Relief   P
Japan Since Recovery of Independence. 1952–1956   P
Russia Since Stalin: Old Trends and New Problems   P
The Public School and Other Community Services   P & C
Ethical Standards and Professional Conduct   P
The Future of the United Nations   P
America and a New Asia   P
Bureaucracy and Democratic Government   P
Congress and Foreign Relations   P
NATO and World Peace   P
Judicial Administration and the Common Man   P
The Search for National Security   P
Medical Care for Americans   P
Toward Family Stability   P
Moscow's European Satellites   P
Formulating a Point Four Program   P
Gambling   P
Aiding Underdeveloped Areas Abroad   P
Military Government   P
Government Finance in a Stable and Growing Economy   P
Critical Issues and Trends in American Education   P
World Government   P
Reappraising Our Immigration Policy   P
Postwar Reconstruction in Western Germany   P
Looking Toward One World   P
Peace Settlements in World War II   P
Progress and Prospects of the United Nations   P & C
Women's Opportunities and Responsibilities   P
Social Implications of Modern Science   P & C
Labor Relations and the Public   P
Belgium in Transition   P & C
Making the United Nations Work   P & C
The Netherlands during German Occupation   P & C
Universal Military Training and National Security   P
Our Muddled World   P & C

Number
of Copies

P	C	
		The Disabled Veteran P
		Postwar Jobs for Veterans P
		Adolescents in Wartime P
		International Frontiers in Education P
		Agenda for Peace P & C
		Higher Education and the War P
		Transportation: War and Postwar P
		The American Family in World War II P
		The United Nations and the Future P
		Our Servicemen and Economic Security P
		Southeastern Asia and the Philippines P
		Nutrition and Food Supply: The War and After P
		Labor Relations and the War P
		Winning Both the War and the Peace P
		The Press in the Contemporary Scene P
		Public Policy in a World at War P & C
		Defending America's Future P & C
		Billions for Defense P & C
		Children in a Depression Decade P
		Our Foreign Commerce in Peace and War P
		When War Ends P & C
		Marketing in Our American Economy P
		Government Expansion in the Economic Sphere P
		Frontiers of Legal Aid Work P
		Democracy and the Americas P
		Refugees P
		Appraising the Social Security Program P
		Ownership and Regulation of Public Utilities P
		Freedom of Inquiry and Expression P & C
		Present International Tensions P & C
		Social Problems and Policies in Sweden P
		Consumer Credit P
		Our State Legislators P
		Revival of Depressed Industries P & C
		The United States and World War P & C
		Consumers' Cooperation P & C
		Current Developments in Housing P
		Improved Personnel in Government Service P
		The American People: Studies in Population P

Number
of Copies

P | C

_____|_____ The Attainment and Maintenance of World Peace P
_____|_____ Problems of Organized Labor P
_____|_____ Education for Social Control P
_____|_____ Toward National Recovery P
_____|_____ Banking and Transportation Problems P & C
_____|_____ Social Insurance P & C
_____|_____ The Crisis of Democracy C
_____|_____ The Administration of Justice P
_____|_____ International Labor Organization P & C
_____|_____ Prohibition: A National Experiment P & C
_____|_____ National and World Planning P
_____|_____ Power and the Public P
_____|_____ An Economic Survey of Australia P
_____|_____ Elements of an American Foreign Policy P
_____|_____ The Insecurity of Industry P & C
_____|_____ The Coming of Industry to the South P & C
_____|_____ Postwar Progress in Child Welfare C
_____|_____ Economics of World Peace P
_____|_____ The Second Industrial Revolution C
_____|_____ Real Estate Problems P & C
_____|_____ The Anti-Trust Laws of the United States C

- **P—Paperbound only; P & C—Paperbound and Clothbound**
- **Quantity and wholesales discounts cannot be applied to this special offer.**
- **Orders for 5 books or less must be prepaid.**
- **Orders for 6 books or more must be invoiced.**
- **All special sales are final.**

Please send me the volumes as indicated above.

☐ Enclosed is $————— (add $.75 for postage and handling)
☐ Please bill me. Postage and handling additional.

Name————————————————————————————————

Address—————————————————————————————————

City————————————————State————————————Zip————

THE AMERICAN ACADEMY OF POLITICAL AND
SOCIAL SCIENCE

3937 Chestnut Street   Philadelphia, Pa. 19104

Origin and Purpose. The Academy was organized December 14, 1889, to promote the progress of political and social science, especially through publications and meetings. The Academy does not take sides in controverted questions, but seeks to gather and present reliable information to assist the public in forming an intelligent and accurate judgment.

Meetings. The Academy holds an annual meeting in the spring extending over two days.

Publications. THE ANNALS is the bimonthly publication of The Academy. Each issue contains articles on some prominent social or political problem, written at the invitation of the editors. Also, monographs are published from time to time, numbers of which are distributed to pertinent professional organizations. These volumes constitute important reference works on the topics with which they deal, and they are extensively cited by authorities throughout the United States and abroad. The papers presented at the meetings of The Academy are included in THE ANNALS.

Membership. Each member of The Academy receives THE ANNALS and may attend the meetings of The Academy. Annual dues for individuals are $15.00 (for clothbound copies $20.00 per year). A life membership is $500. All payments are to be made in United States dollars.

Libraries and other institutions may receive THE ANNALS paperbound at a cost of $15.00 per year, or clothbound at $20.00 per year. Add $1.00 to above rates for membership outside U.S.A.

Single copies of THE ANNALS may be obtained by nonmembers of The Academy for $3.00 ($4.00 clothbound) and by members for $2.50 ($3.50 clothbound). A discount of 5 percent is allowed on orders for 10 to 24 copies of any one issue, and of 10 percent on orders for 25 or more copies. These discounts apply only when orders are placed directly with The Academy and not through agencies. The price to all bookstores and to all dealers is $3.00 per copy less 20 percent, with no quantity discount. It is urged that payment be sent with each order. This will save the buyer the shipping charge and save The Academy the cost of carrying accounts and sending statements. Monographs may be purchased for $4.00, with proportionate discounts.

All correspondence concerning The Academy or THE ANNALS should be addressed to the Academy offices, 3937 Chestnut Street, Philadelphia, Pa. 19104.